21世纪的公共管理
机遇与挑战

第六届国际学术研讨会文集

主编

中山大学中国公共管理研究中心
澳门特别行政区政府行政暨公职局
澳门大学
澳门基金会

中央编译出版社

编委会名单

(以姓氏笔画为序)

马　骏　牛美丽　朱伟干　朱亚鹏
刘伯龙　钟　怡　高炳坤

目 录

Meeting the Challenges of Performance Management
  Andrew Podger ……………………………………………………… 1

The Introduction of Minimum Services Standards (MSS) as the Strategy to Enhance Quality of Basic Public Services in Indonesia's Decentralized System: Potential Benefits and Risks
  Mohammad Roudo …………………………………………………… 16

从管控到服务、嵌入、吸纳：执政党基层组织社会治理行动路线
  孙柏瑛 ………………………………………………………………… 49

澳门博彩业竞争管理政策之研究
  朱顺和　陈海天 ……………………………………………………… 60

澳门公共支出绩效审计探究
  黎宝珊 ………………………………………………………………… 72

小组治国：从政治控制到国家治理
  倪　星　原　超 ……………………………………………………… 87

环境管理与政策——澳门废弃物管制的政策研究
  黄少鸿 ………………………………………………………………… 99

Social Security Administration and Institutional Framework in the Post-aprtheid South Africa: Pitfalls, Challenges and Innovations
  Letlhokwa George MPEDI …………………………………………… 122

政府采购对技术创新的影响效应研究
  朱春奎　李　燕 ……………………………………………………… 144

中国公务人员工资水平地区差异的政治经济学
  张　光　游　宇 ……………………………………………………… 161

Modeling Voluntary Compliance: The Roles of Service Satisfaction, Policy Knowledge, and Trust in Government

  Jesse Campbell Jungho Park Tobin Im ·················· 183

参与式预算的模式：云南盐津分析

  贾西津 ·· 205

中国官员财产公示申报制度——进入立法议程的析论

  孔繁斌 杨淑玲 ·· 228

如何发挥公务人员终身学习理念

  周和根 ·· 243

完善中国基本公共服务体系的公众需求分析

  姜晓萍 田 昭 ·· 248

中西政府治理价值研究的历史嬗变

  丁 煌 ··· 268

Interlocal Agreements and Regional Collaborative Governance Networks in China

  Liming Suo Jie Ma Bin Chen ·· 277

从竞争走向合作：打破土地资源利用的路径依赖

  李永乐 刘玉山 ·· 302

不公平感与反腐败效能感——什么塑造了个体对反腐败的态度？

  李 辉 公 婷 肖汉宇 ·· 311

从女权主义视角探讨澳门女性领导及主管公务员之玻璃天花板

  谢启耀 ·· 331

澳门公务法人制度改革探析——兼比较法的借鉴

  张昇和 ·· 341

Meeting the Challenges of Performance Management

Andrew Podger[①]

Performance management (PM) has emerged internationally as perhaps the most widely adopted initiative from the New Public Management (NPM) agenda of the 1980s and 1990s. Everywhere it raises the following issues: how do we measure performance, how do we judge, how do we reward? Also, vitally, how can we ensure PM is actually used to improve decision-making in the public sector?

Like NPM, PM is interpreted differently in different countries, but amongst its common characteristics are:

(1) A focus on objectives and results, rather than on processes and rules;

(2) A degree of devolution with some flexibility over management processes in order to facilitate capacity to focus on desired results;

(3) The development of appropriate indicators of performance based on results, along with some targets or benchmarks.

Some countries have complemented this approach by opening up competition amongst providers to deliver the most effective and efficient performance, while others have relied more on benchmarking and continuous improvement.

Amongst the many challenges that have emerged over the last 30 years, three in particular remain the subject of continuing debate:

1) The extent to which "results" can be identified and measured in terms of policy impact rather than just program outputs and, more broadly, the nature of the results PM is intended to achieve;

---

① Andrew Podger, ANU Professor of Public Policy.

2) How to ensure organisations have the "capability" to achieve desired results both now and into the future, and how to measure organisational capability;

3) What types of rewards and penalties are most likely to incentivise individuals and organisations to improve performance.

These are the focus of this paper.

1. Defining and Measuring Results

Program budgeting and political vs administrative performance

PM in the 1980s under NPM drew heavily on initiatives in the US in the 1960s and 1970s such as "management by objectives" and "planning, programming and budgeting systems" (PPBS). "Program budgeting" as it was called in Australia involved classifying government activities in programs and identifying for each its specific objective(s); performance indicators were progressively developed for each program to help measure its effectiveness and efficiency. This was built into the budget process so that, with the annual budget, parliament would be advised not only about the proposed allocation of funds across programs but the objectives of those programs and the performance targets expected to be achieved from the funds to be appropriated. At the end of the each year, agencies would report not only on the spending of the moneys appropriated but also on how closely agencies had met the performance targets identified explicitly at the beginning of the year. Expenditure was also subject to auditing by the Australian National Audit Office (ANAO) not only of the propriety of the spending and the accuracy of the financial accounts, but also of performance (MAB – MIAC, 1994).

This highly systematic approach was widely applauded and was complemented by regular evaluations of programs. The politicians took responsibility for the policies and programs, and for articulating the objectives involved and the targets set, while administrators accepted responsibility for management including the regular measurement and reporting of performance against the indicators and targets.

In practice in Australia, program budgeting was always a "work in progress" with performance measures always being refined and improved. And it never operated quite as the designers intended. Parliament scrutiny of proposed budget measures and of annual reports and ANAO reports continued to focus more on inputs and concerns about processes than on the performance information. Much of the public debate and the political context continued to relate to claims of inappropriate or "wasteful" expenditure without much reference to whether the funds contributed or otherwise to program performance, or to whether program performance in terms of efficiency or effectiveness improved. This continues today with populist attacks on "fat cats", travel costs or extravagant expenditures on cars or office accommodation. Sometimes, of course, such debates do have a bearing on program efficiency but they are rarely expressed that way, and far less attention than was hoped has been given by the parliament to program effectiveness as revealed by the performance indicators and evaluations.

Also, evaluation activity decreased after its peak in the mid-1990s partly because government politicians were concerned about the potential ammunition they provided for their opponents in parliament. A cabinet requirement that all new policy proposals identify evidence from past evaluations and set out an evaluation plan were dropped in the late 1990s, ostensibly because it had become too bureaucratic.

There also remains a grey area about what political leaders and what administrative leaders should take responsibility for. To some extent the systematising of PM seems to have contributed to a shift in responsibility toward administrators. A principal-agent separation emerged, in part quite consciously, as NPM measures tried to hold administrators more to account for achieving specified performance targets within the policies and programs established by the politicians. Accountability for political performance continues in Australia, as in other democracies, played out in the legislature, in the media and in the election process, and which only indirectly relates to the efficiency and effectiveness of policies.

In China, where there is no distinction between policies and administration and no democratic election process to settle political performance, the PM system is used to assess what might be regarded as political performance as well as administrative performance (Chan and Gao, 2012).

GBE performance

The question of how to define performance and results was also affected by NPM initiatives involving the use of market-type approaches including the commercialisation and privatisation of certain government organisations. Government business enterprises' performance assessment began to follow private enterprise practice focusing primarily on returns on investment leaving to boards and managers nearly all aspects of administration (Walsh 1987). GBEs' performance was also monitored in respect of any "community service obligations" (CSOs) which were more clearly identified and funded explicitly. In Australia, GBEs remained subject to audit by the ANAO.

Managing performance of non-government agents

Contracting out and other purchaser-provider arrangements reinforced the NPM focus on results rather than processes, with providers, particularly non-government providers (whether for-profit or not-for-profit), allowed significant discretion over the management of inputs whether in terms of staffing or capital or administration, while held firmly to account for specified outputs and, at times, for outcomes (such as employment of the people receiving services). Non-government providers are not subject to ANAO audit, only the actions of the government "purchasers". A continuing debate has been the degree of details in contractual arrangements and the length of contract periods, and whether these allow sufficient discretion for innovation and experimentation that might lead to greater performance in terms of policy and program results. Another issue is the capacity of the government purchasers to make properly informed decisions and to retain strategic capacity while contracting out services.

Measuring overall impact or "outcomes"

Perhaps the biggest challenge remains how far PM can go to focus on overall impact rather than on program outputs and on program efficiency and effectiveness. In the late 1990s, Australia modified its program budgeting approach with what was called an "outcomes and outputs" framework (DOFA 1998, Hawke 2007). This was first implemented in 2000 coinciding with the introduction of accrual accounting.

Under the new framework, programs were aggregated into broad "outcomes" at the individual agency level and within each minister's portfolio responsibility but encompassing a wider range of activities than the former programs. In place of program objectives, the "outcome" statement was intended to indicate more generally the desired impact of the activities involved. This continued to be supported by specified performance indicators and targets, the latter including both output and outcome indicator targets.

This new approach was not particularly successful despite the good intention to better address the impact of policies. There were several significant problems:

(1) First, the outcomes were often described in too broad terms. Indeed, there was a (unsuccessful) High Court challenge over the legal authority to spend funds appropria-

ted by the parliament under such wide terms (High Court, 2005).

(2) Second, associated with this, was concern that the increased discretion involved provided opportunities to fund partisan activities with insufficient scrutiny as the PM arrangements did not provide adequate discipline.

(3) Third, the "outcomes" did not resonate with the parliament or the public in the way that "programs" did. Programs usually had names that reflected clearly understood activities or products (such as "schools" or "hospitals"), whereas outcome statements (such as "better health" or "employment and participation") were too general or not well known or understood even when the objectives were uncontroversial.

(4) There was also no evidence that evaluation of the "outcomes" had been enhanced in line with introduction of the new framework. Indeed, evaluation activity in government agencies received less priority from the late 1990s as mentioned.

(5) Finally, despite the new framework's addressing of the problem of narrowly-defined programs, it was still focussed on each portfolio and did not therefore address the most "wicked" problems like Indigenous welfare or truancy or disadvantaged youth or drugs' abuse, which nearly always cross portfolio boundaries.

In the mid 2000s the framework was modified with the re-introduction of programs under the guise of "sub-outcomes" (ANAO – DOFA, 2004). A major review managed by the Department of Finance in 2011 – 2013 (CFAR, 2012) suggested taking this modification further, in many respects returning the system to the former program budgeting approach while encouraging evaluations of cross-program and cross-portfolio strategies addressing more complex social issues. It proposed that outcomes be retained for performance purposes but appropriation bills no longer appropriate funds to "outcomes". (CFAR also reviewed the 1997 financial management legislative reforms arising from NPM; new legislation was passed by the Parliament in 2013.)

This still leaves somewhat unresolved in Australia the challenge of measuring performance in terms of impact.

Addressing this challenge may be assisted by some clarification of the different levels at which performance might be evaluated:

(1) *Process evaluation* involves mostly internal measures, examining such aspects as whether the program is being delivered to the intended people, whether they are satisfied, and was the administration efficient (e.g. costs per unit of output);

(2) *Impact evaluation* focuses on effectiveness, whether objectives like poverty alleviation, school retention, work force participation, increased life expectancy, are being achieved. It also may address whether there have been unintended effects such as on employment, earnings, savings or fraud and corruption.

Impact evaluation typically requires measures from beyond the agencies delivering the programs, and it in turn can involve different levels of impact:

(1) The *first-round impact* assessment in the static picture of the impact on clients' circumstances, such as the impact of pensions on income distribution or access to education or health services, with no consideration of the behavioural effect he program itself might have induced. Measurement of this impact is typically through surveys of the circumstances of the service clients-their incomes, their location, their housing, their education or workforce participation, their health.

(2) The *second-round impact* assessment involves a dynamic picture of people moving in and out of education, work and welfare, prisons, hospitals etc. Measurement is typically through time series and longitudinal studies and may involve post-hoc examination of the effects of programs on incentives to work, to gain skills, to save etc., requiring surveys of behaviours as well.

(3) A *third round impact* study would address the counter-factual: what might have happened anyway, or under different scenarios and policies. This requires more sophisticated research tools such as randomised trials and dynamic modelling.

Presented this way, it is clear that PM systems cannot be expected to monitor impact beyond the first level on a regular basis within the typical annual cycle that PM systems work to. Even the first round impact may be difficult to conduct in this way.

This suggests that PM systems need to be complemented by ongoing and systematic investment into evaluation studies. Particularly for second and third round impacts, governments will almost certainly rely upon third party experts, and need to allow them professional independence. Statutory authorities with a degree of independence can also play a significant role. In Australia, agencies such as the Productivity Commission, the Australian Bureau of Statistics, the Australian Institute of Health and Welfare and certain economic bureaus continue to be major contributors, working closely with external researchers as well as with government departments.

Such evaluations can also complement PM systems in providing opportunities to examine cross-programs, cross-portfolio and cross-jurisdictional impacts whether this is central to the issue at hand (i. e. "wicked" problems). In other words, PM can continue to focus primarily on programs within portfolios so long as it is complemented by periodic evaluations that include wider impact studies. PM may also be extended to monitor combined programs including across portfolios and jurisdictions where particular complex social or environmental issue are given priority for a period, but it still needs to have complementary evaluation effort to explore impact and effectiveness.

2. Organisational Capability

PM systems generally focus on the current (or recent past) efficiency and effectiveness of government programs and activities, and on individuals' current (or recent past) performance. The idea of assessing capability for future performance either by organisations or by individuals is not new, but does raise many challenges. It is reflected in Kaplan and Norton's, "Balanced Scorecard" and other initiatives aimed at positioning organisations for future performance and looking beyond immediate measures of performance (Kaplan and Norton, 1992).

The UK introduced capability reviews in 2005 under the Blair Government, and Australia drew on the UK methodology in its program of capability reviews between 2011 and 2014 (APSC, 2011; Podger and Harmer, 2014). Capability was defined as the collective expertise of the people in the organisation plus the capacity of its processes and systems.

The components explored in Australia's reviews were:

(1) *Leadership*: in setting the organisation's direction, and in motivating and developing its people;

(2) *Strategy*: having an outcomes-focussed strategy, making choices based on evidence, and collaborating and building a common purpose; and

(3) *Delivery*: having a performance management system, a shared commitment with sound delivery models, good organisational plans that effectively prioritise and allocate resources, and demonstrable innovation in service delivery.

These components are closely interconnected, as illustrated in the capability "wheel" used in both the UK and Australia (Figure 1).

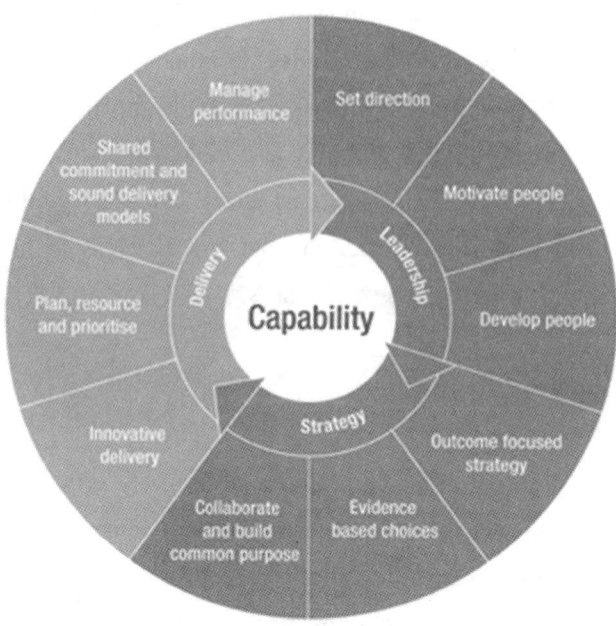

Figure 1　Capability Wheel

Source: APSC, 2011.

The apparent soundness of this approach ot measuring capability has been challenged, however, by the UK's National Audit Office which found a divergence between reported delivery performance and review teams' assessments of organisations' delivery capability (NAO, 2009). That is, the assessments of capability for future performance were not correlated with actual performance. Since the NAO's 2009 report, the UK has stopped its capability review program. It is too early to see whether Australia's capability reviews suffer a similar, apparently devastating, weakness.

Preliminary examination of the first rounds of capability reviews certainly suggested that there was insufficient consistency of standards to allow for reliable comparisons across organisations, even amongst those with similar functions (Podger and Harmer, 2014). Some elements of capability are inherently difficult to measure, such as "leadership", and others are perhaps too vague for even subjective assessment (such as "innovation"). In some cases, the more measurable elements were not as rigorously investigated as they might have been (such as IT capacity and utilisation, skills audits and career planning, financial management).

Nonetheless, in both the UK and Australia, the senior managers themselves found the reviews valuable, providing useful insight into ways to improve strategic planning, leadership and service delivery. Some commentators, however, have been more sceptical [one in the UK referring to "Mandarin-tinted glasses" (Talbot, 2009)].

Notwithstanding the challenges in measuring organisational capability, the initial round of reviews in Australia suggested service delivery capability was generally good, strategic planning was often weak and leadership (including HRM planning) was of mixed quality APSC 2013, Podger and Harmer 2014). Perhaps not unrelated to these findings was that departments were found to do relatively well in working effectively with ministers and the political leadership but there is a high degree of variability in the availability and use of evidence, and almost all rate poorly in internal collaboration and in working with external stakeholders (who are seen by most as outsiders to be managed at arm's length rather than agents to work with collaboratively).

Notwithstanding the challenges of measuring organisational capability, addressing such capability is a central element of performance management. Much of Australia's formal PM system concerns the budget process and the desire that it focus on "results": "*what*" the budget is intended to achieve. For managers, this raises no less important a challenge than "*how*" to achieve the results. Addressing the "how" (and "why") question is the function of strategic planning, complementing the budget aspects of PM with its articulation of objectives and performance targets (Podger, 2009). Strategic planning typically involves clarifying an organisations "vision" of how it wishes to be regarded in the medium-term future, and its "mission" or primary business or function; and identifying key result areas, and specific strategies and targets for each, that would ensure achievement of the vision and mission and the achievement of desired program results in the future. The key result areas identified will depend upon the organisation's functions and environment, and its current performance, but may often include people management, financial and other control systems, information and information technology, and stakeholder relationships. It is not surprising that these bear considerable similarity to the "capability wheel" element used in the UK and Australian capability reviews.

The usefulness of strategic plans depends both on how well they are developed (to gain wide acceptance both within the organisation and amongst stakeholders) and how well the strategies are monitored and reviewed. Too many sit on the bookshelf having little impact on either managers or staff. Quality plans involve tangible action to meet specific targets-not ones related directly to immediate program results but ones that reflect increased capability to do so whether in terms of expertise or systems, processes and assets.

Some Australian agencies have used annual reports to provide information not only on performance against the relevant budget outcomes and output targets, but also on performance against its own strategic plans and related strategies and targets (DHFS, 1998). The new financial accountability legislation (the Public Governance, Performance and Accountability Act, 2013) will require all agencies in future to have corporate plans and to link these to portfolio budget statements and to annual reports.

The Australian Public Service Commission also publishes an annual "State of the Service" report which provides information on the whole of the APS including data on staffing and data from agencies and from a census of APS employees; in recent years it has also drawn on the agency capability reviews. It has become a very substantial and valuable document, attempting to describe the capability and performance of the APS as a whole (including how well the APS values are being upheld) and to draw attention to common challenges that need to be addressed to improve capability. It is not linked to any specific whole-of-APS strategic plan, but it does provide considerable insights into the capability of the APS and has the potential to track whether capability is improving or not and to identify priorities for improving capability (APSC, 2012, 2013).

3. Rewards and Penalties

The very transparency of PM systems, with public reporting of performance, provides incentives for improvement. This is particularly the case where the reports include benchmarking and comparisons of performance across organisations undertaking similar functions. The political (and bureaucratic) reward of being the best, and the penalty of being the worst, may be only reputational but they may have no less an impact for that. In the case of competing organisations, the rewards (and penalties) are highly tangible in terms of winning or losing business contracts in tender processes.

More controversial is the provision of monetary rewards or penalties to individuals or organisations based on performance, particularly for those in the public sector. What is it that best motivates public servants and public organisations to improve performance?

Before addressing the evidence on this issue, it is worth exploring the links between individual performance and organisation performance. High organisational performance depends upon high individual performance, but high individual performance does not always translate into high organisational performance. Amongst the factors contributing to high organisational performance are (APSC, 2014):

(1) Alignment of individual and team goals and targets not only with program objectives and targets but also with the organisation's vision and mission and strategic direction-a clear "line of sight" from the individual to the organisation as a whole;

(2) Timely feedback on individuals' performance that is comprehensive, fair and consistent and generally positive; and

(3) Effective management action to facilitate individual performance, including by removing obstacles to high performance (e.g. good systems, appropriate training and development and a good working environment, and removing consistently poor performers).

In other words, an effective PM system links together "program budgeting" which focuses on results, "strategic planning" which focusses on capability, and individual performance appraisal.

Performance pay for individuals

A key question is whether monetary rewards attached to the performance appraisal encourages better individual performance and, as a result, better organisational 'performance. A 2005 OECD report (OECD, 2005) based on twelve country reports came to the conclusion that performance-related pay is an appealing idea but its implementation is complex and difficult and the impact on motivation is ambivalent-it appears to motivate a minority but a large majority do not see it as an incentive, however it is designed. Much more important motivators are job content and career development prospects. Other studies have also pointed to the risks of a negative impact on organisational performance if individual rewards are seen to be unfair or to undermine desirable team behaviour.

Australian experience also suggests the risks of adverse impact are real (Hawke, 2013) and the effort required to ensure a performance pay system is fair and perceived as such is very considerable and may not deliver commensurate gains in organisational performance. APS employee surveys consistently reveal widespread unhappiness with performance pay arrangements, which in recent years has led most agencies to removing them (the removal process is taking time as performance pay has often been locked into formal enterprise agreements on pay and also because those receiving significant rewards are not happy to see their pay lowered to the average) (APSC, 2004, 2013).

That said, considerable effort is required to ensure that performance appraisal is provided to all staff and managed well, whether or not pay is attached to the results. A link to pay can provide a driver to ensure managers do provide regular and consistent feedback through formal appraisal systems, an essential contributor to organisational performance, even if the pay has no positive impact on incentives.

Notwithstanding the OECD evidence, confirmed by Australian experience, performance pay systems continue to be introduced across the OECD and elsewhere, and there are few examples of public organisations withdrawing their systems. Apart from the continued attraction to the private sector-orientated idea despite the evidence of its limited if any usefulness in the public sector, the OECD report suggests a key reason for such systems continuing to be introduced appears to be their role in facilitating other organisational changes including effective appraisal and goal setting, clarification of tasks, acquisition of skills, improved employee-manager dialogue and increased flexibility in the work place. It may be the catalyst for desired cultural change.

Australia has still not moved entirely away from using performance pay in the public sector. The Abbott Government elected in 2013 has indicated renewed support for the idea reflecting its strong links with private sector leaders who assume performance bonuses will motivate improved performance in the public sector as they believe it does in the private sector. Similarly, some Australian State Governments from the non-Labor side of politics also continue to favour performance pay.

There also continue to be debates in Australia about the design of such performance pay systems. Those who recognise the limited benefits in terms of motivation and the risks of counterproductive effects on organisational performance, but who see sufficient side benefits such as locking in robust performance appraisal, generally favour systems that provide modest benefits for a majority of the staff concerned and that also limit maximum payments even for top performers. On the other hand, adherents of performance pay who believe bonuses are major motivators (as may occur in the private sector) tend to favour schemes with very generous payments for those assessed as top performers, and little or no rewards for those delivering no more than might have been expected. When I was Public Service Commissioner, I advised agency heads using performance pay to adopt the first approach (APSC, 2004). Increasingly, however, I was convinced by the evidence that even this approach offered limited benefits in terms of organisational performance and that the costs involved in avoiding the risk of a counterproductive impact were simply not worth paying (Podger, 2009).

Monetary rewards for organisational performance

Australia has also experimented in providing financial rewards to public sector organisations based on performance. The results again have been mixed. In the case of the National Competition Policy rewards in the mid-1990s, paid to state and territory governments which removed impediments to competition amongst public service providers (and regulatory impediments to competition in the private sector), there is some evidence that even relatively small rewards gained political and bureaucratic attention and helped to drive the reforms (ANAO, 1999). On the other hand, rewards for achieving specific targets such as hospital surgery waiting list numbers and waiting times led to considerable "gaming" amongst jurisdictions able to manipulate administrators data (Canberra Times reference?), and to measures that proved not to achieve sustained performance gains. It may be that such dangers can be reduced over time with experience as consistent data definitions and measures are put into place and audit processes test the integrity of regulatory systems.

But it may also be true that other (non-financial) rewards and penalties have a greater impact on organisational performance. One such approach is "earned autonomy", used originally in the UK NHS in the 1990s (Smee, 2000). This involves rewarding good performance by relaxing central controls such as over financial management, HRM, borrowing and investment etc. Equally, it involves escalating levels of intervention where performance is poor culminating in suspension or dismissal of the relevant organisation's board and/or management. The reputational impact, as much as any administrative cost or relief, would seem to be a key motivator for public organisations and public managers.

Variations of "earned autonomy" have been introduced in Australia particularly at the sub-national level. State governments have the power to dismiss local government and to appoint administrators for a period to address mismanagement and corruption. Increasingly, state governments also establish boards to manage hospitals, allowing them considerable discretion so long as performance reports demonstrate they are meeting standards of efficiency, access and safety and quality. There is debate now about applying such models ot schools.

Critical to any such system is the quality of performance reporting: the relevance of performance indicators, the consistency and timeliness of the data, and the integrity of reporting arrangements. Increasingly, this involves not just reporting on "outcomes" but on inputs and processes that offer insights into service quality such as involvement by service consumers and the wider community. Also critical is the usefulness of the information for organisational learning rather than just external accountability, and the actions that organisations take to explore the data and reflect on management systems and processes.

Conclusion

In many respects, performance management will always be a work in progress. It serves a range of purposes for a range of stakeholders. Australia has been a leader in the PM movement, but is still refining its approach and discovering that variations are needed for the different purposes involved, that each requires a mix of input, output and outcome measures and not all can be managed regularly or systematically.

Particular challenges are involved in measuring impact, requiring external bodies and expertise to assist with evaluations, and acceptance that, while this cannot usually be done on a continuing basis, it is essential for assessing program and cross-program effectiveness.

Assessing organisational capability to achieve high performance into the future is also important but difficult. A critical element is the strength of the links between strategic planning (addressing *how* agencies can achieve the best results) and the performance budgeting framework (*what* is to be achieved).

Australia has also (re)discovered that PM in the public sector is necessarily different from PM in the private sector, and that the use of financial rewards and penalties may not deliver the benefits the advocates claim.

A more general challenge that the Australian experience identifies is how to ensure PM processes do not become so systematised and bureaucratised that they are divorced from the basic role of PM to improve decision-making. There is a risk not only of wasteful administrative effort but of counterproductive effect if incentives are created for gaming or other distorting behaviour. Success depends on the information genuinely contributing to the decisions of ministers, the parliament, agency managers and operational staff, and to learning for the future including by the public at large.

---

[1] Australian National Audit Office (ANAO) and Department of Finance and Administration (DFA), *Better Practice in Annual Performance Reporting*, Canberra, April, 2004.

[2] Australian Public Service Commission (APSC), *State of the Service Report 2003 – 2004*, Canberra, November, 2004.

[3] APSC, *State of the Service Report 2012 – 2013*, Canberra, November, 2013.

[4] Commonwealth Financial Accountability Review (CFAR), *Is Less More ? Towards Better Commonwealth Performance*, Discussion Paper, Department of Finance and Deregulation, Canberra, March, 2012.

[5] Chan, H. S. and Gao, J., "Can the Same Key Open Different Locks? Administrative Values Underlying Performance Management in China", *Public Administration Review*, 91 (2), 2013, pp. 366–380.

[6] Department of Finance and Administration, *Specifying Outcomes and Outputs-Implementing the Commonwealth's Accrual-based Outcomes and Outputs Framework*, Canberra, 1998.

[7] Department of Health and Family Services, *Annual Report 1997 – 1998*, Canberra, October, 1998.

[8] Harmer, Jeff and Podger, Andrew, "Capability Reviews of Australian Government Departments 2010 – 2013", Paper from China Australia Dialogue on Public Administration workshop on public sector HRM, October 2013, held at Sun Yat Sen University Guangzhou, to be published by Australia New Zealand School of Government, Canberra, 2014.

[9] Hawke, Allan, "Performance Management and the Performance Pay Paradox", in Wanna, J., Vincent, S. and Podger, A. (eds), *With the Benefit of Hindsight: Valedictory Reflections from Departmental Secretaries*, 2004 – 2011, ANU Press, Canberra, 2012.

[10] Hawke, Lewis, "Performance Budgeting in Australia", *OECD Journal on Budgeting*, OECD, Paris, 7 (3) 2007, pp. 1 – 15.

[11] High Court of Australia, *Combet v Commonwealth*, Canberra, 2005.

[12] Kaplan, Robert S. and Norton, D. P., "The Balanced Scorecard-Measures that Drive Performance", *Harvard Business Review*, Boston, January-February, 1992, pp. 71 – 79.

[13] MAB – MIAC, *Performance Management: The Integrated Use of Recognition, Rewards and Sanctions*, Management Advisory Board/ Management Improvement Advisory Committee, Public Service and Merit Protection Commission, Canberra, 1994.

[14] NAO (National Audit Office), *Assessment of the Capability Review Programme*, London, February, 2009.

[15] Podger, Andrew, *The Role of Departmental Secretaries: Personal Reflections on the Breadth of Responsibilities Today*, ANU Press, Canberra, 2009.

[16] Smee, Clive, *Speaking Truth to Power: Two Decades of Analysis in the Department of Health*, Radcliffe Publishing Ltd., England, 2005.

[17] Talbot, Colin, "Mandarin-tinted Glasses", *Public Finance Opinion*, London, 27 February, 2009 (http://opinion.publicfinance.co.uk/2009/02/mandarin-tinted-glasses/).

[18] Walsh, Peter, "Policy Guidelines for Commonwealth Statutory Authorities and Government Business Enterprises" (Statement by Minister for Finance), Australian Parliament, October, 1987, Canberra.

The Introduction of Minimum Services Standards (MSS) as the Strategy to Enhance Quality of Basic Public Services in Indonesia's Decentralized System: Potential Benefits and Risks

Mohammad Roudo[①]

1. Introduction

The enhancement of quality of public services becomes the main agenda of Indonesia's decentralization policy.[②] However, after a decade of the implementation, the improvement on the basic public services which becomes the gate way to achieve the better welfare for local people is still unclear and no robust. The high quality of public services can only be seen in some regions as the best practices, yet in general the quality of services at the local level is still below people's desire and inequality on these services still exists (Suwandi, 2002; DSRP, 2009).

As a response to dissatisfaction with that condition, in 2005, the Central Government has introduced Minimum Service Standards (MSS) as the key focus of the decentralization policy aiming to enhance overall quality public services and improve the accountability and performance of local governments to provide basic public services in minimum required quality. While it explicitly refers to minimum quality, it also implicitly set the minimum required quantity and access.

Lying on the intersection on political economics, public finance and organizational

---

① Mohammad Roudo, Ph. D. , in International Development Department, the University of Birmingham (UK).

② Decentralization policy in Indonesia has been initiated in 1999 by the stipulation of the law 22/1999 on local governance and law 25/1999 on fiscal balance between the central government and local governments which later both laws revised into law 32/2004 and law 33/2004.

behaviour concepts and theories such as gains and risks of decentralization, allocative efficiency, principal-agents problems and performance management, we argue that although some potential benefits of decentralization can be captured by the introduction and practice of MSS, some risks and unintended negative consequences can possibly emerge. This paper also concerns with some policy recommendations to ensure the introduction of MSS will attain the promises of and minimize the negative consequences of decentralization.

The paper comprises five parts. The first part will begin by the brief explanation of Indonesia's decentralization policy and its link to the condition of public services in Indonesia after a decade of an implementation. The second will seek the design and institutional arrangements of MSS. The third will discuss the potential benefits from the introduction MSS, while in the fourth will consider its potential risk and unintended negative consequences. In the last part, some policies aiming to ensure the benefits of decentralization and minimize potential risks of decentralization will be presented.

Although there have been many books, studies and reports on Indonesia's decentralization system whether in overall evaluations (UCLG, 2009; Strategic Asia, 2013) administrative and political decentralization (Devas, 1997; Hadiz, 2004, 2010; Turner et al., 2003, 2009), fiscal decentralization (Brodjonegoro and Asanuma, 2000; Vazquez and Vaillancourt, 2013) or even spatial decentralization (Firman, 2003; Bunnel et al., 2011), this discussion on the formulation and implementation of MSS in Indonesia is essential since only few of them link the theories of decentralization with the management of local government performance. If any, there are limited researches specifically seek the potential benefits and risks of MSS as the main focus of decentralization policy to accelerate the improvement of public services across regions in Indonesia.

This paper is also significant to understand the complexities and challenges faced by the Central Government in Indonesia in setting the performance measurements (targets, indicators) of local governments in delivering their basic public services. Besides that, this paper is an essential material for a comparative study to countries which are willing to introduce performance management to their local governments in decentralized system.

2. Decentralization and Public Services

2.1. Understanding the Concept of Decentralization Policy in Indonesia

Decentralization policy in Indonesia can not be separated from the context of political, economic and social reforms introduced in 1997. This reform demanded the transformation of the central-local relationships through setting fair and mutually beneficial central-local relations; effective and efficient resources allocation between the central government and local governments and better quality of public services in all regions. The adoption of this policy follows the trends in many developing Asia and Africa countries in 1980's which was seen by Conyers (1983) as the latest fashion on the model of development during that period as a response to the failure of centralized system in maintaining economic stability from crisis and less concern of the central government to the development issues in the local level (e. g. poverty and inequality on public services).

For Indonesia, the decentralization policy may be defined in terms of two main elements: delimitation of territory and transfer of powers from the central government to local governments, according to the concept of Smith (1985). The delimitation of territory is realized through the creation of 34 provinces as the first tier and 505 districts (93 cities and 412 regencies) as the second tier; while transfer of powers have occurred with almost all government functions to both the first or the second tiers except the 6 main responsibilities①, which belong to the central government, on account of their national and international implications.

In understanding, the concept of MSS, we acknowledge at least 4 unique aspects of the design of Indonesia's decentralization policy. Firstly, the law mandates the devolution on powers and authorities, although it also does not ignore the existence of de-concentration and delegation system in maintaining central-local relationships.② In both delegation and de-concentration, the existence of the local governments is the "extension" of the central government authority to ensure the successful of national objectives, while in a devolved system, the highest level of decentralization, local governments have high autonomy and discretion to determine what their population wants and needs and it is followed by the authorities in making own decision and financial power (Bardhan and Mookherjee, 2006; Rondinelli and Cheema, 2007).

---

① These responsibilities are defence, foreign affairs, finance, monetary, religion and judiciary functions.

② To define the types of central-local relations, we refer to the classifications made by Rondinelli and Cheema (2007), the delegation, the lowest level of decentralization occurs when some power is given to local authorities only to run specific task from the central government (e. g. running Special Economic Zones), while de-concentration applies when the central government transfers powers to local authorities/personnel but they are appointed and are still responsible to the central government.

In Indonesia's devolved system, the central government has transferred most powers and responsibilities to local governments except six main obligations referred above. Since the devolution is taken in the short time and cover almost all government functions, Aspinall and Feally (2003) as well as Hofman and Kaiser (2004) note this policy as the "big bang" policy and characterize Indonesia as the one of the most decentralized countries in the world.

The second key characteristic is that it covers all aspects of decentralization, administrative, political, financial and spatial economic decentralization. Administrative decentralization occurs when policy implementation and managerial tasks are undertaken by the central government's agent at the local level without any authority to make their own decisions. In Indonesia, it is realized by dividing nations into the central government, provincial government as the first tier as well as district (cities and regencies) government as the second tier. After that, the division of authorities amongst different levels/tiers of government is arranged and it is then determined whether it is applied through delegation, de-concentration or devolution, according to the characteristics of the assigned functions. Although it is clear stated in the regulation which sector/area becomes the main responsibilities and authorities of each level of government, the conflicts often occur with jointly powers and responsibilities to authorities between three levels of government what is referred to "concurrent" authorities.[①] Each tier of government will acknowledge tasks as their responsibility if they receive financial benefits whereas they tend to ignore them if these task impose costs refered to what Suwandi (2002) mentions as unfunded mandates

Political decentralization is applied when the Central Government gives more autonomy and high discretion in decision making to local government. Treisman (2007) defines political decentralization when the sub national government has full authority to policy making decision. Similar with this view, Salim and Kombaitan (2009), based on practices in Indonesia, argue that with political decentralization, local authorities and communities have more decision making powers. In Indonesia, political decentralization is consolidated by local democratization whereby local leader and local parliament members are elected and should be accountable to the local people. Local people and local parliament have full authorities to hold local government's accountability as can the central government.

[①] The example of concurrent function or shared competence is the responsibility for road maintenance. This jointly function is clearly divided. The central government is responsible for national roads, while the provincial and districts governments are responsible for the provincial and district roads.

Financial decentralization is crucial to political decentralization, and focuses on the extent which autonomy is given to local government to generate their own revenues and utilize/spend their money. Fengler and Hofman (2009), based on the experience of European, Asian and American Latin Countries, acknowledge fiscal decentralization as the efforts of the central government to give more discretion to local government to generate their own revenues through taxes and other legal financial sources (c. q. charges, selling bonds) as well as guarantee the freedom of local governments to make decisions on their public expenditure. In Indonesia, fiscal decentralization is realized by giving more autonomy in the revenues sides and relatively full authorities on their expenditure side (Brodjonegoro and Asanuma, 2000). In the revenue side, the central government gives more discretion to local governments to raise their own taxes and revenues also transferring more resources through intergovernmental transfer mechanism in the form of Revenue Sharing (*Dana Bagi Hasil*), General Block Grant (*Dana Alokasi Umum*) or Specific Block Grant (*Dana Alokasi Khusus*). Moreover, in the expenditure side, the local governments have relatively full autonomy to spend their budget to achieve their local development objectives based on their own perceived interests and needs.

This idea of fiscal decentralization is also tightly connected to the concept of spatial decentralization, another dimension of decentralization in Indonesia, which focuses on the spatial economic theories about the disparity or inequality amongst regions. Rondinelli (1980) and Firman (2003) define this type of decentralization as the strategy to distribute and diffuse economic concentration across regions instead of concentrate it in only few urban areas. Spatial decentralization policy in Indonesia is addressed through efforts to redistribute resources away from wealth Java Island, to the relatively poor regions of Indonesia. Failure to distribute economic activities from Java into out of Java could increase dissatisfaction among regions then leading to the conflicts among regions to fight for economic and financial resources, such that threat to national integration (Tadjoeddin et al., 2003).

The third characteristic is that it is implemented in a unitary system so the role of the central government is still relatively strong even though most powers and authorities have been transferred to local governments. Ferrazzi (2000) notes that implementation of Indonesia decentralization is contextualized in the unitary system so that the central government has a relatively high degree of control on its local governments compared to a federal system. In another words, unlike the arrangement in federal systems like in the US or Australia where sub-national government (Federal Government) has relatively equal status with the Central

Government and exclusive authority to deal with particular issues that can not be intervened by the central government, the position of local governments in Indonesia is still a subordinate and responsible to the central government as well as to local parliament and people.

Lastly, Indonesia's decentralization policy also focuses on the interactions between different levels of governments; instead of decentralized the powers of governments to the private sectors or directly to local people. This concept is in line with the concept of vertical decentralization defined by Campbell and Denezhkina (2009) or multi-level of governance concept presented by Hague and Harrop (2010); distinguished from horizontal decentralization which emphasised the involvement of non-governmental actors and local communities. However, it does not mean, there is no involvement of non-governmental actors in the implementation of Indonesian decentralization but it does not become the main focus.

2.2. The Quality of Public Service After A Decade of Implementation of Decentralization Policy

Some agendas are mandated by Indonesia decentralization's policy such as reducing dissatisfactions of local governments to the central government on the fiscal balance and avoid disintegration'/balkanise' caused by vertical inequality, prevent the ethnic/tribe conflict caused by inefficient allocation of resources across regions as well as enhancement quality of public services and welfare. While avoiding national disintegration and reducing the horizontal conflict has shown satisfactory results, the enhancement of quality of public services has remained as a main challenge for the implementation of Indonesia decentralization (Strategic Asia, 2013).

The evidence suggests that the current level of satisfaction of population to the access and quality of public services in Indonesia is still low. World Bank (2003, cited in Roudo and Saepudin, 2008) held a survey on the level of people's satisfaction to the services given in 5 cities and 5 districts showing no significant improvement in the level of public services in 2003. Although 34.1% of respondents show the level of satisfaction, 52.5% are still neutral while 13.4% felt unsatisfied with the current condition of services as shown in figure 1 and 2 below.

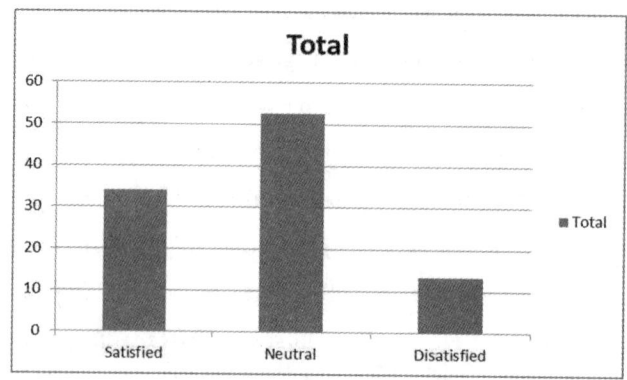

Figure 1 Total Percentage of Population's Satisfaction with the Services Received in 5 Cities and 5 Districts

Source: World Bank (2003, cited in Roudo and Saepudin, 2008).

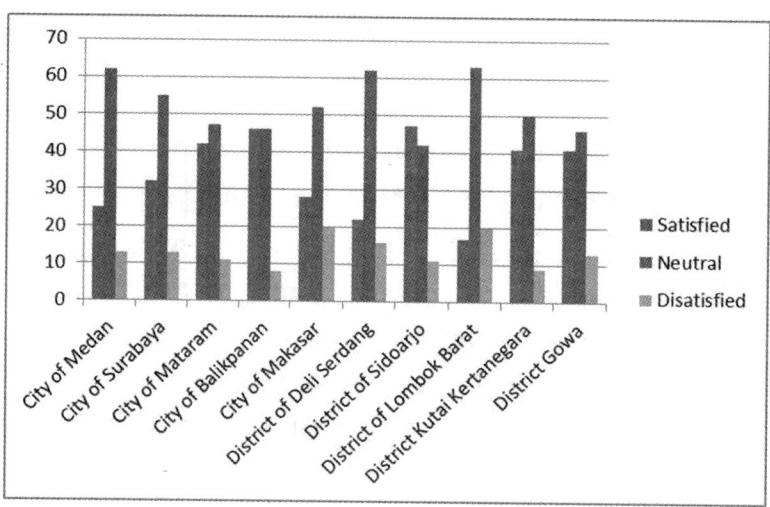

Figure 2 Percentage of Population's Satisfaction with the Services Received in 5 Cities and 5 Districts Segregated by City/District

Source: World Bank (2003, cited in Roudo and Saepudin, 2008).

In addition, Lewis and Pattinasarany (2009) based on the World Bank Governance and Decentralization Survey 2 (GDS2) in 2007 note although 85% of people are somewhat satisfied to the service in the primary education, the satisfaction level is seen to be exaggerated and bias regarding low expectations of population to services that are delivered. Low quality of public services might cause low level of competitiveness as the international business destinations as shown by Indonesia's rank on the Global Competitiveness Index

(GCI) which is positioned in the rank thirty eight in 2012 – 2013 and is relatively lower compared to the neighbourhood such as Singapore and Malaysia which put their rank in the rank second and twenty fourth (Schwab et al., 2013).

Other studies also indicate that basic public services do not reach those who have low income. Kristiansen and Santoso (2006) show that decentralization policy in healthcare in Indonesia causes privatization, does not increase the local government spending to local public health facilities particularly to the poor and does not improve the transparency and accountability in the management of local health unit. Similarly, decentralization policy in the education sector in Indonesia does not improve good governance (c.q. transparency and accountability) and financial allocation to primary and secondary education as well as the inequality of these services still exist across regions (Kristiansen and Pratikno, 2006).

Overall, the improvement of services across regions in Indonesia is not uniform. While there are innovations in some regions, there is still lack improvement across regions. Strategic Asia (2013) shows an improvement of service delivery in some rich and populous areas but the quality of basic services particularly health, education and infrastructure in the remote and poor areas still exist so it increase inequality of services across regions. That is why this problem is mentioned as an "unfinished agenda" in a decade on the implementation of Indonesia decentralization by Strategic Asia (2013). As the responses to this condition, in 2005, the central government introduced Minimum Service Standards (MSS) as the breakthrough strategy and key focus on running decentralization aiming to enhance quality of basic public services.

3. Design and Institutional Arrangement of MSS

3.1. Design of MSS

MSS or in Indonesia's term is called as Standar Pelayanan Minimal (SPM) is actually a form of performance measurement of local governments in Indonesia decentralized system. This is not really new concept since similar measurement of local government performance has been introduced both in developed and developing countries during the 1990s. Ferrazzi (2005) finds similarity of the form of MSS with the application of performance measurement in the Philippines, performance management system in South Africa or best value initiative and comprehensive performance assessment in the United Kingdom (UK). Since it is implemented in the unique decentralized system as explained above, the design of MSS can also be very unique and interesting to observe.

In Law and Government Regulation (GR)[①], MSS is defined as the provision of types and quality of basic public services which becomes part of the "local obligatory function" that should be received by each citizen to a minimum level. While Ferrazzi (2005) sees MSS primarily as a tool to influence and control local governments in fulfilling its "obligatory functions" in delivering basic services at particular standards required, which is set by the central government, Haryanto (2010) interprets MSS as a practical mechanism supporting the delivery of basic public services made by local governments. However, we believe that MSS is not only the strategy of the central government to accelerate the improvement of quality of public services, but also the efforts to reduce regional disparity in the provision of basic public services as part of the implementation of decentralization policy.

From those definitions, we can acknowledge 3 (three) main elements on the design of MSS: basic public services, local obligatory functions and performance measurement of local governments. Haryanto (2010) interprets GR 65/2005 on the guidance of MSS that basic public services refer to minimum socio-economic needs of citizen that should be fulfilled by the government. These services also protect constitutional, basic welfare, public order, national unity, and fulfil commitment of national and international conventions as well as highly demanded by the population in Indonesia like education, health, and infrastructure (Haryanto, 2010).

Moreover, obligatory functions refer to all "concurrent" functions or "shared competence" that is compulsorily implemented by each local government regardless its economic and financial capacities. However, Haryanto (2010) critizes that obligatory functions in the practice in Indonesia do not really represent the obligations or compulsory functions of local governments to fulfil the basic public services as defined above, but it reflects the "newly handed down authority" to districts level and "negative list" of local government's responsibilities to those that central and provincial government has not in charge. There are 26 obligatory functions stated in GR[②] but only few of them are classified as basic public services which are mandated to set MSS, as shown in Figure 3 below.

[①] It refers to Law 32/2004 on Local Governance and Government Regulation (GR) 65/2005 on the guidance of the formulation and implementation of MSS.

[②] This refers to GR 38/2007 on the Division of Authorities/Responsibilities Between the Central Government, Provincial Governments and District Governments.

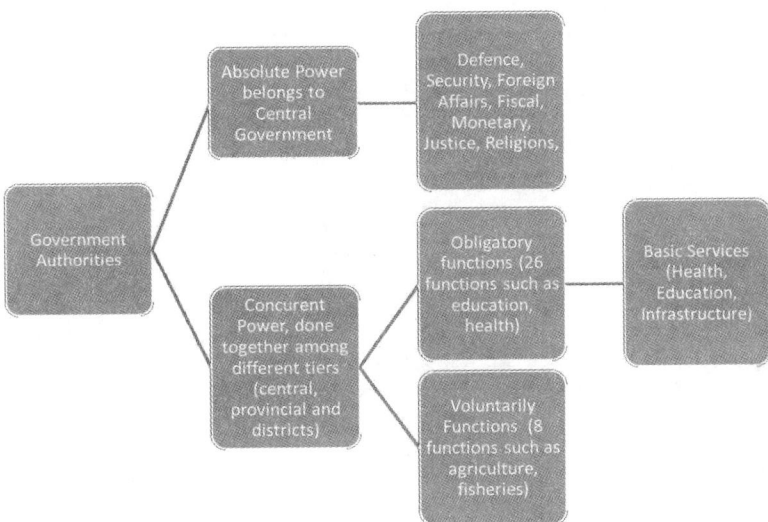

Figure 3 Obligatory Functions in Indonesia's Division of Responsibilities Between Different Levels of Government

Source: Adapted and Modified from GR 38/2007.

However, because the division of responsibilities between different level/tier of government are less clear, bias and inconsistent as mentioned above like which level/tier of government will do what functions, particularly to the concurrent functions whether obligatory and voluntarily functions; in practice, the conflict between different tier/level of government in executing these 'concurrent' functions often can not be avoided.

The last element, the performance measurement is elaborated into some sectors, indicators and targets which is formulated by sectoral ministries (e. g. ministry of education, ministry of health) as Ministry's Decree. In 2012, 15 MSS have been set and applied in district level and 9 in provincial level. All MSS both in district and provincial level consist of 69 services and 169 indicators as shown in Figure 4 below.

Table 1　MSS in Details

No	Sector	Year on Stipulation	Operational Guidance	Financial Guidance	Types of Services	Numbers of Indicators	Target Year
1	Health	2008	Yes	2009	4	18	2015
2	Social	2008	Yes	2010	4	7	2015
3	Environment	2008	Yes	Draft	4	4	2013
4	Administrative Affairs	2008	Yes	Draft	3	6	2011

(Continued)

No	Sector	Year on Stipulation	Operational Guidance	Financial Guidance	Types of Services	Numbers of Indicators	Target Year
5	Housing	2008	Yes	2010	2	3	2025
6	Women Empowerment	2010	Yes	2010	5	8	2014
7	Planning Family	2010	Yes	2010	3	9	2014
8	Basic Education	2010	Yes	2011	2	27	2014
9	General Affairs	2010	Yes	Draft	8	23	2014
10	Labour Affairs	2010	Yes	2010	5	8	2016
11	Communication and Information	2010	Yes	Draft	2	6	2014
12	Food Resilience	2010	Yes	2010	4	7	2015
13	Arts	2010	Yes	Draft	2	7	2014
14	Transportation	2011	No	Draft	4	26	2014
15	Investment	2011	Yes	Draft	7	10	2014
	Total		14	8	65	169	

Source: Author's compilation to Sectoral Ministries Decree.

MSS comprises quantitative and qualitative measurements (indicators and targets) which reflects the principles of the 3E's (economy, effectiveness and efficiencies). At a glance, MSS seems similar to the measurement of local government performance was practiced in the UK as "Best Values" Boyne (2002) notes that under "Best Values", the indicators and targets imposed as the performance measurement were intended to reflect the principles of 3Es. In Indonesia, these 3Es principles are elaborated in 3 types of measurements: inputs, outputs and outcomes. According to Rashid (1999), the measurement at input's level reflects cost imposed and resources utilised; while at output's level refers to goods and services delivered and at outcome's level means the impact or effects to the services delivered.

There is no uniformity among the sectors on their indicators and targets as shown Figure 5. For instance, in the education and health sectors, indicators and targets are dominated by input and output and no outcome can be found, while some indicators and targets in the outcome's level in the infrastructure and food resilience sectors, can be seen. In each sector, it is also very difficult to distinguish between input, output and outcome indicators and targets since most of them are mixed and often less clearly stated and defined.

Table 2 Examples of Indicators and Target in MSS

No	Judgement of Indicators / Targets	Sectors	Types of Basic Services	Indicators of MSS	Target (%)	Time to Achieve (Year)
1	Input	Education	Primary Education Services provided by Districts	In every Primary and Junior High School, there is at least 1 teacher room equipped by chair, desk for the Headmaster, teacher and School staff and should be separated for Headmaster in Junior High School	100	2014
2	Output	Education	Primary Education Services provided by Districts	An education unit is available and affordable by/through walking from permanent housing clusters in isolated areas 3 km's for Primary School and 6 km's from Junior High School.	100	2014
3	Output	Education	Primary Education Services provided by Education Unit	An education unit applies standardized curriculum	100	2014
4	Outcome	Education	–	No information	–	–
5	Input	Health	–	No information	–	–
6	Output	Health	Basic Health Service	Frequency and scope of daily visiting of Pregnant Mother	90	2015
7	Outcome	Health	–	No information		
8	Output	Infrastructure	Water Resources	Availability on clean water to serve daily needs of people	100	2014
9	Outcome	Infrastructure	Building and Environment Re-structuring	Good service to people who arrange the building permit	100	2014
10	Output	Food Resilience	Food Distribution and Access	Availability of Information on supply, price and stock	100	2015
11	Outcome	Food Resilience	Food Availability and Stock	Strengthening food stock	60	2015

Source: Author's Judgement to Some Sectoral Ministries. [1]

---

[1] These Sectoral Ministries refers to of National Education Decree 15/2010 on the MSS of Basic Education in Districts Level, Ministry of Health 741/2008 on the MSS of Health in District Level, Ministry of General Affairs Decree 14/PRT/M/2010 on the MSS of General Affairs and Spatial Plan, and Ministry of Agriculture Decree 65/Permentan/OT.140/12/2010 on the MSS of Food Resilience in Province and Districts.

3.2. Institutional Arrangement

The institutional arrangement refers to the political economic and public administration/management concepts which refer to how organizations are set to achieve their goals/objectives by understanding the actors, the roles of each actor and the rules of the games (Ostrom, 1990; O'Toole and Meier, 2011). Thus, in this part, we will identify actors or/and institutions involve in the practice of MSS, their roles/functions and the rules of the games underpinned the roles of each actor.

Several actors can be identified in overall management of MSS. The first actor is Ministry of Home Affairs (MoHA). This institution is actually the leading actor in the formulation of MSS by making the legal basis and general guidance for the sectoral ministries to set their own MSS, although this institution also takes initiatives as the actors which implement the MSS of General Affairs. Besides that, together with sectoral ministries, MoHA has responsibilities to accelerate the implementation and overcome the "bottle neck" as well as monitor and assess overall achievement of MSS based on the evaluations made by the sectoral ministries.

The second actor is sectoral ministry. Its main role is setting MSS through some indicators and targets (achievement and year) then stipulate them into Ministry Decree by firstly consulted with MoHA. It also monitors and evaluates the implementation of MSS in its sector as well as gives feedback and capacity building to local governments which have low performance in achieving targets set in MSS.

National Development Agency (Bappenas) and Ministry of Finance (MoF) have roles in the process of planning and setting MSS budget. Together with MoHA, Bappenas ensures that MSS will be integrated into local development plan, while MoF makes the financial resources are certain to funding MSS.

Other actors are local governments (districts and provincial governments) which become the leading actor in the level of implementation. Five main local institutions: Regional Secretary, Local Development Plan Agency (Bappeda), Local Finance Agency, Local Auditor and Local Sectoral Agencies (UKPD); become the main actors in the local level. They translate MSS into more practical mechanism and strategies and insert it to local regulations and document plan.

However, the responsibilities of provincial governments become double. They do not only implement MSS mandated to them, but also supervise the implementation of MSS in districts in their regions/territory. Indonesia's GR[①] mandates Governor as the "extension" or "representative" of the Central Government beside its roles as the Head of Province. Since the supervision of MSS is done hierarchical, sectoral ministries usually ask the provincial governments to compile reports on the achievement of MSS from district governments in its regions instead of doing direct supervision into district governments.

The fourth actors are auditors whether the internal (BPKP) or the external auditor (BPK). Both cooperate with local auditors in each district and province and inspectorates in each ministry to avoid fraud reporting and guarantee the success of local government to achieve indicators and targets in MSS. Although both auditors are involved as a supervision team, their roles are not as significant as MoHA. Finally, the last actor to be acknowledged is Special Presidential Unit set up to supervise the success of the national development program set as national priorities which MSS becomes one of those priorities. A simplified overview of the interactions between those actors can be seen in Figure 4.

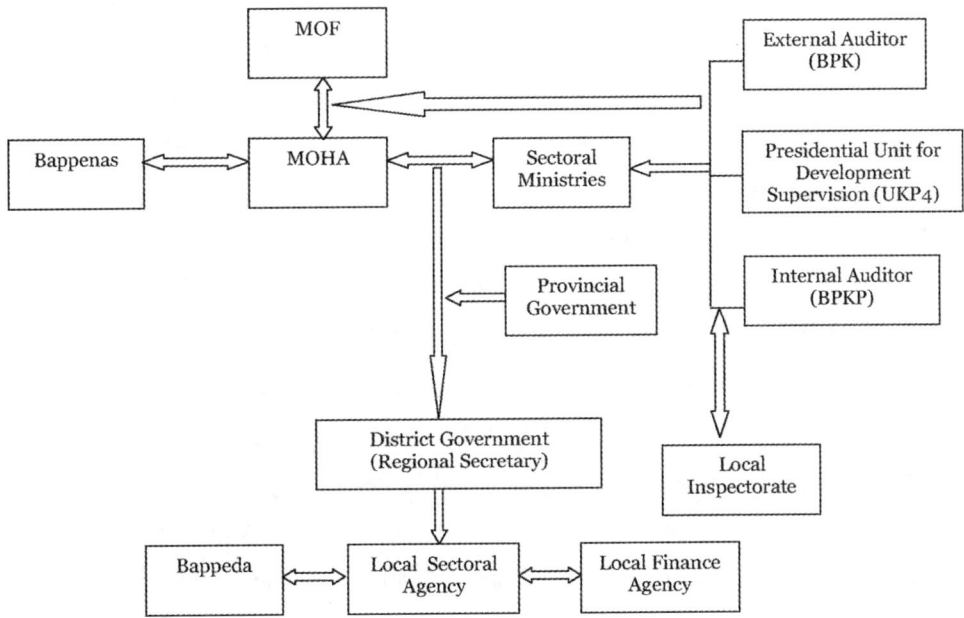

Figure 4 Relations between Actors in the Management of MSS

Sources: Author's interepretation and analysis to Law and GR on MSS.

---

① It refers to GR 19/2010 later revised as GR 23/2011 on the Function of Governor as the Representative of the Central Government.

Finally, in terms of the rules of the games, performance measurement of local governments have been set in MSS are imposed by the central government and should be accepted and implemented by local governments. Compliance is compulsorily which is different from the implementation of local government performance measurement in some OECD countries such as Germany, France and Sweden; where the targets and indicators are voluntarily created by local governments as it is noted by Kuhlmann (2010).

4. Potential Benefits

It seems reasonable to expect that the introduction of MSS could bring many advantages/benefits to the practice of decentralization policy in Indonesia particularly to enhance the quality basic public services across regions. These benefits are called the potential gains of decentralization by some scholars such as Ahmad and Brosio (2009).

The first benefits of MSS, it potentially creates more effective and efficient service which is in line with economic rationale about the optimum size of government and span of services. The idea is big size of state and large span of services will be difficult to capture the real needs and interests of population so the optimum sizes of state and its span of services should be set. MSS makes the government closer to the people because most powers to deliver basic public services have already transferred to the districts as the autonomy units that are closest to the people. Through MSS, local governments will have the powers to make their own strategies to achieve targets set in MSS by considering their financial and human resources capacities as well as the main interests and needs of their population. Gaubatz (2009) and Boasiako and Csanyi (2014), based on experiences of decentralized practices in African, Latin America and Central and Eastern European Countries shows that the effective and efficient service will be provided only if the subsidiarity principle, the principle when the public administration and services are addressed to the lowest level, is applied, regardless of their governmental system whether unitary or federal. Lockwood (2006) explains local governments as the closest entities to the people are better to provide effective and efficient services since they are relatively easier to capture the interest and need of local people, have the better information about the best strategies to deliver it and able to supervise the implementation easier and quicker leading to accurate and update information on the achievement of service delivery.

The introduction of MSS also creates more accountable and transparent as well as high performance of local governments through imposing clear performance measurement and allowing simultaneous scrutiny from the central government, local parliament and local people to local governments. It will lead to more effective and efficient public services delivery as the potential benefits of decentralization.

Performance in public organization refers to results or/and benefits (in terms of outputs, outcomes or impacts) received by people as users.). De Bruijn (2007) and Talbott (2011) define this performance in public organization as a tight connection between inputs (budget and other resources) and outputs/outcomes as the results of programme/activities through particular strategies and plans to achieve aims of public organizations. Polidano (1999) considers this performance as one element of New Public Management (NPM) which was initially developed in the private sectors. Because its successful application in the private sectors, it has been imitated and implemented in many public organizations in 1990s, started in the developed countries then it is followed by many developing countries, not only in the organizations in the central level but also in the local level (Polidano, 1999).

Moreover, Rogers (1999) defines the performance management in local governments is a set of tools and techniques used by politicians and managers in the local level to manage performance of powers have been devolved to them. He also illustrates four main elements in the performance management: clear objectives of organizations, the existence of performance's monitoring and review, the utilization of performance measurement such as indicators and indicators as well as appropriate rewards and punishments for organizations to achieve their objectives (Rogers, 1999). Similarly, Hood (2007) shows three forms of performance measurement, standards, ranks and intelligence, which is commonly adopted by the central and local institutions as described in Figure 4.

Table 3 Application of Performance Measurement

Application	Basic Principles	Example	Variants
Target	Floor standard, change in performance in particular time	Efficiency of savings, staff	Specific vs Global, individual/organization vs sector wide targets
Ranks	Comparison of performance amongst rival units on particular indicators	Sporting leagues	Simple vs composite leagues (number is distilled)
Intelligence	Background information (unpredictable)	Logs-health care episode	Unknown (anonymized) data (near miss reporting) vs attributed data

Source: Adapted and Modified from Hood (2007).

Refer to those definitions and classifications; MSS is one example of the application of performance management in the local level considering some elements presented by Rogers (1999). Now, the objective of local governments can be clearly described to improve their performance in delivering services. Besides that, some mechanisms for monitoring and review the performance are also set. Measurement is clearly set through several indicators and targets which become a focus of performance measurement particularly targets/standards refers to what is presented by Hood (2007). Those characteristics reflects the clear impose of performance measurement as part of performance management which makes the local governments more focus and has stable system to continually improve their performance to achieve indicators and targets have been set in MSS. Thus, this practice is potential to create efficient and effective services.

Moreover, the concept of "contract" to reduce the principal-agent problem and rationale of political decentralization becomes the basis argument why more accountable and transparent local governments and better local government's performance can be captured by allowing more scrutiny from all "principals" of local governments. Firstly, we seek the concept of "contract" in the principal agent relationships. In this relations, several assumptions are set as presented by Mitnick (1980), Laffont and Martimort (2009) and Hughes (2012). Firstly, the goals and objectives of principals and agents are always different so the conflict of goals between principal and agent always exists. Secondly, there is asymmetric information between the principal and agents. The principal often lacks time, interest and expertize while agents often have more information than principals. Nevertheless, agents have few incentives to supply full information to principal. Peters (2001) argues that in principal-agents relations, agents tend to maximize their interests by supplying less information to the principal. Thirdly, unfortunately, agents have obligations to present account and being accountable to their principal on the activities they have done and results have been achieved. Thus, to keep the agents are being accountable to the principal's interests as well as reducing problems lying on the assumption of principal-agent relations, there should be such as agreement that is bounded both the principal and agents. Perrow (1986) and Waterman and Meier (1998) notes that there should be a "contract" between the principal and agents about what agents should do, what information should be received by principals and what kinds of incentives could be gained and disincentive could be imposed to the principals.

In the case of MSS, if we assume that local governments are an agent, at least three main principals can be identified. The first is the central government. The accountability of local governments to this principal works vertically. The second is local parliament. Similarly to the local leader, this institution is also directly elected by local people. The accountability of local governments to this principal works horizontally. The third is local people who will determine whether the local leader will win the election or to be re-elected. Thus, it can be seen that the relation is complex since the agent has interacted with more than one principal.

Furthermore, in the case of MSS, this "contract" is realized as "performance measurement" of local governments consists of indicators and targets. This contract is set with the expectation that agent will be accountable to the principal, the lack of information between principal and agents will be minimized and the overall problems on the principal-agent relations can be reduced. MSS as the contract will be used by the central governments as the information and tools of assessments and control to some extent the powers have been devolved can be well carried out by local governments. As the contract, local parliaments can utilize MSS as tools to measure the accountability of local governments in delivering public services and utilize public money in one year's budget, while it can be used by local people as information and measurement to some extent the rights of citizens in receiving adequate basic public services with required standards in quality have been fulfilled by the local governments.

As the tools to hold the horizontal accountability of local governments to local parliament and people, the introduction and practice of MSS is also in line with the rationale of political decentralization which tightly connects to local democratization and governance in Indonesia. Recalling the discussion in the first part, political decentralization in Indonesia is realized by the direct election of local leaders in all districts as the reflection of the ability of local government to make their own decisions.

This local democratization by setting the obligation of local leaders to be accountable to local people promises an increase in transparency, accountability and performance of local governments through the improvement on the commitment and motivation of local governments in delivering effective and efficient public services as the aims of the organizations. Local leader will put the performance of local bureaucracies in achieving target set in MSS and delivering better services as the main concern. He/she as the head of local bureaucracies will also increase his/her transparency and accountability to local parliament and people, continually improve their performance and increase the satisfaction of their people on service they deliver; as the efforts to win the election or to be re-elected. Thus, the promise that introduction of MSS will improve the governance and performance of local bureaucracies, leading to more effective and efficient public services delivery; could be realized.

The empirical evidence also shows the same result. Devas and Delay (2008) based on experience in Eastern and Central European Countries and Grindle (2007) based on some experience in some American Latin Countries (e. q Mexico, Columbia and Brazil) find that political decentralization through local democratization has positive relations with the improvement of transparency and performance of local governments which leads to the effective and efficient public services. It can be seen that winning the election becomes the big incentives for local leaders to improve their accountability and performance.

Another potential gain of MSS is ability to reduce inequality on the quality of basic public services across regions. As we acknowledge, decentralization policy gives autonomy to local governments to execute their mandated powers in delivering services with their own strategies considering their own financial and human capacity. Regions which are rich in their natural resources have advantages in delivering services since they have big financial and economic capacities. In contrast, the poor regions have many limitations to mobilize its financial, economic and human capacities to execute responsibilities have been devolved.

Moreover, the trickle-down effect which assumes that transfer resources from rich regions to the poor can be automatically occurred, as well as welfare and services in the end will be relatively equal amongst regions, as suggested by some scholars like Myrdal (1957) and Hirschman (1958); have not shown satisfying results. The resources are also dominantly kept in the rich local governments and regions. Besides that the decentralization policy tends to reduce national concern to treat every region equally. As a result, there is an increase on the discrepancy/inequality among regions in terms of financial and economic as well as services after a decade implementation of decentralization as shown by some studies.

Aritenang (2008, 2009) using Gini and Williamson Index, shows the increase in the inequality of the economic and social level between regions after the implementation of decentralization policy in Indonesia, while Firman (2003) notes that, fiscal decentralization and current central-local financial arrangements are relatively successful to reduce vertical inequality (between the central government and local governments) but it tends to raise the horizontal disparity (amongst local governments). Strategic Asia (2013) adds that after a decade implementation of decentralization, the rich regions becomes richer while the poor regions becomes poorer combined with inequality on resources distribution and quality of services which reveal the great challenged to provide the equal access to public services and economic activities for all people in all regions.

The inequality of financial and economic resources is also followed by the disparity on the quality of basic public services among districts in Indonesia, particularly in education and health facilities as well as basic infrastructure (e. g. roads, clean water). Indonesia UNDP (2009, cited in Strategic Asia, 2013) points out that disparities on the quality of public services can be seen clearly amongst districts particularly between the urban areas or cities which can provide superior health and educations facilities, and rural areas or regencies which have many limitations to deliver these services shown by low access and poor quality to healthcare and education centre and facilities. In addition, McCulloch and Malesky (2011) shows the limitation on the access of electricity and communications as well as bad quality of local roads in the poor eastern parts of Indonesia, which is contrast to the condition of the rich western part of Indonesia.

Considering the existence of inequality of public services, MSS is potential to significantly reduce this discrepancy by sets the same standards in the quality of services and ensures each local government fulfil the indicators and targets have been agreed and set. The achievement in each region then will be simultaneously assessed by the central government, local parliament and local people. Here, MSS will create de-polarization on the quality of public services across regions as the efforts to minimize the disparities/inequality traps, as phenomena potentially occurred caused by the decentralization policy as mentioned by Homme (1995) and Fuhr (2011). If de-polarization on the quality public services is occurred, MSS will be able to minimize conflict tensions between the central and local government and among local governments.

5. Potential Risks

As we discussed above, MSS is potential to bring benefits to current the implementation of decentralization policy in Indonesia. Nevertheless, this strategy also contains some potential risks and negative consequences that should be aware. Firstly, MSS will increase the burden of local government budget which possibly causes more dependency of local governments to the central government's transfer grants and resources. Some scholars have counted and roughly predicted amount of money which is required to implement MSS. Lewis (2003) for instance, predicts the needs of local governments to increase routine and development expenditure to the education sector approximately 5 trillion rupiah (250 million pounds) to fulfil education participation standards.① He continues that to fulfil the minimum standards in participation rate of school aged children, local governments need to raise 15% over current budget devoted to education or 7% to current total local government expenditure (Lewis, 2003). However, indicators and targets set for the education sector is not only about the minimum participation rate, it also includes pre-school, special education, adult education and vocational education which covers 24 indicators.② Since the central government sets 15 sectors with 169 indicators③, local governments are required more money for financing these MSS which perhaps over its financial capacity. Here, Lewis (2003) and Ferrazzi (2005) note that sectoral Ministries have less consideration on fiscal implications and affordability of standards when setting the indicators and targets on MSS.

Moreover, to finance MSS, local governments in Indonesia rely whether on their own revenues or the Central Government's transfer grants.④ Since 70 (seventy) percent of local government's revenues in Indonesia come from the central government transfer as identified by ADB (2008), the increase of local governments budget will raise the transfer grants from the central government to local governments. Only some rich local governments which have high own revenues and revenue sharing (DBH) are able to finance MSS.

As a consequence, a dependency of local governments to the central government's budget will increase which potentially downgrade the capacity of local government to rely on their own capacity and blur the meaning of local autonomy have been mandated. Based on the experiences in Latin America (e.g. Mexico), Grindle (2007) calls this phenomena as "dependency traps", while local governments can not avoid its high dependency to the central government which reduces the meaning of political decentralization have been devolved. In addition, more money will be transferred by the central government especially to finance MSS in the poor regions, will raise the burden of national budget and potentially jeopardizes the stability of macro-economic situation. This phenomenon as the consequence

---

① This is realized by increasing physical capital over 15%, fulfil 80% participation rate from primary, junior and secondary school of aged children as it is required as minimum standards.

② See Figure 4.

③ See Figure 4.

④ There 3 main mechanisms of Central Government's transfer grants: Firstly, Sharing Revenues (DBH) which are treated as shared income between the central government and local governments generated from the profit of selling natural resources; secondly, General Block Grant (DAU) which are distributed to each local government with specific formula, treated to reduce horizontal inequality across regions; thirdly, Specific Block Grant (DAK) which is transferred by the central government for specific purposes to maintaion national priorities in regions.

of decentralization policy and strategy, is called as fiscal traps by Homme (1995) and Fuhr (2011).

The second negative consequences, MSS will lead to a slippery slope of political re-centralization through setting equal and same standards in the quality of public services across regions. Based on the experiences of some African countries (e. g. Uganda, Bostwana, Nigeria), Wunsch (2001) notes while decentralization gives higher discretion to local governments to make decision on what they want and how to implement it, re-centralization is a reverse process of decentralization while the central government re-claims autonomy and gradually takes its control and powers have been decentralized.

In case of MSS, it seems that the central government tightly control local governments to provide service in particular required standards with less consideration to human and financial capacity of local government and utilize relatively uniform strategy to achieve targets and indicators set in MSS. As argued by Lewis (2003) targets and indicators in MSS have been set too ambitious and enforce districts to apply uniform strategies which makes some regions are difficult to accomplish these mandates with current human and financial capacities. As a result, it causes the suspicious opinions from some regions that MSS becomes the tools of the central government to re-claim powers have been transferred since the central government never considers the capacity of local governments to achieve those targets and indicators in MSS (Ferrazzi, 2005).

According to experiences in some Latin America Countries (c. q. Brazil and Argentina), Eaton and Dickovick (2004), mention although re-centralization will be good in maintaining the macro stabilization in the crisis, in the normal situation, it will diminish autonomy have been given to local level, hinder the decision making process in the local level, reduce the senses of belongings of policies have been set and make public accountability in the local level absence, which all of them will lead to ineffective provision of services given by the local governments. Similarly, Wunsch (2001) based on cases of African countries shows that re-centralization reduces the sense of belongings of local governments to the central government's policy since local governments felt that they are ignored in the overall policy stage.

In case of MSS, the suspicious opinion of re-centralization to the practice of MSS will diminish sense of belonging of local governments to the indicators and targets have been set in MSS. It will lead to potential risks that the aims of MSS will not be successfully achieved since it is not supported by local governments and is not able to improve motivation and commitment and hinder innovations of local governments to achieve indicators and targets in MSS. This will be realized as the backwards stage in political decentralization in Indonesia.

6. Policy Recommendations

As an effort to minimize potential risks and maximize the potential benefits of MSS, 3 (three) policies are recommended by the author. While, one policy will improve the design of MSS, the rest two policies shall strengthen the institutional arrangements.

6.1. Design of MSS

Reducing number of sectors, indicators and targets have been set in MSS is the necessary part and is recommended to improve the design of MSS. It will ensure that MSS will be doable, feasible and achievable to accomplish by local governments. Indicators and target reflects the political and managerial responses and focuses to achieve the objectives of organization or tasks have mandated (Rogers, 1999). They become a useful tool of control while it is precisely and realistically set. However, these indicators and targets should not be too easy but it should be realistic. Too easy indicators and targets will not bring any significant progress to the achievement of the aims of organizations, while too difficult indicators and targets will de-motivate the members to achieve the target (De Bruijn, 2007; Seddon, 2008; Talbott, 2010). Rogers (1999) adds that too few indicators and targets could cause policy distortions while too many indicators and targets will lead to the unclear focus and overload tasks.

Reducing sectors, targets and indicators in MSS will ensure targets are focus and appropriately encourage local governments to fulfil targets have been set. In line with this idea, Lewis (2003) suggests some actions to makes sector, targets and indicators in MSS are more realistic to achieve, considering financial capacity of local governments as well as human capacity in local level to well implement the tasks, such as reducing number of standards within sectors, lower the level of standards and prioritize some subset of districts obligation functions for immediate actions.

Moreover, to ensure MSS becomes the strong tools of controls, firstly, it should be tightly linked with the current formalized measurement of local government performance. Actually Indonesia has formal instruments to measure the performance of local governments which is called as the evaluation's guidance on the performance of local governments[1] (Evaluasi Penyelenggaraan Pemerintahan Daerah, EPPD). The most important tool in this instrument is Annual evaluation of the performance of local governments or it is called as Evaluasi Kinerja Penyelenggaraan Pemerintahan Daerah (EKPPD) in Indonesia's term since it is measured annually, cover all aspects of performance of local governments where MSS becomes one of its elements and it is published to related parties/actors in league table form.[2]

However, there seems less connection between MSS and EKPPD. Based on our experiences as a member of the evaluation team of EKPPD during 2009 – 2012, MSS is less considered in overall EKPPD although it is clearly stated that MSS becomes one indicator to measure performance of local governments. It is in line to what is explained by Dendi (2010) that EKPPD covers many things from the "soft products" (e. g. relations between the executive and legislative) and "hard products" (e. g. number of excellent condition of roads compared to total roads) but it only extracts less information and adopt few indicators from MSS. In addition, MSS has its own team and mechanism of evaluation which is different with EKPPD so the less connection between MSS and EKPPD can not be avoided.

Secondly, clear incentives to the results have been achieved by local governments in fulfilling indicators and targets set in MSS should be given. This is related to the idea of "performance contract" as we discussed above. As argued by Laffont and Martimort (2009) incentives are essential and required to ensure agent will act as good as principal expect and desire as noted in the performance contracts. Incentives will minimize the problem possibly emerges between principal and agent in principal-agent relations.

The current design of MSS is lack of financial and non-financial incentives to encourage local governments to act in line to mandates are given by the central government as well as

---

[1] Evaluation's guidance on the performance of local governments or Evaluasi Penyelenggaraan Pemerintahan Daerah (EPPD) in Indonesia's term is stipulated in GR 6/2008. This guidance gives some criteria and indicators to monitor and asses the overall performance and capacity of local governments whether through quantitative and qualitative indicators. There are 3 (there) types of evaluation have been arranged in EPPD: Annual evaluation of the performance of local governments or Evaluasi Kinerja Penyelenggaraan Pemerintahan Daerah (EKPPD), evaluation on the performance of the overall of implementation of autonomy (Evaluasi Kinerja Penyelenggaraan Otonomi Daerah, EKPOD) and evaluation to the newly establishing regions (Evaluasi Daerah Otonomi Baru, EDOB).

[2] League table form means that the performance of provinces and districts are placed in order or rank based particular assessment and judgement have been done. It is similar to what Hood (2007) mentions as league table model of performance measurement, one type performance management by numbers.

local parliament and people. In financial terms, it is unclear what incentives will be received by local governments if they are successfully achieved targets in MSS. Learning from experiences in some Latin America, Africa and Southeast Asian countries, Ahmad (et al., 2006) show transfer grants and less scrutiny becomes the effective incentives to endorse local governments improving their services.

This scheme can be imitated in the design of MSS by giving more transfer grants [perhaps in the form of Specific Block Grant (DAK)] or allowing local governments to gain more own revenues (PAD) and borrow money from the central government or market; if they are successfully achieved indicators and targets set in MSS. If this incentive is given, local governments will compete to achieve targets and indicators set in MSS which leads to the improvement of the commitment and motivations of local governments to continually improve their service as the responses to this incentive.

6.2. Institutional Arrangements

The first recommended policy related to the institutional arrangement is setting the clear and consistent roles of each actor involved in MSS. However, setting these roles will not be successful if there is still less clarity and inconsistency in law and regulations which regulate the division of powers among different level/tiers of governments. As it is mentioned by DSRP (2009), unclear and inconsistent division of functions becomes the main obstacles and challenges on the practices of Indonesia's decentralization. Thus, this problem is potential to undermine the practice of MSS as the strategy to accelerate the implementation of decentralization policy in enhancing quality of public services. This is also strengthened by Cohen and Peterson (1999) and Dafflon (2006) based on their experiences in European, Latin America, Asia and Africa countries that regardless unitary or federalism system, the divisions of functions are pre-requisites to successfully implemented any strategies of decentralization policy and minimize conflict and mis-coordination caused by ambiguity on the roles of each level/tier of government.

Related to that point, tasks should be done soon, is to clearly define the tasks of each level of government. Currently, while there is a relatively clear arrangement in education[①], health and transportation, there is still ambiguity in division of authorities in other sectors of

---

① For instance, in the education sector, the district government has responsibilities to primary, junior and senior high school, provincial government has powers to manage special education, while the central government has functions to take care the universities.

MSS such as food resilience and housing. As far as no improvement in the general arrangements of this division of powers, it will be very difficult to arrange the roles of each actor involved in MSS. For instance, it will be very difficult to define and divide the "obligatory functions" which becomes the main core of MSS if the division of powers are not clearly and consistently defined. Currently, the Indonesia's government is in progress to arrange clear and more consistent division of powers. This success of the central government to formulate clear division of powers and endorse each level of government to consistently stick to this rule, will significantly affect the arrangement on the roles of each actor in MSS.

While the roles of each actor have already been clearly defined, the same interpretations to the definition and objective of MSS should be continually constituted. These same interpretations should be binding on all actors in the central, provincial and district level. As it is noted by Watts (2008) and decentralization report's such as UCLG (2009) and Gold (2010), based on the experiences in some decentralized countries in the worlds, the same interpretations of the goal, strategy, and direction of decentralization policies should be agreed and consituted among the central and local government as the pre-requisite to successfully implement decentralization policy.

The creation of a shared interpretation of the goal and direction of MSS is essential. It will make local governments feel that they are the main actor of the practice of MSS. Local governments will think MSS is their tool to improve their accountability and MSS is not the re-centralization strategy of the central government or strategy to re-gain the autonomy has been given to them. If this is done well, it will increase the sense of belonging of each level of government to the practice of MSS and improve commitment and motivation to successfully achieve the goals of MSS.

Endorsing the emergence of inspector and auditor regimes is the last institutional arrangements recommended to improve the practice of MSS. Although the auditor/inspector whether in the central and local level are involved as members of a monitoring team, they play less significant role compared to MoHa or sectoral ministries in the supervision. Ideally, auditors/inspectors have essential roles in measuring performance of public organization and ensure the organization will be on the right track to achieve the goals have mandated to them as shown in practice in the United Kingdom (Game, 2006; Martin et al., 2013).

However, the roles of those actors seem ignored in the practice of MSS and implementation of decentralization policy in general. Thus, the increasing roles of auditors/inspectors (BPK and BPKP) in doing supervision and giving feedback are essential to ensure the central government appropriately set the indicators and targets, and local governments are able to fulfil the indicators and targets set in MSS. However, the cooperation between auditors/inspectors with MoHA, sectoral ministries and other important actors; are still required in doing supervision.

7. Conclusion

In conclusion, decentralization becomes the essential policy in Indonesia to increase the quality of public services and reduce its inequality in terms of services are given by each local government across regions, as the response to the needs of reforms in Indonesia's economic, political and social life. The current data shows that decentralization policy is relatively successful to overcome dissatisfaction of local governments to the central government and avoid conflicts amongst regions yet there are still many challenges to enhance the quality of basic public services and reduce the inequality of these services across regions. Thus, MSS becomes the key focus of decentralization policy to tackle this problem.

Lying on the intersection between some theories and concept such as gains and risks of decentralization, allocative efficiency, principal-agent problems and performance management, and acknowledging the uniqueness on the design and institutional arrangement of MSS; we believe that the introduction of MSS is potential to capture the benefits of decentralization to enhance the quality of basic public services as well as reduce the inequality of these services across regions. These potential benefits are gained through making government is closer to the people; improve accountability, and performance of local governments to effectively and efficiently deliver basic public services and set the same standards to the quality of services delivered to reduce inequality on the services across regions.

However, the potential risks such as the increase of dependency of local governments to the central government's transfer grants and possibility of re-centralization which causes reluctance (no commitments and motivations) of local governments to implement and achieve indicators and targets have been set in MSS, should also be anticipated.

Moreover, to ensure these potential gains can be reinforced into the "real" gains and minimize the potential risks, 2 main policies are recommended. Firstly is the improvement to the design of MSS. It comprises reducing number of sectors, indicators and targets which is adjusted to the financial and human capacity of local governments as well as tightly connects MSS with the current formal measurement of local government performance and gives clear incentives to local governments which are successfully achieve indicators and targets have been set in MSS. Secondly is the institutional arrangement. This policy consists of better roles of arrangements amongst related actors; building the shared interpretations of the objective and direction of MSS as well as endorsing the emergence of auditor/inspector's regimes in Indonesia's decentralization system.

Finally, future research is required to check whether some potential benefits of decentralization can be well captured and realized to the "real gains". Some questions such as whether the introduction of MSS cause polarization in the quality of public services across regions or whether the introduction of MSS could increase motivation and commitment of local governments or it creates the reluctance of local governments to implement this policy caused by re-centralization, should be proved by taking some examples of particular sectors in the MSS in some pilot regions.

---

[1] ADB, "Managing Asian Cities: Sustainable and Inclusive Urban Solutions", The Philippines: Asian Development Bank, 2008.

[2] Ahmad, E. and Brosio, G., "What Do We Know? Evidence on Decentralization and Local Service Provision", in Ahmad, E. and Brosio, G. (eds.), *Does Decentralization Enhance Service Delivery and Poverty Reduction?*, United Kingdom: Edward Elgar, 2009, pp. 125 – 160.

[3] Ahmad, J., Devarajan, S. and Khemani, S., et al., "Decentralization and Service Delivery", in Ahmad, E. and Brosio, G. (eds.), *Handbook of Fiscal Federalism*, United Kingdom: Edward Elgar, 2006, pp. 240 – 268.

[4] Aritenang, A., "A Study on Indonesia Regions Disparity: Post Decentralization", *Munich Personal RePEc Archive (MPRA)*, Paper No. 25245, 2008 (on line), Available from: http://mpra.ub.uni-muenchen.de/25245/1/MPRA_paper_25245.pdf (Accessed 21 June, 2014).

[5] Aritenang, A., "The Impact of Government Budget Shifts to Regional Disparities in Indonesia: Before and after Decentralisation", *Munich Personal RePEc Archive (MPRA)*, Paper No 25243, 2009 (on line), Available from: http://mpra.ub.uni-muenchen.de/25243/1/MPRA_paper_25243.pdf (Accessed 21 June, 2014).

[6] Aspinall, E. and Fealy, G., "Introduction: Decentralisation, Democratisation and the Rise of Local", in Aspinall, E. and Fealy, G. (eds.), *Local Power and Politics in Indonesia: Democratisation and Decentralisation*, Singapore: Institute of Southeast Asian Studies, 2003.

[7] Bardhan, P. and Mookherjee, D., "The Rise of Local Governments: An Overview", in Bardhan, P. and Mookherjee, D., *Decentralization and Local Governance in Dveloping Countries: A Comparative Perspective*, Massachusetts: MIT Press, 2006, pp. 1 – 52.

[8] Boasiako, K. B. A. and Csanyi, P., "Introduction: Decentralization from Global Perspective", in Boasiako, K. B. A. and Csanyi, P. (eds.), *The Theories of Decentralization and Local Government: Implementation, Implication and Realities, a Global Perspective*, The United States: Stephen F. Austin State University Press, 2014.

[9] Boyne, G. A., "Concepts and Indicators of Local Authority Performance: An Evaluation of the Statutory Frameworks in England and Wales", *Public Money and Management*, 22 (2), 2002, pp. 17 – 24.

[10] Brodjonegoro, B. and Asanuma, S., "Regional Autonomy and Fiscal Decentralization in Democratic Indonesia", *Hitotsubashi Journal of Economics*, 41, 2000, pp. 111 – 122.

[11] Bunnel, T., Miller, M. A. and Phelps, N. A., et al, "Urban Development in a Decentralized Indonesia: Two Success Stories?", Paper on The Joint Conference of The Association of Asia Studies (AAS) and International Convention of Asia Scholar, Hawaii, 2011.

[12] Campbell, A. and Denezhkina, E., "Vertical and Horizontal Coordination in Russian Local Government", Paper on the European Political Research Consortium Conference, University of Postdam, 11 September, 2009.

[13] Cohen, J. M. and Peterson, S. B., *Administrative Decentralization: Strategies for Developing Countries*, Connecticut: Kumarian Press, 1999.

[14] Conyers, D., "Decentralization: The Latest Fashion in Development Administration", *Public Administration and Development*, 3 (2), 1983, pp. 97 – 109.

[15] Dafflon, B., "The Assignment of Functions to Decentralized Government: From Theory to Practice", in Ahmad, E. and Brosion, G. (eds.), *Handbook of fiscal federalism*, United Kingdom: Edward Elgar, 2006, pp. 271 – 305.

[16] De Bruijn, H., *Managing Performance in the Public Sector*, 2nd ed., London: Routledge, 2007.

[17] Dendi, A., "Assessment of Local Governance and Development Performance in Indonesia: Current Models, Challenges and Future Perspectives", Paper on IASIA International Congress, Bali-Indonesia, 2010.

[18] Devas, N., "Indonesia: What Do We Mean by Decentralization?", *Public Administration and Development*, 17 (3), 1997, pp. 351 – 367.

[19] Devas, N. and Delay, S., "Local Democracy and the Challenges of Decentralizing the State: An International Perspective", in Coulson, A. and Campbell, A. (eds.), *Local Government in Central and Eastern Europe: The Rebirth of Local Democracy*, The UK: Routledge, 2008, pp. 135 – 153.

[20] DSRP, *Stock Taking on Indonesia's Recent Decentralization Reforms*, Jakarta: Decentralization Support Facility, 2009.

[21] Eaton, K. and Dickovick, J. T., "The Politics of re-centralization in Argentina and Brazil", *Latin American Research Review*, 39 (1), 2004, pp. 90 – 122.

[22] Fengler, W. and Hofman, B. , "Managing Indonesia's Rapid Decentralization: Achievements and Challenges", in Ichimura, S. and Bahl, R. , *Decentralization Policies in Asian Development*, Singapore: World Scientific, 2009, pp. 245–262.

[23] Ferrazzi, G. , "Using the 'F' word: Federalism in Indonesia's Decentralization Discourse", *The Journal of Federalism*, 30 (2), 2000, pp. 63–85.

[24] Ferrazzi, G. , "Obligatory Functions and Minimum Services Standards for Indonesia Regional Government: Searching for a Model", *Public Administration and Development*, 25 (2), 2005, pp. 227–238.

[25] Firman, T. , "Potential Impacts of Indonesia's Fiscal Decentralisation Reform on Urban and Regional Development: Towards a New Pattern of Spatial Disparity", *Space and Polity*, 7 (3), 2003, pp. 247–271.

[26] Fuhr, H. , "The Seven Traps of Decentralization Policy", *International Journal of Administrative Science and Organization*, 18 (2), 2011, pp. 88–93.

[27] Game, C. , "Comprehensive Performance Assessment in English Local Government", *International Journal of Productivity and Performance Management*, 55 (3), 2006, pp. 466–479.

[28] Gaubatz, K. T. , "City-state Redux: Rethinking Optimal State Size in an Age of Globalization, *New Global Studies*, 3 (1), 2009, pp. 1–211.

[29] Gold, "Local Government Finance: The Challenges of 21th Century, Second Global Report on Decentralization and Local Democracy", Barcelona: United Cities and Local Government and The World Bank, 2010.

[30] Grindle, M. S. , *Going Local: Decentralization, Democratization and the Promise of Good Governance*, The US: Princeton University Press, 2007.

[31] Hadiz, V. R. , "Decentralization and Democracy in Indonesia: A Critique of Neo Institutionalist Perspectives", *Development and Change*, 35 (4), 2004, pp. 697–718.

[32] Hadiz, V. R. , *Localising Power in Post-authoritarian Indonesia: A Southeast Asia Perspective*, Stanford: Stanford University Press, 2010.

[33] Hague, R. and Harrop, M. , *Comparative Government and Politics: An Introduction*, 8th ed. , London: Palgrave Macmillan, 2010.

[34] Haryanto, A. , "Improving Service Quality of District Education Offices (DEO) in Indonesia Decentralized Education System", Unpublished PhD Thesis, The School of Management, College of Business, RMIT University, 2010.

[35] Hirschman, A. O. , *The Strategy of Economic Development*, Yale: University Press, New Haven, 1958.

[36] Hofman, B. and Kaiser, K. , "The Making of the "Big Bang" and Its Aftermath: A Political Economy Perspective", in Alm, J. , Vasquez, J. M. and Indrawati, S. M (eds.), *Reforming Intergovernmental Fiscal Relations and the Rebuilding of Indonesia: The "Big Bang" Program and Its Conse-*

quences, Massachusetts: Edward Elgar Publishing Limited, 2004, p. 15 – 46.

[37] Homme, R. P., "The Dangers of Decentralization", *The World Bank Research Observer*, 10 (2), 1995, pp. 201 – 210.

[38] Hood, C., "Public Service Management by Numbers: Why Does It Vary? Where Has It Come from, What Are the Gaps and the Puzzles?", *Public Policy and Management*, 27 (2), 95, 2007, p. 102.

[39] Hughes, O. E., *Public Management and Administration*, 4th ed., UK: Palgrave Macmillan, 2012.

[40] Kristiansen, S. and Pratikno, "Decentralising Education in Indonesia", *International Journal of Educational Development*, 26, 2006, pp. 513 – 531.

[41] Kristiansen, S. and Santoso, P., "Surviving Decentralization? Impacts of Regional Autonomy on Health Services Provision in Indonesia", *Health Policy*, 77 (2006), pp. 247 – 259.

[42] Kuhlmann, S., "Performance Measurement in European Local Governments: A Comprehensive Analysis of Reform Experiences in Great Britain, France, Sweden and Germany", *International Review of Administrative Sciences*, 76 (2), 2010, pp. 331 – 345.

[43] Laffont, J. J. and Martimort, J. J., *The Theory of Incentives: The Principal-agent Model*, Princeton: Princeton University Press, 2009.

[44] Lewis, B. D. and Pattinasarany, D., "Determining Citizen Satisfaction with Local Public Education in Indonesia: The Significance of Actual Service Quality and Governance Conditions", *Growth and Change*, 40 (1), 2009, pp. 85 – 115.

[45] Lewis, B. D., "Minimum Local Public Service Delivery Standards in Indonesia: Fiscal Implications and Affordability Concerns, Research Triangle Institute International", 2003, Available from: http://www1.worldbank.org/publicsector/decentralization/Feb2004Course/Background%20materials/Lewis.pdf (Accessed 6 December 2013).

[46] Martin, S., Downe, J. and Grace, C., et al., "New Development: All Change? Performance Assessment Regimes in UK Local Government", *Public Policy and Management*, 33 (4), 2013, pp. 277 – 280.

[47] McCulloch, N. and Malesky, E., "Does Better Local Governance Improve District Growth Performance in Indonesia?", *IDS Working Papers*, 2011, 369, pp. 1 – 48.

[48] Mitnick, B. M., *The Political Economy of Regulation*, New York: Columbia University Press, 1980.

[49] Myrdal, G., *Economic Theory and Underdeveloped Regions*, London: Duckworth, 1957.

[50] Ostrom, E., *Governing the Commons: The Evolutions of Institutions for Collective Actions*, Cambridge: Cambridge University Press, 1990.

[51] O'Toole, L. J. and Meier, K. J., *Organization, Governance and Performance*, Cambridge: Cambridge University Press, 2011.

[52] Perrow, C., *Complex Organizations: A Critical Essay*, 3rd, ed., New York: McGraw-Hill. 1986.

[53] Peters, B. G., *The Politics of Bureaucracy*, 5th ed., London: Routledge. 2001.

[54] Polidano, C., "The New Public Management in Developing Countries", *IDM Public Policy and Management Working Paper No. 12*, Institute for Manchester: Development Policy and Management, 1999.

[55] Rashid, N., *Managing Performance in Local Government*, London: Local Government Series, 1999.

[56] Rogers, S., *Performance Management in Local Government*, 2nd ed., London: Financial Times, 1999.

[57] Rondinelli, D. A., "Government Decentralization in Comparative Perspective: Theory and Practice in Developing Countries", *International Review of Administrative Sciences*, 47, 1980, pp. 133 – 145.

[58] Rondinelli, D. A. and Cheema, G. S., "Implementing Decentralization Policies: An Introduction", in Rondinelli, D. A. and Cheema, G. S. (eds.), *Decentralizing Governance: Emerging Concepts and Practices*, Washington: Brooking Institution Press, 2007, pp. 1 – 20.

[59] Roudo, M. and Saepudin, A., "Enhance Public Services through Formulation and Implementation Minimum Service Standards in Indonesia: Concepts, Urgency and Challenges" (*Meningkatkan pelayanan publik melalui penyusunan dan penerapan Standar Pelayanan Minimal: Konsep, Urgensi dan Tantangan*), *Riptek*, 2 (1), 2008, pp. 1 – 6 (online), available from: http://bappeda.semarangkota.go.id/uploaded/publikasi/Meningkatkan_Pelayanan_Publik_Melalui_SPM_-_ROUDO.pdf (Accessed on 22 June, 2014).

[60] Salim, W. and Kombaitan, B., "Jakarta: The Rise and Challenge of Capital", *City*, 13 (1), 2009, pp. 120 – 127.

[61] Schwab, K., Martin, X. S. and Brende, B., "The Global Competitiveness Report: 2013 – 2014" (online), Geneva: World Economic Forum, Available from: http://www3.weforum.org/docs/WEF_GlobalCompetitivenessReport_2013 – 14.pdf (Accessed August 8, 2014).

[62] Seddon, J., *Systems Thinking in the Public Sector: The Failure of the Reform Regime and a Manifesto for a Better Way*, The United Kingdom: Triachy Press, 2008.

[63] Smith, B. C., *Decentralization: The Territorial Dimension of the State*, London: Allen and Unwin, 1985.

[64] Strategic Asia, *Decentralization Assessment Report*, Jakarta: UNDP and Strategic Asia, 2013.

[65] Suwandi, M., "The Implementation of Regional Autonomy: The Indonesian Experience", Paper on the conference "Can Decentralization Help Rebuild Indonesia", Atlanta, May, 2002, pp. 1 – 3.

[66] Suwandi, M., "The Indonesian Experience with the Implementation of Regional Autonomy,

in Alm, J., Vazques, J. M. and Indrawati, S. M. (eds.), *Reforming Intergovernmental Fiscal Relations and the Rebuilding of Indonesia: The Big Bang Program and Its Economic Consequences*, Edward Elgar Publishing Limited, 2004, pp. 272 - 288.

[67] Tadjoeddin, M. Z., Suharyo, W. I. and Mishra, S., "Aspiration to Inequality: Regional Disparity and Centre-regional Conflicts in Indonesia", in the UNU/WIDER Project Conference of Spatial Inequality in Asia United Nations University Centre, Tokyo, March 2003, pp. 28 - 29.

[68] Talbott, C., *Theories of Performance: Organizational and Service Improvement in the Public Domain*, The United Kingdom: Oxford University Press, 2010.

[69] Treisman, D., *The Architecture of Government: Rthinking Political Decentralization*, Cambridge: Cambridge University Press, 2007.

[70] Turner, M. M., Podger. O., Sumardjono. M., et al., *Decentralisation in Indonesia: Redesigning the State*, Canberra: Asia Pacific Press, The Australian National University, Canberra, 2003.

[71] Turner, M. M., Imbaruddin, A. and Sutiyono, W., "Human Resource Management: the Forgotten Dimension of Decentralization in Indonesia", *Bulletin of Indonesian Economic Studies*, 45 (2), 2009, pp. 231 - 249.

[72] UCLG, *Decentralization and Local Democracy in the World: First Global Report*, Barcelona: United Cities and Local Government and the World Bank, 2009.

[73] Vazquez, J. M. and Vaillancourt, F., "An Overview of the Main Obstacles to Cecentralization", in Vazquez, J. M. and Vaillancourt, F. (eds.), *Decentralization in Developing Countries: Global Perspectives on The Obstacles to Fiscal Devolution*, The United Kingdom: Edward Elgar Publishing Limited, 2013, pp. 1 - 22.

[74] Waterman, R. W. and Meier, K. J., "Principal-agent Models: An Expansion?", *Journal of Public Administration Research and Theory*, 8 (2), 1998, pp. 173 - 202.

[75] Watts, R. L., *Comparing Federal Systems*, 3rd ed., Canada: McGill Queen University Press, 2008.

[76] Wunsch, J. S., "Decentralization, Local Governance and 'Recentralization' in Africa", *Public Administration and Development*, 21, 2001, pp. 277 - 288.

从管控到服务、嵌入、吸纳：
执政党基层组织社会治理行动路线[*]

孙柏瑛[**]

研究的缘起

近10年来的中国社会经历了从经济转轨到社会转型的全面洗礼。一系列由社会结构变迁和利益关系调整诱发的社会矛盾冲突，给现有秩序带来冲击，也对党和政府的执政合法性形成了挑战。为回应社会问题，重构合法性，党和政府做出政策调整，其间涉及的政策议程和行动策略被概括为加强和创新"社会管理"。

基层是国家权力控制与民间自治力量的交接部，是社会治理前沿：第一，社会矛盾冲突发生在基层。位置决定了它是最先触及问题并做出反应的主体，承担着为"阻隔危机"而"冲锋陷阵"的维稳功能。第二，社会管理服务事务向基层转移和聚集。基层面对从大规模流动人口到由此衍生的城市生活"新族群"及其社会排斥、从人口老龄到底层贫困、从食品安全到社会治安等诸多新问题。[1]为了有效回应并降低上级党政组织的压力，加强属地化管理是必然的选择。[2]服务管理事务下沉，基层承担着从"了解需求"到"实现服务"的多重职责。第三，基层社会的组织化需要。计划体制下，单位作为国家与个体的中间层，发挥着控制、规范社会成员行为和调整关系的作用。一方面，单位制瓦解，导致中间层"塌陷"，社会的规范能力急剧下降，呈现原子化和"碎片化"趋势。另一方面，受所有制结构改革、经济与社会领域分权、民间组织成长以及人口流动性等因素影响，社会逐步发展成为自主的领域和力量。基

---

[*] 基金项目：2011年国家社会科学基金重大项目"基层政府社会管理体制机制创新研究"（项目编号：11&ZD032），教育部"211工程"三期中国人民大学公共管理学院"中国特色的公共管理与公共政策学科平台建设"子项目与中国人民大学行政管理国家重点学科项目资助。

[**] 孙柏瑛，中国人民大学公共管理学院行政管理学系主任，教授，博士生导师。

层正是转型中社会空间和社会领域的载体，它聚集了多元的社会力量，自下而上表达权利和多样性利益，要求更大的自主性。据此，以新的思路和形式整合社会力量，实现有序的利益表达，直接关系党的执政基础。基层体现政社关系的联结途径和方式，担负着"整合资源"且"形成互动"的复合责任。

为适应治理环境变化和治理结构变迁，党着手对其基层党组织系统（下简称为"基层组织"）的结构、功能与行动方式进行改革，寻求新的路径来维系党在基层的政治影响力，重构其权威合法性，巩固领导地位。为此，党采取了一系列行动策略，努力体现其在基层社会治理中的结构转型、功能转型和角色转型。本文以近10年来影响颇广几个案例（见表1）为焦点，对演化路径及其内在逻辑进行分析。

表 1 文内案例要点

案例名称	发生地	时间	推动部门	要点
大调解	江苏南通市	2003	市委、政法委	以政法综治部门为中心，建立"一综多专、专业调处、专家咨询"的行政调解、司法调解、民间调解三大系统横向协同，市、县、乡镇三级纵向联动的矛盾纠纷调解机制。
网格管理	北京东城区、朝阳区	2005—2007	区委、政法委	各地广泛应用。运用数字化网格技术，在划定的区域内建立区、街、社区、工作站四级工作平台，在掌握辖区人、业、物、事信息的基础上，形成快速知晓问题、分级分层处理并责任到人的联动机制。
群工部	河南义马市	2005	市委、政法委、信访局	在党委下设群众工作部，督导各部门联合处理信访事务，由市委常委、政法委书记兼任部长。信访局更名为群工局，除信访职能外，新增原属民政部门、人劳社保部门、司法行政部门和科技部门的一些职能。下设巡回法庭，提供便民的矛盾纠纷调处机制。
复合主体	浙江杭州市	2008	市委	党政部门、知识界、行业、媒体等多元身份的组织或个人共同参与、主动关联，形成网状联结、功能融合新型创业主体，通过资源、信息、知识共享，促社会事业、知识创业等领域的服务创新。行会作为复合主体中间层发挥居间联动作用，建立战略合作联盟。

(续表)

案例名称	发生地	时间	推动部门	要点
基层服务型党组织	浙江湖州市 湖北宜昌市	2010	市县委、组织部	以"片组户民情联系、区域化统筹服务"为两翼，构建基层党建工作模式。乡村实行"上提下分"，村建党委、组建支部，党支部建在村民小组、专业合作社、各类协会，服务于村民；城市通过"支部小班化"，党支部建在"两新"组织、楼道、居民小组、专业协会，做"企业的保姆"，为居民和企业服务。
三级理事会	广东云浮云安县	2010	云安县委	公共服务前移，下沉到乡镇一级，延伸至村，提供土地流转、劳动力、林业、农技推广服务。基层政府精简，将原"七站八所"简化为"大部制""三办两中心"，即党政办、农经办、宜居办和综治信访维稳中心、社会事务服务中心。自然村、行政村、乡镇建三级理事会，实现"民事民办、民事民治"。
全响应	北京西城区	2011	区委社会工委	自上而下建立制度化的"听民情、访民忧、解民难"，知晓民需；依托网格自下而上建立问题快速反应、分析研判与科学决策系统；建立八条"响应链"，联动区、街道和社区，整合多元社会力量参与社会事务管理，并将党组织建在楼门、楼宇、"两新"组织中，延伸社会管理的触角。
区域化党建	上海静安、长宁等区	2011	区委组织部	打破原有辖区地域限制，党组织在更大区域范围内整合社会资源，实现顶层设计。建立"联席会议"协商机制区，建立"共同行动理事会"，由行业工作委员会牵头组织，下设办公室，吸收"两新"组织领导人加入。街道层成立大口工委，下设专业委员会，统筹集合辖区优势资源，形成协会+党组织、商会+党组织的工作模式；提供组团式服务，通过广泛征集意见、民主协商，为辖区内企业提供信息资源，服务于辖区居民需求；以项目拉动资源聚合，夯实社区的服务平台和服务的人财物资源。

资料来源：笔者根据调研和参阅媒体报道自制。

行动策略的演化

10年来,基层组织社会治理的目标模式、管理方式和策略选择经历了渐进的变化,体现了其治理思维与逻辑的演化。

以维稳为主导的信息化防控体系构筑

2003年中央将政府职能定位于"宏观调控、市场监管、社会管理、公共服务"四方面。彼时,"社会管理"的内涵指向并不明确,文件表述比较抽象,知识界讨论2005—2006年才密集起来。[3]但国内社会局势对中央加强社会管理的意图做了诠释。2003年不仅遭遇"非典",还是信访的"洪峰年"。这一年,信访数量急剧攀升,越级访数量增长尤甚①,反映出矛盾多发、冲突加剧、抗争升级的特征。在农民失地、城市拆迁、国企改制、劳资纠纷、土地收益分配、环境污染、业主维权、流动人口、党群干群关系领域中,由分配不公引发的权利、利益纷争,影响了社会,导致了秩序失衡。同期社会分配指数显示,2002年基尼系数升至0.45,超过国际公认的警戒线。其中,人均财产最多的20%人口拥有59.3%的财产,人均财产最少的20%人口仅有2.8%的财产,两者比率为21.18:1。如以财产最多的10%人群与财产最少的10%人群比对,两者拥有财产比率为60.89:1[4],社会分化和贫富悬殊十分严重。

面对增长的社会风险,消除危机扩散,有效防范并处置危机事件,抑制信访数量和规模,控制越级访和京访,快速、有效地解决矛盾成为社会管理的首选目标。统领社会管理事务的政法委系统迅速加强了其组织建制,整合了组织资源,建立起社会管理体制架构。这时,"社会管理"核心内涵是"维稳",即以秩序稳定为中心,建立危机事件快速响应和处置机制,在事前、事中、事后环节形成实时监测、动态控制、有效回应的能力。由此,基层防控网络建设的宗旨是"向前""向下"延伸。"向前"为察觉问题,提前预警;"向下"为强化基层、责任到人,管理的目标是"纵向到底""横向到边""全面覆盖"。行动策略为:以数字信息技术为支撑,以联动机制为纽带,以管理流程改造为工具,以精细化管理为追求,力求将知晓问题、研判问题、分类分级问题与风险控制链接起来,形塑整合型的危机防控体系。"大调解""网格管

---

① 2003年信访数量估计在800万件以上,增速迅猛。1994年到2003年,全国群体性事件从大约1万起递增到6万起,参与人数由73万多人增加到307万多人,平均每年增长12%。2004和2005年,群体事件分别为7万多起到8.7万起。国家信访局局长周占顺承认,"2003年以来,群众信访总量仍呈现上升趋势,群众集体访、重复访和群众赴京访上升幅度大,人数多,规模大,持续时间长、行为激烈,在一些地方和行业引起连锁反应,严重影响首都和局部地区社会稳定。"

理""群工部"为这一思路下的经典案例。

第一,整合资源。整合现有分散的、处于条块分割的部门资源,运用协同联动、"无缝隙"的运行机制将纵向层级与横向部门联系起来,聚合体制内资源,实现"三位一体":问题知情——信息上传、研判动员——多部门协同处理、结果导向——问题处置绩效评估,形成一个系统的闭路环,以达到跟踪问题、快速解决的功效。

第二,关口前移。通过自上而下"问责"和自下而上"倒逼"的方式,强化基层对危机事件的回应和处置责任。责任下沉的具体行动方案为:一是增加投入、增强动员。加强对基层人力、财力的投入,在正式编制的公务员和事业编之外,还有为数不少的"编外"协管人员参与到社会管理中;二是"划片到组""分片到组"。在网格的基础上,将基层管辖区域划分为组别,党组织按照地域或界别,由党委或支部成员分别管理,建立联系,倾听诉求,上门服务,解决问题或在新型组织中建立党支部和发展党员;三是搜集信息、防控前移。将问题的获取渠道前移,通过街道的信息平台以及下沉的社区管理员以及楼宇、庭院中的楼门长和院长,及时上传下情,做到全面知晓,"不留死角"。

第三,单位协同。为维护稳定,基层组织迫切需要广泛动员社会力量,形成广泛的社会网络,"齐抓共管"。参与的力量主要来自驻区的体制内组织,如中央或地方的党政机关、事业单位和国有企业等,以及在民政部门注册的社团。基层党组织透过与单位的共建项目,融通单位协力邀请单位退休知名人士参加社区活动、向单位布置保卫任务等方式,试图让辖区中分散在条条块块上的单位组织形成协同合力。

第四,网格技术与精细化管理。基层组织成功运用界定管理事务、明确职能、精细分级分类、再造流程等核心管理技术,建构了纵横交叉联动机制和网格管理系统。这些技术以预判问题发生、风险状况以及控制途径为导向,在采集辖区内"人、事、物、业"信息的基础上,按照人员、问题、事件的性质进行分类和分层,有针对性地编组管理流程,形成"集问题(或对象)性质—事务分级—防控过程—责任到人—绩效考评"于一体的管理预案,将管理不断向庭院、楼宇、单元、楼门延伸,实现"全覆盖"目标。

在建立维稳防控体系中不断发展的信息化、精细化和协同联动机制,对推动基层党政组织及时发现问题,关注矛盾并寻求解决方案有工具性价值,为集中统一指挥、提升管理效率搭建了基础平台,并开始探索问题源头治理的途径。但是,由于其核心理念包含强烈的管控、弹压甚至反人性的色彩,既有悖于法治政府观念,又制造了威胁长期秩序稳定的困局。在此目标驱动下,民意表达受到遏制,利益冲突的深层问题没有得到解决。同时,由于基层组织工作重心扭曲,角色异化,与民众对立更加严重,出现越维越不稳的现象,使得以维稳主导的社会管理模式日益遭到质疑。

以服务为导向的基层党组织建设

基层社会管理遭遇的困惑让党组织进一步思考其治理的合法性来源问题。"服务型政府"观念带来了新的逻辑指引。在科学发展观和构建和谐社会总体目标下,基层"服务型"党建成为获得合法性重要的理论资源。以体察民需、关注民生、解决民难、完善社保、提高福利为基本任务,党依托基层组织建设、网格传输和协同联动等机制,将服务功能嵌入到基层社会管理体系中。

2007年,北京西城区委在关于社区"九养"政策的文件中,首次使用"社会服务管理"概念,后被广泛应用。社会管理加入了"公共服务"内涵,迅速衍生出一系列新表述,如"寓管理于服务""瞄准民需""一刻钟服务圈""服务零距离""接地气"、服务"无缝隙"等。南京建邺区建立基层"一委一居一站"服务体系时,以"一资三民",即"资源向下、民生优先、民主向前、民心向上"来描述管理目标。各地在党委、组织部、社会工委等部门推动下,把"党委领导"下的"服务型党建"作为方向。后面案例体现了倡导民本、服务民生的价值追求。先前以管控为导向的网格管理技术,也以服务功能加注,被定义为改进流程、提升服务的有效工具。

第一,以洞察民需为导向,确定社区服务供给的方向。倾听民意,知晓"民需",解决"民难"是基层组织服务输送的三个面向。连接需求表达、服务决策与服务供给的渠道,集知情—识别—回应—解困—反馈于一体是基层组织的工作重点。知晓民生需求是服务的前端,目的在于界定服务供给方向,形成相适宜的服务项目。基本工作方式是:在辖区内划分片组,自上而下地将区、街道(乡镇)党政主要领导划分到指定片组,定期走访群众,访情、听民意,将建议汇集到政策层;支部成立"党员志愿服务队",分片包组到社区居民,了解需求;组织专项民意调查,发问卷采集民情等等。自下而上由延伸至楼门、楼宇、庭院的网格管理员即时上传信息,或社区党支部、居委会采集信息并逐级上传,并在决策层转化为台账、折子工程等服务事项。从应用效度看,自上而下的需求信息搜寻和识别起着主导作用。由于官僚系统自身特征以及居委会的行政化,自下而上表达渠道及其影响力依然弱化。

第二,加大服务设施投入,服务机构大幅向基层下沉。适应服务责任下放的要求,基层组织以设立直接面向居民、包容基本服务项目、功能齐全的服务机构为要务,建立起包括社务、政务、党务事务服务机构。在乡镇街道层面,不仅设立有综合性的"一站式"服务中心,还建有针对老人和残疾人的专项服务中心,为社区弱势群体提供生活便利和救助。为培育草根民间组织,基层多设立有"社会组织服务中心",除在资金扶助和项目购买方面给予支持外,提供场所和活动空间成为服务中心的主要服务方法。在居民社区层面,基层也同步建立了一定规模的综合服务中心,招聘社工作者，提供助残、社保、养老、文体、康健等多项服务。总体看，在发达地区，服务基础设施建设已相当完备，在比较落后的乡村，服务设施的框架已经形成。

第三，拓展服务功能，扩充服务内容。适应居民需求增长，基层组织服务事项也在随之拓展。起初的服务事项主要针对居民日常基本生活需要，如买菜不方便，平房区上厕所困难以及相关证照办理困难、老年人与残疾人餐饮、办事困难等，后逐步发展到围绕居民文体精神生活和心理健康开展活动。社区建立了形式多样的文娱体育队，设立了图书报刊阅览室，引入了心理咨询机构和小型体检中心，举办了丰富多彩的文体活动和健康讲座。在白领密集的商务楼宇中，针对白领婚恋困难，驻商圈楼宇的党支部定期举办青年联谊会，提供交友的空间。随后，应对居民的一些利益冲突问题，基层党组织进入利益协调领域，在存在利益冲突的问题上推动邻里寻求斡旋解决问题的方案。例如，北京老城区停车困难，邻里为此纠纷不断，西城"全响应"机制启动，在街道工委协调下，社区召开包括社区党支部、居委会和居民利益相关人参加的协商讨论会，共商车位划分配置问题，取得解决问题的共识。上海基层组织通过业主委员会形成业主与物业管理公司的利益协调机制，就物业费、设施维修、环境管理等涉及业主利益的事项逐步确立协商谈判制度。

第四，应用一系列管理技术，改进服务方式，以提升民众对基层服务的满意度。为切中民需并将基本服务提供给最有需要的人群，实现快捷便利、供给高效和民众满意目标，基层组织运用了网格技术、分类管理、流程再造、绩效评估等管理工具，将服务责任与服务对象精细分类，建立分级服务供给策略，提高资源应用效率。与此同时，针对基层组织内部管理问题，通过全面质量管理、ISO9000、职责清单和任务规划等管理方案，不断强化基层的服务责任，规范服务行为，建立服务标准，提高服务能力。

以组织化为导向的利益调适与社会资源整合

以服务谋求合法性的路径，为基层组织获得了活动空间。但是，两方面挑战依然对基层组织形成压力：一是不断增长的权利、分化的利益与自下而上的利益表达渠道封闭、政策输入和转换途径不畅之间存在着紧张；二是"两新"组织大量涌现，成为基层社会中具有一定自主性的重要主体力量。传统的社会控制方式与社会新生力量整合之间存在着张力。新时期如何构建和调适党社关系，党组织能否有效掌控社会领域，直接关系到其执政基础及在基层社会的领导地位。作为回应，基层组织将联系民众、吸纳并代表利益、动员力量、聚合资源、协商参与作为目标，以组织嵌入和组织化利益表达为行动策略。复合主体、服务型党组织建设、三级理事会、"全响应"机制、区域化党建案例表达了基层组织通过再组织化过程，形成核心领导地位的诉求。

组织化包括互为条件的两个方面：一是强化基层组织的自身建设。主要针对很多地方基层组织"四无"（无人员、无经费、无场所、无规划）状况[5]，中共中央组织部推动了"三有一化"项目[6]，即实现"有人管事、有钱办事、有场地议事以及推进城市基层党建区域化"，加强街道社区基层组织开展工作的能力，让党的领导成为基层经济发展和社会事业发展"双轮驱动"的核心力量和政治保障。[7]二是基层组织在"两新"组织中建立党支部，发展党员，完善组织体系的过程，目标是联络群众，获取需求信息，吸纳和代表利益，提供服务和达成协同共治。

第一，基层党建通过组织嵌入辐射辖区内"两新"组织，为党实现引领功能奠定组织基础。基层组织化的优先行动是在"两新"组织中集中开展组建工作，即将党的组织建制向"两新"组织延伸和覆盖，在"两新"组织中建立党支部，承担党务工作职能并发挥引领作用。党组织覆盖设置方式主要有三种：一是按照属地设置原则，在非公从业人员密集的相关区域，如商圈、商务楼宇、集贸市场内设立涵盖多组织的党支部；二是按照界别与领域设置原则，依托商会或作为枢纽型社会组织的人民团体、行业协会党委，向下延伸至所辖组织，建立党支部；三是按照单位为基础的设置原则，在有三名党员的"两新"组织单独设立党支部，或两个以上的单位组合建立联合党支部。[8]党支部履行的党务工作职责包括：为亮明身份的党员重建组织关系、管理党员事务、完成上级指定的工作和开展组织生活等。更重要的责任是，在组织建设的同时能够充分发挥党居间协调聚合利益、团结各种力量、促进党社互动的作用。

第二，将服务导入基层党建过程，运用群众路线方法，获知服务需要，回应利益需求，以满意度绩效获得支持。基层党建向"两新"组织的嵌入过程，主要是通过提供公共服务、满足民众需求的方式实现的，服务功能成为基层组织与群众连接的中介，具有作为组织嵌入媒介的策略意义。服务事项直接面向社区居民日常生活需求、企业组织及其员工需求、社会组织发展需求等三大类，服务功能的履行方式则是群众路线。从群众中来：建立群众需求分析会商和群众顾问团等制度，以制度化的形式调查并获知居民、企业、社会组织的需求信息，将信息汇集评估，作为决策依据并给予反馈，形成了集党群互动、民意汇集、确定需求、实现服务的通道。到群众中去：除延续先前分片包组党员干部联系群众的办法外，党员服务中心及其志愿服务队为社区提供了便民维修、环卫维护、治安巡逻、助残养老、文体康乐等多方面的服务。

第三，以基层组织系统为中心，汇集辖区内多元主体的力量，克服"碎片化"现象，整合治理资源。基层党建承担的另一个功能是借助组织系统，将区域内的多元社会治理资源整合起来。这些社会资源既包括辖区内公有的单位组织，如党政机关、事业单位、国有企业，也包括社区中的自治组织，如居委会、业委会，还包括有代表性的"两新"组织，基层组织采用的整合方法是党建联建。在纵向上，以区县一级党的部门为发起者和推动者，在地缘关系的基础上，在城市的区、街道、社区与乡村的县、乡镇、行政村建立三级联席会议或理事会制度，突破原有组织建制的界限，按照整体性原则，将分散在各部门、互不隶属的党组织资源整合起来，形成联动的"响应链"；在横向上，以区域属地内的党组织为主导，居中推动，以行业界别或业缘为基础，将行业党组织、单位党组织与区域党组织共建互联，建立共同行动理事会，下设办公室，形成日常联系沟通机制。据此，在党委统一领导下，以属地组织为依托，联动单位党组织，延伸组织至"两新"组织，形成纵横交织的组织网络，作为聚合并整合社会资源的平台。同时，借助这一组织网络平台，建立起各种利益汇集和各方协商对话的互动机制。

第四，基层组织运用协商讨论的民主形式，居间调适利益关系，解决矛盾，谋求共识。在吸取民意、汇集民间利益的过程中，基层组织不仅采用群众路线方法，而且还运用协商民主的形式，通过利益相关人间的讨论对话，实现民意采集、利益协调和决策民主的目标。基层协商实践通常针对经年存在的、与居民生活密切相关且存在多方利益博弈的社区事务展开，例如，稀缺的停车位分配、物业费收取与支出、基层政府预算支出、邻里矛盾等，这些事务只有在利益相关人间平衡利益，达成共识，确立分配规则，才能得到有效解决。为此，基层组织担当起居间倡导和发动的角色，组织利益相关方进行商讨，在不断优化协商规则和程序设计的基础上，逐步建立规范的代表人推选、商谈方式、议事与投票规则、参与和监督制度，促成利益相关人在互动与彼此理解的过程中找到各方接受的解决问题的方案。协商民主在基层社会管理事务中的应用，基层组织不仅发挥了利益协调和服务供给的双重作用，而且为党社互动、利益汇集与推动自治提供了有益的探索经验。

简要的结语

在社会组织不断发展、新的社会力量不断成长的基层社会空间中，党实现领导权和影响、支配能力无疑是其重要的目标。而在新形势下运用怎样的治理方式达成目标，才能在因应潮流、增进社会活力与有效统合社会力量之间取得平衡，在顺应民意与引领民意之间取得平衡，既关乎党执政稳定的社会基础，也关乎党组织合法性的来源。

透过10年来基层组织社会治理制度演进与行为变化的考察，不难看到，围绕目标，党的基层组织进行了多重转型：在功能上，从依靠管控功能逐步转向强化服务功能或以服务拉动管理；在结构上，从以自上而下垂直管理为主体的组织系统转向横向延伸、覆盖与纵向统领、嵌入相交错的组织网络；在行为方式上，从单向的政治动员和意识形态统御逐步转向整合资源、聚合与协调利益以实现领导权；在管理技术上，既有限度地应用了政治议程中的协商、投票民主参与形式，也比较广泛地采用了行政管理的组织变革工具，诸如信息化、精细化、流程再造、协同与整体性机制构建，将其纳入党在基层的再组织化过程，使组织的行动纲领得以有效贯彻执行。

基层组织的变化景象，演示了社会治理结构重构中党组织的行动路径及其逻辑。概括而言，其路线是：在党委领导和推动下，党的工作部门通过组织嵌入和资源下沉的双元工作机制，将组织系统的触角不断延伸，建造基层组织网络的基础，从而加强对社会空间、社会组织的覆盖和渗透，实现以党为核心领导的基层社会服务与管理功能。在推进基层组织化的实践中，党组织采用了传统政治动员方法与现代管理理念和工具相结合的工作方式，一方面维系党强有力的政治统合能力，另一方面使党组织适应现代社会治理观念与潮流，体现与时俱进的适应能力和合法性来源。传统方式包含了自上而下的推动、运动式执行、分片包组、群众路线等，而应用的新的管理工具集中在努力整合多元力量、提高服务满意度和增进治理开放性三个领域，诸如整体性与协同机制、无缝隙流程再造与规范精细化、网络化与信息公开透明、商谈讨论对话等。一系列混合治理工具的运用，给党的基层组织带来了新的空间，提升了其回应能力和治理弹性。一是，以关注民生和强化公共服务功能，将需求表达—利益满足—服务供给三位一体连接起来，形成了以服务为媒介的党和社会联系纽带和互动渠道。这一通道不仅使组织嵌入获得了实务的支撑，而且为基层组织向社会的融入提供了合法的依据，增强了党执政的社会性质和意义。二是，以利益关系协调维系各方互动与合作，党组织成为利益吸纳和传导的中枢。在多元利益结构中，基层组织实践扮演了居间利益协调的角色，运用组织化整合，基层组织吸纳、聚合了多元社会力量，以需求为导向汇集共同的关注，以协商讨论为手段，促进关系调整和共识形成。以利益调适实现利益的吸纳和代表，发展了基层组织向社会融入的能力。由此可见，基层的实践行动旨在显示打造与社会良性互动的开放性党组织的强烈意图，有学者将其概括为"开放式党建"。[9]在这里，开放性不仅是指基层党组织权力运作的公开透明与接受群众监督，而且是指党组织建立与社会的新型关系秩序，以及以创新社会治理工具回应现实问题的观念与制度框架。

基层社会治理变迁中党组织的实践历程，也留下了一些需要深思和进一步探讨的问题。从近年来党的基层组织几个阶段的演化方式看，自上而下的推动依然是改革的基本路径，强有力的上层支持有助于清除障碍，让改革项目顺利推进。但同时意味着，改革的原发动力并非来自于基层组织和社区、"两新"组织，前者是执行机构，后者则作为被嵌入的对象，那么，基层组织与社区、"两新"组织进入被整合的组织网络之中的动力机制或者相互兼容的利益关系结构究竟是什么？换句话说，党组织的覆盖和渗透是否促进了组织网络中各组织成员的共同利益，以及维系共同利益的条件是什么？其次，基层组织的嵌入与组织化过程将利益表达和多元社会力量纳入了既定的管道，被有序吸纳与整合。然而，在这一利益统合方式的设计下，源自民间自主性能否得到充分发展，社区自治能否获得广泛的空间而不是行政化的不断扩张，也就是说，在现代治理框架下，组织嵌入、吸纳可否促进自治和公共参与？迄今，我们没有回答这些问题的现成答案，只能在实践探索中不断地追问和回应。

---

[1] 何增科：《中国社会管理体制改革总论》，见何增科主编：《中国社会管理体制改革路线图》，国家行政学院出版社2009年版，第3—5页。

[2] 北京第五次城管会议，定位街道管理功能为"统筹辖区发展、监督专业管理、组织公共服务、指导社区建设"，上海确立"两级政府，三级管理"原则，突出街道和社区在城市管理中的作用。林尚立：《社区民主与治理：案例研究》，社会科学文献出版社2003年版。

[3] 中国行政管理学会课题组：《加快我国社会管理和公共服务改革的研究报告》，《中国行政管理》2005年第2期；李学举：《加强社会建设和管理，促进社会和谐与发展》，《求是》2005年第7期；陈振明、李德国、蔡晶晶：《政府社会管理职能的概念辨析——"政府社会管理"课题的研究报告之一》，《东南学术》2005年第4期。

[4] 薛澜、张扬：《构建和谐社会机制治理群体性事件》，《江苏社会科学》2006年第4期。

[5] 魏礼群主编：《社会管理创新案例选编》（中册），人民出版社2011年版，第525—526页。

[6] 中共中央组织部：《关于加强街道党的建设工作的意见》，1996年；《中办转发中共中央组织部关于进一步加强和改进街道社区党的建设工作的意见》，中办发〔2004〕25号。

[7] 中共上海市静安区委组织部：《深化完善区域化党建格局，积极探索社会管理创新》，2012年。

[8] 张超：《组织嵌入、合法性重构与功能拓展：中共在社区中的调适》，清华大学博士学位论文，2014年。

[9] 韩福国：《开放式党建：协商民主与群众路线的融合》，上海人民出版社2013年版。

澳门博彩业竞争管理政策之研究

朱顺和　陈海天[*]

一、绪言

2001年澳门实施博彩自由化政策，允许本地与外国的博彩投资者在澳门投资新设赌场。开放外国博彩企业可以进入澳门博彩市场，可以引进外国博彩企业的管理经验与技术；相对的，也带来本地博彩市场经营竞争的压力。2009年中国国务院颁布《珠江三角地区改革发展规划纲要（2008—2020年）》，澳门定位为世界旅游休闲中心，加上受惠于中国经济快速成长及港澳自由行旅游政策，澳门旅游业持续蓬勃地发展，博彩业的博彩收入亦呈现增长趋势。2013年澳门博彩收入高达澳门币3607亿元，较2012年持续增长18.61%。以博彩收入而言，澳门自2006年迄今已位居全球第一大赌城。同时，博彩业为澳门第一大产业，生产总值约占全澳生产总值45%，其重要性充分反映在其对政府财政税收的贡献上（朱顺和、陈海天、罗迪，2013）。

近年来，澳门政府陆续批准现有博彩公司在路凼金光大道上新建或扩建赌场，面对来自本地博彩市场与邻近国家博彩市场的激烈竞争，此已成为澳门博彩业者首要关注的经营问题；同时，也成为博彩监管机构管理政策必须考量的重要因素。Porter（2008）指出产业的过度竞争会导致企业投资报酬率降低，如接近经济学家所称完全竞争产业的投资报酬率，会造成企业的亏损或者倒闭。Demsetz（1973）指出，大型企业的获利能力优于小型企业，主要是因为企业效率（efficiency），而非企业之间共谋串通（collusion）或是市场垄断（monopoly）。因此，若政府政策采取分散政策或是反合并政策，可能导致企业无效率。Round（1975）探讨澳洲产业的市场结构、市场竞争与公共政策，研究结论认为市场集中度高，会提升大型企业获利力。

据此，本研究尝试以结构—行为—绩效（Structure-Conduct-Performance；SCP）模

---

[*] 朱顺和，澳门科技大学商学院助理教授；陈海天，澳门科技大学商学院硕士生。

式为基础（Bain，1951），以集中度（Concentration）模型来检视澳门博彩市场结构状况；同时，以 Panzar-Rosse 模型来检验澳门博彩长期市场竞争状况。其次，基于实证分析结果，本研究提出澳门博彩竞争管理政策之具体建议，提供澳门博彩监管机构作为管理政策之参考，以确保本地博彩市场的公平经营与竞争，并维持博彩业的长期可持续发展。

二、文献综述

关于企业竞争的理论基础，学者提出智慧资本理论及资源基础理论，前者是无形资产为重心，后者以有形资产及无形资产为重心；同时，两者都强调企业资源是形成企业竞争优势的重要来源。

智慧资本理论是基于知识基础理论，智慧资本与知识管理存在密切关系（朱顺和、卓宪、鄢铄，2013）。Galbraith（1969）首先提出智慧资本（Intellectual Capital）概念，认为智慧资本是企业运用组织营运、决策及脑力行为所产生出的价值。学者进一步提出对智慧资本的不同定义与见解，并强调无形资产是企业竞争力的重要依据。Stewart（1997）定义智慧资本，是指员工能为企业带来竞争优势的一切知识及能力的总和。Bontis（1998）将智慧资本可分为人力资本、顾客资本及结构资本；其中，人力资本是企业产生创新的源头，员工努力工作可以带来顾客价值及结构资本的效率；顾客资本即指顾客的价值，衡量指标如市场占有率、顾客满意度、顾客贡献度等；结构资本是指不会随着员工下班带回家的知识，可成为企业的财产。Edvinsson and Malone（1997）则提出斯堪地亚市场价值结构（Skandia Market Value Structure），认为智慧资本是企业掌握的知识、组织技术、实际经验、顾客关系及专业技能，使其具有市场竞争优势。

其次，关于资源基础理论的源起，Wernerfelt（1984）首先提出资源基础观点（resource-based view），认为企业资源包括有形资产与无形资产。采取多角化经营的企业在规划战略时，其企业资源可作为处理重要问题的基础。Barney（1991）认为企业资源包括所有资产、能力、组织流程、企业属性、信息、知识等，能使企业构想与执行改善企业经营效率与效果的战略；同时，提出战略规划体系（strategic planning system），强调企业资源的异质性与不可移动性，可产生企业可持续竞争优势。Grant（1991）提出战略分析的企业资源基础方法（resource-based approach to strategy analysis），分析企业资源，以评估企业能力，并据之以分析企业竞争优势，以形成企业战略。Peteraf（1993）则提出竞争优势的基础（cornerstones of competitive advantage）架构，认为异质性、不完全移动性、竞争的事前限制及竞争的事后限制等情况，可作为企业可持续竞争的基础。美国哈佛大学教授麦克·波特（Michael Porter）提出竞争策略概念，新企业的加入、被人取代的威胁、客户议价能力、供应商议价能力及现有竞争者之间的对立态势等五个竞争作用力之总合,可以决定一产业的竞争程度与获利程度。

近年来有国内外学者关注博彩业竞争之研究议题,主要偏重于探讨竞争对博彩业经营的影响。Walker and Nesbit(2013)研究1997年至2010年间美国密苏里州区域内博彩公司的市场竞争对博彩收入的影响。研究结果显示:1. 角子机、赌桌与营业面积对博彩收入有正向影响;2. 角子机与营业面积与市场竞争呈负相关;赌桌与市场竞争有正向相关性;3. 市场竞争对博彩收入有负向的影响。Chu,Wu and Zhang(2014)提出澳门放宽博彩市场管制,允许本地及国外投资者新建赌场,是否影响澳门博彩市场的集中度及竞争程度。实证研究指出,澳门博彩市场为垄断性竞争(monopolistic competition)的市场,博彩公司应采取扩大经济规模策略,提升市场竞争能力。

三、竞争衡量方法

竞争的衡量方式可分为两大类:结构性与非结构性竞争衡量方式(Bikker and Haaf,2002)。其中,结构性竞争衡量方式,以外生因素(exogenous factors)来衡量市场结构;非结构性竞争衡量方式,以内生因素(endogenous factors)来衡量市场竞争状况。

2.1 结构性竞争衡量方式

根据结构—行为—绩效模式(Bain,1951),市场结构为企业竞争战略规划的重要影响因素,基于产业的市场结构状况,企业拟定竞争决策,可预期其经营绩效。本研究采用学者常用的结构性衡量指标为:市场集中比率(Concentration Ratio;CR)、赫芬达尔-赫希曼指数(Herfindahl-Hirschman Index;HHI)(Bikker and Haaf,2002)。

(1)市场集中比率

市场集中比率是指某一特定市场或产业,少数的较大企业所占市场的份额,反映出市场竞争程度(杨菁、陈艳,2009)。其计算公式为:

$$CRn = \sum_{i=1}^{n} X_i / \sum_{i=1}^{N} X_i$$

其中,

X_i = 第 i 家企业以资产、营业收入或其他业务指标计算的市场占有率;

n = 产业中市场占有率较大的前几家企业;

N = 产业中的所有企业家数。

市场集中比率一般以3家、4家、5家或8家企业代表一个产业中市场占有率较大的前几家企业。若 CRn 值越高,表示该一产业的竞争程度较低;若 CRn 值越低,表示该一产业的竞争程度较高。以 CR4 为例,CR4 值大于 0.75,表示该一行业为集中度极高的市场;CR4 值介于 0.65—0.75,表示该一产业为较高集中度的市场;CR4 值介于 0.65—0.35,表示该一产业为中度集中度的市场;CR4 值小于 0.35,表示该一产业为低度集中度的市场。

(2) 赫芬达尔 – 赫希曼指数(赫氏指数)

赫氏指数是衡量市场集中度的综合性指标之一,衡量一个产业中各竞争企业所占该行业的比重(Bikker and Haaf, 2002),其计算公式为:

$$HHI = \sum_{i=1}^{n} S_i^2$$

其中,

n = 产业中企业数量;

S_i = 第 i 家企业以资产、营业收入或其他业务指标计算的市场占有率。

赫氏指数的范围从 0 到 1,数值高表示市场高度集中水平,缺少竞争(Stanek, 2012)。若 $HHI < 0.1$,表示该产业属于低度集中水平,显示该产业为竞争市场形态;若 $0.1 < HHI < 0.18$,表示该产业属于中度集中水平;若 $HHI > 0.18$,表示该产业属于高集中水平,显示该产业为寡占或垄断市场形态。

2.2 非结构性竞争衡量方式

非结构性竞争衡量方式包括三种模型:Iwata 模型,Bresnahan 模型及 Panzar-Rosse 模型(Bikker and Haaf, 2002)。其中,Panzar-Rosse 模型则被前人广泛运用于银行业研究(Al-Muharrami, Matthews and Khabari, 2006)。

Panzar and Rosse 于 1987 年提出 Panzar-Rosse 模型,其表现了银行在面对逐渐下降的收入时,将会采取的竞争行为(Bikker and Haaf, 2002)。其公式如下:

$$Ln(TREV_{it}) = \alpha_0 + \alpha_1 Ln(PL_{it}) + \alpha_2 Ln(PK_{it}) + \alpha_3 Ln(PF_{it}) + \alpha_n \sum Ln(Bank\text{-}specific\ Factors_{it}) + \varepsilon_{it}$$

其中:

$TREV_{it}$ = 银行 i 在 t 期的总收入与总资产之比率;

PL_{it} = 银行 i 在 t 期的人事费用与总资产之比率;

PK_{it} = 银行 i 在 t 期的营运费用与总资产之比率;

PF_{it} = 银行 i 在 t 期的利息费用与存款及债务之和的比率;

Bank-specific Factors$_{it}$ = 银行 i 在 t 期的特有因素;

ε_{it} = 银行 i 在 t 期的误差项。

Panzar-Rosse 模型采用一个衡量指标,称之为 H 统计值。H 统计值表现了银行由成本数值变化而引起的利息收入变动(Bikker and Haaf, 2002)。其公式如下:

$$H = \sum_{k=1}^{m} \frac{\partial R_i^*}{\partial w_{ki}} \cdot \frac{w_{ki}}{R_i^*}$$

其中：

R_i^* = 银行 i 在平衡时的收入方程；

W_{ki} = 银行 i 的投入价格因素；

m = 对投入价格影响因素的数量。

H 统计值是 Panzar – Rosse 模型中的三个参数系数之和（α_1，α_2，α_3）。H 统计值的区间为负 $-\infty$ 到 1 之间。当 $H=1$ 时，表示银行业为完全竞争（perfect competition）市场；当 $H\leq0$ 时，则说明银行业为垄断（monopoly）市场；当 $0<H<1$ 时，说明银行业为垄断性竞争（monopolistic competition）市场（Coccorese，2004）。

四、研究方法

3.1 研究样本

本研究资料来源为在香港证券交易所上市的澳门博彩公司年报财务数据。研究对象包括银河娱乐集团有限公司（Galaxy）、新濠娱乐集团有限公司（Melco）、美高梅中国控股有限公司（MGM）、金沙中国有限公司（Sands）、澳门博彩控股有限公司（SJM）及永利澳门有限公司（Wynn）等六家澳门博彩公司。样本期间为 2008 年至 2013 年，并以年为样本区间。

3.2 研究模型

竞争的衡量方式可分为两大类：结构性方式与非结构性方式（Bikker and Haaf, 2002）。本研究以结构性竞争衡量方式，来衡量澳门博彩市场的市场结构；此外，以非结构性竞争衡量方式，来衡量澳门博彩市场的长期市场竞争状况。

3.2.1 市场结构分析模型

本研究采用市场集中比率（Concentration Ratio；CR）、赫芬达尔 – 赫希曼指数（Herfindahl – Hirschman Index；HHI）作为市场结构衡量指标。

（1）市场集中度

本研究市场集中比率是分别以博彩公司的博彩收入或总资产为基础，并以市场占有率为前三大企业的市场占有率之合计数来衡量。其计算公式为：

$$CR3 = \sum_{i=1}^{n} X_i / \sum_{i=1}^{N} X_i$$

其中，

X_i = 第 i 家澳门博彩公司的博彩收入或总资产市场占有率；

n = 博彩收入或总资产为基础之市场占有率的前三大澳门博彩公司；

N = 所有在香港证交所上市之澳门博彩公司。

（2）赫芬达尔－赫希曼指数（赫氏指数）

本研究赫氏指数也是分别以博彩公司的博彩收入或总资产为基础，并以所有企业的市场占有率之平方和来衡量。其计算公式为：

$$HHI = \sum_{i=1}^{n} S_i^2$$

其中，

n = 所有在香港证交所上市之澳门博彩公司；

S_i = 第 i 家澳门博彩公司的博彩收入及总资产市场占有率。

3.2.2 市场竞争模型分析

本研究在 Coccorese（2004）的研究模型基础上，建立市场结构研究模型。其中，因变量为总收入与总资产的比率；自变数包括人事费用与总资产的比率、利息费用与总资产之比率及折旧及摊提费用与总资产之比率；另选取财务杠杆（Leverage）、资产规模（Size）及以总资产为基础之赫氏指数（HHI）作为控制变量。本研究以 H 值为模型系数 α_1, α_2, α_3 的合计数，进行 Wald test；当 H 值 = 0 时，虚无假设为市场结构是垄断性市场结构；当 H 值 = 1 时，虚无假设为市场结构是完全竞争市场结构。

$$Ln(TREV_{it}) = \alpha_0 + \alpha_1 Ln(PE_{it}) + \alpha_2 Ln(PF_{it}) + \alpha_3 Ln(PK_{it}) + \alpha_4 Ln(LEV_{it}) + \alpha_5 Ln(SIZE_{it}) + \alpha_6 Ln(HHI_t) + \varepsilon_{it}$$

其中，

$TREV_{it}$ = 第 i 家博彩公司在第 t 年的总收入与总资产的比率；

PE_{it} = 第 i 家博彩公司在第 t 年的人事费用与总资产的比率；

PF_{it} = 第 i 家博彩公司在第 t 年的利息费用与总资产之比率；

PK_{it} = 第 i 家博彩公司在第 t 年的折旧及摊提费用与总资产之比率；

LEV_{it} = 第 i 家博彩公司在第 t 年的总负债与总资产之比率；

$SIZE_{it}$ = 第 i 家博彩公司在第 t 年的总资产；

HHI_t = 第 t 年的以总资产为基础的赫氏指数；

ε_{it} = 第 i 家博彩公司在第 t 年的误差项。

其次，本研究参考 Coccorese（2004）的研究模型基础上，建立市场竞争长期均衡研究模型。其中，因变量为资产回报率，由于部分博彩公司营运初期产生亏损，因此采用（1+资产回报率）作为因变量；自变数包括人事费用与总资产的比率、利息费用与总资产之比率及折旧及摊提费用与总资产之比率；另选取财务杠杆、资产规模及市场竞争的赫氏指数作为控制变量。本研究进行 Wald test，以 H 值为 α_1, α_2, α_3 的合计数，当 H 值 = 0 时，虚无假设为市场竞争状况是长期均衡。

$$Ln(1+ROA_{it}) = \alpha_0 + \alpha_1 Ln(PE_{it}) + \alpha_2 Ln(PF_{it}) + \alpha_3 Ln(PK_{it}) + \alpha_4 Ln(LEV_{it}) + \alpha_5 Ln(SIZE_{it}) + \alpha_6 Ln(HHI_t) + \varepsilon_{it}$$

其中，

ROA_{it} = 第 i 家博彩公司在第 t 年的资产回报率；

PE_{it} = 第 i 家博彩公司在第 t 年的人事费用与总资产的比率；

PF_{it} = 第 i 家博彩公司在第 t 年的利息费用与总资产之比率；

PK_{it} = 第 i 家博彩公司在第 t 年的折旧及摊提费用与总资产之比率；

LEV_{it} = 第 i 家博彩公司在第 t 年的总负债与总资产之比率；

$SIZE_{it}$ = 第 i 家博彩公司在第 t 年的总资产；

HHI_t = 第 t 年博彩业以总资产为基础的赫氏指数；

ε_{it} = 第 i 家博彩公司在第 t 年的误差项。

3.3 实证分析结果

3.3.1 市场结构实证分析结果

表 1 所示为市场结构分析结果。其中，就以博彩收入为基础 $CR3$ 值，介于 0.659649 至 0.709157 之间，显示澳门博彩业属于高度集中的市场结构；然而，$CR3$ 值先呈缓慢减低，再呈缓慢上升，此乃受银河度假村路凼第一期赌场开始投入营运影响；就以总资产为基础 $CR3$ 值，介于 0.700599 至 0.730251 之间，显示澳门博彩业属于高度集中的市场结构，唯 $CR3$ 值则呈缓慢减低。

其次，就以博彩收入为基础 HHI 值，介于 0.197011 至 0.219392 之间，显示澳门博彩业属于高度集中的市场结构，HHI 先呈缓慢上升，再呈缓慢减低，此乃受银河度假村路凼第一期赌场开始投入营运影响；就以总资产为基础 HHI 值，介于 0.207994 至 0.231928 之间，显示澳门博彩业属于高度集中的市场结构，HHI 值则呈缓慢减低。

表 1 市场结构实证分析结果表

年度	CR3		HHI	
	博彩收入	总资产	博彩收入	总资产
2008	0.703017	0.730251	0.207856	0.231928
2009	0.709157	0.724700	0.219134	0.223260
2010	0.681000	0.727868	0.219392	0.227325
2011	0.659649	0.721839	0.205321	0.222996
2012	0.693413	0.712304	0.201568	0.210132
2013	0.694195	0.700599	0.197011	0.207994

资料来源：作者整理。

3.3.2 市场竞争状况实证分析结果

本研究以 Eviews 7.0 版软件进行实证分析。表 2 为变量描述性分析结果表, 说明变量的数据特征。其中, 折旧及摊提费用与总资产之比率的变动度相对较高, 显示澳门博彩公司仍不断扩大经营规模。表 3 为自变数之间的相关性分析结果表, 说明自变数之间不存在共线性。

本研究以面板数据 (data panel), 采用固定效应模型 (fixed effect model) 进行多元回归实证分析。表 4 为 Panzar-Rosse 模型对市场竞争状况的实证分析结果。模型的 H 值为 0.833268, 经 Wald test 检验 $H=0$ 的统计分析结果, F 统计值为 15.13095, 在 0.01 水平下显著, 拒绝垄断性市场结构之虚无假设; 接着 Wald test 检验 $H=1$ 的结果, F 统计值为 18.20140, 在 0.01 水平下显著, 拒绝完全竞争市场结构之虚无假设。实证结果显示: 澳门博彩市场属于具高集中度的垄断性竞争市场。

其次, 本研究进一步分析澳门博彩市场是否为长期均衡状态。表 5 为 Panzar-Rosse 模型对澳门博彩市场是否为长期均衡的实证分析结果。模型的 H 值为 -0.10866, 经 Wald test 检验 $H=0$ 的结果, F 统计值为 10.68218, 在 0.01 水平下显著, 拒绝澳门博彩市场为长期均衡之虚无假设。实证结果显示: 澳门博彩市场不处于长期均衡状态。

表 2 变量描述性分析结果表

变量	最大值	最小值	平均值	标准差
$Ln\ TREV$	0.834830	-1.294287	-0.083836	0.573021
$Ln\ PE$	-1.723204	-3.903185	-2.533095	0.548208
$Ln\ PF$	-0.071721	-16.21501	-3.497513	2.301155
$Ln\ PK$	-1.734353	-3.714133	-2.414011	0.438307
$Ln\ LEV$	-0.024305	-3.109141	-0.610534	0.503329
$Ln\ SIZE$	18.30898	16.11991	17.18802	0.646815
$Ln\ HHI$	-1.461329	-1.570247	-1.512165	0.040338

资料来源: 作者整理。

表 3 自变数相关性分析结果表

变量	$Ln\ PE$	$Ln\ PF$	$Ln\ PK$	$Ln\ LEV$	$Ln\ SIZE$	$Ln\ HHI$
$Ln\ PE$	1.000000					
$Ln\ PF$	0.478927	1.000000				
$Ln\ PK$	0.626573	0.627899	1.000000			
$Ln\ LEV$	0.109519	-0.002849	0.033525	1.000000		
$Ln\ SIZE$	-0.545378	-0.094679	-0.532849	-0.473861	1.000000	
$Ln\ HHI$	0.032032	-0.284750	-0.174405	0.426065	-0.383336	1.000000

资料来源: 作者整理。

表4 多元回归分析结果表 [以 $Ln(TREV)$ 为因变量]

变量	系数	标准误差	t 统计值	概率
C	-10.98844	2.641588	-4.159784	0.0004*
Ln PE	0.679483	0.228407	2.974875	0.0066*
Ln PF	-0.023819	0.024197	-0.984376	0.3348
Ln PK	0.177604	0.159853	1.111047	0.2776
Ln LEV	-0.013893	0.092141	-0.150776	0.8814
Ln SIZE	0.878403	0.267549	3.283150	0.0031*
Ln HHI	1.412058	1.905347	0.741102	0.4658
R2	0.917581			
Adj. R2	0.879805			
F-statistic	24.29030			
D-W stat	1.477779			
H = 0	15.13095*			
H = 1	18.20140*			

注：* indicates $p<0.01$。The Wald test 以 F 统计值检验 $H=0$ 的垄断市场之虚无假设，检验 $H=1$ 的完全竞争市场之虚无假设；以1%为信赖水平。

资料来源：作者整理。

表5 多元回归分析结果表 [以 $Ln(1+ROA)$ 为因变量]

变量	系数	标准误差	t 统计值	概率
C	-6.668358	1.939299	-3.438540	0.0021*
Ln PE	0.277149	0.167683	1.652813	0.1114
Ln PF	0.017482	0.017764	0.984080	0.3349
Ln PK	-0.403291	0.117365	-3.436516	0.0022*
Ln LEV	-0.026100	0.067645	-0.385840	0.7030
Ln SIZE	0.0333071	0.196419	1.695720	0.1029
Ln HHI	-0.530585	1.398794	-0.379316	0.7078
R2	0.650373			
Adj. R2	0.490127			
F-statistic	4.058596*			
D-W stat	2.177209			
H = 0	10.68218*			

注：* indicates $p<0.01$。The Wald test 以 F 统计值检验 $H=0$ 的长期均衡状态之虚无假设；以1%为信赖水平。

资料来源：作者整理。

四、结论与建议

经实证分析结果,本研究获致结论:澳门博彩市场属于具高集中度的垄断性竞争市场,但不是处于长期均衡状态的市场。

高集中度的垄断性竞争市场能带来博彩企业的高经营效率,此一研究结论与Demsetz(1973)及Round(1975)的见解一致。若澳门博彩监管机构为强调公平性,使得CR值或HHI值降低,导致澳门博彩市场结构由高集中度转趋于中集中度的市场结构,将减低经济规模的优势。因此,本研究建议:澳门博彩监管机构应适度地维持澳门博彩市场为高集中度市场结构,获取经济规模效益,维持博彩业可持续经营,以确保澳门经济稳定发展。

然而,台湾义守大学国际观光餐旅学系主任苏锦俊博士表示,比较澳门与美国赌场经营模式,澳门博彩业太过注重于博彩经营,不若美国博彩业注重博彩与休闲娱乐之结合,澳门博彩业经营应适度多元化。此观点与Porter(2008)见解一致。澳门博彩业具有单一产品经营之行业基本特征,博彩收入约占总收入的93%—98%,在缺乏产品差异化的产业,客户会以价格及服务质量作为其选择往来的主要依据(Porter,2008)。因此,本研究建议:澳门博彩监管机构应规范澳门博彩公司适度多元化业务,结合精品商店、餐饮美食、会议展览、文化创意、影艺表演等主题,提高服务质量;同时,应结合澳门所拥有世界文化遗产与非物质文化遗产等丰富旅游资源,以增强澳门博彩业整体之竞争优势。

其次,澳门博彩市场目前不是处于长期均衡状态的市场,此一结论可能归因于澳门博彩监管机构批示现有澳门博彩公司在路氹金光大道陆续扩建及新建赌场;当澳门博彩业随着路氹金光大道新设赌场完成,澳门博彩市场发展将会步入成熟期阶段。因此,本研究建议:澳门博彩监管机构应制定澳门博彩市场长期均衡监管指标,避免恶性竞争,以维持澳门博彩市场的长期稳健发展。

---

[1] 朱顺和、卓宪、鄢铄:《澳门博彩业财务资本与智慧资本对企业价值影响之研究》,《澳门经济》2013年第34期,第35—47页。

[2] 朱顺和、陈海天、罗迪:《宏观经济因素对澳门博彩业风险承担影响之研究》,《澳门经济》2013年第35期,第14—25页。

[3] 杨菁、陈艳:《澳门银行业市场结构分析》,《澳门经济》第28期,第42—54页。

[4] Al-Muharrami, S., Matthews, K. G. P. and Khabari, Y., "Market Structure and Competitive Conditions in the Arab GCC Banking System", *Journal of Banking & Finance*, 30 (12), 2006, pp. 3487–

3501.

[5] Bain, J. S. , "Relation of Profit Rate to Industrial Concentration American Manufacturing, 1936 – 1940", *Quarterly Journal of Economics*, 65 (3), 1951, pp. 293 – 324.

[6] Barney, J. , "Firm Resource and Sustained Competitive Advantage", *Journal of management*, 17 (1), 1991, pp. 99 – 120.

[7] Bikker, J. A. and Haaf, K. , "Competition, Concentration and Their Relationship: An Empirical Analysis of the Banking Industry", *Journal of Banking and Finance*, 26 (11), 2002, pp. 2191 – 2214.

[8] Bontis, N. , "Intellectual Capital: An Exploratory Study that Develops Measures and Models", *Management Decision*, 36 (2), 1998, pp. 63 – 76.

[9] Chu, S. H. , Wu, S. H. and Zhang, J. , "Concentration and Competition in Macanese Casino Industry: Panzar – Rosse Approach", 2014 International Conference on E-commerce and Contemporary Economic Development, 2014.

[10] Coccorese, P. , "Banking Competition and Macroeconomic Conditions: A Disaggregate Analysis", *Journal of International Markets, Institutions & Money*, 14 (3), 2004, pp. 203 – 219.

[11] Demsetz, H. , "Industry Structure, Market Rivalry, and Public Policy", *The Journal of Law and Economics*, 16 (1), 1973, pp. 1 – 9.

[12] Edvinsson, I. and Malone, M. S. , *Intellectual Capital: Realizing Your Company's True Value by Finding Its Hidden Manpower*, New York: Harper Business, 1997.

[13] Galbraith, J. K. , *The Affluent Society*, London: Hamish Hamilton, 1969.

[14] Grant, R. M. , "The Resource – Based Theory of Competitive Advantage Implications for Strategy Formulation", *California Management Review*, 33 (3), 1991, pp. 114 – 135.

[15] Panzar, J. C. and Rosse, J. N. , "Structure, Conduct and Competitive Statistics", Economic Discussion Paper, No. 248, Bell Lab, 1982.

[16] Panzar, J. C. and Rosse, J. N. , "Testing for Monopoly Equilibrium", *Journal of Industrial Economics*, 35 (4), 1987, pp. 443 – 456.

[17] Peteraf, M. A. , "The Cornerstones of Competitive Advantage: A Resource-based View", *Strategic Management Journal*, 14 (3), 1993, pp. 179 – 191.

[18] Porter, M. E. , "The Five Competitive Forces that Shape Strategy", *Harvard Business Review*, 2008, pp. 78 – 93.

[19] Round, D. K. , "Industry Structure, Market Rivalry, and Public Policy: Some Australian Evidence", *The Journal of Law and Economics*, 18 (1), 1975, pp. 273 – 281.

[20] Stanek, R. , "Competition and Risk-Taking in Banking Industry", *Financial Assets and Investing*, 3 (1), 2012, pp. 7 – 19.

[21] Stewart, T. A. , *Intellectual Capital: The New Wealth of Organizations*, New York: Bantam Doubleday Dell Publishing Group, Inc. 1997.

[22] Walker, D. M. and Nesbit, T. M., "Casino Revenue Sensitivity to Competing Casinos: A Spatial Analysis of Missouri", *Growth and Change*, 45 (1), 2013, pp. 21 – 40.

[23] Wernerfelt, B., "A Resource-Based View of the Firm", *Strategic Management Journal*, 5, 1984, pp. 171 – 180.

[24] Upneja, A., Kim, H. and Singh, A., "Differences in Financial Characteristics between Small and Large Firms: An Empirical Examination of the Casino Industry", *Journal of Hospitality Financial Management*, 8 (1), 2000, pp. 23 – 35.

澳门公共支出绩效审计探究

黎宝珊[*]

政府绩效审计发展于20世纪70年代，而建议"绩效审计"的统一称谓则开始于1986年第12届最高审计机关国际组织（INTOSAI）国际会议上，在这届会议发表的一篇文章《关于绩效审计、公营企业审计和审计质量的总声明》中指出："除了合规性审计，还有另一种类型的审计，它涉及对公营部门管理的经济性（Economy）、效率性（Efficiency）和效果性（Effectiveness）（即"3E"）的评价，这就是绩效审计。" INTOSAI于2004年出版的《公共机构内部控制标准的指导方针》中关于"3E"的内容如下[1]：

表1 "3E"内容说明表

经济性	效率性	效果性
维持低成本	最好地利用资源	提供人们希望从政府获得的内容
资源的合理数量、合格品质在合适的时间和地点以最低的成本进行分配	用最小的资源投入来获得一个既定的产出数量和质量，或用既定的数量和质量的资源投入来获得最大的产出	行动的结果与目标或行动的既定效果匹配的程度

资料来源：INTOSAI《公共机构内部控制标准的指导方针》（2004）。

关于绩效审计的称谓各国不尽相同，加拿大审计长公署（Office of the Auditor General，OAG）将绩效审计与常规审计结合称为"综合审计"（Comprehensive Auditing）；英国称为"货币价值审计"或"物有所值审计"（Value-for-money Audit）；美国政府责任办公室（Government Accountability Office，GAO）称为"绩效审计"；中国称为"经济效益审计"；香港及澳门则称之为"衡工量值式审计"。

---

[*] 黎宝珊，澳门公职人员协会助理秘书长。

绩效审计与财务审计的目的、对象和作用略有不同，绩效审计不仅审计政府部门的财务收支状况，而且对其管理活动的效益做出评价并且提出改进建议，故此绩效审计发挥的作用较财务审计作用更大。

一、澳门政府绩效审计的发展

澳门政府实行绩效审计的工作始于澳门 1999 年回归中国之后，开展绩效审计的工作由按照《澳门特别行政区基本法》成立的澳门审计署进行。澳门审计署根据《基本法》第六十条依法设立，它是一个独立机关，享有行政财政自治权，由审计长领导，对行政长官负责。

审计署按照法规开展澳葡政府管治时期所欠缺的各种审计活动，审计署依法对政府部门的公共收支表、资产负债表、享有财政自治权的部门及机构的管理账目，以及预算外资金的管理和使用情况进行"账目审计"，以此作为撰写澳门特区总账目审计报告的基础。同时亦依法开展"衡工量值式审计"，对公共资源管理上或投资管理所达到的效益、效率及节省程度标准进行审查，并对被审计单位提出建议。审计署亦依法开展"专项审计"，对预算管理、内部管理、管理模式及财政活动之效益进行审查。[2]审计署开展各样审计工作的目的是为改善及提升政府部门的管治水平及善用公帑的观念。

除此之外，审计署于 2011 年亦开始推行跟踪审计的工作，同时对涉及大量财政资源的公共项目或计划的合同执行、预算执行，以及在管理或决算前的所有财政活动等开展各项审计工作。

审计工作的顺利开展，在一定程度上依赖有关审计方面的法律颁布，它能提供法律基础及明确审计的职责，更好地推行公共支出绩效审计的工作，澳门政府应尽快制定有关政府公共支出绩效审计的专门法律，以及相关法规、部门规章及实施细则等，进一步提升绩效审计的法律地位。

绩效审计对澳门来说是一项崭新的审计工作，澳门审计署于澳门回归后开展绩效审计工作已有十余年时间，截至 2014 年 2 月，澳门审计署完成审计报告并向公众公布的共有 57 份，当中包括账目审计 17 份，占总审计报告的 29.8%；专项审计有 10 份，占总审计报告的 17.5%；衡工量值式审计（绩效审计）有 30 份，占总审计报告的 52.6%。从数据资料可明显知悉澳门审计署完成的绩效审计工作超逾所有审计工作的一半。

二、澳门公共财政支出绩效审计的作用

澳门这十年间受惠于博彩业的发展，政府的收入以倍数增加，经济发展的同时，亦带动澳门不少大型项目及基建的建设，随着经济社会的持续发展，不少大型建设项目陆续开展，可以预见政府投资开支将继续增加，政府公共开支对澳门经济社会的影响亦日趋增加。故此，提高公共财政支出的绩效尤其重要，特别是有的部门轻支出的理财观念，使财政支出绩效不高；又或大型建设的预算金额以各种各样理由不断追加，使追加后金额与原来预算的金额相差甚远；一些有问题工程更使政府日后负担高昂的维修费用。为监督政府公共支出的效率及效益，推行绩效审计能提高公共支出的绩效水平，确保公共资源免被浪费，保证公共资源合法合理地运用，至于开展公共财政支出绩效审计有如下几方面的作用：

（一）统一财政规范及完善运作机制

政府推行绩效审计的目的在于监督及评估政府对公共资源及公帑能合法及合理地运用，通过对政府公共财政的绩效审计，能完善政府部门及机构的预算执行及对财务处理的重视，绩效审计的推行能统一各政府部门及机构财务法规方面的规范，例如管理、登录、采购等方面。此外，绩效审计亦能促进政府部门机构重视优化自身的内部运作系统，以补足原有财务管理机制上的不足及缺陷。

（二）提高公共资源的有效利用

随着澳门经济快速增长，政府公共支出日益增大，资源越来越不能满足社会的需求，故政府必须提升公共资源的高效使用，绩效审计的实施可以从效益及效果两方面来评价公共资源的使用程度，透过绩效审计能揭露政府公共资源使用效益效果的突出问题，特别是公共资产的损失浪费、流失等重大问题，借此使被审计对象重视及保障公共资源高效利用及合理的管理。

（三）提升监督作用及增加透明度

按照公众受托经济责任理论分析，社会公众是公共资源的最初拥有者即委托人，而委托人聘用另一个人即代理人代表他们履行某些服务，包括把若干决策权托付给代理人即政府。透过绩效审计可以有效地将委托人的监督力外部化，即通过完善的政府绩效审计制度将审计结果公开，并提出改善建议，通过报告的公开逐步建立起外部监督机制，让社会大众可以直接监督政府。绩效审计可对代理人即政府的

行为进行监控，了解政府管理公共资源的状况，对政府经济责任的履行情况进行评价。此外，向被审计对象提出改善建议，给政府部门构成压力，无形中提供了责任的监督管道，审计报告的披露加强了市民大众对政府工作及使用公帑的监督，从而亦消除了官僚主义。

（四）利于构建高效及廉洁的政府

由于澳门现行执行率的情况，政府部门及机构均以耗尽编制的预算金额为最终目的，至于是否达致效率及效果则不予考虑。故开展绩效审计可以从政府收支的成本效益、效果方面来衡量其物质资源、人力资源配置与消耗之间的合理性及效果性，借以反映政府机构设置是否合理，责任有否推卸，能力与责任是否匹配，员工是否负责，有否更好地提高公共部门的信息质量，借以促进公共部门正确决策及提高服务效能。此外，透过绩效审计可以找出浪费及行政性腐败存在的根源，提出改善建议方案，从源头上预防及遏制腐败情况的发生，借以建立高效廉洁的政府。

（五）强化制约及监督权力

随着政府事务透明度的开放，市民大众对政府履行职务、管理及使用公共资源的绩效情况较以前更为关注及重视，澳门审计署在权力制约和监督方面有其重要的职能作用，审计署开展绩效审计，借披露报告可减少及解决由于滥用权力或监督不力所导致的错误或决策失误，从而发挥对公权力的监督及制约作用。

三、澳门公共财政支出执行率的评价

在澳门政府推行绩效审计工作前，政府开展的仅是对公营部门财政活动做出稽核及审计，至于绩效审计本质的"3E"——"经济性""效率性""效果性"的内容并未纳入当时的审计范围内，充其量亦只是监督工作完成后执行率所占的百分比。

公共支出是市民收入分配与再分配的重要组成部分，是国家或地区满足社会需要而进行的资源配置活动，是公共财政的一个重要部分。这些年来，澳门审计署所披露的关于政府部门的不合理公共开支个案不少，有的甚至是违规事件，故加强政府公共支出的绩效审计与监督，提高公共资金的使用效率及效果，是现今澳门政府所迫切要进行的工作。

按照澳门法律赋予澳门财政局的权力，澳门财政局负责指导、统筹及监察本地区行政公营部门或机构之财政活动，当中规范公共财政支出的职责是：组织"公共会计系统"及"本地区总预算"，促进并指导其运作及执行，以及确保本地区财政之正常管理，确保行政当局投资与发展开支计划之编制及执行，确保公库与代理银行及其他实体之联系，监管公款之调动及进行出纳活动，并组织有关之账目系统及做记账活动等职责。[3]澳门政府透过公共财政支出提供公共产品、公共服务以及履行其公共责任，而财政的监控则透过各政府部门及机构依法按时向澳门财政局递交财务资料以实施。

澳门各政府部门及机构每年皆按照年初批核的预算而执行工作，一般而言，部门及机构每年均依照上年度预算的项目做出有需要的相关调整而制定下年度预算，经由经济财政司司长向澳门立法会引介，后经立法会通过、批准及颁布后，预算案立即生效。

至于监控部门的财政运作情况是否在预算之内，则透过部门向澳门财政局递交的各种报表及资料所体现，其中执行率的计算，是由财政局负责计算该部门在相应的实际开支项目内对比预算支出金额的比率。澳门财政局没有开展对政府部门及机构的绩效审计工作，在预算中的监控内容根本不存在经济性、效率性及效果性的稽核内容，充其量将执行率作为考虑机构所预计的工作是否完成的参考，若执行率达到百分百，说明该年度相应开支项目的工作全部完成，当中完成工作的成本多少、效率高低及效果如何都不在计算及监督之列。

由于法制规范存在缺陷，监控目的不完善，欠缺善用公帑的意识及存有花费人家钱的观念，故或会有各政府部门举办不应办活动的情况出现及为耗尽不该耗的预算金额以满足执行率的现象发生。

四、澳门公共财政现存问题的原因

澳门政府部门及机构每年透过批核的年度预算对公共产品及公共服务的提供而做出开支，而此等公共开支按照预算法及相关法规依法支付，但至于公共产品及公共服务所达到的效果及效益，如何分配公共资源，预算法中则没有列明，这样便为管理者提供了滥用或浪费公共资源的方便，利用公权力不适当地挪占公共资源，又由于政府就财政开支方面计算执行率的方法与绩效审计的要求有异，导致在绩效审计报告的披露中屡屡出现浪费公帑的情况发生。

澳门预算法制度采用的是过程导向预算，即政府或其他部门以上一财政年度的预算支出为依据而进行编制的预算模式，过程导向预算关注的是预算资源在管理过程中的具体分配和使用，而不是预算资源的使用效果和绩效目标的实现程度。由于政府本质的特殊性，往往着重于提供公共服务而不惜大量投入公共资源，至于提供公共产品及公共服务后的效果，政府根本无考虑，政府亦没有机制及法规要求部门衡量或评估。政治决策追求的是行政效率，而非财政效率，但财政效率恰恰就是反映政府支出的社会效果。

此外，政府部门及机构在当年所剩余的预算余额，由于部门没有权力支配这些剩余预算，故此，原则上必须将预算的余额交还政府，除此之外，另一更深远的影响是部门恐怕下一财政年度的预算可能被削减，原因是政府可能认为该部门不需要太多的预算亦可以完成工作，这样无疑是对该部门节约资源的变相惩罚。故此，各部门会想方设法耗尽剩余的预算资源，以争取下一财政年度获更多的预算拨款。

财政支出的另一浪费根源，在于现行财政制度存在拨款与效果不挂钩的原因，同时一些手握大权的政府官员在执行任务时缺乏节约意识。

政府应逐步加强公共支出纪律约束，防止错误的公共开支安排，严格规范公共资金的使用，对于公共资金的滥用、过度的拨款承诺以及错误的公共支出安排应有相应的惩罚措施。世界各国采用的结果导向公共支出管理技术已经广泛应用于提供公共服务，并与结果问责联系，它加强了经济责任追究制度，使审计机关在追究相关单位和人员的行政责任、法律责任和经济责任时有理有据。

五、澳门公共财政支出绩效审计的缺陷与原因

澳门回归后审计署完成的 30 份绩效审计工作报告所涵盖的审计范围非常广，当中包括医疗设备购置、使用、保养维修及报废、公共部门向社团发放财政资助的研究、政府车辆使用及监管制度、澳门保安事务局资产及劳务之购置及管理、澳门奥林匹克游泳馆及东亚运动会兴建工程的使用及质量监管、环境委员会办公室搬迁及装修工程处理情况、公务人员出外公干费用规定、教育暨青年局辖下部门服务设施、持续进修发展计划、交通违例检控工具的使用及监管等一系列审计报告。

就审计过程中所发现的不正常及不正当情况，审计署会将其撰写在审计报告中，通过审计报告的对外披露从而建立监督机制，但由于澳门审计署并无惩处的权限，故当发现被审计单位违规，公共资源被闲置，甚至浪费公共资源等情况出现时，只能向被审计单位提供改善建议，提出的建议由于缺乏强制性规定，故改善与否在于被审计单位的态度，被审计单位或官员亦无须因审计带出的各种违规问题而承担相关的责任，形成有权无责的情况出现。而绩效审计的开展恰恰就是要加强对权力的制约和监督，及督促政府机构认真履行职责。在现行体制下，政府部门及机构在行使行政职能时的职权颇大，它拥有对人、财、物的决策权及执行权，透过绩效审计报告的公布能揭露政府部门或相关管理者对权力的运用及职责履行的情况。故此，认真落实问责制能使管理者支配公共资源及公共资金时重视其责任，责任机制作用在于有效地督促政府自律，从而使政府的行为按法定的程序运行，通过法律的颁布及运行，可以在权力

上对管理者进行有效的制衡，在行为上对其实施有效监督或追责，及时发现问题及消除隐患，否则，审计机关实施的绩效审计工作会完全失去应有的作用。

澳门政府迄今并没有一套以法律颁布的绩效审计准则，对绩效审计的目的、审计对象、审计内容及操作方法等都缺乏统一明确的法定规则，这样不利于公共财政支出绩效审计具体操作过程中的规范，同时给公共支出绩效审计的开展带来一定的难度，澳门政府亟须就政府绩效审计方面，以法律形式颁布绩效审计准则，使其增加绩效审计的法律地位及其权威性。

六、美国政府绩效审计的实践

美国政府责任办公室在绩效审计方面一直处于前列位置，其审计准则及相关法规均被世界各国因应各自的社会经济情况局部或全部所采用，美国政府绩效审计工作有着悠久历史，其所累积丰富的审计工作经验亦值得借镜及学习。

政府责任办公室按照法规负责对政府部门的会计资料、公共资金收入、支出及运用进行审查和监督，审计机关完成审计工作后，向国会递交审计报告，并向市民大众披露审计报告，这制度除可增加政务的透明度外，更促使政府部门重视构建高效廉洁及公共责任的态度。政府责任办公室独立于行政部门，故此为政府绩效审计能够保持客观和公正创造了条件，亦因此推动了政府绩效审计的发展。

20世纪50—60年代，随着美国政府改革政府预算体制，绩效预算被引进到预算制度中，绩效预算是将业绩的指标、成本核算和执行结果都纳入预算体系中。

美国政府绩效审计工作有统一的审计准则作指导，1972年美国政府责任办公室历时两年研发出版了第一部美国政府审计准则《政府机构、计划项目、活动和职责的审计标准》，后来这套准则的名称更改为《政府审计准则》（俗称"黄皮书"），是政府责任办公室开展项目评估后制定的一部政府审计准则，它对绩效审计起着指导作用。[4]《政府审计准则》确立了具体的公共部门绩效审计测试与评估准则，它对难以量化的标准建立了"优先实践"原则，并实行"金额化"法，新修订的《政府审计准则》使政府审计有规可循，保证了审计质量。

1974年美国国会颁布了《立法机关重组法案》及《国会预算与拨款控制法案》，授权美国政府责任办公室可以超越原来纯粹的财务事项审计范围，转向依法对政府机构的项目管理活动进行评估与分析。

1993年美国国会颁布了《政府工作绩效与结果法案》，规定政府机构每年必须提交绩效规划和报告，政府财政预算必须与政府部门挂钩，并且须向公众通报各自的绩效状况，这无疑提高了政府工作项目的效果和认真履行公共责任的态度。

至于开展绩效审计不可或缺的审计人员问题，美国政府责任办公室从20世纪70年代开始，聘用许多不同行业的专业技术人士，以应付办公室不断扩大的任务，及不断增加的项目评估工作，当中不乏属于管理学、统计学、经济学、法律学、计算机等各方面的专业人士，为办公室组成了一支复合型的人才结构，促进了审计人员素质的提高，亦为办公室进行绩效审计工作提供不同工作范畴的专业建议及改善意见。

七、英国政府货币价值审计的方式

绩效审计在英国被称为"货币价值审计"或"物有所值审计"。在20世纪，英国主计审计长将货币价值审计的运用，发展到政府部门财务管理的多方面，而货币价值审计在1983年的《国家审计法》中开始以法律形式确认并于1984年1月1日起实施，首次为审计署开展绩效审计提供了法律基础，该法律规定，审计署可就政府执行的计划、项目或其他工作活动及其结果进行审查并报告。[5]

英国国家审计署开展的绩效审计是检查公共资金使用情况的方式与效果，其中对经济性的审计关注在保证质量的前提下降低资源消耗，将政府支出降到最低水平；对效率性审计主要是对比产出与投入的关系，保证资金支出的合理性；对效果审计主要是对比实际效果和预期效果的关系，保证资金支出达到理想效果。最后将这三方面内容结合起来考察，判断其项目或活动的支出是否物有所值。

在绩效审计规范性建设方面，英国《国家审计法》授权审计长开展政府绩效审计，并对其具体职责做了明确规定，国家审计署制定了绩效审计手册，随后，就开展绩效审计的过程中，又陆续出台了绩效审计指南、绩效审计项目设计指南、绩效审计案例指南、绩效审计成本效益分析指南等一系列的绩效审计工作指南，其对绩效审计的指导规范起到关键作用。

国家审计署每年根据议会关注的重点领域或问题，以及公众关注的社会热点、焦点及难点等问题确定审计项目，审计署在广泛收集资料后，对项目进行成本效益分析及制订工作方案。国家审计署不对绩效审计的程序、步骤要求过多的硬性规定，反而倡导灵活和创新的原则，要求审计人员根据审计项目的类型和特点选择适当的方法、程序和报告方式。

国家审计署广泛利用绩效审计成果，将完成的绩效审计报告制定和出版为先进经验指南并向全社会公布绩效审计报告，冀通过指南介绍及推广先进的审计经验和方法，另外又通过网络、报刊、议会听证会等形式，向社会公布绩效审计的结果。

国家审计署非常重视审计人员的培训和岗位交流，审计署根据审计人员的职位不同，针对性地开展培训工作，对新招聘人员制定岗位培训制度，对较高级别的人员制定了持续职业计划。同时，为了使审计人员全面熟悉工作和拓宽视野，建立了专业人员轮换交流制度，即要求审计人员在某个工作单位的工作期限一般不能超过五年，否则要进行岗位交流。另外，每年还会聘请经济管理等具有各方面专门知识的专家组成联合小组，以便用多学科的方法教授绩效审计工作。

八、香港政府衡工量值式审计的做法

香港政府绩效审计称为衡工量值式审计，香港审计署于20世纪70年代开始衡工量值式审计，而立法会于1978年成立政府账目委员会，成为立法会的常设委员会，负责处理审计报告所提事项，它与审计署一起对政府公共开支的合法有效进行审查。由于账目委员会是立法机构的组成部分，负有对政府权力制衡和执法监督的职责，因此更有权威性，这是香港公众问责制的开始，伴随着衡工量值式审计工作准则的颁布，为香港衡工量值式审计及公众问责揭开序幕。香港衡工量值式审计到20世纪80年代形成规范，覆盖的审计范围亦扩展至接受政府资助的机构，公众问责的发展亦随着衡工量值式审计的推行而发展起来。

香港审计署根据自身的权限，依法进行两类工作，一类为政府账目审计，另一类为衡工量值式审计。前者每年须向立法会提交一份报告书，数量占审计署全年工作量的三分之一；后者每年须向立法会提交两份报告书，工作量占全年总工作量的三分之二。账目审计工作的开展是透过审核政府会计账目及其他相关资料，确认财务收支的真实性与合规性，随后向立法会提供独立的审计报告。由于审计资源的限制，香港审计署一般不对被审计单位做全面审计，而只选择被审计对象的部分业务进行审计，当完成现场审计后，审计署会向立法会递交一份审计报告，其报告中载有要求被审计单位提升管理水平、加强问责制度、提高成本效益等改善建议。衡工量值式审计是对被审计单位在履行职务时所达到的经济性、效率性及效果性进行审计。[6]

按照《香港特别行政区基本法》规定，香港审计署拥有完全独立的地位，审计署审计长可直接向立法会提交审计报告，不须经过行政长官及其他政府官员的审定和批准，依法安排和执行审计工作，无须听命任何机构或个人。审计署审计长在提交报告时拥有很大的自由度，可以披露对于政府部门和公共机构的审计过程中所发现的任何不当情况及涉及的财政问题。

然而，香港审计署没有权力对被审计单位下达具有法律约束力的文书，为达致审计的效果，审计署不断加强与被审计单位的沟通和合作，借以使被审计单位接纳其提供的措施和认同其改善的建议。

绩效审计不同于财务审计，绩效审计更需要知识面广及能力较强的工作人员，在培训综合素质人才方面，香港审计署除通过持续培训以促进审计人员更新知识及提高技能外，每年还派选员工到海外培训，培训课程由英国国家审计署和美国政府责任办公室提供协助，让受训员工到有关机构接受学习，吸收先进的审计方法和审计技术。

九、完善澳门公共财政支出绩效审计的建议

澳门政府开展绩效审计工作的时间仅十余年，若与国外比较，完成的绩效审计报告数量、经验的成熟程度及制度之完善范围仍与之相距甚远。澳门政府可借鉴西方发达国家及邻近地区政府绩效审计方面的丰富经验及成果，构建澳门政府绩效审计理论，加强绩效审计综合人才的培养，增加对接受政府财政资助的社团开展绩效审计，构建绩效审计的评价体系，探索及改善切合澳门实际情况的绩效审计规范及标准等举措，使绩效审计能够深入地朝着经济性、效率性、效果性、甚至公平性及环保性（即"5E"）等五个方向前进。

（一）完善绩效审计体制和明确审计职责

审计体制很受各国法律环境的制约，历史的经验证明，审计在其发展过程中，发展速度的快慢、独立性的强弱、制衡作用的大小，审计体制的形式、权威性的高低以及运行效率的优劣，很大程度上取决于法律的推动。

澳门回归后用以监督政府是否合法合规地运用公权力的手段在于对政府部门及机构实施绩效审计的工作，绩效审计不同于财务审计，绩效审计的有效执行得依赖一套完善的政府审计准则包括评价指标及评价标准，以审核其审计事项是否偏离标准，甚至有否违规违法。因此，建立一套切合澳门实际情况的绩效审计准则至为重要，并且它亦能起到有法可依及其独立性的作用。

澳门审计署开展的绩效审计工作只有调查权和建议权，至于处理处罚权则欠奉。为达致被审计单位重视其审计报告中揭示出来的违规、浪费公帑、滥权等事项，政府应加快立法对绩效审计的问责力度，明确绩效审计的问责主体及扩大问责的范围，问责制法律的颁布及执行，能促使被审计单位依循绩效审计报告的建议进行纠正，从而达致惩治腐败、改善工作、提高公共资源使用或公共资金管理的绩效目的，更重要的是若没有惩治权，这将为其他尚没有受到审计监督的部门提供了一个避责的先例，最终影响政府的威信及法治。审计体制本身无所谓好或劣之分，只要适合自身情况，能真正发挥经济监督和制衡作用，该体制就是最有效的。

（二）提升审计执行人员的素质与能力

绩效审计是一项系统工程，属于高层次的审计监督，对审计人员的专业性及综合性要求较高，审计人员除需要掌握传统的财务知识、审计业务知识及计算机应用技能之外，还需要掌握其他学科，如法律、统计、管理、经济、工程等多方面的专业知识，从而进行绩效审计。

因此，政府须培训及建立一支拥有不同领域知识的复合型审计人员队伍，储备大量不同专业的优秀人士及协助提供改善措施，同时，尚要对现有审计人员进行专业培训，提高审计水平。除此之外，亦须培养人员的综合分析能力及判断力。

绩效审计能否达到目的及审计人员如何发挥作用，很大程度上取决于素质高的审计人员及对公共支出绩效审计方法体系的掌握和运用的程度。

（三）建立财政绩效评价标准体系

"绩效审计的评价标准"是审计人员用以衡量公共部门及机构绩效状况的基本尺度和依据。绩效审计评价标准各种各样，如对公共资金使用合规性的评价主要以法律、法规作为标准，对经济性的评价以公共部门及机构一般支出水平为标准，对效果性的评价主要以预先确定的目标为标准等。[7]而政府绩效评价是通过选用某种程序和方法，参照一个既定的标准，对已发生的工作项目或已使用及支付的公共资金进行评价。

实施公共财政支出绩效审计评价，首先要建立一套科学及完善的公共财政支出绩效审计评价指标体系，根据这些指标需要事先制定评价标准，及后根据各指标的实际水平进行比较评价，指标体系是从不同角度及不同层面来反映公共部门及机构所从事的管理活动内容，如资源投入情况、资源利用情况、资源节约情况、产出情况、政府职能履行情况、公众满意情况等。为了判断各指标实际水平的高低，审计人员需要参照一个基准进行判断，而这个参照基准就是绩效审计的评价标准。[8]

审计署现有《审计质量监控措施》及审计手册，《审计质量监控措施》规范审计前期工作及审计过程所应遵循的要求规定，如立项前所应遵循而缺一不可的五个原则：重要性原则、风险性原则、时效性原则、可行性原则及增值性原则；搜集审计证据时所应采用的方式，如书面证据、实物证据、电子资料、口头证据、勘验笔录等；审计工作底稿有否如实地记录资料；审计报告有否准确及客观地撰写其审计发现；完成审计工作的所有资料有否储存于审计档案内并妥为保存。审计手册包括《账目审计手册》及《衡工量值式审计手册》，它们是规范审计人员在开展相关审计工作时所应遵循的审计工作程序及流程，而数年前制定的《内部守则》则规范审计人员的内部工作程序及应遵的规定。[9]

(四) 建立绩效预算体制

澳门政府现阶段尚未实施绩效预算的模式运作，而所施行的"预算纲要法"则从1983年开始运作至今，澳门政府在对公共支出施行公共支出绩效审计工作时，可建议对现行的预算运作模式及内容进行改革，因绩效评估工作的开展，最终是为促进财政支出预算改革，并为提高政府部门的管理水平，财政预算管理法制若不加强，实在难以对政府绩效审计制定评价标准。

政府绩效评价模式是随着预算管理的加强而发展的，澳门现行的财政预算主要按投入进行编制，注意力集中在投入以及执行过程的合规性方面，而不是产出及支出后的绩效方面，在这种预算管理模式下，公共支出缺乏明细的公共资金产出指标和绩效预算的约束，公共部门及机构主要以预算执行情况为基础，列出公共部门及机构所完成的工作清单而已，至于是否全面履行职责，以及工作业绩如何实难以准确予以评价。可以说，财政管理上对绩效的关注不重视，财政预算只存在合规性合法性的监督，这样的执行模式会对财政资金的使用绩效有严重的影响，极易造成浪费公共资源的情况出现。政府应建立以结果为导向的公共财政绩效预算机制，在提高公共资金使用的经济效益和社会效益的同时，亦为澳门审计署全面实施公共财政绩效审计提供可操作的平台。

推行绩效预算可以提高财政资金的效益，而效益是绩效审计的最终目标，此外，绩效预算的施行能防止公共部门及机构千方百计地扩大预算，漠视降低行政成本的情况出现，亦能防范财政风险，促进政府机构改革，创新运作机制，抑制浪费，提升政府绩效及施政能力。同时，绩效预算也是一种公民监督下的预算方式，对于强调构建服务型的澳门政府，绩效预算可以强化政府为公众服务观念的同时，亦能够提高政府的管理水平及加强财政监督的作用。绩效预算的核心就是建立一套能够反映政府公共活动绩效的评估体系，在绩效预算的模式下，要压缩公共预算支出，就必须对政府的政策项目及方案进行绩效评估，故此，实施绩效预算是建立财政绩效评价体系的大前提，而绩效评估和绩效预算恰恰是构建政府绩效审计密不可分的两个元素。[10]

(五) 确立财政支出绩效审计的内容重点

传统审计是以会计资料为基本载体的经济资料，而绩效审计却是以业务资料为基本载体的管理活动。从世界各国开展绩效审计的主要内容来看，都是围绕着经济性、效率性和效果性即"3E"审计开展的。绩效审计的核心都是衡量资源是否被有效利用和是否达到了目标或结果。经济性、效率性和效果性都是整个绩效审计核心的价值判断标准，各国的绩效审计内容和范围也有许多共同的和相互重叠的部分。

以经济性、效率性及效果性的"3E"为评价内容的绩效审计是一个系统过程，它透过审计的程序及方法来评价审计物件就经济性、效率性及效果性的执行情况，借以对履行受托经济责任加以评价和监督。随着"3E"的长时间推行，审计理论研究进一步深化，审计领域逐步扩展到公平性（Equity）及环保性（Environment）等事项，公共支出绩效审计的内容亦从以前的"3E"加上新增的"2E"改称为"5E"审计，即增加了对社会效益和环境影响的审计。

澳门审计署开展绩效审计时所施行的的内容重点亦按照西方发达国家对绩效审计工作开展的操作模式，即以节省程度（经济性）、效率和效益方面进行审计。

随着社会经济的发展及公民意识的提高，市民大众对政府受托管理及分配公共资源的要求不只局限及满足于"3E"的审计内容，公众对政府分配公共资源时所持的公平性要求同样强烈。此外，经济的高速发展，某程度上是以破坏自然环境所换来的，因此，开展环保性审计是刻不容缓的一个重要绩效审计内容。

澳门审计署可以尝试加入公平性审计及环保性审计，将原来的"3E"绩效审计增至"5E"审计，就公平性审计方面，可加入审查政府投入资源的应用是否体现了公平原则，确认接受公共服务的团体或个人是否受到公平的待遇，需要特别照顾的弱势社群是否能够公平享受到更多的服务。而环保性审计方面则审查政府机关或公共投资项目的环境管理活动，包括污染防治审计和生态恢复与建设审计，以及资源的可持续开发与利用审计等，以确认投入资源的应用是否符合可持续发展的战略，减少对生态环境的影响程度，以及监管环境状态等。

（六）采用财政支出绩效审计的恰当类型和方法

因应不同的绩效审计对象及内容，采用与之配合的绩效审计类型，能协助被审计单位适时纠正错误，防止公共资源被浪费的情况出现。澳门审计署开展绩效审计多年来所采用的类型多是"事后绩效审计"类型。即审计署对被审计单位完成的经济活动，开展与公共支出有关的绩效审计工作，评判被审计单位的公共资源使用及管理是否合法、合理并从中发现问题，就涉及设备的购置及公共竞投的程序是否符法、是否按照既定标准等而进行分析及评价并找出问题的根源，以及查找被审计单位哪些环节出现浪费资源或闲置资源的情况。

公共投资或工程项目的监督方面若采用跟踪审计类型，可及时发现问题并予以纠正，跟踪审计是以经济业务的实施情况与事前的预测、预算、计划和标准等进行分析比较，从中找出差距和存在的问题，及时采取有效措施加以纠正。跟踪审计能及时堵截漏洞及适时遏止公共资源被滥用的情况出现,事实上,审计署亦于2011年完成了针对轻轨一期建设的首项跟踪审计报告,该报告披露政府缺乏一个完整投资预算规划,采购方面采用直接批给一间供应商而放弃议价制度等问题出现。跟踪审计在专项资金审计中能预早发现问题,从而加强管理,同时使用效益的分析,以及注重产生问题的原因并提出建议。

澳门审计署可深入研究绩效审计类型及方法,从而带动整个政府部门及机构对绩效审计的重视及合法合规地使用公帑的观念。此外,对公共部门及机构财政资金使用效益的具体目标难以准确预料,并且缺乏现成的标准参照时,审计人员可利用现代管理理念和科学方法进行分析和判断,评价公共资金使用的绩效。[11]

结　语

自20世纪70至80年代开展的绩效审计,发展至今已成为世界政府审计趋势及主流,从绩效审计的工作中充分证明,政府绩效审计在加强政府权力的制约、提高政府办事效率及效果、增加政府透明度等方面发挥了重要的作用。

政府绩效审计从效益和效果两个方面的审查发现问题,从而提供政策优劣信息,找出根源,提出改进建议,帮助管理者改进决策,提高财政支出效益,避免损失及浪费。

公共财政支出绩效审计是政府绩效审计的一个重要组成部分,我们必须承认经济活动中或多或少存在违规的情况,只要将世界各国绩效审计成功经验按照澳门实际情况套用,必定创出一条适合澳门情况的公共支出绩效审计之路,同时,借鉴国外经验,逐步完成从财务合法合规性审计向全面的绩效审计迈进。

[1] 国外绩效审计理论与实务课题组:《国外绩效审计理论与实务》,中国时代经济出版社2010年版。

[2] 澳门审计署,网址:http://www.ca.gov.mo/cn/about/knowus.php。

[3] 澳门财政局,网址:http://www.dsf.gov.mo/about/about_duty.aspx。

[4] 李晔:《美国政府审计的启示与借鉴》,中华人民共和国审计署,网址:http://www.audit.gov.cn/n1057/n1072/n1747922/1939582.html,2012年1月19日。

[5] 闵晓蕾:《关于政府绩效审计理论的文献综述》,《科技与经济》2006年第23期。

[6] 陈志刚:《香港政府绩效审计研究与借鉴》,深圳市审计局,2005年8月21日。

[7] 公共支出绩效审计研究课题组:《公共支出绩效审计研究》,中国时代经济出版社2007年版,第106页。

［8］祁敦芳、叶鹏飞、叶忠明等：《政府绩效审计》，中国时代经济出版社2009年版，第43页。

［9］《审计质量监控措施》，澳门审计署。

［10］周亚荣：《政府治理视角下的中国政府绩效审计研究》，武汉大学出版社2010年版，第115页。

［11］公共支出绩效审计研究课题组：《公共支出绩效审计研究》，中国时代经济出版社2007年版，第107页。

小组治国：从政治控制到国家治理[*]

倪 星 原 超[**]

一、引论

"中国的政治体制中充满了尚未成为制度的组织"[1]。"领导小组"作为一种中国传统的理政策略和治理工具，即中国政治过程和治理场域中典型的"亚正式制度"之一。小组治大国，大事立小组。通过成立跨部门领导小组来组织实施重大战略任务，是我们党和政府在长期实践中形成的一种有效的工作方法，是中国共产党在对国家治理经验不断总结和提升过程中形成的。

其实，任何一个新阶段的起点都是基于以前阶段的经验、政治行为和观点。[2]不同历史阶段的领导小组虽然其在性质、结构、功能和运行逻辑方面均有所不同，但这并不意味着这些历史片断是孤立的、无意义的。相反，只有从历史的关联中才可以对这些片断有深刻意义的理解。遗憾的是，海内外学者对于"领导小组"的研究似乎有意地回避了对这种历史关联的探讨，而更多的是试图直接地、孤立地以西方的政策过程框架和理论视角去诠释和解释这种特殊机制。①而对于中国的政治行动者来说，这

---

[*] 本文为国家社会科学基金重大项目（13&ZD011）；中山大学"985工程"三期建设项目。

[**] 倪星，中山大学政治与公共事务管理学院教授；原超，中山大学政治与公共事务管理学院博士研究生。

① 海内外学者关于领导小组的研究详见：Barnett, A. Doak, *The Making of Foreign Policy in China: Structure and Process*, Boulder: Westview Press, 1985; Hamrin, Carol Lee and Zhao Suisheng (ed.), *Decision-Making in Deng's China*, Armonk, New York: M. E. Sharpe, 1995; Lieberthal, Kenneth and Lampton David (eds.) *Bureaucracy, Politics and Decision Making in Post-Mao China*, Berkeley and Los Angeles: University of California Press, 1992; Lieberthal, Kenneth and Oksenberg Michel, *Policy making in China: Leaders, Structures, and Processes*, Princeton, New Jersey: Princeton University Press, 1988; Alice Miller, "The CCP Central Committee's Leading Small Groups", *China Leadership Monitor*, No. 26, 2008; 邵宗海：《具有中国特色的中共决策机制——中共中央工作领导小组》，韦伯文化出版社2007年版；吴晓林：《小组政治研究：内涵、功能与研究展望》，《求实》2009年第3期；陈玲：《官僚体系与协商网络：中国政策过程的理论构建与案例研究》，《公共管理评论》2006年第2期；赖静萍：《当代中国党政关系的演进与现代国家的成长——以领导小组的历史变迁为观察点》，《江苏社会科学》2009年第2期；程同顺：《当代中国组政治分析》，《云南行政学院学报》2001年第6期。

种关联属于个人经验，也许无须去分析，但局外的观察者必须经常地问自己：这种历史关联如何构造了政治行动并赋予其意义？[3]因此，对于"领导小组"的研究，其内在意义就在于寻求对中国政治的整体理解，特别是以"领导小组"的历史沿革为研究起点，对"领导小组"的形成、运行和沿革的历史脉络和演变逻辑进行梳理，总结不同时期"领导小组"在中国特色政治过程和国家治理领域中的组织定位，能够帮助我们厘清其中的历史关联，更好地把握和理解中国政治和绘制中国国家治理图景，推进国家治理体系和治理能力现代化进程。

二、领导小组的历史沿革

（一）革命时期的探索

1. 长征时期

1935年3月，长征途中的红军二渡赤水后，中央政治局在遵义县鸭溪镇召开扩大会议讨论下一步的作战计划时产生了分歧。在会议上，毛泽东放弃攻打打鼓新场的提议无法得到会议多数成员的赞同，其前敌总指挥的职务也被撤销。会后，毛泽东半夜里提马灯一一说服周恩来和朱德，最终放弃攻打计划，使中央红军幸免于覆灭。为了使军事指挥能够机动灵活，避免在会议中关于军事路线和行动方针出现争执不休的局面，政治局会议决定成立由毛泽东、周恩来、王稼祥组成的新"三人团"①，即后世所称的"三人军事领导小组"②。"三人军事领导小组"的成立改变了中共在江西瑞金时期模仿苏联建立起的党、军队、政府三套相对独立的中共领导体制，将军队与党融为一体。

"三人军事领导小组"作为党中央委托的负责军事指挥的临时性机构，是在长征途中为了便于集中军事指挥权力而设立的。在红一和红四方面军会师后，"三人军事领导小组"的职能被中央政治局和红军司令部所取代。[4] "三人军事领导小组"虽然作为一个具有特殊意义的军事指挥范畴内的临时性机构，与之后的领导小组的运作方式有很大不同，其象征意义远远大于实际成效，但是它的成立和运作奠定了中共之后在处理党政事务上"遇大事，立小组"的思路。

---

① 新"三人团"的表述是为了和老"三人团"相区别，遵义会议之前，由博古、李德和周恩来组成的老"三人团"是当时党、政、军的领导核心和最高权力机构。老"三人团"在遵义会议之后被撤销。

② "三人团"是当时成立之初的名称，关于"三人军事领导小组"的提法，最早是周恩来于1972年6月10日在《批林整风汇报会议上的讲话》中提出的，后世的研究文章均沿用"三人军事领导小组"的说法。

2. 延安整风时期

"小组思路"首次得到充分彰显是在延安整风运动时期。1941年9月至10月毛泽东在延安政治局扩大会议会议上宣布要"实行两条路线的斗争,反对主观主义和宗派主义",全面清算并重新解释1931年至1935年中共的历史。会议决定成立"清算过去历史委员会",主要任务是引导党的高级领导人将目光转到回顾过去历史问题,重新建立改写党史的框架。[5] "清算过去历史委员会"以《关于四中全会以来中央领导路线问题结论草案》的完成而宣告起使命结束。同时成立的还有以下几个临时机构:以康生为主任的"中央党与非党干部审查委员会",以毛泽东为组长的"中央高级学习组"和以陈云为首的"复查过去被错误打击干部委员会",前两个机构成为了毛泽东领导整风运动最重要的工具。中央政治局和书记处的许多功能被中央高级学习组所取代。

1942年6月,中央总学习委员会(中央总学委)宣告成立,由毛泽东担任主任。中央总委会的设立标志着中央高级学习组成立后开始的权力转移过程得到了进一步深化。在延安整风运动期间,中央总学委并非是一个固定的实体机构,而是一个实际上凌驾于政治局和书记处之上的中共最高决策和权力的临时机构。

随着延安整风运动的顺利完成,中央总学委已完成其使命,在1944年5月中共六届七中全会中宣布撤销中央总学委,由毛泽东、刘少奇、周恩来、朱德、任弼时五人组成主席团,代行政治局和书记处的职权,成为了延安整风运动后新的中共最高领导核心。

(二)新中国成立及社会主义建设时期的经验得失

1. 新中国成立初期(1953—1958年)

建国初期,为了保证中共对社会主义建设进程全面而绝对的掌控,中共中央引进借鉴苏联的"干部分级分类管理制度"。1953年11月,中共中央做出《中共中央关于加强干部管理工作的决定》,决定逐步建立在中央及各级党委统一领导下,在中央及各级党委组织部统一管理下的分部分级管理干部的制度。按照工作需要,把目前全体干部划分为九类,在中央及各级党委组织部的统一管理下,由中央及各级党委的各部分分别进行管理。[6] 例如在中央设置了中央农村工作部①、中央工业交通工作部②、

---

① 1952年11月,中共中央农村工作部成立,其任务是贯彻执行农村工作的政策方针,组织与指导农民互助合作运动;1962年11月被撤销,业务合并入国务院农林办公室。

② 1956年1月,工业交通工作部成立,后拆分为工业工作部和交通工作部,任务主要是管理工业和交通系统干部,检查各部门对党的决议、政策的执行情况;1960年被撤销。

中央财政工作部①等。但是,从实际运作状况来看,工作部的职能不限于干部管理,也兼及于行政领导。

2. "大跃进运动"时期(1958—1966年)

1958年,中共希望能够更为有力地透过党组织动员大众进行社会主义建设,因此在6月,中共八届四中全会结束后,中共中央发出《关于成立财经、政法、外事、科学、文教各小组的通知》,决定成立财经、政法、外事、科学及文教等小组,将政府工作划分为五大块,各由专人负责分口领导。《通知》指出:"这些小组是党中央的,直隶中央政治局,向它们直接作报告。大政方针在政治局,具体部署在书记处。只有一个'政治设计院',没有两个'政治设计院'。大政方针和具体部署,都是一元化,党政不分。具体执行和细节决策属政府机构及其党组。对大政方针和具体部署,政府机构及其党组有建议之权,但决定权在党中央。政府机构及其党组和党中央一同有检查之权。"[6]在这一时期,除了上述成立的小组外,又相继成立了中央精简干部和安排劳动力五人小组、国家机关编制小组、中央学制问题研究小组等。这些小组大部分随着其任务的结束而被撤销。

3. "文化大革命"时期(1966—1976年)

1960年以后,在中国全面进行社会主义建设过程中,对怎样建设社会主义、社会主义社会的主要矛盾等一系列问题上,中央一线领导与毛泽东产生了很大分歧。在毛泽东看来,当前自己在与中央一线领导意见分歧中的不利局面很难通过正式的沟通协调等正常程序得以解决,必须"同时批判混进党内、政府、军队里和文化领域的各界里的资产阶级代表人物,清洗这些人,有些则要调动他们的职务"[7],采取非常规程序,利用自己在党内的地位和高度权威,设立中央文革小组,从而取代中央书记处。

1966年5月,中央召开政治局扩大会议,通过了《中国共产党中央委员会通知》,宣布设立文化革命小组,隶属于政治局常委之下。[8]领导小组成立之初,是作为政治局常委的参谋秘书班子角色,没有办公机构,也没有发挥实质意义上对一线工作的指导功能。为了加强中央文革小组的领导力,在八届十一中全会上通过了《关于无产阶级文化大革命的决定》,提出了文化大革命运动的目的、重点、依靠力量、方法,还规定各级文革小组是"无产阶级文化革命的权力机构","不应当是临时性组织,而应当是长期的常设的群众组织"。[8]同时,全会还改组了中央领导机构,将文革小组的部分成员进入政治局常委,在组织上保证并加强了文革小组的权力。与中央文革小组地位变化相联系,其组织机构也得到充实,办公室改成办事组,并相继成立了文艺

---

① 1956年1月,中共中央财政贸易工作部成立,其任务是管理财政贸易系统干部,检查财政贸易部门对当的决议政策的执行情况;1960年被撤销。

组、理论组、宣传组、档案组等职能机构。[9]中共九大后，随着毛泽东认为文化大革命取得全面胜利，为重建党组织，将国家各项工作纳入正轨，中央文革小组被撤销，从而结束了它的政治使命。

（三）改革开放以来的新发展

随着改革开放的启动，中共开始反思"文革"中严重混乱的党政关系，为了推动政治体制改革的现代化建设，开始逐步以"党政分开"作为指导思想对行政机构进行改革，其中对"领导小组"的改革也包含在内。党政机关开始逐渐恢复正常运行，中共各领导小组也相继恢复设置。如中央财经领导小组、中央对台工作领导小组以及中央政法小组等。恢复的领导小组大多以"议事机构"为主，主要负责政策指导、政策调整等，不处理具体事务，不设专门机构和职员，而由行政事务机构处理。[10]原来的交通工作部、工业工作部等并没有得以恢复，而是转变为中央书记处下属的相关政策研究室，如中央科学研究协调委员会，中央党史领导小组等。

同时，随着改革开放的深化，出现了大量以前没有遇到的新的任务和情况，因此，大量以"协调工作"为主要职能的新的领导小组出现，这些领导小组大部分是任务导向，周期性短，任务结束则撤销。如中央和国家机关机构改革工作小组、中央引进国外智力以利"四化"工作领导小组、中央落实政策小组等。

"领导小组"在这一时期的变化与中共在新时期大规模的机构改革密不可分，其性质、结构、运作制度和章程也逐步呈现出规范化和制度化的趋势。"领导小组"第一次进入了中国特色的政治话语体系之中。1986年国务院出台《国务院关于清理非常设机构的通知》，这是第一个关于"领导小组"的专门性文件。《通知》指出，"各级国家机关在常设机构之外设置的不少委员会、领导小组、办公室等统一更名为'非常设机构'"[11]。随着机构改革由改革初期"党政分离"的思路向市场经济背景下"理顺关系"的逻辑转变，对"领导小组"也出现了整合、废除和合并的不同思路。1993年4月，国务院出台《关于国务院议事协调机构和临时机构设置的通知》（国发〔1993〕27号）中，将国务院的"非常设机构"更名为"议事协调机构和临时机构"。政治话语体系中对"领导小组"的功能和性质进行了重新定位。进入新世纪以后，随着社会主义现代化建设的推进，"领导小组"等议事协调机构进一步得到了广泛关注和重视。2008年的国务院机构改革中，在十六届四中全会通过的《中共中央关于加强党的执政能力建设的决定》中第一次做出了"规范各类领导小组和协调机构，一般不设实体性办事机构"的表述。随后，国务院出台《关于议事协调机构设置的通知》（国发〔2008〕13号），指出了议事协调机构的改革发展方向："严格控制议事协调机构的设置，凡工作可以交由现有机构承担或者由现有机构进行协调可以解决的，不另设议事协调机构。一般不单设实体性办事机构，不单独核定人员编制和领导职数"[12]。

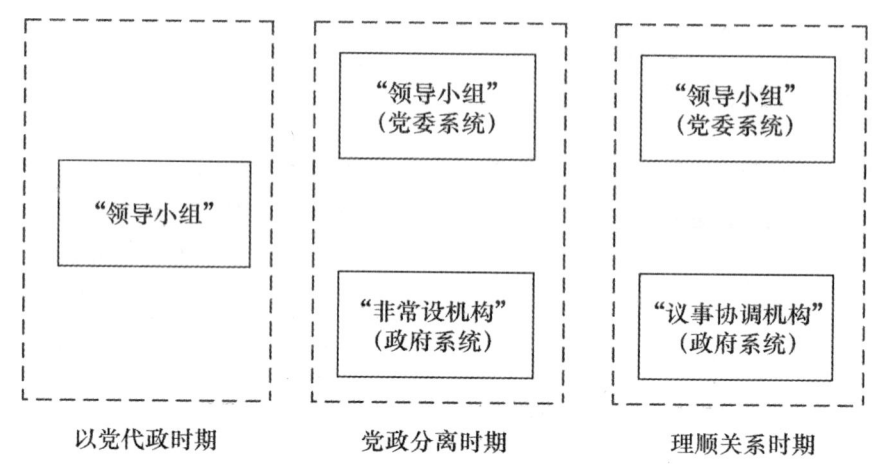

图 1　不同时期"领导小组"的称谓变化图

三、领导小组在历史沿革中的组织定位

自中国共产党在革命战争时期的积极探索起，历经新中国成立后的社会主义建设、"文革"十年动乱和改革开放新时期的建设等不同历史阶段的洗礼后，"领导小组"被大规模运用于中国这一历史悠久、超大规模的政治共同体的党政领导、现代化建设和深化改革进程中。在这一过程中，"领导小组"已经逐渐发展成为有中国特色的党政协调机制和国家治理动员机制，由原来单一的经验层面的组织形态逐渐发展为多元的规范运作的组织形态。

（一）性质：从"以党代政"协调机制到"党政分离"协调机制

各个历史时期的领导小组事实上都体现为中共党政关系的一部分，是党对政府运作控制的一个重要的手段和机制。在政策规划及制定上，党抓所谓的整体方向及原则，而由政府部门加以执行其细节部分，党还是主控及领导着政府部门。在运作上，整合党与政府部门之间的共识，并在党中央的主导下对政府各部门的执行政策进行协调。[13]

虽然领导小组是中国特色的由党主导下的党政协调机制，但是从"领导小组"的历史分期来看，这种党政协调机制总体上呈现出由"以党代政"的协调机制向"党政分离"的协调机制转变。

"以党代政"协调机制的领导小组在革命战争年代和建国初期最为明显，在文化大革命十年动乱中,"以党代政"的领导小组的地位达到顶峰,功能发挥到极致。在革命战争年代,特别是延安整风时期的"中央高级学习组""中央总学委"这两个"领导小组"的成立,彻底凌驾于并且取代了中央政治局和中央书记处。毛泽东依靠坚强的组织机构"中央总学委",通过党的意识形态的学习和教化,高效、有力地对文艺领域、宣传领域和干部教育系统领域的组织领导机构进行了重组和改造,使得党的意志超越并掌控了政府的运作,从而无论在机构运作上还是在政府的干部系统中均体现出"以党代政"的形态。中共在建立政权后的十年间,首先是在1953年将政府的各部门整合为若干直接对中央负责的"口",紧接着在1956年进一步地由中央各小组直接领导国务院的各"口","领导小组"的成功地将其政治体制的结构与功能转而成为一种高度集权的模式:把宪法规定向国家权力机关负责的政府变成了党中央的执行机关,因而党中央取代了国家权力机关,把本来属于政府的"具体部署"权收归中央,在政府部门,党组决定一切重大事务和问题。[13]

在"文化大革命"十年动乱期间,"中央文革小组"由松散的参谋性的临时机构最终发展为党的法定最高决策机构之上,使得原有的制度规定和集体决策框架失灵。文革时期的"中央文革小组",相比于延安整风时期的"中央总学委",正是表现为"以党代政"的临时机构取代正式机构做法的重演。

改革开放后,中共中央充分反思新中国成立以来尤其是文革十年来"以党代政"给国家、党和人民带来的巨大灾难,以及对政府决策的法治化和民主化的破坏,同时,随着改革的进一步深入,大量新的复杂的事务涌现,中共主张在"党政分开"的框架内发展新的党政关系。在中共中央范畴下的领导小组大多数以"政策参谋"的角色出现,对政府政策和其他公共事务具有政策咨询和间接指导意义;而在中央和地方政府范畴下的领导小组,党在其中的色彩已经逐步减弱,而是逐步转变为以"沟通协调"为主要职能的议事协调机构或临时机构。

(二) 功能:从"政治控制"工具到"国家治理"工具

作为中国特色的由党主导的党政协调机制,领导小组始终都是为了围绕不同时期的中国共产党面对的生存、发展和转型的历史任务需要而展开的。因此,领导小组的功能的变化自然取决于不同时期中共面临的历史环境。从某种程度上来说,领导小组功能的变化反映了不同历史时期中共为了发展和转型而进行积极的组织调适。

在革命战争年代,中共作为一个新成立的革命党,面临的是组织如何生存的重要问题。"三人军事领导小组"的成立就是为了能够保证以毛泽东为首的中共领导人根据面临的实际情况灵活、机动地指挥党的军队,将党对军队的绝对领导牢牢地掌握在手中。"中央总学委"的成立和撤销均由毛泽东的个人意志决定,借助这样一个领导小组，能够在延安整风期间对各领域的组织领导机构进行重组和改造，就是为了能够维护党的绝对领导地位以及作为一个政治家拥有对党组织的绝对话语权。

建国初期，中共面临的是如何能够尽快地完成民主主义革命进行社会主义建设。"中共中央工作部""中共中央领导小组"的成立初衷也是为了保证中共对社会主义建设进程全面而绝对的掌控。①"文革"时期，"中央文革小组"作为发动"文化大革命"而成立的特殊的组织机构，同时也是毛泽东为发动文化大革命非程序性控制中央权力的需要。[9]

改革开放后，领导小组的功能发生了较大的变化。随着"党政分离"的改革逻辑的逐步演进，中共面临的是如何能够高效地整合和利用资源进行国家治理。领导小组也出现了两种不同的发展路径，其中，中共中央领导小组不断精简并最终基本稳定下来，仍然代表政党对一些诸如保密、政法、扶贫等重要工作起着宏观掌控和间接指导的作用，这些分管不同事务的"领导小组"，在中共党组织结构中，拥有协调政策、提出新构想、监督政策执行以及人事安排的建议权等职能。[15]而政府序列的领导小组则呈现出大增大减的态势，一方面不断地根据部门主义的现状和复杂的现实情况，在一段时间内，大量领导小组以具有议事协调为名被设计和创造出来，另一方面，又受制于臃肿的机构现状和行政改革的深入开展，大量的领导小组又被撤销。领导小组的功能不仅仅是呈现出"以党领政"的形态，更多地是以"参谋议事""沟通协调""推进改革"的形态在优化国家治理体系、提升国家治理能力方面发挥其作用。

（三）结构：从"一元经验"组织形态到"多元规范"组织形态

从总体上看，领导小组的结构呈现出从一元化经验的组织形态向多元化规范的组织形态的转变。但是从不同的历史阶段来看，在改革开放之前，无论是革命时期还是建国初期，领导小组均表现为从临时机构向实体机构的发展；在改革开放之后，领导小组表现为从实体机构逐渐向多元化的任务导向性的组织形态转变。

改革开放前，在延安整风时期，"中央高级学习组"和"中央总学委"成立时的定位是为整风运动进行准备工作的加强领导干部学习的临时性组织，后来发展为取代政治局的最高决策机构，有专门的机构、办公室和人员配置，成为了实质意义上的实体机构。"文革"时期，"中央文革小组"以及其他下属小组成立之初是作为秘书参谋的临时机构，组织结构较为松散，最后发展为取代政治局和书记处的拥有最高决策

---

① 尤其是薄一波在《若干重大决策与事件的回顾》中提到，1953年春，薄一波在财政部任上出台新税制因为没有事先向中央报告受到毛泽东严厉批评，毛泽东认为政务院犯了分散主义错误，因此强调要加强中央对政府工作机构的领导。这一事件也成为了"中共中央工作部"成立的导火索。

权和决定地方干部的任免权的实体性机构。而建国初期的"工作组"和"中央领导小组"自成立起就是拥有独立人员编制、办公机构的实体组织。

改革开放后，领导小组并没有呈现出单一的发展模式，而是小部分保留其实体机构的属性，大部分转变为临时机构，同时，在中国政治话语中由"非常设机构"向"议事协调机构"转变。另外，关于领导小组的结构和运行规则方面也较前期更加的制度化和规范化。从中央到地方均出台了关于成立领导小组的结构、组成人员、运行机制和办公室运行规则等，对领导小组的规范运行奠定了制度化基础。

四、"小组治理"与国家治理现代化

大国治理是中国国家治理的现实基础，集中体现了中国国家治理过程中有限的社会资源总量与超大规模社会对国家治理资源大规模需求之间的矛盾。[16]有学者将中共对这样一个历史遗产丰富、超大规模的国家的治理方法和思路称为"适应性治理"。[17]"适应性治理"作为一种有弹性的治理，治理主体能够在面对新挑战和外部的不确定性时适时做出变化和组织调适的治理过程。在"适应性治理"过程之中，既包括中共在推动治理结构和治理过程方面的规范化和制度化努力，同时也包括在"务实主义治理模式的历史传统"中寻找经验，建构具有高度适应能力的存在于正式制度之外的治理机制和治理结构。

"小组治理"作为存在于正式制度外的"亚正式"的治理机制，以其"精巧的治理结构设计""高效的资源整合能力"和"广泛的共识决策框架"灵活机动地消解了日常治理结构的负荷和治理能力的匮乏，因而成为了深植于中国国家治理中的一个特殊机制。

首先，作为有中国特色的党政协调机制，领导小组中的权力关系与中共的组织体制、中国的国家治理结构形式及条块分割的行政管理体制之间有着内在的契合性。改革开放以来，中国的国家治理进入了转型期，"在中央意识形态削弱的情况下，除了广泛的协商，没有什么其他方式能让这种体制有效运转"[1]，中国的政策制定受到"碎片化的威权主义"影响，决策过程充满了讨价还价，效率低下。"小组治理"的运作机制打破了常规治理遇到的困境，通过对国家治理过程中，尤其是在治理政策的制定过程的重构，将中共民主集中决策机制和政府的政策制定过程有机结合在一起，增强了决策的民主性和有效性。

作为拓宽多元治理主体参谋议事的吸纳机制，领导小组作为一个意见搜集和意见整合的平台，以政策议题为导向，大量相关领域的专家、学者、群众、人大和政协的官员的意见和建议得以在领导小组内得以吸纳和整合，大大拓宽了中共政策制定和决策的民主化、科学化。[18][19][20]与此同时，正如古德诺所说，要使得政府协调运转，就必须找到某种使国家意志的表达和执行相一致的办法。这种办法在政府体制内部不能找到，所以必须从法外的一些制度中寻找。事实上，可以在政党中找到它。[18]在中国，各个职能部门的政策执行都是在党的领导下进行，不可能超然于党的政策之外，它们与党委的关系不是平行的，而是一种上下级关系，因此借助以党委为核心的"领导小组"治理形式，通过"高位推动"的模式，有益于促进党政各部门之间进行非正式的意见交换，最终形成集体政策。[21]

"小组治理"中，这种将中共集体领导机制内嵌于政府政策制定过程的机制，使得政府的政策制定和决策过程实际上转变为党的民主集中制决策，通过这样一种富有弹性的决策机制，既充分调动了部门决策和部门协商的积极性，又保证了在融合各方意见的基础上适时拍板定案、形成决策。

其次，高效的资源整合和动员机制，也是"具有中国特色党主导下的公共政策执行机制"[21]，一方面，领导小组有着高效率的组织结构和管理方式——矩阵式组织，这样的结构反应迅速，责任明确，管理成本低，能够有效地整合复杂与相互依赖的活动[22]，同时加强了信息的横向流动促进了部门之间的沟通和互信，减少了信息不对称带来的政策执行困难；另一方面，领导小组将具有实权的部门负责人纳入其中，同时通过其职务层级代表的权力以及"附加权力"对小组内的普通成员予以统驭，从而能够充分运用政治资源协调各成员单位的行动，保证协调机制的有效运作。[23]"小组治理"还包括一系列配套机制：建立自下而上逐级高频次的信息反馈和信息报送机制，通过设立专门的领导小组办公室，使得关于专项任务的完成情况及协调沟通通过高频次的信息报送机制及时从各个部门传递至办公室，由办公室收发并直接回馈，减少了信息流经的层级，从而降低信息不对称带来的不利影响；建立了自上而下的督查和督导机制，领导小组同时也是责任小组，专人专项的督导督查有利于及时有效地督促各成员部门形成责任意识和问责机制；建立了自上而下的会议和文件传递机制，在这一过程中，上级的权力话语随着信息自上而下的逐级传递得到了确认和彰显，这种动员型的治理过程也被逐步整合到这种以会议和文件为驱动形式的制度化和仪式化体系之中。[24]

中国已经进入了国家改革与治理转型的深水区，党的十八届三中全会提出将"推进国家治理体系和治理能力现代化"作为全面深化改革的总目标。在国家转型期不断衍生出各种高度复杂、异常和相互依赖的社会问题，使得地方政府在政策执行过程中遇到大量的技术性困难。[24]这些技术性困难是在常规治理制度和规则框架内难以克服的，同时，现有的治理制度设计和规则在推动国家治理现代化尤其是治理主体多元化、治理手段多样化和治理结果的有效性方面收效甚微。而"小组治理"在"务实主义治理模式的历史传统"中积极汲取经验,作为中国特色的党政协调机制、多元治理主体参谋议事的吸纳机制和高效的资源整合动员机制,一方面充分调动了部门决策和部门协商的积极性,有效地保证了治理政策制定的民主化和科学化,另一方面,通过"高位推动"实现对资源的积极整合和有效利用,使得政令能够迅速得到地方贯彻和落实,推动了治理手段的多样性,消解了常规治理制度和治理结构的负担和紧张。

"小组治理"作为一种依靠小组领导、权威训诫的方式开展的治理行为,同时也作为一种"亚正式"的治理机制,既来源于总体性社会的内卷动力,同时又适应分化多元社会的外卷压力,以权力先导、体制发动及法制化人治的方式沿袭和因循着总体性支配权力的国家治理路径,同时又将不断运用作为技术性智力的政策工具手段[25],能够迅速有效地对常规治理制度和规则进行优化,充实、巩固和完善中国现有的基本治理体系。

---

[1] 李侃如:《治理中国:从革命到改革》,胡国成等译,中国社会科学出版社2010年版,第192—209页。

[2] 倪星、原超:《从二元到多元:海外中国政治精英研究述评》,《中山大学学报》(社会科学版),2011年第6期,第127—128页。

[3] 詹姆斯·R. 汤森:《中国政治》,董方译,江苏人民出版社2007年版,第2—3页。

[4] 曾景忠:《遵义会议后中央三人军事领导机构研究》,《中共党史研究》1989年第4期。

[5] 逄先知主编:《毛泽东年谱》(中卷),中央文献出版社2013年版,第333页。

[6] 中共中央组织部等编:《中国共产党组织史资料:1921—1997》(第9卷),中共党史出版社2000年版,第187—190页。

[7]《中共中央关于中国共产党中央委员会的通知》,中发〔1966〕267号文。

[8] 国防大学党史党建政工教研室编:《"文化大革命"研究资料》(上册),中央文献出版社1989年版,第1—2页。

[9] 沈传宝:《中央文革小组的历史沿革及立废原因探析》,《中共党史研究》,2007年第1期,第51页。

[10] 唐亮:《现代中国的党政关系》(日文),庆应义塾出版会株式会社1997年版,第48—50页。

[11]《国务院关于清理非常设机构的通知》,国发〔1986〕100号文。

[12]《国务院关于议事协调机构设置的通知》,国发〔2008〕13号文。

[13] 邵宗海:《中共决策机制之研究》,见《中共中央领导小组的党政协调运作》,台湾"行政院国家科学委员会"专题研究计划成果报告,2005年。

[14] 庞松、韩刚:《党和国家领导体制的历史考察与改革展望》,《中国社会科学》1987年第6期,第22页。

[15] 许志嘉:《中共外交决策模式研究》,台北:水牛出版社2001年版,第138页。

[16] 王沪宁:《社会资源总量与社会调控:中国意义》,《复旦学报》1990年第4期。

[17] Sebastian Helimann, Elizabeth J. Perry (eds.), *Mao's Invisible Hands: The Political Foundations of Adaptive Governance in China*, Cambridge, Mass: Harvard University Press, 2011.

[18] Jean-Pierre Cabestan, "Is China Moving towards 'Enlightened' but Plutocratic Authoriarianism?", *China Perspectives*, 55, 2004.

[19] Jean-Pierre Cabestan, "Consultative Leninism: China's New Political Framework", *Journal of Contemporary China*, 18, 2009, p. 62.

[20] Bo Kong, "China's Energy Decision – Making: Becoming More Like the United States?", *Journal of Contemporary China*, 18, 2009, p. 62.

[21] F. J. 古德诺:《政治与行政》,王元、杨百朋译,华夏出版社1987年版。

[22] 贺东航、孔繁斌:《公共政策执行的中国经验》,《中国社会科学》2011年第5期。

[23] 童宁:《地方政府非常设机构成因探析》,《中国行政管理》2007年第3期。

[24] 倪星、原超:《地方政府的运动式治理是如何走向"常规化"的》,《公共行政评论》2014年第2期。

[25] 杨志军:《中央与地方、国家与社会:推进国家治理现代化的双重维度》,《甘肃行政学院学报》2013年第6期。

环境管理与政策——澳门废弃物管制的政策研究

黄少鸿[*]

一、引言

环境问题与每个人的生活息息相关，遍及全球每一角落的气候变化，地区性的空气污染，以至城市的废弃物、空气质素、噪声污染、光污染等问题，都需要国家、地区以至个人，放弃一些过往被认为是权利的既得利益，一点一滴去换取环境延缓恶化，换取可持续发展。因此，有必要透过公共管理，以调整社会成员对保护环境的权利和义务。

在城市的环境管理工作中，世界各地在近几十年均致力对城市废弃物做出管制，作为整体环境政策的重要组成部分，以及可持续发展的其中一项重要目标。澳门在处理废弃物方面的工作，逐渐由以往着重宣传教育，过渡到教育与管制并重的政策方向。在2014年特区的施政方针首次提出面向全体市民的环境管理强制性措施的政策方向[①]，引入了污染者付费、环境成本内部化以及使用经济手段等的管理概念。然而，由邻近地区推行环境政策的经验可以看出，政府在实行环境管理工作时，需要面对重大的挑战，但亦蕴藏不少的机遇。与邻近地区比较，本澳环境管理工作步伐较缓慢，有必要总结经验以提升工作效益。

---

[*] 黄少鸿，澳门群力智库中心政策研究部委员。
① 2014年财政年度施政方针关于运输工务范畴部分，指出将"继续强化自愿性减塑措施，为过渡至下一阶段包括胶袋征费等强制性措施进行前期工作铺排"。《2014年财政年度施政方针》，第224版，网址：http://images.io.gov.mo/cn/lag/lag2014_cn.pdf。

二、澳门城市废弃物管理及发展现况

(一) 概况

澳门自回归及2003年赌权开放后,进入较高速的经济增长期,与此同时所产生的城市废弃物数量也随之上升,问题日益引起关注。2013年所产生固体废弃物的总量约为31.8万公吨,建筑废料3925千立方米,但回收的资源废料只有1425公吨。(见表1)

表1 近年本澳产生各类废弃物及回收情况

年份	2011	2012	2013
期中人口数 (较去年同期之增长量)	558100 (2.48%)	568700 (1.90%)	591900 (4.08%)
固体废料[①](公吨) (较去年同期之增长量)	265663 (3.50%)	282688 (6.41%)	317943 (12.47%)
建筑废料(千立方米) (较去年同期之增长量)	1618 (-17.20%)	2420 (49.57%)	3925 (62.21%)
废料焚化[②](公吨) (较去年同期之增长量)	334698 (2.41%)[③]	370682 (10.75%)	401542 (8.33%)
废料堆填[④](公吨) (较去年同期之增长量)	73171 (N/A)[⑤]	81116 (10.86%)	89547 (10.39%)
回收资源废料(公吨) (较去年同期之增长量)	622 (81.34%)	1017 (63.50%)	1425 (40.12%)

注:①包括家居垃圾、工商业垃圾、从海中捞取的垃圾、特殊和危险品,以及其他需要堆填的垃圾。
②包括固体垃圾、特殊和危险品、医疗垃圾和污泥。
③统计暨普查局2010年统计数字不包括焚化的污泥数字,故只以相同基准部分进行比较。
④包括焚化后残余物以及其他需要堆填的垃圾,另外建筑废料直接用作堆填。
⑤统计暨普查局没有公布2010年之相关统计数字。
资料来源:澳门统计暨普查局,2014。

表2 过去十年废弃物的累积增幅

年份	2004	2013	累积增幅
期中人口数	454300	591900	30.3%
家居废料(公吨)	154527	207810	34.5%

(续表)

年份	2011	2012	2013
工商业废料（公吨）	51508	107054	107.8%
建筑废料（千立方米）	583	3925	573.2%
废料焚化（公吨）	256224	401542	56.7%

资料来源：澳门统计暨普查局，2014。

由表1及表2的数字可以看出，澳门在社区所产生的废弃物数量、废料焚化量以及堆填的废料数量一直持续增加。即使近年政府一直提倡减少废物，以及推出资源垃圾分类回收的相应措施，而且相关政府部门亦指近年回收资源废料数量的增长理想，但实际回收废料的数量相对于产生量仍处于相当低的水平，政策的效果并不理想。

表3　本澳及邻近城市/地区人均每天垃圾产生量

城市/地区	2011年每日人均生活废弃物产生量（公斤/人/日）	资料来源
北京	0.86[①]	《北京统计年鉴2012》，北京
上海	0.82[①]	《中国统计年鉴2012》，中国
广州	0.75[①]	《广州统计信息手册2012》，广州
澳门	1.64[②]	《环境统计2011》，澳门
香港	1.27[③]	《香港固体废物监察报告——二零一二年》，香港
台北	0.39[④]	台北市统计数据库，台北

注：①每日人均生活垃圾清运量=生活垃圾清运量/常住人口（年末）/当期日数。
②每日人均运往焚化中心处理的废弃物量=运往焚化中心处理的废弃物量/年中人口/当期日数。
③每日人均都市固体废物量=都市固体废物量（每日平均量）/年中人口；都市固体废物量包括：家居废物+商业废物+工业废物。
④每人每日垃圾清运量=垃圾清运量/当期日数/清运区期中人口数。垃圾清运量包括：焚化及卫生掩埋之废弃物、沟泥，但不含回收资源、事业废弃物及迁移旧垃圾。

资料来源：转引自《澳门环境状况报告2011》，第80页，澳门环境保护局，2013。

按上表标准计算，澳门在2013年每日人均生活废弃物产生量已上升至1.86公斤。无论由澳门近年的废弃物增长量来看，或是比较邻近城市或地区的情况，在管制废弃物和分类回收的环境管理问题上，本澳都有很大的改善空间。

（二）专责部门

在1979年，当时的澳葡政府成立了保护自然及环境地区委员会，为维护自然、保护环境和生活质素展开工作。1989年9月成立环境委员会，作为协助制定澳门环境政策并协调行政当局推动及执行有关计划、措施及活动的咨询组织。其后鉴于世界各地及地区内对环境保护的呼声日益高涨，特区政府在2009年6月正式成立环境保护局①（下称环保局），取代先前负责本澳环保范畴的咨询机构环境委员会。

环保局为澳门特别行政区负责研究、规划、执行、统筹和推动环境政策的公共部门。成立以来，环保局分别制定和推行不同范畴的环保政策和措施，开展研究、咨询和立法等工作，目的是更有效地持续进行防治、监察和控制环境污染的工作；推动环境影响评估、环境规划和管理；加强环境宣传和教育，提升居民环保意识；持续优化生态保护区及其他环保基建设施；并透过加强区域合作，共建优质生活环境。同时把过往分别由民政总署及建设发办公室所管理的卫生堆填事务以及促进和协调固体废弃物焚化中心的工作，转移到环保局执行。

在废弃物处理工作上，除了环保局外，民政总署负责公共卫生设施包括垃圾房、垃圾站及垃圾桶的设立，会定期派员巡查各区的垃圾收集设施，确保设备的正常运作；同时负责资源垃圾分类回收工作的执行。

（三）废弃物管理工作

1. 废弃物的收集及清运

在澳葡政府时期，当时的市政厅②负责全澳的卫生设施、街道清洁、废弃物的收集及运送，以及相关的处理工作。1992年行政当局把城市清洁、垃圾桶清洁、废弃物的运送及固体废料回收的专营权批给予澳门清洁专营有限公司，市政厅则负责监督专营公司的工作。在2013年5月，澳门清洁专营有限公司再次投得特区政府"澳门城市清洁及垃圾收集清运服务"10年合约。

截至2014年3月，全澳共有垃圾房138个（例见图1，当局按地区及空间状况设置相应大小的垃圾房）。除了传统的垃圾收集方式，现时于澳门黑沙环新填海区设有固体垃圾自动收集系统，每天可收集35—40公吨垃圾，透过管道输送至垃圾压缩系统，被压缩装箱后以专车运送至澳门垃圾焚化中心处理。

2. 资源垃圾分类回收工作

1999年本澳开始推行资源垃圾分类回收工作，初期以学校宣传教育为重点，其后逐步扩大回收计划的层面，推广至社团、商业机构、政府部门以及于全澳各区设置公

---

① 参阅第6/2009号法律。

② 在回归之前，澳门在葡萄牙管治时代设有澳门市政厅及海岛市政厅，负责管理多项市政及部分民生事务。回归后，两个市政厅被撤销，过渡成为临时澳门市政局及临时海岛市政局；2002年1月正式合并成为民政总署。

图 1 设置在社区的垃圾房

共回收点等。截至 2012 年年底,民政总署在全澳门设置了资源垃圾公共回收点 286 个,玻璃樽公共回收点 40 个,以及衣物公共回收点 8 个① (例见图 2);另外有 318 个单位(包括学校、政府部门、社团及机构)以及三千多个屋苑参与回收计划。② 环保局和民政总署定期举办回收资源废弃物的有奖活动,鼓励市民参与回收工作。近年,

图 2 设置在社区的资源废弃物回收箱、玻璃樽及衣物回收箱

---

① 截至 2014 年 7 月。资料来源:http://www.iacm.gov.mo/sal/c/info/default.aspx。
② 《2013 澳门年鉴》,澳门新闻局 (2013),第 326 页。

民政总署多次表示，透过经年的资源垃圾分类回收计划，回收物料的数字有所上升，计划渐见成效。分类回收所得的物料，主要透过城市清洁及垃圾清运服务的营运公司做定期收集，并运往指定的回收商做初步处理，再运往外地进行循环再造。

在回收厨余方面，民政总署于2008年起开始陆续在街市、酒店及学校开展厨余回收计划，推广及协助设置小型干式厨余机，把厨余发酵转化为肥料、堆肥等，应用于山林、绿化带、苗圃及有机农耕活动等。

3. 末端处理

20世纪80年代末90年代初，行政当局决定采用"焚化为主，堆填为辅"的废弃物处理方案，耗资5.5亿澳门元建设了有三条处理线的垃圾焚化处理中心，于1992年开始投入运作。约十多年后，垃圾处理能力渐趋饱和，特区政府从2005年开始、2008年完成了垃圾焚化中心的扩建，新增了三座焚化炉，将每日处理能力提升至1728吨，预计可满足至2020年后的垃圾处理需求。

建筑废料方面，2006年3月位于氹仔机场大马路的建筑废料堆填区开始启用，用作填埋由开挖、拆建、兴建等活动产生的惰性固体废弃物，包括瓦砾、混凝土块、软土、海泥及熔渣等等。近年被运往建筑废料堆填区掩埋的建筑废弃物每年平均达225万立方米，对堆填区造成沉重的压力。

4. 源头减废

除了传统的废弃物处理工作外，因应近十多年世界各地区和城市纷纷对废弃物采取更积极的应对措施，"源头减废"成为特区政府近年的重要研究项目之一。根据环保局的调查结果，2012年澳门平均每人每日使用约2.2个塑料袋，全年总用量则约为4.5亿个，当中被丢弃的塑料袋约占澳门整体废弃物总重量的4%，反映澳门市民在购物时仍然很大程度地依赖胶袋。

作为"源头减废"的措施之一，根据逐步实践"污者自付"原则，澳门消费者委员会于2008年初发起"无胶袋日"，与多间商号定于每月28日不主动向顾客提供胶袋，以养成顾客自备购物袋的习惯；至2011年4月增加至每月两天。另外，在2013年环保局与多个社团合办为期两个月的"减塑有着数"有奖活动，鼓励购物时不索取胶袋或自备购物袋。在2014年6月环保局除继续上述活动外，亦表示就胶袋征费方案，将于2015年初展开咨询工作。

（四）废弃物管制法规及环保规划

澳门在1991年颁布《环境纲要法》，规定澳门环境政策须遵从的一般纲领和基本原则，其后在各个环境领域颁布相关法规，有关废弃物管制的法律规范包括以下各项：

表4 现行有关废弃物管制的法律规范

序号	颁布日期	法例编号	法例名称/内容
1	1991年3月11日	第2/91/M号法律	《环境纲要法》
2	1995年11月14日	第58/95/M号法令	刑法典第二百六十八条——防止污染罪行
3	1997年8月25日	第35/97/M号法令	规范在海事管辖范围内禁止投掷或倾倒有害物质
4	2004年8月16日	第28/2004号行政法规	《公共地方总规章》

资料来源：澳门环保局，2014。

政府在施政方针的层面，是在2010年首次引入废弃物管制的概念，之后逐步具体化。

表5 2010年至今运输工务范畴施政方针有关废弃物管制的相关内容

年份	与废弃物管制相关的内容
2010	本着从"规划入手，源头管理"的思路，将有序地开展全面的环境规划工作，制定《澳门环境保护概念性规划构想》。
2011	坚持"规划入手，源头管理"的理念，制订本澳资源垃圾再利用的方案，并开展探索长远解决本澳惰性物料的处理途径，以及电子废物污染控制的管理方案。
2012	将全方位展开科学调查和分析研究，搜集有关塑料袋的生产和使用的统计资料，订定本澳限塑生产和使用的政策建议方案。
2013	为推动发展区域循环经济，妥善处理各类废弃物，政府与广东省达成初步共识，首先以澳门惰性拆建物料作为跨境处置的工作重点，日后将根据社会发展需要，逐步深化合作内容。
2014	继续强化自愿性减塑措施，为过渡至下一阶段包括胶袋征费等强制性措施进行前期工作铺排。

资料来源：澳门施政报告，网址：http://www.policyaddress.gov.mo/policy/home.php?lang=cn。

在具体的环境保护规划方面，2012年9月特区政府公布了《澳门环境保护规划（2010—2020）》（下称《规划》），围绕可持续发展、低碳发展、全民参与和区域合作等四大理念为核心，以"构建低碳澳门、共创绿色生活"为规划愿景，将改善人居环境及保障居民健康为环境保护规划的重要目标。

在《规划》中指出，当局将根据固体废弃物产生的数量、种类和性质分类管理，加强危险废弃物监控，制定固体废弃物污染防治管理指引等，并逐步引入"污染者自付"或"生产者责任制",建设成完善的固体废弃物信息管理体系。① 对于资源垃圾的回收及再生,《规划》中的策略方向定为加强废弃物源头减量控制,以及推动废弃物的资源化及多元化利用。建立以"源头削减、分类收集、分类运输、回收利用、综合处理"为原则的城市垃圾处理系统。

三、邻近地区城市废弃物管制的经验

处理城市废弃物是各大城市近几十年环境政策需要解决的重大问题之一,"垃圾围城"几乎伴随每一个城市的发展而相继出现,各地政府均投入大量社会资源去面对这个问题,以免社会发展被窒碍。本部分探讨邻近地区一些城市对废弃物管制的经验,发展概况如下:

表6 本澳及邻近地区(城市)废弃物管理政策及措施时间表

城市	年份	政策及措施
台北市	1990	兴建垃圾焚化炉
	1997	推行垃圾不落地政策及资源回收四合一计划(实施生产者责任制)
	2000	废弃物按量收费计划
	2002	推行限塑政策(针对免洗具及胶袋)
	2004	建立厨余回收系统
	2005	实施强制垃圾分类回收
	2006	实施强制厨余回收
韩国	1990	兴建垃圾焚化炉及废弃物堆填区
	1995	废弃物按量收费计划
	1998	建立厨余回收系统
	2003	实施生产者责任制及饮品容器回收计划
	2005	实施废弃物堆填区废置厨余禁令
	2010	推行101个减少厨余的运动
	2013	实施厨余按量收费计划

---

① 《澳门环境保护规划(2010—2020)》,澳门环保局(2012),第23页。

（续表）

城市	年份	政策及措施
香港	1990	逐步停用及清拆垃圾焚化炉
	1995	启用新垃圾堆填区
	2002	研究废弃物处理方案
	2005	建筑废物处理收费计划
	2009	实施胶袋征费计划
	2013	提出兴建垃圾焚化炉及扩建堆填区的综合治理方案
澳门	1992	垃圾焚化炉投入运作
	1999	实施自愿性垃圾分类回收计划
	2005	垃圾焚化炉进行扩建
	2012	推出《澳门环境保护规划(2010—2020)》

注：台北市及韩国资料整理自《香港资源循环蓝图2013—2022》。

表6显示台北和韩国开展有关工作的时间较早，而且成绩亦比较好；澳门仍然处于起步的阶段。以下就与澳门关系较密切的两个城市，探讨其对废弃物管制政策及措施执行情况。

(一) 台北市

台北市由以往把垃圾任意弃置，继以焚化为主、掩埋为辅的处理方式作为主轴，进而成功推行源头减废、垃圾分类，以至垃圾不进掩埋场、垃圾全回收，2013年资源回收率高达56.15%，成绩非常亮丽，成为很多城市处理废弃物的参考和仿傚对象。

自1984年制订"都市垃圾处理方案"开始，政策以掩埋为主，协助地方政府兴建卫生掩埋场，以妥善处理垃圾。其后因社会对环境质量要求日益提升，加上焚化技术愈见成熟，于1991年制订以"焚化为主、掩埋为辅"的"垃圾处理方案"，逐步提升至2002年垃圾焚化处理率64%以上。除设备上的政策措施外，台北市早于1991年开始依用水量随水费征收垃圾费，于2000年改为垃圾费随袋征收，垃圾收集车只会收集环保局指定的专用垃圾袋，垃圾袋售价为每公升新台币0.5元，市民可以在指定的地方如便利店购买，但资源回收则不用收费，以提供经济诱因让市民减少废物，多回收。2005年进一步实施垃圾强制分类，把垃圾分为一般垃圾、资源垃圾和厨余，分别处理及回收。违规者可被科处罚款新台币1200至6000元不等，使用伪造垃圾袋更可被重罚高达新台币 10 万元，举报的市民可以获得 20% 的罚款作为奖金；而为了堵截非法弃置垃圾，政府亦会透过各区、各巷、各里等地区组织纠察义工，协助捉拿非法弃置的市民，而罚款就转交作该区的民用基金。2011 年每日平均家户垃圾量较随袋征收前减少 65%，人均每天生活废弃物产生量仅为 0.39 公斤，并逐步达成垃圾不进掩埋场、垃圾全回收、零废弃①之目标。

台北市在应对城市垃圾方面的成绩并非偶然，早在 1997 年政府曾推行类似分类回收的计划，但以失败告终，原因在于倡导不足，未能与市民建立良好的沟通渠道，也并非由整个市政府共同推动政策。其后在实施垃圾费随袋征收措施上，政府在两年之前在少部分地区试办，经检讨可行后，对整个措施进行规划及立法工作。在政策实施前半年进行大规模的宣传，在地区举办说明会 349 场，特别为大厦管理员和清洁人员举办说明会 401 场，训练了 2100 人作为训练其他市民的"种子教师"，到 415 个宗教团体解释政策。在民间组织方面，不少环保团体在台湾反对以焚化炉作为解决废弃物问题主要手段，但对于政府的回收分类计划则十分支持。在环保团体的推动下，市民组织环保义工队在每一个垃圾收集点进行宣传和监察，使制度的推行较顺利，效果亦较理想。此外，政府各部门的配合和大力推动亦起了重要的作用，由市长牵头亲自拍摄宣传海报，市政府的主要官员出席公众场合时必定协助宣传；市长及副市长也会抽问部门首长有关垃圾费随袋征收制度的问题，如答错会被罚新台币 100 元。在地区方面，倡导的工作由"民政署"负责，学校方面由"教育署"负责，警察部门在推行初期每日有 4500 人次检举违规人，部门各司其职，由上而下做好由倡导至执法的工作。

在回收废料的工作方面，台湾早于 1998 年已推行计划，由上游生产商出资，补助下游合资格的回收厂拆解废物，并配合"资源回收基金"监管制度，回收处理当地 14 类废物资源，包括废旧电器及计算机。1998 年的"资源回收四合一"（即生产者责任制）要求生产商补助回收业处理废物，奖励市民回收。台湾垃圾管理政策的成功，可以追溯到政府 1998 年制定的一笔鼓励资源回收的资金。根据 33 种商品类别，制造商和进口商估算垃圾的回收成本支付费用。"环保署"把这些收费分配给资源回收公司。这些年来，曾经是小型而且营运方式危险又简陋的资源回收业，已经发展出自己的高科技专业。台湾已经有把铝箔和塑胶与纸分离的技术。抽取出的塑胶和铝可以用于其他产品，纸则以高温加压成为纸板，用来制造家具或是当作建材。

---

① 根据台湾"行政院"环境保护署资料，"零废弃"观念之定义为，以"源头减量、资源回收"为垃圾清理之方向，具体订定以 2001 年为计算基准，至 2007 年、2011 年及 2020 年之总减量目标分别为 2001 年垃圾产生量（831 万吨/年）之 25%、40% 及 75%。

(二) 香港

香港在过去的 30 年，人口增长约为 36%，而都市固体废物总量增加 80%，同一时期的人均每天都市废弃物产生量由 0.97 公斤增加至 2011 年的 1.27 公斤。[①] 香港在 2003 年之前，都市废弃物产生量一直持续上升，其后开始下降。

香港在 20 世纪 90 年代，因旧式焚化炉产生严重污染而改用堆填区处理垃圾，焚化炉其后全面停用并陆续清拆。然而，在 1994 年至 1995 年启用之三个垃圾堆填区，预计将于 2015 年至 2019 年相继爆满。香港政府于 2002 年开始积极研究废物处理技术，包括向全球 15 个国家和地区的公司寻求解决方案，当中提议的技术主要为生物处理和热能处理两大类。到了 2007 年，香港政府开始研究扩建其中一个垃圾堆填区，但由于受到堆填区附近居民与市民的大力反对，计划在 2010 年立法会辩论时遭到否决，同时亦令使用焚化炉处理废弃物的议题重新进行研究。其后，在兴建焚化炉和扩建垃圾堆填区等的议题上，政府一直有提出不同的方案，但受到不同组织和人士反对，包括环保组织指焚化炉对环境有所影响，应先进行减废回收工作；堆填区附近受影响市民反对抗建，以及市民不满绿化区因而减少；对于征收排污及垃圾费一类的措施，亦受到商户反对。另一方面，根据"污染者自付"原则，香港在 2005 年实施建筑废物处置收费计划，以及 2009 年 7 月的胶袋征费措施。

在规划方面，香港政府在 2005 年底发表"都市固体废物管理政策大纲（2005—2014）"，订下规划目标每年减少产生都市固体废物量 1%，至 2014 年或之前，把都市固体废物回收率提高至 50%，把弃置于堆填区的都市固体废物总量减少至 25% 以下。在 2006 年实施建筑废物处置收费计划后，由过往每日产生接近 5 万公吨建筑废物，逐步减少至约 3300 公吨，但仍占总废物接收量的 25%；实施胶袋征费措施后，每人每天消耗的胶袋量由过往的 1.5 个下降至约 1 个。在 2013 年 5 月推出了《香港资源循环蓝图 2013—2022》[②]，规划由 2011 年开始，透过不同的措施，把人均每天都市废弃物产生量由 1.27 公斤减少至 2022 年的 0.8 公斤。而资源废弃物回收和堆填的比例，由 2011 年 48% 和 52%，规划至 2022 年分别为 55% 和 22%，其余 23% 则透过焚化技术转废为能。

在 2014 年 1 月发表最新的固体废物监察报告[③]中指出，香港 2012 年每日平均固体废物为 13844 公吨，而每人每日平均弃置 1.3 公斤固体废物，数字与过去四年相若，但回收率却下跌 9 个百分点至 39%，回落至 2004 年水平。原因是环保署沿用多年的

[①] 《香港资源循环蓝图 2013–2022》，香港环境局（2013），第 4 版。

[②] 参考网址：http://www.enb.gov.hk/sites/default/files/WastePlan–C.pdf。

[③] 参考网址：https://www.wastereduction.gov.hk/chi/materials/info/msw2012tc.pdf。

废物回收率一直有偏差,将一些回收物料的转口数字"误报"在内①,并且预料 2013 年的回收率或跌至 20%。

在回收废弃物方面,政府在 2010 年就废电器电子产品生产者责任计划进行公开咨询,提出要求电器及计算机产品的生产者(入口、零售及消费者)缴纳回收处理费,补助下游回收业处理电子垃圾,但受到工商政党、电器入口及批发等生产商的一面倒反对②。回收业在香港的发展受到土地贵、成本高所影响,回收到的废料几乎都只是平价出口往外地,中国内地自 2013 年中开始拒收废塑料、废纸等,令回收业的经营雪上加霜。有政府认可的回收商指,虽然香港废物回收率有 48%,但当中只有约 1% 的物料在本地回收再造,80% 回收得来的塑胶被直接送往堆填区③,影响废弃物回收再造的效益。

四、澳门实施废弃物管制的挑战、机遇和对策

(一) 管制废弃物的必要性

在全球环保呼声日渐高涨的情况下,各地纷纷开展其环保工作,澳门行政当局早在 1999 年已经开展了自愿性的资源垃圾分类回收工作,显示当局意识到环保工作的重要性。然而,多年来的环保宣传教育工作成果却未能具体反映在环境数据上,废弃物、焚化垃圾、堆填废料的数量近年均呈现增加的趋势;虽然回收率亦有显著的增长,但仍远不及废弃物的增长量。

使用堆填作为处理废弃物的方法,由于堆填区的占地面积大,使用寿命有限④,且对环境有一定的影响,与澳门土地面积细小、地价高昂产生极大的矛盾。当年行政当局以长远而持久的方法解决问题,即推动使用"焚化为主,堆填为辅"的废弃物处理方案,时至今日已经受到相当大的挑战,包括城市高速发展而引致废弃物数量的增加、土地资源持续短缺、市民对废弃物处理的卫生要求有所提高等等。此外,去年环保局已经表示建筑废料堆填区接近饱和,政府正积极觅地增设堆填区,并与内地商讨

---

① 香港文汇网,2014 年 1 月 29 日,网址:http://paper.wenweipo.com/2014/01/29/HK1401290016.htm。
② 香港明报,2011 年 11 月 7 日,第 A34 版。
③ 香港经济日报,2013 年 7 月 3 日,第 A30 版。
④ 在 1948 年以前澳门的垃圾会送到中国内地堆填,其后政府把垃圾运往毗邻珠海的鸭涌河填埋,1983 年鸭涌河填埋区的容量饱和,不宜继续使用,珠海亦拒绝为澳门设置固体垃圾填埋区。随后几年间,澳门的垃圾先后被运到氹仔鸡颈山和石排湾堆填。

透过区域合作，处置本澳经筛选的建筑废料。① 所有这些因素的影响，使本澳有必要从"焚化为主，堆填为辅"的废弃物处理方案，在更高层次的政策角度作全盘考虑，形成"规划入手，源头管理"的施政方针，以及"源头减废、资源回收"的工作部署。

（二）现时在管制废弃物工作上所遇到的问题及挑战

1. 规划及评估

环保局在2012年9月发布《规划》，对多项环保工作进行规划和制定工作目标，当中指出对废弃物资源回收率的规划目标，近期目标（2010—2012年）为20%，至2015年（中期）及2020年（远期）分别达到30%及45%（见表7）。《规划》同时指出应持续透过宣传推广和激励手段，推动居民将废弃物减量化、增加公众参与回收的意欲，以及进行建筑废弃物资源利用的研究。在2014年6月，环保局发布了《澳门环境保护规划（2010—2020）近期实施成效评估》，（下称《成效评估》），当中指出除废弃物资源回收率一项未能达到规划目标外，其余各项环境规划均达标。《成效评估》比对2009年和2012年的废弃物资源回收率，分别为18.6%和19.1%，未达到规划目标的20%。

以下分析回收率的构成情况，本澳过去数年人口和固体废弃物的产生量，除2009年出现轻微下降外，趋势是持续上升的，数字如表7所示：

表7　澳门特别行政区环境保护指标体系及工作目标

资源能源利用水平					
指标名称	单位	2009	2012	2015	2020
单位GDP能耗	太焦耳/亿澳门元	17.0	12.0	10.0	8.5
清洁能源使用率	%	12.6	18	25	35
再生水回用率	%	—	—	<2	4
环境质量					
指标名称	单位	2009	2012	2015	2020
环境空气质量年达标率①	%	98	98	≥98	99
沿岸水体水质总评估指数	/	0.77	0.77	0.75	0.70

---

① 《澳门日报》，2013年5月19日，第A1版。

(续表)

污染物控制与资源化					
指标名称	单位	2009	2012	2015	2020
城市生活污水集中处理率	%	95	95	97	99
区域噪声平均消减量	dB(A)	0	0.2	1.0	2.3
废弃物资源回收率	%	18.6[②]	20	30	45
特殊及危险废弃物资源化处理率	%	4	5	10	15
电子电器废弃物集中回收率	%	—	—	20	60
生态保育					
指标名称	单位	2009	2012	2015	2020
城市绿地率	%	39.1[③]	41.5	43.5	45.0

注：①自2012年7月2日起，澳门的空气质量指数标准将提升至世界卫生组织建议的过渡时期目标值（IT-1）的水平，由于暂时未能积累足够的历史数据，为此有关规划目标仍以2009年的原有标准作为基准年，未来经全面评估后视实际情况再做滚动式修订。

②由于本澳回收的废弃物基本运往外地循环再造，为此根据统计暨普查局进出口资料中包括废纸、废塑料及废金属等数量估算得2009年废弃物资源回收率。

③根据《澳门园林建设与绿地系统规划研究》制定的澳门城市绿地分类标准，澳门绿地面积的统计于2010年做出了较大的更改，为此，此指标规划值的编订以2010年为基准，且该基准值根据《环境统计（2010）》及前述研究中的统计数据计算。

资料来源：《澳门环境保护规划（2010—2020）》，澳门环保局，2012年9月，第16页。

表8　2007—2012年固体废弃物回收率概况

资料来源	年份	2007	2008	2009	2010	2011	2012
统计暨普查局	固体废弃物（公吨）	244,272	255,320	247,656	254,415	263,561	290,294
	焚化的固体废料（公吨）	288,243	298,491	324,808	321,409	329,154	365,648
	期末人口	538,100	549,200	542,200	552,300	557,400	582,000
	回收物料（公吨）	124	343	298	343	622	1,017
环保局	废弃物资源回收率	26.0%	24.0%	18.6%	19.7%	20.6%	19.1%

注：关于环保局2007年、2008年废弃物资源回收率，《澳门环境状况报告2011》第81页列出1999年至2011年之废弃物资源回收率统计图（见图3），但没有准确数字，故根据图示列出接近之数值。

根据表8统计暨普查局（下称统计局）的数字，澳门过去数年在人口、固体废弃物产生量、焚化的固体废料数量以及回收物料的数量，呈同一趋势持续上升。但环保局方面的回收率数字，在环保政策及措施没有重大改变的情况下，出现了相对波动的变化（见图3），趋势亦较难做出预测和部署，原因在于废弃物"总回收量"的计算。就这方面，国际上普遍采取的回收率计算方法如下①：

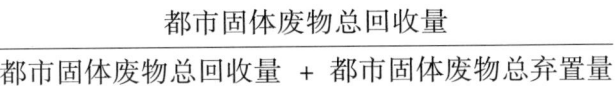

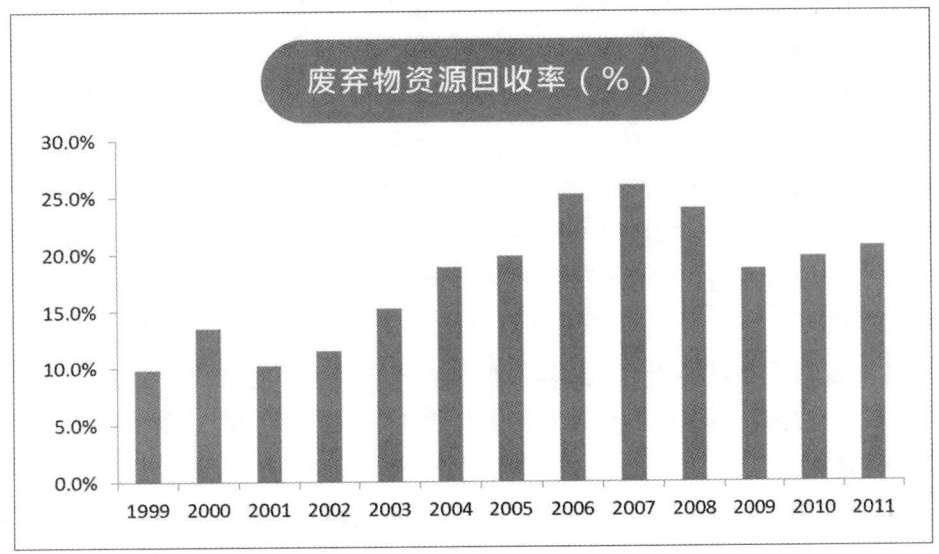

图3　废弃物资源回收率数字

资料来源：《澳门环境状况报告2011》，第81页。

对于"都市固体废物总回收量"，没有统一的计算标准，各地方的计算方式不尽相同，情况亦相当复杂。例如已遭弃置的旧衣服或物品，经部门收集转赠予其他人，即从来没有落入"废弃物"行列，是否用作计算回收物品？而且这些数据的收集存在困难。香港方面，固体废物总回收量的计算，是由香港海关从出口商经出口报关呈报，得出可回收物料自香港出口至外地的全年总出口量；加上都市固体废物在本地循环再造的全年总量（由环境保护署向本地回收再造商作统计调查的结果估计）计算出来。然而，香港环保署在2014年1月指出沿用多年的废弃物回收率一直存在偏差，根据出口数字计算的回收率误将转口废塑料计算在内（参阅第三部分第二点），可见回收率的计算相当复杂而且具争议性。

---

① 资料来源：香港立法会环境事务委员会就都市固体废物回收率及处理进口废物事宜的特别会议，2013年7月26日。参考网址：http://www.legco.gov.hk/yr12 - 13/chinese/panels/ea/papers/ea0726cb1 - 1620 - 1-c.pdf.

澳门方面，环保局鉴于本澳回收到的废弃物基本运往外地循环再造，因此根据统计局进出口资料中包括废纸、废塑料及废金属等数量估算得出废弃物资源回收率。[①] 数字显示过去数年回收物料总量确有所上升，但由于人口及商业活动的增加，废弃物产生量上升，加上复杂的出口数字估算，使回收率呈不规则变化的同时，实际的情况是，无论回收率的变化如何，送入焚化炉和堆填区的废弃物数量基本维持上升趋势。也就是说，规划目标（短期回收率达到20%）与改善环境情况的目标不一致；因为虽然回收率上升，却没有反映出澳门环境问题持续恶化的事实。

台北市对回收工作的目标是"垃圾不进掩埋场、垃圾全回收"，以制定规划的年度为基准（2001年垃圾产生量为每年约831万吨），至2007年、2011年及2020年之总减量目标分别为之25%、40%及75%，目标明确清晰并有针对性，可以预期达到工作目标的同时，环境问题亦必然有所改善。

因此，现时澳门在废弃物管制的规划和评估基准应做出调整，检讨沿用多年的"焚化为主，堆填为辅"废弃物处理方案，规划和政策目标是废物减量及分类回收，以缓解堆填区爆满的压力以及废弃物对环境的负面影响。

2. 法律规范

人们意识到过去在发展及生活过程中恣意破坏自然环境的活动，必需透过强制执行力予以调整，保障自然资源的合理利用、维护生态平衡、保护人类的未来以及可持续发展，环境法律及其规范在这种人类的认识和客观形势下产生和发展起来。

正因为环境法律规范（及具体表现在环境政策及管理措施）的效果是改变过去大多数人在发展及生活过程中对自然环境的破坏，加上自然资源的有限性，所以法律规范的制定必须有效率以及具备一定的社会基础，规范的内容要适时、适度、宏观及具前瞻性。

澳门社会对废弃物进行管制的意见存在已久，过去行政当局基于未有专责部门，故迟迟未有起步。2009年环保局成立后，在有关的问题上仍然进展缓慢。至2014年6月，环保局才表示计划在2015年开始胶袋征费的法规咨询，作为首个引入污者自付原则的法规咨询工作。然而，澳门立法工作的效率一直为社会所诟病，一个较近期、同样在社会已经存在较广泛共识的《预防及控制吸烟制度》（即控烟法），在获得超过七成市民支持修订的民意基础上，由法规咨询至开始实施共耗时四年多，可以看到立法效率亟须改善。事实上，无论是胶袋征费，还是强制性的资源废弃物分类回收计划，以及垃圾收费计划一类的废弃物管制措施，在邻近地区如北京、广州、香港、台湾、东京、首尔、新加坡等，已经以不同的形式出现，本澳市民对此绝不陌生，甚至

---

① 《澳门环境保护规划（2010—2020）近期实施成效评估》，澳门环保局，2014年6月，第8页注6。另外在《澳门环境状况报告》系列报告中，采取同样的估算方法来估算废弃物资源回收率。

在旅游期间已经习惯与澳门不一样的弃置废物方式。政府在对废弃物管制的立法工作上，在地区中已经大为落后，实在没有合理理由仍在有关工作上放任自流。再加上十多年来的自愿性废弃物分类回收计划的成效已经不能回应社会的环保要求，使用法律规范的手段是整个废弃物管制措施的基础和行动的依据，特区政府应该确切投入资源加速立法以及其法律推广工作。

3. 基建设施及社会动员

澳门虽然拥有较先进技术的废弃物焚化设施，但在整体处理废弃物基础建设上仍有不足之处，其中较为明显的是至今未有大规模的厨余回收及处理基建设施及相关的计划。

根据环保局的资料，现时本澳每天所产生的废弃物当中，厨余的数量占20%—40%，即每天生产出400至800公吨厨余，对焚化炉及堆填区均造成压力。虽然当局在街市、酒店及学校推广厨余回收，并协助设置厨余机，但由于这类厨余机每天处理厨余的能力有限（每天约30—100公斤），而且未有开放予市民使用，厨余机的能力和效益均处于有限的水平。

香港在2014年4月通过预算拨款约15.3亿港元于离岛区兴建首个有机资源回收中心，第一期计划在2016年运作。中心每日处理量厨余上限为200公吨，当局希望日后共六期的回收中心能适用至全香港。[①] 就邻埠及其他已建立较完善厨余回收及处理的经验来看，本澳在加强厨余回收及处理基建设施方面需要提高工作效率。

然而，即使在社会已经共识需要兴建废弃物处理基建设施的同时，近年出现不少相关的社会问题。例如澳门部分学校所设置的小型干式厨余机，由于在发酵过程多少会产生异味，故必须把设施放置于校舍的天台；这与香港把厨余回收中心设置在离岛的原因大同小异。近年香港在兴建焚化炉及扩建现有垃圾堆填区的问题上闹得满城风雨，澳门亦曾经发生居民反对兴建垃圾站的个案[②]，突显了一个在环保政策中较难处理的问题——邻避效应（Not in My Back Yard，NIMBY）[③]。

近年澳门在发展社区设施方面进行了不少工作，如研究兴建安老院、社区中心、停车场、垃圾回收站等，当中更不乏已研究多年以及已经进行公众咨询的发展项目，

---

① 澳亚卫视新闻，2014年4月8日，网址：http://www.imastv.com/news/article.php? id=38990。

② 民政总署在2010年9月，因为计划于本澳著名世遗景点之一的圣老楞佐堂（俗称风顺堂）古地基石墙外兴建风顺堂地下升降式垃圾桶，结果惹来社会一片反对之声。另在2012年7月约20名东望洋新街居民反对于该街道兴建压缩式垃圾房站，到政府总部递信，居民忧虑垃圾房会发出臭味和引发环境卫生问题，希望民署另觅地址兴建。

③ 邻避效应是一个形容新发展计划受到该区或邻近地区居民反对的贬义词语。一般而言，受到反对的发展计划都会为地区带来长远的利益，但短期内可能会对附近的居住环境造成一些负面影响。为了保护自己的居住环境，附近居民会反对这个计划，或提议在其他地区兴建。

最后都因为受到设施附近居民的强烈反对而终止计划，这不但耗费了社会资源，亦阻碍了环保建设发展。最后由于多个社区建设未能顺利展开，政府在推动新项目时，便步履维艰，形成恶性循环。在最近的胶袋征费问题上，环保局表示需要在取得社会共识的基础上进行，明年开始征询社会意见，舆论因而直指本澳的污者自付及强制性废弃物分类回收工作实施无期，实在有其道理。环保工作多涉及改变人们的生活习惯，以及处理废弃物为一种厌恶性工作，无论在兴建设施（焚化炉、堆填区、回收站等）、征费、立法强制分类、监管（处罚）等环节，都必然会遇到不同的社会阻力，如无法动员社会成员在多个环节共同努力参与行动，体谅和支持基建设备，以及政府从中大力推动，实行环境政策只会阻力重重。

4. 对回收行业的支援

回收再造行业是"循环经济"的一个关键元素，其经济活动所产生的可循环再造物料将因重复使用、回收和循环再造而重回消费环当中。本澳回收行业近年的发展，由于土地资源匮乏，而且回收业具其特殊性，在选址上必须充分考虑并确保环境、卫生及景观等问题，避免造成负面影响和二次污染，因此寻找合适的地点作为回收业用地存在一定的困难和制约。回收行业多年来面对租金上涨、土地缺乏等问题，经营空间及物料储存空间均严重不足。此外，由于回收过程繁复，很多时候要进行人工再处理，加上回收后附加价值不高，所以愿意投资的人也不多，总体而言行业发展与环保气候背道而驰。

另外，社会上没有污者自付的概念，一直以来扔掉垃圾零成本，回收行业要客户付费提供服务时，便选择扔掉废物。此外，除了平日在街上或屋苑见到的回收箱外，更多的可回收物品是无序地落入一般的废弃物当中而落入堆填区，或者回收箱内的废料未有经过适当的处理而无法回收，都会直接影响废弃物回收处理的成效。例如政府早前推出环保节能基金，鼓励节能。基金推出后大量公司更换节能产品，不少回收公司收到查询如何回收旧光管，但由于要付钱回收而没有成功个案。甚至有数以千计完好光管想卖出，但因为光管的回收价值低，且要处理光管内的气体，在近乎没有经济利益的情况下，政府即使有意推动社会节能，却对废弃物不加以合适的政策措施或指引，结果造成二次污染。

上述提到的厨余回收工作，政府一直未有大力推广到屋苑及食肆，多年来停留在宣传及试验阶段。学校及酒店所设置的厨余机可再造肥料，但处理量低，若由私人投资发展成商业活动，同样面对由于厨余掉进垃圾桶是免费的，加上需要因应厨余的分类程度去选择所投资的机器，再者就是肥料在澳门的出路较狭窄，难以发展成有利可图的生意。在整个社会不注重分类回收，没有强制执行分类回收，没有政策或指引支持回收行业，市民和店铺大多会选择直接扔掉，甚至向回收公司讨费，回收再造行业无法发挥"循环经济"的作用,对于整体废弃物处理的成效,同样造成相当的负面影响。

(三) 应对废弃物问题的优势、机遇及对策

环境政策及其管理工作的特点是,涉及参与的市民数目多,层面非常广泛,可以说基本都是全民参与,而且很多实质措施均涉及人们生活习惯的改变,这些改变需时很长,政府要不断因应形势去调整政策。从台北市管制废弃物的经验可知,相应的政策和管理工作必须具备全局性的考虑,单项措施必然存在局限性,影响实施的效果。澳门现时在管制废弃物产生及处理方面的情况未如理想,情况与台北市早期推行的垃圾分类回收计划相似,在缺乏全局性的政策及措施考虑的情况下,个别的环保工作计划均以失败告终。因此建议行政当局采用国际上公认的多层次废物管理架构来引导政策和措施(见图4),包括:

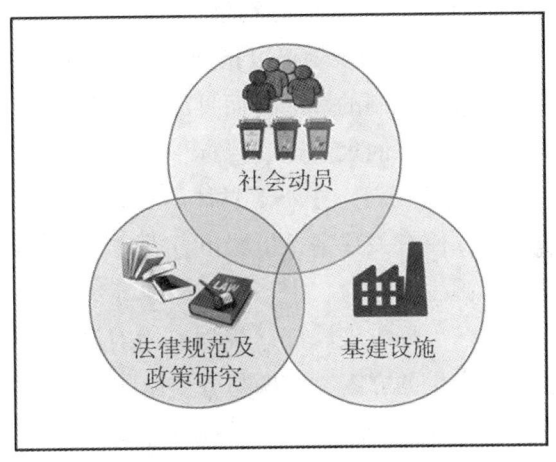

图4 多层次废物管理架构示意图

1. 兴建及提升现有基建设施,加强区域环保建设及产业合作

澳门使用焚化及堆填方式处理废弃物,在基建设施及相关管理经验方面均处于较好的水平①,各项硬件设施预计可满足至2020年后的废弃物处理需求。但是,在现时每年废弃物净产生量(即产生量减去回收量的净值)持续上升的情况下,在能够有效控制废弃物增长前,焚化中心及堆填区仍存在不敷应用的风险。因此有必要积极开拓各种各样的废弃物分类回收基建设施,即规划及兴建大型的厨余回收处理设施,以及建筑废料分类回收中心等,并尽快把设施推广至建筑业、屋苑及社区,方便业界和市民使用。此外必须持续优化垃圾焚化中心的处理技术,规划及建设符合规范的飞灰填埋场,强化"焚化为主,堆填为辅"的废弃物处理方案。

另一方面,由于澳门土地面积的限制以及对回收再造品的市场较狭窄,因此应该与邻近地区积极研究合作拓展废弃物处理的基建设施,以及再造品的市场。本澳近年与珠海已经开展多方面的合作,例如澳门大学横琴校区、中医药产业园、粤澳新通道等等,两地正全面开展新时代的区域合作。在环保工作上更加是唇齿相依,

---

① 焚化中心自2008年完成扩建后,现时每天可处理1728吨废弃物,噪声、污水等指标均达到国际先进水平,垃圾处理过程中产生的热能可用于发电,尾气的排放符合欧盟2000/76/EC指引。

空气素质、水资源、能源、废弃物等方面都几乎面对共同的问题和挑战，加强区域合作和研究可以使本澳在环保基建选址及规模上更具弹性，提升两地的废弃物处理技术和效能的同时，亦可以更好地支援狭窄的本澳市场诸如回收行业等的环保产业的发展。

2. 加速研究及实施制度化建设

本澳多年来对废弃物的管理工作只停留在教育宣传阶段，边际效应已经接近临界，必须尽快完善管制废弃物的规划，并同时完善管制废弃物及处理工作的规范及制度，以有效控制其增长及做好分类回收工作，包括：

（1）良好的规划可以指出工作的方向，减低不确定的风险，减少资源的浪费与重叠以及提供控制的标准，而且应该确立清晰和具体的目标。再根据规划内容制定各项工作计划、时间表及达到目标，用以分配各项资源及其他必要行动。

现时《规划》中不乏具体的工作目标，如城市绿地率的规划数字为短期目标达41.5%，而有关数字是指城市各类型绿地（除水面以外的休闲游憩绿地、道路交通绿地、苗圃生产绿地、生态保护绿地等）合计面积占城市总面积的比率，具有评估的可操作性。当局应该修订《规划》中对废弃物管制的目标和行动框架，科学化研究减少废弃物产生的方案，考虑与分类回收工作的协同效应，制定具体的工作目标，例如引入目标时间减少废弃物总量的百分比，按目标部署相关的工作。

（2）废弃物管制的规范包括很多方面，基本的法律法规如台湾的"都市垃圾处理方案"是现时最刻不容缓的，必须依照"污染者自付"及"生产者责任制"原则定立法律框架；细则性的措施及其规范、罚则等可以行政法规来补充，另需要强化现时本澳"公共地方总规章"，监管市民及商铺适当地弃置垃圾。再根据固体废弃物产生的数量、种类和性质分类管理，制定固体废弃物污染防治管理指引等，建设成完善的固体废弃物信息管理体系等一系列的法律及制度。

在实践"污染者自付"原则方面的废弃物征费措施，澳门消费者委员会在2008年初推出每月一次的"无胶袋日"活动，鼓励市民少用胶袋，其后环保局亦加入推广工作。2010年消费者委员会进行有关工作的成效问卷调查[①]，结果显示活动实施两年多后，大部分商铺耗用胶袋数量有所减少，但市民自备购物袋的意识仍较薄弱。此外，消费者及商铺均支持"无胶袋日"活动，并认为可以推广活动的范围及时间，由此可见社会对减塑有一定的共识。2014年6月环保局表示将于稍后提出胶袋征费措施的公众咨询工作，其后在网络上有意见调查支持有关措施，虽然问卷的对象和结果存

---

① 参考网址：http://www.consumer.gov.mo/c/active/210-c1.pdf。

在局限性，但亦一定程度地反映出民意的倾向（见图5）。① 因此，行政当局应该加快对胶袋征费，以至实践"污染者自付"及"生产者责任制"原则的法律咨询工作，促使早日落实减废回收的具体政策及措施。

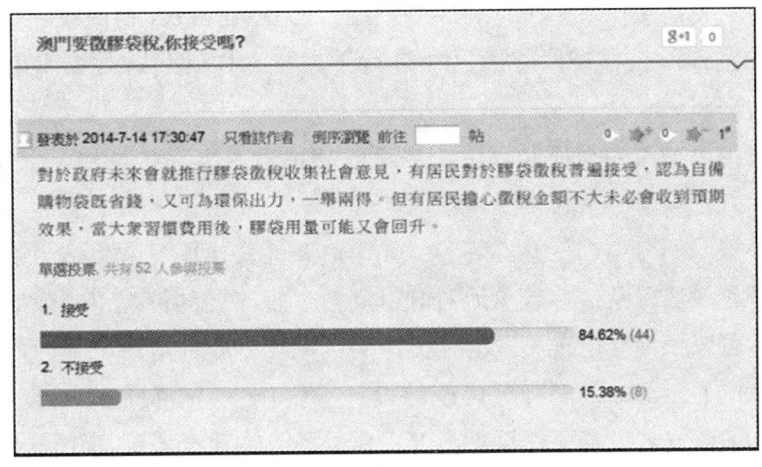

图5 网上讨论区对胶袋征费之投票情况

（3）推行废弃物管制措施必然引起市民生活习惯的改变，再完善的法规如果没有到位的监管措施，失败的风险会非常高。台北市在推行"垃圾不落地"政策初期，市民需要定时把已分类的垃圾送到收集车辆，有市民未赶及指定时间，或随意把不合分类规格的垃圾装入回收袋中。政府为此需要组织社区的纠察义工、透过闭路电视监察、抽查垃圾袋等，逐渐把市民的生活习惯改变过来。因此，在设计废弃物管制制度时，必须考虑可行及有效的监督措施，以配合制度的执行。

此外亦应该考虑采取适当的经济诱因以提高执行效益，例如上述台北市组织社区的纠察义工，如发现市民违规弃置垃圾而施行罚款，有关款项将投入该区的社区建设，有关做法便有效调动了监察团队的积极性。香港在实施第二阶段胶袋征费措施时，规定商铺无须把所征得的胶袋费上缴政府，亦是采用经济手段以补偿商铺实施胶袋征费时所带来的额外工作。在本澳的分类回收工作中，民政总署可免费向屋苑提供三色回收桶，但须由屋苑负责联系回收商处理，故建议由回收计划收集所得之资源垃圾交由清洁工人卖给回收商，以赚取相应之报酬，充分发挥清洁工人在回收计划中所担当之角色，提高他们的积极性。由此可见，监督和激励的配合在人性化管理措施之中可以起积极的作用。

---

① 澳门电讯公司网上讨论区，网址：http://forum.cyberctm.com/forum/forum.php? mod = viewthread&tid = 11237769&extra = page%3D1。

3. 提升居民社会意识

基建设施和制度规范是环境政策和管理工作的基础，要在环境保护工作中取得成功，最重要的一点是有效地引导全民参与，提升居民的环保和社会意识。澳门虽然在过去十多年未有太多实质性的废弃物管制措施，而且资源废弃物回收率数字存疑，但在分类回收的宣传及教育推广方面已经进行了大量工作，渐渐为本澳市民带出环保意识。

接着即将推出的废弃物环保政策，包括胶袋征费、废弃物征费、强制分类回收，以至设置厨余处理设备、焚化炉及堆填区扩建等，以及对废弃物的管制进行监督如惩处违规扔掉垃圾或不分类进行弃置等等，无不涉及改变市民日常生活习惯及工商业运作模式。在邻避效应以及或多或少地对既得利益产生改变的情况下，政府推动有关的环保政策时，可以预期会出现不同的社会阻力。因此，政府应该把握时间和机会，主动加强与市民沟通，清晰讲解有关设施的设计、科技、安全措施、对废弃物的清运、气味处理等相关配套，以释公众疑虑，并提出补偿方案供受影响居民参考，否则将来方案出台，亦难以获得市民及议会支持。

此外，自2009年起特区政府大力兴建公共房屋以满足社会需求，多个高密度大型屋苑近年相继落成。政府应该把握契机，在新屋苑推行各类减废及回收的试验措施，收集数据以评估和研究市民生活习惯与政策措施的关系。加上积极引导民间团体参与政策制定和推广工作，有效吸取坊间的主流意见并融入措施中，从多方面向市民传达废弃物管制的意义和目的，提高公民意识，共同为自身和社会发展而努力。

五、总结

环境管理及政策所涉及的范围十分广泛，对废弃物进行管理是环保工作中重要的一项。近十多年邻近地区不断致力推动源头减废和分类回收工作，台北市的成功成为了很多地区的学习对象；香港虽然起步较迟及遇上社会阻力，但亦有一定成绩，港、台两地与澳门的社会情势较为接近，其废弃物管制之路各有值得借镜的地方。

澳门已经推行十多年的废弃物分类回收工作，在全球环保意识高涨的带动下，近年的回收数字虽然有所上升，但废弃物所带来的威胁却有增无减。多年来人均废弃物产生量高，资源化程度低，除了是社会现象，也是政策的结果。行政当局应检讨规划和措施的成效，调整政策目标和内容，以最大的决心与市民共同应对废弃物问题。

环境问题的产生并且日益严重的根源在于人们自然观上的错误，这导致人类社会行为的失当，最终使自然环境受到超过能够自我修复程度的干扰和破坏。环境管理的目的是协调社会发展与环境的关系，透过持续而且动态的过程，运用各种手段限制人们损害环境的行为。因此它必须适应社会、经济、技术的发展，及时调整政策内容以及相关的措施。政府是社会上唯一具有行使环境保护的权威性、强制性以及综合性的组织，必须责无旁贷地负起保护属于大家的环境和未来的责任，以实现社会的可持续发展。

[1] 赵莹：《垃圾能源化利用与管理》，科学技术出版社 2013 年版。

[2] 罗振：《垃圾资源化，你应该做的 50 件事》，化学工业出版社 2013 年版。

[3] 黄明健：《环境法制度论》，中国环境科学出版社 2004 年版。

[4] 赵由才：《生活垃圾资源化原理与技术》，化学工业出版社 2002 年版。

[5] 北京市环境保护科学研究院：《环境影响评价典型实例》，化学工业出版社 2004 年版。

[6] 乔艳洁、曹婷、唐华：《从公共政策角度探析邻避效应》，《航空工业管理学院学报》2007 年第 26 卷第 1 期。

[7] 谭鸿仁、王俊隆：《邻避与风险社会：新店安坑掩埋场设置的个案分析》，《地理研究》2005 年第 42 期。

[8] 澳门特别行政区政府新闻局：《澳门年鉴 2013》，2014 年。

Social Security Administration and Institutional Framework in the Post-aprtheid South Africa: Pitfalls, Challenges and Innovations

Letlhokwa George MPEDI *

1. Introduction

The purpose of this paper is to critically assess the past, present and envisaged reforms pertaining to the administration of social security in South Africa. The paper discusses the drivers of good public administration reforms from a social security perspective [e. g. courts of law (particularly the Constitutional Court of South Africa), policy makers and Non-Governmental Organisations (NGOs)], success and failures of as well as lessons to be learnt from such reforms. While at it, the paper examines the advantages and disadvantages of each of the aforementioned catalysts of social security administration reforms in South Africa. It proceeds by analysing the importance of having constitutionally protected social security and pertinent rights and a specific chapter in the Constitution dealing with the public administration, particularly in a developing country context, as the basis for social security administration reform endeavours. Furthermore, the paper discusses lessons to be learnt by other developing countries from the South African social security administration reform experiences.

---

* Letlhokwa George MPEDI, Professor and Director: Centre for International and Comparative Labour and Social Security Law, Faculty of Law, University of Johannesburg.

2. Social Security Administration in South Africa

2.1 Brief historical overview

The social security administrative and institutional framework[1] is generally built on and influenced by the pertinent legislative and policy framework. As it could be expected, the South African social security administration of the apartheid era was largely influenced by the laws and policies of that time. These laws and policies generally perpetuated the differentiated treatment of the various race groups in South Africa. The outcome of this approach in the social security provisioning sphere is that certain race groups, particularly the Whites, received beneficial treatment as regards the quality of services and benefits.[2] Within the same breath, racial groups such as Black Africans were excluded and marginalised or treated unfavourably by social security institutions.[3] This resulted in, among others, racial, gender and geographic inequities in social security provisioning endeavours.[4] As correctly asserted by the Constitutional Court in *Mashavha v President of the Republic of South Africa and Others*[5]:

> Gross inequalities were deliberately and legally imposed as far as race and also geographical areas are concerned. Not only were there richer and poorer provinces, but there were "homelands", which by no stretch of the imagination could be seen to have been treated on the same footing as "white" South Africa, as far as resources are concerned. These inequalities also applied to social assistance-an area of governmental responsibility very closely related to human dignity.

---

[1] Olivier and Smit (Olivier M. P. and Smit N., "Social Security Law", in Joubert W. A. (ed.), *The Law of South Africa*, Vol. 13, Part 2, Butterworths, 2002, at paragraph 157) explain an "institutional framework" as follows: "The institutional framework can be understood to include the system of government in the country, the financial framework, the administrative framework, the legislative framework, governance issues as well as service delivery and support systems."

[2] Patel P., "Social protection in South Africa: History, Goals and Strategies", in Midgley J. and Piachaud D. (eds.), *Social Protection, Economic Growth and Social Change: Goals, Issues and Trajectories in China, India, Brazil and South Africa*, Edward Elgar, 2013.

[3] Ibid.

[4] See, for example, Mpedi L. G., "Diversity and Respect: Perspectives from the South African Social Security System", in Lutz R. (ed), *Diversity and Respect: Problems of Perception in the Global Agenda for Social Work*, Paulo Freire Verlag, 2013, p. 69 at 73 – 75.

[5] 2005 (2) SA 476 (CC); 2004 (12) BCLR 1243 (CC) at paragraph [51].

In addition, the administration of the social security system was fragmented. For instance, the social welfare system during the apartheid period was administered by fourteen departments for different population groups and homelands.①

2.2 Present-day position

2.2.1 Relevant constitutional provisions

2.2.1.1 *Duty to abide by the Constitution of the Republic of South Africa*

Each and every one of the social security institutions operating in the country (be they public or private) have a duty to abide by the *Constitution of the Republic of South Africa*, 1996.② This obligation stems from the supremacy of the Constitution③; the obligation on the state to *respect*, *protect*, *promote* and *fulfil* the rights enshrined in Bill of Rights④; the binding effect of the Bill of Right on all organs of state⑤; and the binding effect of the provisions contained in the Bill of Rights on natural and juristic persons.⑥ To this end, social security institutions must abide by section 33 of the Constitution. This section, which deals with the right to just administrative action⑦, provides every person with the right to

---

① The "homelands" were quasi-sovereign enclaves established for Blacks in South Africa and were abolished in 1993. The Republic of South Africa is now one sovereign state (s 1 of the *Constitution of the Republic of South Africa*, 1996).

② Act 108 of 1996.

③ Ss 1 (c) and 2 of the Constitution.

④ S 7 (2) of the Constitution. The rights entrenched in the Bill of Rights include social security (related) rights such as the right to equality (s 9 of the Constitution), the right to human dignity (s 10 of the Constitution), the right to life (s 11 of the Constitution), the right to privacy (s 14 of the Constitution), the right of access to housing (s 26 of the Constitution) and the right of access to social security [s 27 (1) (c) of the Constitution].

⑤ S 8 (1) of the Constitution. Section 239 of the Constitution defined an 'organ of state' as "any department of state or administration in the national, provincial or local sphere of government; or (b) any other functionary or institution (i) exercising a power or performing a function in terms of the Constitution or a provincial constitution; or (ii) exercising a public power or performing a public function in terms of any legislation, but does not include a Court or a judicial officer." See *Directory Cost Cutters CC v Minister of Post and Telecommunications* 1996 3 SA 800 (T).

⑥ S 8 (2) of the Constitution.

⑦ According to s 1 (i) of the *Promotion of Administrative Justice Act* 3 of 2000 (PAJA) "administrative action" means "any decision taken, or any failure to take a decision, by – (a) an organ of state, when – (i) exercising a power in terms of the Constitution or a provincial constitution; or (ii) exercising a public power or performing a public function in terms of any legislation; or (b) a natural or juristic person, other than an organ of state, when exercising a public power or performing a public function in terms of an empowering provision, which adversely affects the rights of any person and which has adirect, external legal effect…" See, for further reading on the meaning of "administrative action", Henderson AJH "The meaning of 'administrative action'" 1998 *South African Law Journal* 634.

administrative action that is lawful, reasonable and procedurally fair and with the right to written reasons[1], where that person's rights have been adversely-affected by the administrative action in question. Furthermore, section 33 of the Constitution obliges the state to enact national legislation, in order to give effect to the foregoing rights and to: provide for the review of administrative action by a Court or, where appropriate, an independent and impartial tribunal[2]; impose a duty on the state to give effect to the rights in subsections (1) and (2); and promote an effective administration.[3] The right to just administrative action may appear straight forward. Nonetheless, in practice social security institutions do not always comply with this right. The series of cases brought against the various provincial departments of social development for their failure to conform with the right to just adminis-

---

[1] See, generally, Barrie G. N., "The Giving of Reasons for Administrative Decisions in English and United States Law", *Tydskrif vir die Suid-Afrikaanse*, 2000, p. 595. See also, for an illuminating discussion on the right to administrative justice in South Africa, Dlamini C. R. M., "The Right to Administrative Justice in South Africa: Creating an Open and Accountable Democracy", Prat 1, *Tydskrif vir die Suid-Afrikaanse*, 2000, p. 697; and Dlamini C. R. M., "The Right to Administrative Justice in South Africa: Creating an Open and Accountable Democracy ", Part 2, *Tydskrif vir die Suid-Afrikaanse*, 2001, p. 53.

[2] Section 33 of the Constitution, in essence, reinforces the common law administrative law framework developed over the years in South Africa. In *President of the Republic of South Africa v South African Rugby Football Union* 1999 BCLR 1059 (CC) the Constitutional Court pointed out at 1117E – F that: "the principal function of section 33 is to regulate conduct of the public administration and, in particular, to ensure that where action taken by the administration affects or threatens individuals, the procedures followed comply with the constitutional standards of administrative justice. These standards will, of course, be informed by the common law principles developed over decades."

[3] In consequence of section 33 of the Constitution, the legislature enacted the *Promotion of Administrative Justice Act* 3 of 2000 (PAJA). The PAJA (together with the *Promotion of Access to Information Act* 2 of 2000 (PAIA)) (See, for further reading about the PAIA, Currie I and Klaaren J *The Promotion of Access to Information Act Commentary* (Siber Ink (2002)) is also aimed at the promotion of *efficient administration* and *good governance*, as well as the *creation of accountability*, *openness* and *transparency* in the public administration or in the exercise of a public power or the performance of a public function, by giving effect to the right to just administrative action (Preamble to the *Promotion of Administrative Justice Act*. See, for further reading about the PAJA, Currie I. and Klaaren J., *The Promotion of Administrative Justice ActBenchbook*, Siber Ink, 2001), Pfaff R. and Schneider H., "The Promotion of Administrative Justice Act from a German perspective", *South African Journal of Human Rights*, 200, p. 59; and Plasket C., "Administrative Action: The Constitution and the Promotion of Administrative Justice Act 3 of 2000", paper presented to a Legal Resources Centre seminar on the Promotion of Administrative Justice Act 3 of 2000, Johannesburg, 23 October 2001.

trative action are the case in point.[1] The non-compliance with the right to just administrative action was not only observed in the social assistance sphere but in the social insurance field as well. For example, in *Tseleng v The Chairman, Unemployment Insurance Board & Another*[2] the Court held that failure on the part of the Unemployment Insurance Board to bring policy to the attention of the applicant that no further benefits are payable to applicants who failed to seek employment is unjust and contrary to the right to procedurally fair administrative action. It argued that:

> Perhaps the policy is a sound one, but if a statutory body considers that such a consideration is so material as of itself to determine the fate of an application, then it should at the very least afford an applicant the opportunity of dealing with its difficulty and not keep the policy to itself…To hold otherwise would be to countenance injustice since persons who might otherwise be fully able to justify their application would be deprived of the opportunity of doing so.[3]

2.2.1.2 *Basic values and principles governing public administration*

The Constitution makes provision for basic values and principles governing public administration which public social security institutions should respect and uphold. In accordance with s 195 (1) of the Constitution:

> Public administration must be governed by the democratic values and principles enshrined in the Constitution, including the following principles:

---

[1] See, for example, *MEC, Department of Welfare v Kate* [2006]2 All SA 455 (SCA); *Ntame v MEC, Department of Social Development, Eastern Cape*; *Mnyaka v MEC, Department of Social Development, Eastern Cape*; *Mnyaka v MEC, Department of Social Development Eastern Cape* [2005]2 All SA 535 (SE); *Vumazonke v MEC for Social Development, Eastern Cape, and three similar cases* 2005 (6) SA 229 (SE); *Jayiya v MEC for Welfare, Eastern Cape Government and another* [2003]2 All SA 223 (SCA); *Mbanga v Member of the Executive Council for Welfare and Another* 2001 (8) BCLR 821 (SE); *Mahambehlala v Member of the Executive Council for Welfare, Eastern Cape Provincial Government and Another* 2001 (9) BCLR 889 (SE); *Bushula and others v Permanent Secretary, Department of Welfare, Eastern Cape Provincial Government and another* 2000 BCLR 728 (E); *Rangani v Superintendent-General, Department of Health and Welfare, Northern Province* 1999 (4) SA 385 (T); and *Bacela v MEC for Welfare (Eastern Cape Provincial Government)* 1998 1 All SA 525 (E). Also see Olivier M "The role of law in extending protection to welfare beneficiaries: Innovative perspectives from South Africa" in Instituut voor Sociaal Recht K. U. Leuven (ed) *Sociale Bescherming op Nieuwe Paden: Liber Memorialis Béatrice Van Buggenhout* (Universitaire Pers Leuven (2003)) 667 at 668 – 672.

[2] (1995) 16 *ILJ* 830 (T).

[3] At 846.

(a) A high standard of professional ethics must be promoted and maintained.

(b) Efficient, economic and effective use of resources must be promoted.

(c) Public service must be development-oriented.

(d) Services must be provided impartially, fairly, equitably and without bias.

(e) People's needs must be responded to, and the public must be encouraged to participate in policy-making.

(f) Public administration must be accountable.

(g) Transparency must be fostered by providing the public with timely, accessible and accurate information.

(h) Good-human resource management and career-development practices, to maximise human potential, must be cultivated.

(i) Public administration must be broadly representative of the South African people, with employment and personnel management practices based on ability, objectivity, fairness, and the need to redress the imbalances of the past to achieve broad representation.

The preceding principles apply to administration in every sphere of government; organs of state; and public enterprises. Accordingly, the national, provincial and local spheres of government[1] have to abide by these principles in their social provisioning endeavours. The same applies to those organs of state that administer both social assistance (e.g., the South African Social Assistance Agency (SASSA)) and social insurance schemes (e.g., the Unemployment Insurance Fund, the Road Accident Fund and the Compensation Fund).

In light of the objectives of the *Promotion of Administrative Justice Act* (PAJA) and the *Promotion of Access to Information Act* (PAIA)[2] and the position of public

---

[1] In terms of s 40 of the Constitution the Government of the Republic of South Africa is constituted as national, provincial and local spheres of government which are distinctive, interdependent and interrelated.

[2] Such as giving effect to the constitutional obligations of the state of promoting a human rights culture and social justice [s 9 (c) of PAIA] as well as promoting transparency, accountability and effective governance of all public and private bodies [s 9 (e) of PAIA].

administration under the Constitution①, it can be opined that the PAJA and PAIA are in conformity with the basic values and principles governing public administration, as stipulated in s 195 of the Constitution, as well as with the eight principles of *Batho Pele*.②

2.2.2 Social security schemes and funds

The South African social security institutional framework is divided between the public sector and the private sector. Public institutions administer both statutory social assistance③ and several social insurance④ schemes. The South African Social Security Agency is respon-

---

① The position of public administration under the Constitution has been highlighted by the Constitutional Court, in *President of the Republic of South Africa v South African Rugby Football Union* 1999 10 *BCLR* 1059 (CC) 1115B – D (at paragraph 133), in the following terms: "Public administration, which is part of the executive arm of government, is subject to a variety of constitutional controls. The Constitution is committed to establishing and maintaining an efficient, equitable and ethical public administration which respects fundamental rights and is accountable to the broader public. The importance of ensuring that the administration observes fundamental rights and acts both ethically and accountably should not be understated. In the past, the lives of the majority of South Africans were almost entirely governed by labyrinthine administrative regulations which, amongst other things, prohibited freedom of movement, controlled access to housing, education and jobs and which were implemented by bureaucracy hostile to fundamental rights or accountability. The new Constitution envisages the role and obligations of government quite differently."

② The eight principles of *Batho Pele* are as follows: *Consultation* – Citizens should be consulted about the level and quality of the public services they receive and, wherever possible, should be given a choice about the services that are offered. *Service Standards* – Citizens should be told what level and quality of public services they will receive, so that they are aware of what to expect. *Access*-All citizens should have equal access to the services to which they are entitled. *Courtesy* – Citizens should be treated with courtesy and consideration. *Information* – Citizens should be given full and accurate information about the public services they are entitled to receive. *Openness and transparency* – Citizens should be told how national and provincial departments are run, how much they cost, and who is in charge. *Redress*-If the promised standard of service is not delivered, citizens should be offered an apology, a full explanation and a speedy and effective remedy; and when complaints are made, citizens should receive a sympathetic, positive response. *Value for Money*-Public services should be provided economically and efficiently in order to give citizens the best possible value for money. The *Batho Pele* principles are analogous to the principles contained in the United Kingdom's *Citizens Charter* of 1991. The key principles of this interesting document, as cited by Bynoe (Bynoe I., *Beyond the Citizen's Charter: New Directions for Social Rights*, Institute for Public Policy Research, 1996) include that: "Standards should be set and published, with performance measured against them; full and accurate information on public services should be readily-available; value for money in services should be pursued, together with independent validation of performance against standards; mistakes and failures should be put right with an apology, a full explanation, and a swift and effective remedy."

③ According to s 1 of the *Social Assistance Act* 13 of 2004, "social assistance" means a "social grant including social relief of distress."

④ "Social insurance", as defined by s 1 of the *Social Security Agency Act* 9 of 2004, means "contribution based benefit payments aimed at income maintenance."

sible for the administration of the social assistance scheme in South Africa. The national and provincial departments of Social Development are responsible for the administration of welfare benefits. The Department of Labour, on the one hand, fulfils a supervisory role over funds (such as the Unemployment Insurance Fund and the Compensation Fund) which administer their own occupational-based schemes (*viz.*, unemployment insurance and occupational injuries and diseases scheme, respectively). The Department of Transport, on the other hand, plays a supervisory role over the Road Accident Fund-a fund responsible for the compensation of road accident victims. Private institutions are involved in the administration of private insurance institutions (such as the occupational injuries and diseases schemes in the mining and building industries, medical aid schemes and retirement schemes). However, this is within the private regulated markets. In addition, the role of civil society should also be recognised, as it plays a pivotal role in the "informal welfare sector". The *White Paper for Social Welfare*[①] provides that the formal welfare sector is, in general, accepted to consist of welfare organisations that are government-subsidised, and religious organisations delivering welfare services, some of which are government subsidised. The informal welfare sector comprise of organisations that are currently not government subsidised and these informal social networks consist of networks such as family, friends, neighbours and indigenous helping systems.[②]

Table 1 Key South African Social Security Funds/Schemes

Public		Private/voluntary
Agency	*Funds*	*Schemes / Funds*
☐ South African Social Security Agency	☐ Unemployment Insurance Fund ☐ Compensation Funds ☐ Road Accident Fund	☐ Medical Aid Schemes ☐ Retirement Funds

---

① Chapter 3 at item 2 in Government Gazette 18166 Government Notice 1108 of 8 August 1997.

② See, for a discussion on informal social security, Dekker A. H. and Oliver M. P., "Informal Social Security", in Olivier M. P. et al (eds.), *Social Security: A Legal Analysis*, LexisNexis Butterworths, 2003, p. 559; and Olivier M. P. and Mpedi L. G., "Extending Social Protection to Families in the African Context: The Complementary Role of Formal and Informal Social Security", 4th International Research Conference on Social Security, Antwerp, Belgium, May 2003, pp. 5 – 7.

2.2.3 Social risks and responsible institutions

2.2.3.1 *Social assistance*

(1) *South African Social Security Agency*: The South African Social Security Agency, established pursuant to a recommendation by the Committee of Inquiry into a Comprehensive System of Social Security for South Africa (hereinafter the Committee), [1] has been established to act, eventually, as the sole agent that will ensure the efficient and effective management, administration and payment of social assistance; serve as an agent for the prospective administration and payment of social security; and render services relating to such payments. [2] Its main functions are to administer social assistance in terms of Chapter 3 of the *Social Assistance Act*[3]; collect, collate, maintain and administer such information as is necessary for the payment of social security, as well as for the central reconciliation and management of payment of transfer funds, in a national data base of all applications for and beneficiaries of social assistance; and establish a compliance and fraud mechanism to ensure that the integrity of the social security system in maintained. [4] In a nutshell, SASSA is responsible for the efficient and effective management, administration and payment of social assistance benefits[5] in South Africa. [6] SASSA has, among others, the following traits: (i) it is a *creature of statute*[7]; (ii) it is a *juristic person*; (iii) it is subject to *policy control* by the Department of Social Development; and (iv) it is headed by a *Chief Executive Officer*[8] who reports directly to the Minister of Social Development. [9]

---

[1] Committee of Inquiry into a Comprehensive System of Social Security for South Africa *Transforming the Present—Protecting the Future* (Committee of Inquiry into a Comprehensive System of Social Security for South Africa (2002)) (at 122 – 123). It should be noted that the Committee of Inquiry into a Comprehensive System of Social Security for South Africa, when proposing the establishment of SASSA, suggested that consideration be given to functions of the social security agency in the following spheres: *social assistance*, *social insurance* and the *intermediary services*. SASSA is yet to incorporate the social insurance and intermediary services in its activities.

[2] S 2 of the *South African Social Agency Act* 9 of 2004.

[3] 13 of 2004.

[4] S 4 of the *South African Social Agency Act*.

[5] Namely, (aged persons) old age grants and grant-in-aid; (people with disabilities) disability grants and grant-in-aid; (war veterans grants) war veterans grants, grant-in-aid and supplementary grants; (children) child support grant, care-dependency grant and foster-care grant.

[6] Preamble and s 3 of the *South African Social Security AgencyAct* 9 of 2004.

[7] *South African Social Security Agency Act* 9 of 2004.

[8] S 5 of the *South African Social Security Agency*.

[9] S 6 of the *South African Social Security Agency*.

(2) *Government departments*: In accordance with Schedule 4 of the Constitution, health services, public works and welfare services are functional areas of concurrent national and provincial legislative competence. Accordingly, there are several government departments (both at national and provincial levels) which provide tax financed benefits geared at poverty alleviation as well as the provision of indirect social security[①] to the needy. These departments include the Department of Social Development (social welfare services[②])[③], the Department of Health (free basic health care to pregnant women and children under six years of age, primary school feeding schemes and poverty relief) and the Department of Water Affairs and Forestry (free basic water). Government departments, unlike statutory bodies such as SASSA, have *inter alia* the following distinctive features: (i) they are directly supervised and controlled by the responsible ministry; (ii) they are staffed by civil servants who are recruited in terms of rules and policies applicable in the civil service; (iii) since they are not legally incorporated, these institutions do not invest funds in their own names; and (iv) their funds are usually invested on their behalf in the name of the Treasury, thereby giving the Treasury string influence over investment and supply of funds to the government.[④]

[①] Indirect social security refers to "those services (such as those relating to the provision of food and nutrition, water and sanitation, housing, basic education, energy etc.) that are not part of direct or traditional social security, but are nonetheless crucial in preventing human damage and imperative in aiding human beings in living dignified lives" (Mpedi L. G., "Indirect social security", in Olivier M. P. et al (eds.), *Social Security: A Legal Analysis*, LexisNexis Butterworths, 2003 p. 535 at 537). See, for further reading on the notion of indirect social security, Mpedi L. G., "Indirect social security", in Olivier M. P. et al (eds.), *Social Security: A Legal Analysis*, LexisNexis Butterworths, 2003, p. 535.

[②] National Treasury (Republic of South Africa) described 'social welfare services' as "services aimed at supporting the aged, needy children, people with disabilities and victims of crime" (National Treasury (Republic of South Africa) *Provincial Budgets and Expenditure Review*: 2003/04 – 2009/10 (National Treasury (Republic of South Africa) (2007)) 51).

[③] According to the *White Paper for Social Welfare* (the White Paper): "the national Department of Welfare (now the Department of Social Development) will be responsible for the following functions which will be carried out in conjunction with provincial governments and other role players in the private sector: coordination, national policy and planning, legislation, marketing: social welfare governance structures, human resource development, national programmes, social welfare financing, national information system, capacity and institution building, parliamentary liaison and international liaison.

[④] Sylva A. G., "Managerial Problems in the Dministration of Social Security Schemes", in International Social Security Association, *Workshop on Organization and Methods for Chief Executives of Social Security Institutions in English Speaking Africa*, Swaziland, 7 – 10 November 1989, p. 41 at 43 – 44.

(3) *Local government*: The functions of local government①, as listed by the Constitution, are to: provide democratic and accountable government for local communities; ensure the provision of services to communities in a sustainable manner; promote social and economic development; promote a safe and healthy environment; and encourage the involvement of communities and community organisations in matters of local government.② Furthermore, the Constitution obliges municipalities to structure and manage their administration, budgeting and planning so as to give priority to the *basic needs* of the community, to promote the *social and economic development* of the community and to participate in national and provincial development programmes.③ In addition, municipalities have the right to administer, among others, child care facilities, municipal health services and municipal public works.④

2.2.3.2 *Social and private insurance*

The institutional administration of social and private insurance⑤ is spread over a variety of institutions. Social insurance is chiefly administered by public institutions. These institutions are to a large extent created by an act of parliament and are directly supervised by the

---

① Chapter 7 of the Constitution makes provision for local government in South Africa. In accordance with s 151 (1) of the Constitution, the local sphere of government consists of municipalities, which must be established for the whole of the territory of South Africa. In addition, the executive and legislative authority of a municipality is vested in its Municipal Council [s 151 (2) of the Constitution]. Furthermore, a municipality has the right to govern, on its own initiative, the local government affairs of its community, subject to national and provincial legislation, as provided for in the Constitution [s 151 (3) of the Constitution]. Lastly, the national or provincial government may not compromise or impede a municipality's ability or right to exercise its powers or perform its functions [s 51 (4) of the Constitution].

② S152 (1) of the Constitution.

③ S 153 of the Constitution. Also see the *Municipal Systems Act* 32 of 2002.

④ S 156 (1) and Schedule 4 (Part B) of the Constitution.

⑤ Igl (Igl G., "Social Insurance: Legal Aspects", in Elsevier Science, *International Encyclopedia of Social & Behavioral Sciences*, 2001, p. 14325 at 14325) distinguishes social insurance from private insurance as follows: "The difference between social and private insurance can be found in the goals, the techniques of protection, the legal form of the insurance bodies as private or public organizations, and the way of financing the benefits. But there is no clear distinction between them. Sometimes, the goals of social insurance are attained by compulsory private insurance and, in some countries, the bodies responsible for social insurance are private bodies. One of the main distinctions between social and private insurance concerns the ways in which risk is calculated and financed. In the field of private insurance, the basis of calculation of the premiums is the risk. In the field of social insurance, the risk is less important, and social aims (such as health and welfare) prevail against the economic criterions. Private insurance, moreover, distributes the burden of an individual risk across a group. Social insurance has the same effects, but it also effects income redistribution between those who are healthy and sick, richer and poorer, younger and older people, or households without and with family members."

responsible ministry.[1] Furthermore, certain of the social insurance institutions (for example, the Road Accident Fund, the Compensation Fund and the Unemployment Insurance Fund) in South Africa are run as though they were a part and parcel of the conventional civil service structure.[2] This is the case despite the fact that "these institutions are engaged in specialised functions with a need for a high degree of operational flexibility."[3] The end result of this is, as the Committee of Inquiry into a Comprehensive System of Social Security for South Africa puts it, "that the public service structures tend to reprioritise key aspects of the social insurance functions, thus contributing to a significant reduction in the institution's ability to achieve basic operational functionality."[4]

Private insurance, on the other hand, is administered by private institutions-mostly commercial enterprises (insurance companies) and private employers (pension funds). To put it differently, private insurance is largely financed and delivered in a regulated private market. It should be noted that the government is responsible for the policy and regulatory framework within which these private institutions operate. However, there are some policy co-ordination issues which still need to be addressed in South Africa. As the Committee of Inquiry into a Comprehensive System of Social Security for South Africa points out:

> Since 1994 the government has made significant strides in policy co-ordination through institutions such the cluster of cabinet ministers. There are, however, still a number of policy areas in which policy co-ordination is lacking. For instance, with regard to retirement and old age, the Department of Social Development develops policy for old age grants, whereas the National Treasury develops the policy for private old age provision. These two environments are not viewed holistically. The specific areas of social security identified by the [Committee of Inquiry into a Comprehensive System of Social Security for South Africa] as having no clear over-riding policy responsibility or lead Ministry are:
> (1) Old-age and retirement
> (2) Disability

---

[1] E. g., the Unemployment Insurance Fund, the Road Accident Fund and the Compensation Fund.

[2] Committee of Inquiry into a Comprehensive System of Social Security for South Africa *Transforming the Present—Protecting the Future* [Committee of Inquiry into a Comprehensive System of Social Security for South Africa (2002)] 121.

[3] *Ibid.*

[4] Committee of Inquiry into a Comprehensive System of Social Security for South Africa "Committee Report No. 12: Institutional framework for comprehensive social protection"-accessed at http://www.sarpn.org.za.

(3) Maternity benefits and support.①

Table 2 Social risks and responsible institutions

Social risks	Social assistance	Social Insurance
Unemployment	–	☐ Unemployment Insurance Fund
Disability	☐ South African Social Security Agency	☐ Road Accident Fund ☐ Compensation Fund
Old age	☐ South African Social Security Agency	☐ Private and occupational-based funds
Survivors' benefits and funeral benefits	–	☐ Unemployment Insurance Fund ☐ Compensation Fund ☐ Road Accident Fund ☐ Private funds
Health care	☐ Provincial Department of Health ☐ Local authorities	☐ Medical Aid Schemes ☐ Road Accident Fund ☐ Compensation Fund ☐ Private insurance
Maternity	☐ Provincial Department of Health	☐ Unemployment Insurance Fund ☐ Private insurance ☐ Occupational health schemes
Child benefits	☐ South African Social Security Agency	☐ Unemployment Insurance Fund ☐ Compensation Fund ☐ Road Accident Fund
General poverty	☐ South African Social Security Agency ☐ Provincial Departments of Public Works, Human Settlements, Health, Labour and Rural Development and Land Reform	–

Source: Partly based on Liffmann R. et al. "Administration" in Olivier MP et al. (eds.) *Social Security Law: General Principles*, Butterworths (1999), pp. 77–78.

---

① Committee of Inquiry into a Comprehensive System of Social Security for South Africa, *Transforming the Present—Protecting the Future*, Committee of Inquiry into a Comprehensive System of Social Security for South Africa, 2002, pp. 121–122.

2.2.4 Ensuring the accountability of social security institutions

There is a variety of supervisory bodies in South Africa which (should) ensure that (public) social security institutions are accountable. These supervisory bodies include the following:

(1) *Office of the Public Protector*: The office of the Public Protector, which is cited as one of the state institutions that strengthens constitutional democracy in South Africa[1], has the power to: investigate any conduct regarding state affairs, or the public administration in any sphere of government[2], that is alleged or suspected to be improper or to result in any impropriety or prejudice; report on that conduct; and take appropriate remedial action.[3] As is apparent from the powers of the office of the Public Protector, its main concern revolves around administration, whereas investigation of crimes, and related issues, are referred to the police.

(2) *South African Human Rights Commission*: The South African Human Rights Commission has a Constitutional duty to: promote respect for human rights and a culture of human rights; promote the protection, development and attainment of human rights; and monitor and assess the observance of human rights in South Africa.[4] It has the power to investigate and to report on the observance of human rights; to take steps to secure appropriate redress where human rights have been violated; to carry out research; and to educate.[5] Incensed by the inefficiency of the Department of Social Development (Eastern Cape) in its administration of the social assistance scheme, the Court in *Vumazonke v MEC for Social Development, Eastern Cape, and three similar cases*[6] ordered that a copy of

---

[1] S 181 (1) (a) of the Constitution.

[2] Public Protector South Africa, *Report on an Investigation into an Allegation That the South Africa Social Security Agency Suspended Payment of a Child Support Grant without Furnishing Written Reasons*, Report No. 23 of 2009/10; Public Protector South Africa, *Report on an Own Initiative Investigation into an Allegation That the South African Social Security Agency suspended the Social Security Grant of MS NS Mphephu without Good Cause*, Report No. 27 of 2008/09; Public Protector South Africa, *Report on an Investigation into Allegations of Maladministration against the National Department of Social Development and the KwaZulu-Natal Provincial Department of Social Services and Population Development*, Report No. 4 of 2008/9.

[3] S 182 (1) of the Constitution. It should be noted, however, that in terms of s 182 (3), the office of the Public Protector has no power to investigate Court decisions. This provision is in line with s 165 of the Constitution, which guarantees the independence of the judiciary.

[4] S 184 (1) of the Constitution.

[5] S 184 (2) of the Constitution.

[6] 2005 (6) SA 229 (SE).

the judgment be served on the Chairperson of the Human Rights Commission. ① In addition, the South African Human Rights Commission has an obligation to require relevant organs of state to provide it with information on the measures that they have taken towards the realisation of the rights in the Bill of Rights concerning housing, health care, food, water, social security, education and the environment. ② Pursuant to this requirement, the South African Human Rights Commission compiles and releases reports on the economic and social rights in South Africa. ③ This, however, has throughout the years proved not to be an easy task. As Khoza points out: "The [South African Human Rights Commission] has consistently reported that government departments have not always been co-operative in giving information required for the reports-often providing inadequate and/or incorrect information or submitting it late-and this has led the [South African Human Rights Commission] to invoke its powers to subpoena government officials. Such problems doubtless influence the quality of the reports…" ④

(3) *Auditor-General*: The Auditor-General has an obligation to audit and report on the accounts, financial statements and financial management of: all national and provincial state departments and administrations; all municipalities; and any other institution to be audited by the Auditor-General. ⑤ Furthermore, the Auditor – General has discretion to audit and report on the accounts, financial statements and financial management of: any institution funded by the National Revenue Fund or a Provincial Revenue Fund or by a municipality; or any institution that is authorised in terms of any law to receive

---

① In this decision, Plasket J. stated at paragraph [18] that: "I am aware of the fact that when a previous crisis in the administration of social assistance in the province was brought to the Human Rights Commission, it concluded that, despite trying, there was nothing it could do but to support a class action for the reinstatement of a substantial number of disability grants. Many would have expected that the attention that that crisis has received would have spurred the respondent and her officials out of their lethargy and indifference and instilled in them a sense of responsibility and commitment. That has not happened. As the crisis deepened, I have decided that it is appropriate to order that a copy of this judgement be served on the chairperson of the Human Rights Commission so that he can consider whether to institute an investigation into the conduct of the respondent's department, with a view to proposing concrete steps to ensure that it begins to comply with its constitutional and legal obligations and ceases to infringe fundamental rights on the present grand scale."

② S 184 (3) of the Constitution.

③ Soft copies of the South African Human Rights Commission's reports on economic and social rights can be accessed at http://www.sahrc.org.za.

④ Khoza S. "Review of the sixth report of the South African Human Rights Commission: An Introduction", 8, 2007, *ESR Review* 15 at 16 – 17.

⑤ S 188 (1) of the Constitution.

money for a public purpose.[1]

(4) *Public Service Commission*: The Public Service Commission (PSC), established in accordance with section 196 of the Constitution, is a: "constitutionally-mandated, national body responsible for the important tasks of: promoting the democratic values and principles enshrined in the Constitution of the Republic of South Africa; investigating, monitoring and evaluating the organisation, administration and personnel practices of the public service, and advising national and provincial organs of the state accordingly; providing directions to ensure that personnel procedures comply with constitutional values and principles; proposing measures to ensure effective and efficient performance within the public service; investigating employee grievances; and reporting on its activities and performance."[2] In light of the foregoing important tasks of the PSC, it may be asserted that the PSC: "promotes the development of ethics and accountability, in that it ensures that government departments follow the sound principles of public administration to ensure efficient, economic and effective use of resources, and that people's needs are responded to."[3] It is, indeed, clear that public administration in South Africa is not at liberty to act as it pleases. Institutions such the PSC are there to ensure that. Accordingly, it is not surprising that the Court in *Vumazonke v MEC for Social Development, Eastern Cape, and three similar cases* deemed it appropriate to, in addition to the South African Human rights Commission, serve a copy of its judgment on the PSC.[4]

---

[1] S 188 (2) of the Constitution.

[2] *Report on the State of the Public Service* (November 2001), accessed at: http://www.gov.za/-reports/2001/spservice.pdf.

[3] Mafunisa M. J., "Enhancing Accountability and Ethics in the Public Service: The Case of the Republic of South Africa", in Frimpong K. and Jacques G. (eds.), *Corruption, Democracy and Good Governance in Africa: Essays on Accountability and Ethical Behaviour*, Lightbooks, 1999, p. 238 at 244.

[4] Justifying such a move, Plasket J. pointed out (at paragraphs [19], [21] – [22]) that: "In my view it is also necessary to bring the crisis to the attention of the Public Service Commission because a large part of the problem in the respondent's department appears to be maladministration and inefficiency in the administration of social assistance. The Public Service Commission is created as an independent and impartial institution with the express purposes of maintaining an 'effective and efficient public administration' and 'promoting 'a high standard of professional ethics in the public service'…As with the Human Rights Commission, it seems to me to be appropriate to have this judgement served on the chairperson of the Public Service Commission so that he can consider instituting an investigation into the respondent's department. There appears to me to be no reason why both institutions, with their complementary focuses and expertise should not conduct joint investigation. I stress, however, that much as I hold the view that an investigation by these institutions is appropriate and necessary, I am not making an order to that effect: the decision to investigate or not is one that is vested in the institutions concerned and must be taken by them…the time for talk and no action has long passed. Something drastic and concrete must be done to remedy a serious, systemic infringement of the Constitution and law-and the principles of good administration-by the respondent's department."

The aforementioned supervisory bodies are independent, and subject only to the Constitution and the law, and they must be impartial and must exercise their powers and perform their function without fear, favour or prejudice.① In addition, the Constitution proscribes any interference with the functioning of these institutions be it from natural and juristic persons or from an organ of state.②

2.2.5　Developing a sound social security administrative and institutional framework: A work in progress

It goes without saying that the apartheid injustices which were propagated in the course and scope of the governance and administration of the social security institutions have no place and cannot be tolerated in a democratic South Africa.③ Meaningful progress has been made towards the goal of ensuring good administration and operational efficiency of social security institutions in South Africa. For instance, the social grant scheme which was administered by nine provincial departments is currently managed by the SASSA. Secondly, the number of cases that were brought against several provincial departments of social development for failure to comply with rules of natural justice when handling the social grants applications has declined. Furthermore, significant progress has been registered by SASSA in its quest to improve the social grant payment process. This process has yielded some positive spinoffs in the form of financial savings as well as job creation for unemployed youth.④ An-

---

①　S 181 (2) of the Constitution.

②　S 181 (4) of the Constitution

③　As aptly pointed out by the Constitutional Court: "The history of our country and the need for equality cannot be ignored… Equality is not only recognized as a fundamental right in both the interim and 1996 Constitutions, but is also a foundational value. To pay, for example, higher old age pensions in Johannesburg in Gauteng than in Bochum in Limpopo, or lower child benefits in Butterworth than in Cape Town, would offend the dignity of people, create different classes of citizenship and divide South Africa into favoured and disfavoured areas" (*Mashavha v President of the Republic of South Africa and Others* 2005 (2) SA 476 (CC); 2004 (12) BCLR 1243 (CC) at paragraph [51]).

④　According to South African Social Security Agency (South African Social Security Agency, *Annual Report* 2012/13, South African Social Security Agency, 2013, pp. 10 – 11): "The project entailed the mass re-registration of existing beneficiaries, children receiving grants and procurators so as to root out fraud and corruption and review incomplete files in order to ensure the correct payment of grants. As part of the transition to the new payment system, a new biometric-based payment solution for social grants was implemented. While a total of 18.9 million people have been successfully re-registered onto the new system, the new biometric solution also resulted in over 150 000 social grants being cancelled, leading to a saving of R150 million per annum for SASSA. The highest affected grant was the CSG [Child Support Grant], with 22 432 cases, followed by the OAG [Old Age Grant], with 12 367 grants being cancelled. Another pleasing spin-off of the re-registration project was the creation of jobs for some 8 000 youths, of which 3 000 are permanent positions."

other way in which SASSA improved the social grant payment process was through the introduction of a SASSA smart payment card. This card was issued to over 10 million social grants recipients and it ensured that a large number of the so-called previously unbanked social grants recipients were integrated into the South African banking system.① It also reduced the transaction costs from a reported average of R32 to R16. 44 per transaction.② In the social insurance sphere, the Unemployment Insurance Fund and the Compensation Fund have reported some surpluses.③ This is positive, particularly when one takes into account the fact that funds such the Unemployment Insurance Fund were at some point in their existence declared technically insolvent.④

Notwithstanding the preceding pronouncements, there are a number of challenges that still require (further) attention. For instance, the South African Social Security Agency and most social insurance schemes are beset by problems such as corruption and fraud.⑤ Secondly, the administration of the social assistance programme is still characterised by inefficiency. This problem is apparently more pronounced in the former homelands due to a shortage of the requisite skills among certain officials.⑥ Furthermore, the South African social security institutional and administrative framework is disjointed. As a result, there is a duplication of services. For instance, there are several welfare databases (e. g. the Labour Centre

---

① Report of the Portfolio Committee on Social Development on Social Development on the 2013/13 Annual Report of the South African Social Security Agency (SASSA), dated 18 February 2014-accessed at http://db3sqepoi5n3s. cloudfront. net/files/140303pcsocdevreport2. htm.

② South African Social Security Agency, *Annual Report* 2012/13, South African Social Security Agency, 2013, p. 96.

③ The Unemployment Insurance Fund has, as 31 March 2013, a net surplus of R16. 01 billion (Department of Labour, *Unemployment Insurance Fund Annual Report* 2013, Department of Labour, 2013, p. 104). The Compensation Fund, on the other hand, reflected a surplus of R9. 2 billion in the 2012/2013 financial year (Department of Labour, *Annual Report of the Compensation Fund for the Year ended March* 2013, Department of Labour, 2013, p. 10).

④ See, for example, News24 "UIF is 'technically insolvent'", accessed at http://www. news24. com/xArchive/Archive/UIF-is-technically-insolvent – 20010313 and IOL News "R400m in the red-that's the UIF's plight"-accessed at http://www. iol. co. za/news/politics/r400m-in-the-red-that-s-the-uif-s-plight – 1. 61987#. U_B352UcS1I.

⑤ See, for example, Department of Labour, *Annual Report of the Compensation Fund for the Year ended March* 2013, Department of Labour, 2013, p. 10; and Special Investigating Unit, *Annual Report* 2012/2013, 2013, pp. 25 – 27, 58 – 60.

⑥ Mpedi L. G. , "Current Approaches to Social Protection in the Republic of South Africa", in Midgley J. and Piachaud D. (eds.), *Social Protection, Economic Growth and Social Change: Goals, Issues and Trajectories in China, India, Brazil and South Africa*, Edward Elgar, 2013, p. 217 at 238.

data, South African Social Security Agency data, Unemployment Insurance Fund data etc.) operating alongside each other. It must be said that the rationale behind the establishment of the South African Social Security Agency was that it would eventually serve as an administrative and institutional hub of the social security system. Regrettably, the South African Social Security Agency is yet to incorporate social insurance and related services in its scope of responsibilities. It should be noted that the South African National Planning Commission has recommended that the various welfare databases be consolidated into one. [1]

3. Key Facilitators of Good Public Administration Reforms: A Social Security Perspective

Depending on, *inter alia*, the legislative framework and, at times, the political dispensation (i.e. democratic or dictatorial) as well as the socio-economic context policy-makers as well as individuals and non-governmental organisations (NGO) can play a pivotal role in prompting reforms aimed at ensuring that social security institutions are appropriately governed. [2] In South Africa, the rights enshrined in the Bill of Rights have been used, albeit in different ways, to reform the social security administrative framework of a variety of social security institutions. Policy-makers have and continue to develop social security policies that will ensure that the post-apartheid social security institutions are managed in line with the new constitutional dispensation. In pursuit of this quest committees have been established to identify issues and possible solutions. An example of such committees is the Committee of Inquiry into a Comprehensive System of Social Security for South Africa. [3] In ad-

---

[1] National Planning Commission, *National Development Plan: Vision for* 2030, South African National Planning Commission, 2011, pp. 347 – 378.

[2] As rightly pointed out by the Committee of Inquiry into a Comprehensive System of Social Security for South Africa (Committee of Inquiry into a Comprehensive System of Social Security for South Africa, *Transforming the Present—Protecting the Future*, 2002, p. 119): "Major shifts become possible, as in the case of South Africa, with changes from undemocratic to democratic forms of Government and through the introduction of a Constitution. Such shifts may preface the development of new policy, organisations and legislation that previously could not evolve due to imbalances in political and economic power. Nevertheless, the degree to which institutions and organisations change, and the manner in which they change, depends on the influence different stakeholders exercise on policy-making."

[3] See, for instance, Committee of Inquiry into a Comprehensive System of Social Security for South Africa, *Transforming the Present—Protecting the Future*, 2002.

dition, certain social security laws were repealed[1], some amended appropriately[2] and, in some instances, new ones enacted. [3] Furthermore, there are plans to revamp some social security schemes. The Road Accident Fund is the case in point. [4]Individuals, in the form of juristic and natural persons, and NGOs have on a number of occasions successfully approached the courts of law to lobby and compel social security institutions to respect and fulfil the rights, principles and values ingrained in the Constitution. For instance, in *Mashavha v President of the Republic of South Africa and Others*[5] the Constitutional Court confirmed an order of the High Court in *Mashavha v President of the Republic of South Africa and Others*[6] that Presidential Proclamation R7 of 1996, which professed to assign the administration of certain sections of the *Social Assistance Act* 59 of 1992 to provincial governments, is inconsistent with the (interim) Constitution and for that reason invalid. Most recently, the Constitutional Court has found a contract between the South African Social Security Agency and a company contracted (i.e. Cash Paymaster) to pay social grants to be invalid. Accordingly, it ordered that the tender process be re-run. [7]

In spite of the probable role that policy-makers can play as promoters of good public administration, particularly in the field of social security, it should be mentioned that their efforts can at times be hindered by a variety of factors. For instance, the implementation of plans or recommendations devised by policy-makers is habitually a protracted exercise due to official rules and processes. In addition, policy-makers often struggle to speak in one voice due to different vested interests. Individuals and NGOs also have their challenges. For

---

[1] For example, the *Unemployment Insurance Act* 63 of 2001 repealed the *Unemployment Insurance Act* 30 of 1966. The *Social Assistance Act* 13 of 2004 repealed the *Social Assistance Act* 59 of 1992. The objects of the *Social Assistance Act* 13 of 2004 are closely aligned to good administration of the social assistance scheme in South Africa. Section 3 states the objects of the act as follows: "The objects of this Act are to – (a) provide for the administration of social assistance and payment of social grants; (b) make provision for social assistance and to determine the qualification requirements in respect thereof; (c) ensure that minimum norms and standards are prescribed for the delivery of social assistance; and (d) provide for the establishment of an inspectorate for social assistance."

[2] See, for example, *Compensation for Occupational Injuries and Diseases Act* 130 of 1993 as amended by the *Compensation for Occupational Diseases Amendment Act* 61 of 1997.

[3] See, for example, the *South African Social Security Agency Act* 9 of 2004.

[4] See the *Road Accident Fund Benefit Scheme Bill* of 2014.

[5] 2005 (2) SA 476 (CC); 2004 (12) BCLR 1243 (CC).

[6] 2004 (3) BCLR 292 (T).

[7] *Allpay Consolidated Investment Holdings (Pty) Ltd and Others v Chief Executive Officer of the South African Social Security Agency and Others (No 2)* 2014 (6) BCLR 641 (CC); 2014 (4) SA 179 (CC).

example, they are in some instances compelled to approach courts of law in their quest to enforce their rights. While there is nothing wrong with this approach, the problem is that litigation invariably requires financial resources and know-how which is not always readily available to most individuals and NGOs. Another point to be noted is that court decisions have an undesirable tendency of developing social policy in a fragmented fashion.

4. Lessons to Be Learnt from the South African Experience

The South African social security administrative and institutional framework is far from perfect. Nonetheless, there are few lessons that can be learnt from the South African experience. Firstly, the social security administrative and institutional framework of that country draws its inspiration from a Constitution which embodies a number of enforceable fundamental rights (e. g. the right to just administrative action) and state institutions supporting constitutional democracy which are essential for good social security administration. The rights-based approach, which is followed in South Africa, is essential for ensuring that those who administer as well as those who benefit from the social security institutions can be held accountable. Secondly, a rights-based approach on its own is not adequate. It has to be supported by an independent judiciary and autonomous institutions supporting constitutional democracy (such as the Human Rights Commission) that can be approached to enforce rights and monitor compliance and accountability by those responsible for the administration of social security institutions. Furthermore, greater cooperation between social security institutions and NGOs has to be fostered. The point is that NGOs, as part of civil society, serve as a link between the state and its institutions and are a crucial component in efforts to ensure good governance. For this reason, they should be viewed as associates and not opposition in any state's efforts to ensure good social security administration. The quest for good social security administration is an ongoing struggle and requires a concerted effort among all the stakeholders. When all is said and done, the prevalent social, political and economic environment are instrumental in shaping the development of institutions and organisational structures and, thus, cannot be ignored.[①]

[①] Committee of Inquiry into a Comprehensive System of Social Security for South Africa, *Transforming the Present—Protecting the Future*, 2002, p. 119.

5. Conclusion

In conclusion, the importance and relevance of a sound social security administrative and institutional framework should not be underestimated.[1] This is largely due to the fact that social security institutions are crucial for ensuring that social security benefits are properly administered. To make sure that this is done, it is essential that a social security administrative and institutional framework is built on a legislative foundation that clearly spells out the rights and duties of those responsible for administering the system as well as those who benefit from it. The rights-based approach which is outlined in a Constitution as found in South Africa is appropriate. However, as highlighted in the paper, a rights-based approach which is not undergirded by monitoring and enforcement institutions to ensure good governance and accountability is meaningless. At the end of the day, social security institutions cannot monitor and hold themselves accountable. To expect them to fulfil such a role is nothing but a recipe for disaster.

---

[1] See, for example, Ruck S., "Good Governance as the Key to an Effective Social Security Scheme", *ILO SRO-Harare Newsletter*, December, 2006, p. 11.

政府采购对技术创新的影响效应研究

朱春奎　李　燕[①]

一、引言

关于政府采购在创新活动和经济发展中应扮演何种角色的问题上，新古典经济学和演化经济学一直存在着较大分歧。新古典经济学家们普遍认为，自由贸易与自由竞争会促使企业不断创新，提高生产率，降低产品价格，促进经济增长，即创新源于以价格为基础的自由竞争。演化经济学则认为，竞争力并非来源于以价格为基础的自由竞争，而是源于创新，因此有必要将促进创新作为包括政府采购在内的国家政策的主要目标之一。

事实上，利用政府采购促进创新的合理性可以从新兴产业的保护政策中找到依据，类似的政策已经伴随着资本主义走过了五百多年，最远可追溯至文艺复兴时期（Reinert，2007），而且已经被几乎所有的经济学流派及其分支所接受（Evans and Alizadeh，2007）。即使在新古典主义经济学的框架下，市场失灵也为政府运用政府采购介入创新活动提供了依据。

20世纪80年代初，创新政策领域的学者就开始关注政府采购对创新活动的重要促进作用（Rothwell and Zegveld，1981；Rothwell，1984；Geroski，1990），但由于当时的创新政策聚焦于通过增加技术供给来推动创新发展，政府采购在促进创新活动方面的潜能在之后的一段时期内始终未能得到充分挖掘。近年来，随着创新政策范式由供给侧向需求侧的逐渐转变（Edquist and Hommen，1999，2000），创新导向型的政府采购再次进入人们的视野，引发了创新政策学者和政策制定者的广泛关注。

[①] 朱春奎，复旦大学国际关系与公共事务学院教授；李燕，复旦大学国际关系与公共事务学院博士研究生。

政府采购在我国是20世纪90年代中期从国外引进的,自1996年在上海、深圳试行政府采购制度以来,中国政府采购规模迅速扩大,从1998年的31亿元发展到2012年的13978亿元,约占当年GDP的2.7%。随着政府采购规模的不断扩大和创新驱动发展战略的实施,一个亟待回答的问题是,我国的政府采购是否促进了技术创新?而对于这一问题,一直缺乏有说服力的经验研究(胡凯、蔡红英、吴清,2013)。

本文旨在运用2001—2011年的跨省面板数据,对我国政府采购与技术创新之间的关系进行实证研究。本文引言之后的余下部分将做如下安排:第二部分在文献综述基础上,探讨了政府采购对技术创新的影响机理;第三部分建立了计量经济模型,以实证检验中国政府采购的创新影响效应;第四部分展示并简要分析了模型计算结果;第五部分总结了本次研究的主要发现,并提出了相应的政策建议。

二、文献综述与理论探讨

作为一项重要的需求侧创新政策,学者常常使用不同的称谓来描述政府采购在促进创新方面的重要性和潜能,如创新导向型政府采购(innovation-oriented public procurement)(Rotehwell and Zegveld,1981)、创新促进型政府采购(public procurement of innovation)和创新友好型政府采购(innovation-friendly public procurement)(Rolfstam,2012)、创新型政府采购(innovative public procurement)(Edler and Georghiou,2007)、发展型政府采购(developmental public procurement)(Weiss,2013)、政府技术采购(public technology procurement)(Edquist and Hommen,2000)、创新政府采购(public procurement for innovation)(Edler and Georghiou,2007)、远期承诺采购(forward commitment procurement)(UK DBIS,2011)、战略型政府采购(strategic public procurement)(Edler,2010)或启发式政府采购(enlightened public procurement)(Williams and Smellie,1985)。

政府采购促进研究与创新的途径主要有以下五个方面:一是政府采购为创新型服务或产品创造需求,从而激励创新(Schmookler,1966;Rosenberg,1972;Mowery and Rosenberg,1979);二是通过签订购买前商业化创新成果(研发服务)的合同,帮助创新型企业解决其创新型产品和服务的前商业化阶段所面临的问题,促进新产品和服务的成功应用,为企业顺利进入市场提供机遇,降低企业面临的技术风险和市场风险;三是政府采购者以"领先使用者"(lead-user)的身份建立起"先导市场"(lead-market)(von Hippel,1986;Poter,1990;Rolfstam,2012b),为新产品和新服务开拓市场产生示范效应,降低消费者对采用新技术风险的担忧(Georghiou,2007;

Edler et al.,2013);四是政府采购帮助创新型企业降低价格,提升竞争力,加速新产品和服务商业化、扩散和应用(OECD,2011);五是通过与企业签订政府购买合同,使企业更容易地获得第三方的私人投资。

近年来,在欧盟的积极倡导下,政府采购的创新激励效果逐渐引起了世界各国政府的高度重视,并在实践中充分发挥政府采购在促进创新活动方面的潜能。总体来看,关于创新型政府采购政策效果的实证研究为数不多,学者们运用案例分析、多案例比较分析、描述性统计与计量模型等方法围绕以下两个核心问题对创新型政府采购的政策效果进行了分析:一是实践中,政府采购作为一种创新政策,是否真的能够对创新的生产、扩散和应用起到积极的推动作用?二是与其他创新政策相比,政府采购在促进创新活动、增加创新需求的过程中是否存在着比较优势?对于以上两个问题,大部分学者给出了肯定的答案,但对政府采购作用于创新活动的具体方式及其效果则持不同意见(Rothwell and Zegveld,1981;Rothwell,1984;Lichtenberg,1988;Geroski,1990;Edquist and Hommen,2000;Aschoff and Sofka,2009;Rolfstam,2009;Yaslan,2009;Uyarra and Flanagan,2010;Flanagan et al.,2011;Lember et al.,2008;Brammer and Walker,2011;Guerzoni and Raiter,2012)。

在作为整体的需求侧创新政策的政策效果尚不明确的情况下,政府采购对创新活动的实际影响亦仍无定论。事实上,政府采购对创新的促进作用只体现在一小部分案例(主要是在国防领域)中,并由于缺乏明确目标、贸易保护主义与对国内产业巨头的过度支持而极可能被误用;公共需求与私人需求可能互不相同甚至相互冲突,同时服务于公共需求和私人需求的工业企业很可能倾向于专注于公共市场;公共部门也将优先选择那些曾与其有过合作经历的企业签约以保障服务质量或避免转换成本。这些都会降低企业的创新动力,也将对新市场和新应用的进一步拓展产生抑制作用。

中国对政府采购创新激励功能的认识经历了一个从无到有、逐步深化的过程。长期以来,政府采购工作都围绕着提高公共资金使用效率这一核心目标,并将资金节约率作为评价政府采购工作绩效的主要标准,从而忽视了政府采购的创新激励功能。2003 年开始实施的《政府采购法》规定了政府采购应在"保护环境、扶持不发达地区和少数民族地区、促进中小企业发展"等方面发挥积极作用,并以公开招标为主的政府采购方式为企业通过公开竞争扩大其新产品或新服务的公共需求提供了机遇。2006 年,中国政府确立了提升自主创新能力、建设创新型国家的战略目标,并在《国家中长期科学和技术发展规划纲要(2006—2020 年)》及《实施〈规划纲要〉的若干配套政策》中正式提出将政府采购作为推动自主创新的重要政策工具。

有关中国政府采购创新效应的文献以理论分析和政策阐释为主，实证研究则极其缺乏，加之数据来源、变量选择、模型设定与估计方法的差异，导致为数不多的实证研究得出的结论也各不相同。艾冰（2009）运用2001—2005年的时间序列数据，建立灰色关联矩阵模型与多元回归测度政府采购在促进自主创新的主要因素中的重要程度，结果显示，随着政府实际购买水平的提高，自主创新水平也相应提高，政府采购在促进自主创新中具有拉动作用。万启伟（2012）以2010年中国大陆31个省（自治区、直辖市）的截面数据，运用多元线性回归方法，检验政府采购与自主创新的关系，结果表明政府采购规模对提高当地自主创新活动具有积极的促进作用。王亮（2013）以汽车产业为例，运用2000—2010的时间序列数据，分别计算了政府采购活动与汽车工业创新投入、创新产出的皮尔逊相关系数，结果显示政府采购活动的各变量与汽车工业的创新投入、创新产出的各变量之间均呈显著的正相关。然而，胡凯等人（2013）运用2000—2010的省级面板数据建立静态和动态面板模型，研究发现中国的政府采购没有促进技术创新，甚至阻碍了技术创新。

本文拟运用2000—2011年中国大陆30个（除西藏之外）省（自治区、直辖市）的面板数据，建立计量经济学模型，考察中国政府采购对技术创新的影响效应，并探索这一影响效应在不同地区、对不同创新产出的差异情况，以期深化政府采购与技术创新关系的认知。

三、模型设定与变量说明

（一）模型设定

为研究政府采购对技术创新的影响效应及其时间与地区效应，本文以中国大陆30个（剔除西藏）省、自治区、直辖市2001—2011年的面板数据为基础，构建了以下计量模型：

$$Patent_{it} = \beta_1 proc_{it} + \beta_2 x_{it} + \alpha_i + \varepsilon_{it} \tag{1}$$

$$Invention_{it} = \beta_1 proc_{it} + \beta_2 x_{it} + \alpha_i + \varepsilon_{it} \tag{2}$$

$$Utilitymodel_{it} = \beta_1 proc_{it} + \beta_2 x_{it} + \alpha_i + \varepsilon_{it} \tag{3}$$

$$Design_{it} = \beta_1 proc_{it} + \beta_2 x_{it} + \alpha_i + \varepsilon_{it} \tag{4}$$

公式（1）为基本模型，i 和 t 分别表示省份和年份，被解释变量 $patent_{it}$ 表示 i 省在 t 年的技术创新水平，$proc_{it}$ 为模型的解释变量，即 i 省在 t 年的政府采购规模，x_{it} 为一组控制变量，α_i 表示时间上恒定的，无法观测到的影响各省技术创新水平的其他因素，ε_{it} 为随机误差项。模型（2）至（4）中，方程左边的 *invention*、*utilitymodel*、*design* 为被解释变量，分别表示不同类型的创新产出，下文将对此做出详细说明。

以基本模型为基础，本文将样本进行拆分，分别建立对东、中、西部地区模型，以探索不同地区政府采购对技术创新的影响效应。进一步，由于2006年国家正式提出运用政府采购促进自主创新，因此，本文以2006年为分界点，将样本拆分为2001—2006年和2007—2011年两部分，以探究将政府采购正式确立为创新政策工具的前后，政府采购对技术创新的影响影响是否存在差异。

（二）被解释变量

patent 表示各省专利申请数，本文用这一指标表征各省的技术创新水平。技术创新水平的测度，既包括技术创新投入指标，如研发投入等，也包括技术创新产出指标，如专利申请数量及授权数量、新产品销售数量及新产品销售收入等。由于本文旨在研究政府采购对技术创新结果的影响作用，故选取专利申请数量作为技术创新水平的代理变量。之所以选择专利申请量而非专利授权量与新产品指标衡量各地区的技术创新产出水平，一是由于按照中国现行的专利审查制度，从专利的最初申请到最终授权之间存在较长的时延，最长可达三至五年，故不能较为准确地反映出政府采购对技术创新活动的当期影响；二是由于实践中，政府对新产品提供的税收优惠政策，导致一些企业夸大新产品数量及其销售收入，从而造成统计数据失真（宣烨、李光泗，2008），且新产品指标也无法反映出将除企业之外的其他创新主体的创新产出水平。

为进一步探究政府采购对不同水平的技术创新能力的影响，本文将专利申请量划分为发明专利申请量、外观设计专利申请量、实用新型专利申请量三种类型，建立了模型（2）至（4）。其中，发明是指对产品、方法或者其改进所提出的新的技术方案；实用新型是指对产品的形状、构造或者其结合所提出的适于实用的新的技术方案；外观设计是指对产品的形状、图案、色彩或者其结合所做出的富有美感并适于工业上应用的新设计。由此可知，三种创新产出的创新程度依次增高。模型（2）至（4）中，*invention* 表示各省发明专利申请数的对数，*utilitymodel* 表示各省实用新型专利申请数的对数，*design* 表示各省外观设计专利申请数的对数。各专利申请数据来源于历年《中国科技统计年鉴》。

(三) 解释变量

proc 表示各省的政府采购金额,本文使用这一指标来测量各省的政府采购规模。为消除物价水平的影响,本文以 2001 年为基期,利用各地区居民消费价格指数对各省政府采购金额进行了平减。政府采购金额数据来源于《中国政府采购年鉴》。

(四) 控制变量

x 表示一组控制变量,具体包括:

(1) 经济发展水平 (*Pgdp*)。本文用人均 GDP 的对数来衡量各省经济发展水平。所用数据源于历年《中国统计年鉴》。

(2) 创新人力资本 (*Human*)。人力资本是影响地区技术创新能力的重要禀赋,人力资本的丰裕程度决定了技术创新水平的高低。本文用研发人员数量来表征各省的创新人力资本状况。相关数据来自历年《中国科技统计年鉴》。

(3) 创新经费投入强度 (*rd-indensity*)。资金投入是技术创新活动的基础,是影响技术创新水平的要素,强大的资金投入为技术创新活动提供了有力的物质保障。本文使用研发支出占 GDP 的比重来测量各省的创新经费投入强度。相关数据来自历年《中国科技统计年鉴》。

(4) 经济开放度 (*Fdi*)。大量研究证实,一个地区的经济开放程度和吸引外资的能力将直接或间接地影响其技术创新水平。外商直接投资 (FDI) 将通过示范—模仿效应 (Kokko,1992)、竞争效应 (Caves,1971)、联系效应 (林毅夫、平新乔、杨大勇,2000) 与培训效应产生技术溢出,从而对当地的技术创新活动产生影响。因此,本文利用各省外商投资总额占当年全国外商直接投资总额的比重来衡量该省的经济开放度。另外,文本还引入了各省进出口总额占当年全国进出口总额的比重 (*im-export*) 作为 fdi 的替代变量,用以检验模型的稳健性程度。相关数据来源于历年《中国统计年鉴》。

(5) 知识产权保护 (*Ipp*)。知识产权保护通过影响研发资源配置和技术创新主体的激励机制,进而促进或阻碍技术创新活动。本文借鉴胡凯等人 (2012) 的观点,认为一个地区技术市场交易成交额能够在一定程度上反映出该地区的知识产权保护水平,使用各省技术成交额占当地 GDP 的比重来度量各省知识产权保护水平。相关数据来自历年《中国统计年鉴》。

模型中各变量说明和样本描述性统计分别如表 1、表 2 所示。

表 1　模型变量说明

变量类型	变量名称	缩写	变量定义	单位
被解释变量	创新活动水平	$Patent$	各省专利申请受理数	项,取对数
		$Invention$	各省发明专利申请受理数	项,取对数
		$Utilitymodel$	各省实用新型专利申请受理数	项,取对数
		$Design$	各省外观设计专利申请受理数	项,取对数
解释变量	政府采购规模	$Proc$	各省政府实际采购金额,以2001年价格折算	万元,取对数
控制变量	经济发展水平	$Pgdp$	各省人均GDP,以2001年价格折算	元,取对数
	创新人力资本	$Human$	各省R&D研究人员数量	人,取对数
	创新投入强度	$rd-indensity$	各省R&D经费占GDP的比重	%
	经济开放度	Fdi	各省外商投资总额占当年全国外商直接投资总额的比重	%
		$im-export$（替代变量）	各省外贸进出口总额占当年全国进出口总额的比重	%
	知识产权保护	Ipp	各省技术交易成交额占本省GDP的比重	%

表 2　样本描述性统计

变量名称	观测数	均值	标准差	最小值	最大值
$Patent$	330	19094.53	35990.33	124	348381
$Invention$	330	4822.515	8955.293	40	84678
$Utilitymodel$	330	6901.173	10999.38	44	81097
$Design$	330	7370.055	18014.32	30	182606
$Proc$	330	1205163	1458022	11792	8052830
$rd-indensity$	330	1.16097	0.977114	0.14	5.82
Fdi	330	5.058035	6.456036	0.0331538	29.53369
$im-export$	330	3.332271	6.259886	0.025367	35.61646
$Pgdp$	330	18654.23	13872.62	2895	68977.77
Ipp	330	0.766995	1.526122	0.005294	11.63111
$Human$	330	55992.51	60821.3	848	410805

四、实证结果与分析

(一) 模型设定检验与估计方法选择

1. 多重共线性检验

多重共线性是多元回归分析中的常见问题之一,该问题将直接导致方程回归系数估计的标准误差变大,系数估计值的精度降低。直观上看,政府采购规模、经济发展水平、创新人力资本、创新投入强度、经济开放度、知识产权保护之间很可能相互影响,存在相关关系。虽然计量软件会自动剔除完全的多重共线性,但出于研究的严谨性,确保模型设定的正确性,本文首先对模型的多重共线性进行了诊断。由各变量的相关系数可知(见表3),模型存在着近似多重共线性的可能,但不能据此做出定论。应通过计算各解释变量与控制变量的方差膨胀因子,以判断模型是否存在设定偏误。模型中解释变量最大的 VIF 为 6.86(见表4),小于 10 的临界值,可认为该模型并不存在严重的多重共线性。本文将采用逐步回归的方法依次引入各控制变量,不断改进模型,既可避免模型设定出现偏误,又可捕捉每个控制变量对创新活动的可能作用,从而考察政府采购对创新活动的实际影响。

表3　各变量相关系数矩阵

	Proc	human	fdi	rd – indensiy	pgdp	ipp
proc	1					
human	0.6812***	1				
fdi	-0.0188	-0.0481	1			
rd – indensity	0.3221***	0.5889***	0.0234	1		
pgdp	0.704***	0.5397	-0.0769	0.5948	1	
ipp	0.102*	0.3181***	-0.028	0.8447***	0.4241***	1

注:***、**、*分别表示1%、5%、10%的显著性水平。

2. 异方差性与序列相关检验

由于本文使用全国各省的相关数据开展研究,不存在对总体进行随机抽样的情况,所以,本文初步判定使用固定效应模型,模型估计后的 Hausman 检验结果也支持了以上判断。考虑到模型可能存在着异方差性和序列相关,本文对模型进行了异方差性和序列相关检验。修正后的 Wald 组间异方差性检验结果拒绝了"随机误差项具有同方差"的原假设,所以在固定效应模型估计中计算异方差稳健标准误,以解决模型存在的异方差问题。本文使用伍德里奇(Wooldridge, 2002)和德鲁克(Drukker, 2003)的提出的面板数据序列相关检验方法(Wooldrige test),判断模型是否存在自相关问题。结果显示,模型随机误差项之间存在序列相关。

表4 解释变量与控制变量的方差膨胀因子(VIF)

变量	方差膨胀因子(VIF)
rd – indensity	6.86
ipp	4.33
proc	3.45
pgdp	3.09
human	3.06
fdi	1.05
平均 VIF	3.64

当存在异方差性和序列相关时,原有的标准估计方法(剔除平均值方法)将无法产生一致性的估计结果,德里斯科尔和克雷(Driscoll and Kraay, 1998)基于渐进理论提出了一种新的非参数估计方法,该方法放松了截面数量对估计可行性的限制,修正了原有的协方差矩阵估计方法,从而产生了有效克服空间相关性和时间相关性的一致性估计量。蒙特卡罗实验证明,该方法在 T(时间数量)大于 N(截面数量)的情况下更为有效,但只要 T 大于10,即便是在 N 大于 T 的情况下,面对异方差性和序列相关,该方法仍能够产生较为稳健的估计结果。因此,本文借鉴德里斯科尔和克雷(1998)的方法,以保证系数估计的有效性和一致性。

(二)估计结果与分析

如表5所示,随着各控制变量的逐渐引入,政府采购对技术创新的影响效应的方向及其显著性均发生了较大变化。在仅考虑了创新人力资本(human)与经济开放度(fdi)两个控制变量的情况下[列(1)至列(3)],政府采购对技术创新呈现出显著的促进效应,但当逐个控制了经济发展水平(pgdp),创新投入强度(rd – indensity)与知识产权保护(ipp)的影响之后,政府采购(proc)的系数由正值变为负值,且不再显著。因此,从整体上看,政府采购并未对技术创新产生积极的推动作用。

表5 政府采购对技术创新的影响

变量	(1)	(2)	(3)	(4)	(5)	(6)
	\multicolumn{6}{c}{Patent}					
Proc	0.543***	0.439***	0.439***	-0.0613	-0.0648	-0.0651
	(0.0331)	(0.0332)	(0.0338)	(0.0553)	(0.0477)	(0.0473)
Human		0.522***	0.521***	0.00153	-0.196***	-0.173***
		(0.152)	(0.151)	(0.0674)	(0.0578)	(0.0583)
Fdi			-0.00126	0.00278	0.00114	0.00102
			(0.00306)	(0.00183)	(0.00176)	(0.00165)
Pgdp				1.549***	1.374***	1.367***
				(0.175)	(0.146)	(0.143)
rd-indensity					0.743***	0.726***
					(0.0655)	(0.0658)
Ipp						0.0499*
						(0.0291)
常数项	1.576***	-2.283	-2.266	-5.266***	-2.409***	-2.589***
	(0.430)	(1.537)	(1.525)	(0.974)	(0.745)	(0.818)
样本量	330	330	330	330	330	330
R^2	0.658	0.677	0.677	0.829	0.868	0.870

注：括号中为各系数标准误；***、**、* 分别表示1%、5%、10%的显著性水平。

如表6所示，政府采购对于不同类型创新产出的影响效应存在明显差异。具体来看，政府采购对发明专利申请量和外观设计专利申请量并没有产生正向的推动作用，政府采购对实用新型专利申请量则呈现出显著的负效应，即在5%的显著性水平上，政府采购规模扩大1%，实用新型专利申请量就减少0.0075%。因此，对不同创新程度的创新活动而言，政府采购对发明类创新活动和外观设计类创新活动均未起到正向的激励作用，且对实用新型类创新活动产生了显著的抑制作用。

表6 政府采购对技术创新的影响：对不同创新产出影响的差异

变量	(1) Invention	(2) Utilitymodel	(3) Design
Proc	−0.0407 (0.0810)	−0.0775** (0.0441)	−0.0903 (0.0376)
Human	−0.0312 (0.182)	−0.463*** (0.0622)	0.120 (0.0831)
Fdi	−0.000231 (0.00331)	0.00131 (0.00214)	0.000259 (0.00167)
Pgdp	1.576*** (0.150)	1.322*** (0.169)	1.269*** (0.143)
rd-indensity	0.778*** (0.0796)	0.870*** (0.0692)	0.592*** (0.119)
Ipp	0.0281 (0.0261)	−0.000587 (0.0302)	0.0382 (0.0410)
常数项	−7.767*** (0.614)	−0.0569 (0.732)	−5.407*** (1.412)
样本量	330	330	330
R^2	0.902	0.854	0.607

注：括号中为各系数标准误；***、**、*分别表示1%、5%、10%的显著性水平。

为探究不同地区中，政府采购对技术创新的影响效应有何不同，我们将样本划分为东部、中部、西部三个部分进行回归。估计结果表明［见表7中第(1)至(3)列］，政府采购对不同地区技术创新活动的影响作用各不相同。政府采购对东部地区的技术创新活动具有明显的抑制作用，即在5%的显著性水平上，政府采购规模扩大1%，东部地区的专利申请量就降低0.135%；政府采购对中部地区的技术创新活动呈现出并不显著的激励作用；而政府采购对西部地区的技术创新活动则未表现出显著的影响效应。

以2006年为分界点的分阶段回归结果显示［见表7中第(4)(5)列］，将政府采购正式确立为创新政策工具的前后，政府采购对技术创新的影响影响存在较大差异。在将政府采购确立为创新政策工具之前(2001—2006)，政府采购并没有显著地影响技术创新活动，而在将政府采购确立为创新政策工具之后(2007—2011)，政府采购却对技术创新活动产生了显著的抑制作用，即在1%的显著性水平上，政府采购规模扩大1%，专利申请数量就降低0.105%。

表7 政府采购对技术创新的影响：东、中、西部的地区比较与分阶段比较

变量	(1) 东部地区	(2) 中部地区	(3) 西部地区	(4) 2001—2006	(5) 2007—2011
Proc	-0.135** (0.0546)	0.0712 (0.0938)	-0.0665 (0.0401)	0.0623 (0.0421)	-0.105*** (0.0208)
Human	0.00168 (0.0347)	-0.415 (0.254)	-0.443*** (0.0413)	-0.0905 (0.0726)	0.0289 (0.0460)
Fdi	-0.00260 (0.00338)	-0.00179 (0.00240)	0.00501 (0.00418)	$-3.75e-05$ (0.00153)	0.000260 (0.00105)
Pgdp	1.347*** (0.120)	1.226*** (0.192)	1.507*** (0.122)	0.622*** (0.0504)	0.391*** (0.0351)
Ipp	-0.00678 (0.0238)	0.520 (0.353)	0.139*** (0.0400)	0.841*** (0.119)	1.856*** (0.0492)
rd-indensity	0.909*** (0.0923)	0.973*** (0.208)	-0.0637 (0.0542)	-0.0355* (0.0183)	0.0999*** (0.0329)
常数项	-3.469*** (0.553)	-0.455 (2.575)	-1.147* (0.606)	0.0204 (0.306)	-8.554*** (1.032)
样本量	121	88	121	180	150
R^2	0.935	0.874	0.863	0.792	0.83

注：括号中为各系数标准误；＊＊＊、＊＊、＊分别表示1％、5％、10％的显著性水平。

（三）模型稳健性检验

为确保实证结果的稳定性和研究结论的可靠性，本文同时使用变量替换的方法对基本模型进行稳健性检验。我们使用各省外贸进出口总额占当年全国进出口总额的比重（$im-export$）作为各省经济开放度的代理变量，替换原基本模型中的各省外商投资总额占当年全国外商直接投资总额的比重（fdi）。稳健性检验的结果如表8所示，政府采购规模（$proc$）系数的方向和显著性与原模型估计结果保持一致，表明实证结果并未随着参数设定的改变而发生变化，模型具有较好的稳健性。

表8 模型稳健性检验

变量	(1)	(2)	(3)
	Patent		
Proc	-0.0599	-0.0640	-0.0644
	(0.0563)	(0.0485)	(0.0481)
Human	-0.00118	-0.197***	-0.174***
	(0.0691)	(0.0579)	(0.0583)
Im-export	0.00258	0.000836	0.000792
	(0.00204)	(0.00170)	(0.00161)
rd-indensity		0.743***	0.726***
		(0.0658)	(0.0660)
Pgdp	1.547***	1.372***	1.366***
	(0.177)	(0.148)	(0.145)
Ipp			0.0502*
			(0.0290)
常数项	-5.236***	-2.392***	-2.576***
	(0.980)	(0.753)	(0.826)
样本量	330	330	330
R^2	0.829	0.869	0.87

注：括号中为各系数标准误；***、**、*分别表示1%、5%、10%的显著性水平。

五、结论与建议

本文运用2000—2011年的省际面板数据，建立计量经济学模型，检验了中国政府采购对技术创新的影响效应。结果表明，政府采购并没有对技术创新产生积极的推动作用：对不同创新类型的创新活动而言，政府采购对发明类创新活动和外观设计类创新活动均未起到正向的激励作用，对实用新型类创新活动则产生了显著的抑制作用；就不同地区而言，政府采购并未对中、西部地区的技术创新活动产生显著的影响作用，对东部地区的技术创新活动则表现出明显的抑制作用；2006年将政府采购确立为创新政策工具之后，政府采购不但没有发挥其应有的创新激励效应，反而阻碍了技术创新活动。

长期以来，中国政府采购的政策取向主要侧重于节约资金、预防腐败等方面，没有体现通过政府采购强化对企业创新活动支持的政策取向；政府采购对普通货物与创新产品基本上是不加区别的,未能给市场化初期的创新产品创造一个强大的需求市场;政府采购的创新激励功能尚未得到法律法规的确认;缺乏一个公平、公开、公正的市场竞争环境,政府部门常常倾向于优先选择那些曾与其有过合作经历的企业签约以保障服务质量或避免转换成本,政府采购过程中普遍存在着地方保护主义现象。所有这些问题的存在,使得政府采购对创新活动的支持和拉动作用十分有限。要强化政府采购对技术创新活动的支持与激励功能就必须解决这些问题。

我国已启动加入《政府采购协议》谈判,面临发达国家高技术产品进军国内政府采购市场的压力。减缓这一冲击,就需要强化政府采购支持企业创新的政策取向,通过立法建立有别于传统政府采购的创新型(或创新导向型)政府采购制度;丰富政府采购支持企业创新活动的工具选择,形成创新导向型政府采购的政策支撑体系;扩大政府采购规模,加大对技术创新产品的倾斜,为自主创新产品开拓市场需求;引入竞争机制,努力营造一个公平、公开、公正的市场竞争环境;根据技术/产品/市场的生命周期的不同阶段,适时调整政府采购政策,保证政府采购促进自主创新的有效性。

[1] Aschhoff, B. and Sofka, W., "Innovation on Demand-Can Public Procurement Drive Market Success of Innovations?", *Research Policy*, 41, 2009, pp. 1757 – 1769.

[2] Cabral, L., Cozzl, G., Denicolo, V., Spagnolo, G. and M. Zanza, "Procuring Innovations", in N. Dimitri, G. Piga and G. Spagnolo (eds.), *Handbook of Procurement*, Cambridge University Press, 2006.

[3] Caves, R. E., "International Corporations: The Industrial Economics of Foreign Investment", *Economics*, 38 (141), 1971, pp. 1 – 27.

[4] Chen Jin and Cheng Chunzi, "The Legislation of Public Procurement Policy for Innovation in China", in Lember V. et al. (eds.), *Public Procurement, Innovation and Policy*, Springer – Verlag Berlin Heidelberg, 2013, pp. 93 – 108.

[5] Dalpé, R., "Effects of Government Procurement on Industrial Innovation", *Technology in Society*, 16 (1), 1994, pp. 65 – 83.

[6] Drukker, D. M., "Testing for Serial Correlation in Linear Panel-data Models", *Stata Journal*, (3)2, 2003, pp. 168 – 177

[7] Driscoll, J. C. and A. C. Kraay, "Consistent Covariance Matrix Estimation with Spatially Dependent Panel Data. Review of Economics and Statistics", 80 (4), 1998, pp. 549 – 560.

[8] Edquist, C. and Hommen, L., "System of Innovation: Theory and Policy for Demand Side", *Technology in Society*, 21, 1999, pp. 63 – 79.

[9] Edquist, C. and Hommen, L., "Public Technology Procurement and Innovation Theory", in Edquist, C., Hommen, L. and Tsipouri, L. (eds.), *Public Technology Procurement and Innovation. Economics of Science, Technology and Innovation*, Kluwer Academic Publishers, Vol. 16, 2000, pp. 5 – 70.

[10] Edquist, C. and Zabala-Iturriagagoitia, J. M., "Public Procurement for Innovation as Mission-oriented Innovation Policy", *Research Policy*, 41 (10), 2012, pp. 1757 – 1769.

[11] Edler, J. and Georghiou, L., "Public Procurement and Innovation-Resurrecting the Demand Side", *Research Policy*, 36 (7), 2007 pp. 949 – 963.

[12] Edler, J., "Demand Oriented Innovation Policy", in Smits R., Kuhlmann S. and Shapira P. (eds.), *The Theory and Practice of Innovation Policy: An International Research Handbook*, Cheltenham: Edward Elgar, pp. 275 – 301.

[13] Edler, J. et al., "Impacts of Innovation Policy: Synthesis and Conclusions", Compendium of Evidence on the Effectiveness of Innovation Policy Intervention Project, 2013.

[14] Geroski, P. A., "Procurement Policy as a Tool of Industrial Policy", *International Review of Applied Economics*, 4 (2), 1990, pp. 182 – 198.

[15] Guerzoni, Marco and Raiteri, E., 'Innovative Public Procurement and R&D Subsidies: Hidden Treatment and New Empirical Evidence on the Technology Policy Mix in a Quasi-experimental Setting", Working paper, Department of Economics "Cognetti de Martiis", University of Turin.

[16] Gregersen, B., "The Public Sector as a Pacer in National Systems of Innovation", in Lundvall, B. A. (ed.), *National Systems of Innovation. Towards a Theory of Innovation and Interactive Learning*, London, pp. 129 – 145.

[17] Kokko, A., "Foreign Direct Investment, Host Country Characteristics and Spillovers", The Economic Research Institute, Stockholm, 1992.

[18] Lichtenberg, F. R., "The Private R and D Investment Response to Federal Design and Technical Competitions", *The American Economic Review*, 78 (3), 1988, pp. 550 – 559.

[19] Lundvall, B. A., "Innovation as an Interactive Process: From User-Producer Interaction to the National System of Innovation", in Dosi, G., Freeman, C., Nelson, R., Silverberg, G. and Soete, L. (eds.), *Technical Change and Economic Theory*, Pinter, London, 1988, pp: 349 – 369.

[20] Moors, E., Enzing, C., van der Giessen, A. and Smits, R., "User-producer Interactions in Functional Genomics Innovations. Innovation Management", *Policy & Practice*, 5, 2003, pp. 2 – 3.

[21] OECD, "Demand-side Innovation Policies: Theory and Practice in OECD Countries", in *Demand-side Innovation Policies*, Paris: OECD Publishing, 2011, http://dx.doi.org/10.1787/9789264098886-en.

[22] Porter, M. E., *The Competitive Advantage of Nations*, Macmillan, London and Basingstoke, 1990.

[23] Rolfstam, M., "Understanding Public Procurement of Innovation: Definitions, Innovation Types and Interaction Modes", available at SSRN, http://ssrn.com/abstract=2011488, 2012.

[24] Rosenberg, N., "Factors Affecting the Diffusion of Technology", *Explorations in Economic History*, 10 (1), 1972, pp. 3 – 33.

[25] Rothwell, R., "Technology Based Small Firms and Regional Innovation Potential: the Role of

Public Procurement", *Journal of Public Policy*, 4 (4), 1984, pp. 307 – 332.

[26] Smits, R., "Innovation Studies in the 21st Century, Questions from a User's Perspective", *Technological Forecasting and Social Change*, 69, 2002, pp. 861 – 883.

[27] Schmookler, J., *Innovation and Economic Growth*, Cambridge, MA: Harvard University Press, 1966.

[28] Slavtchev, V. and Wiederhold, S., "Government Demand Composition and Innovative Behavior in Industries", Ifo Working Paper, 35, 2011.

[29] Uyarra, E. and Flanagan, K., "Understanding the Innovation Impacts of Public Procurement", Manchester Business School Working Paper, 2009.

[30] Von, Hippel, E., "Lead Users: A Source of Novel Product Concepts", *Management Science*, 32 (7), 1986, pp. 791 – 805.

[31] Weiss, L., "US Technology Procurement in the National Security Innovation System", in Lember V. et al. (eds.), *Public Procurement, Innovation and Policy*, Berlin Heidelberg: Springer – Verlag, 1986, pp. 259 – 283.

[31] Williams, R. and Smellie, R., "Public Purchasing: An Administrative Cinderella", *Public Administration*, 63 (1), 1985, pp. 23 – 29.

[32] Wooldridge, J. M., *Econometric Analysis of Cross Section and Panel Data*, Cambridge, MA: MIT Press, 2002.

[33] Yasla, "Public Software Procurement and Its Impacts on the Technological Capability and the Competitive Advantage of the Software Industry", unpublished PhD t[34]hesis, Manchester Business School, University of Manchester, 2009. Cited in Uyarra, E. and Flanagan, K., "Understanding the Innovation Impacts of Public Procurement", Manchester Business School Working Paper, 2009.

[35] 艾冰:《政府采购促进自主创新的关系及效果研究》,中南大学博士学位论文,2009年。

[36] 林毅夫、平新乔、杨大勇:《可口可乐罐装系统对中国经济的影响》,北京大学中国经济研究中心讨论稿,No. C2000001,2000。

[37] 吴静、周曼、白志远:《政府采购扶持自主创新研究文献综述》,《中国政府采购》2011年第4期,第75—78页。

[38] 王宏、郑上福:《基于省际面板数据分析的政府采购与技术创新关系研究》,《湖南财政经济学院学报》2011年第5期,第82—85页。

[39] 万启伟:《政府采购与自主创新的实证研究》,西南交通大学硕士论文,2012年。

[40] 王春晖、李平:《政府扶持企业技术创新的政策效应分析》,《科技进步与对策》,2012年第2期,第106—109页。

[41] 胡凯、蔡红英、吴清:《中国的政府采购促进了技术创新吗?》,《财经研究》2013年第

9期,第134—144页。

［42］沈木珠、徐升权:《促进技术创新的政府采购政策研究》,《中国政府采购》2006年第1期,第24—26页。

［43］王亮:《我国汽车产业技术创新与政府采购关系研究》,《经营管理者》2013年第13期,第147—148页。

［44］宣烨、李光泗:《FDI对国内企业技术创新影响的实证研究》,《中南财经政法大学学报》2008年第3期,第108—114页。

中国公务人员工资水平地区差异的政治经济学*

张 光　游 宇**

一、导论

自改革开放以来，中国尽管取得了高速的经济增长，从低收入国家变为中等收入国家，但也付出了收入分配不平等的代价。这一点，甚至表现在政府公务人员工资的地区分布上。2012年，公务人员工资收入最高的上海（人均90622元）比收入最低的山西（人均32672元）高了1.77倍。而在1995年，工资最高的上海（人均9005元）比最低的贵州（人均4161元）仅高了1.16倍。在1980年，公务人员平均工资最高为青海的1097元，最低的是四川的772元，前者仅比后者高了42%（国家统计局，2013，1996，1987）。那么，究竟是什么因素决定公务人员工资在中国地区之间的差距，为什么在有的地区工资增长得更快，有的地区增长得较慢？显然，这是一个典型的政治分配问题。借用拉斯韦尔（Lasswell, 1950）的经典命题来表述：公务人员在何地、何时以何种方式获得多少工资收入。这个问题因为公务人员的工资完全来自于依靠国家权力从社会强制征收的收入，从而具有高度的政治和道德敏感性，这一点在中国的两会期间体现的尤其明显。

然而，学术界却并未对这一重要的公共行政问题提供丰富且有分量的研究。正如李应芳（Fang Lee Cooke）教授对中国公共部门工资问题的回顾性研究所言：尽管中国的公共部门在定性与定量研究中均具有无可争议的重要性，但那些能够增进我们对于其工资政策、实践及由于向市场经济转型而导致的变迁的研究仍然是不足的（Cooke, 2004: 895）。尽管如此，基于定性访谈资料或统计数据形成的实证研究与相

---

* 本文系由"厦门大学繁荣哲学社会科学项目"资助。
** 张光，厦门大学公共事务学院教授，中山大学中国公共管理研究中心研究员，三亚学院教授。游宇，西南财经大学公共管理学院讲师。

关的政策分析（如 Chew，1990a，1990b；Chan and Suizhou，2007）依然为我们积累了重要的研究成果。比如，李应芳（Cooke，2004）运用其与中国学术界友人等访谈资料对于国家所驱动的公共部门改革进行了分析；吴木銮（2009，2011）从中国分权下的集权与政策执行中的目标扭曲等视角对公务员的工资政策改革及其执行效果进行了分析；就"高薪养廉"的争论，公婷与吴木銮（Gong and Wu，2012）的分析结果则表明，本世纪初以来，我国公务员薪酬水平较快上升与腐败程度的加深是同时发生的，而公务员薪酬和廉政建设有着复杂的关系；陈汉宣与马骏的研究（Chan and Ma，2011）则利用相关年鉴数据并对比其他国家分析了中国的公务员收入水平，并回答了社会与学术界均较为关心的问题——中国公务员的收入到底是高还是低：在相对于其他社会部门的中下层次的工资收入与较高的福利、补贴等隐性或非工资收入（non-wage pay）并存的情况下，中国公务员收入并不低。然而既有的研究大多或依靠历史叙述，或借助国际比较理论论述工资政策，或相对于其他行业分析公务人员工资水平，鲜有论者就我国公务人员工资水平地区差异的决定因素进行实证研究。本文意欲填补这个空白。本文结构为：除导论外，本文的第二部分主要论述一个可行的理论分析框架；第三部分则梳理新中国成立以来主要的工资政策；第四部分则根据理论框架与相关分析，论述变量设置与研究假设；第五部分是实证发现与讨论；最后部分为结论。

二、解释公务人员工资水平的地区间差异：一个理论框架

大量的研究表明，在现代社会中，劳动者之间的收入和工资水平差异主要是由市场（或经济）因素和政治因素共同决定的（Beramendi and Cusack，2009；Erickson and Ichino，1995；Soskice，1990）。这一点也应适用于国家公务人员的工资水平及其差异。不过，作为一个直接依靠国家财政资金获得工资收入的职业，公务人员的工资水平对政治因素的依赖程度，应当显著高于不直接依靠财政的职业，如制造业、建筑业，等等。

一般而言，工资水平的市场决定机制主要是通过对劳动力的供求关系完成的。理论上，当欲进入一门职业的劳动者越多时，即劳动者供给越多时，其工资水平即下降；而当一门职业需要的劳动者越多时，即雇佣者对劳动者的需求越大时，其工资水平上升。关于工资的跨地区差异的决定因素，各地的经济发展水平是一个重要的市场性决定变量。经济发展水平高，通常意味着对劳动力有较高的需求且劳动者面对的生活成本也越大，从而推高工资水平。既有的研究还发现，与市场接触程度越强的地方，其工资水平越高。这是因为，企业在与市场接触容易的地方投资经营，流通成本

较低，利润较高，因此，能够聚集较多的企业，从而产生较高的雇佣需求，推高该地的工资水平（Hering and Poncet，2010）。

而对于公务人员这一处于高度"计划"内的群体，其供求关系在很大程度上则是由政府主导。正如经典的公共选择理论文献所论述的那样，作为理性经济人，官僚们的目标在于追求预算规模的最大化与政府规模的扩张（Niskanen，1971；Brennan and Buchanan，1980）。然而在现代社会中，政府"利维坦"式的扩张倾向却不得不受到诸多经济因素与公共舆论的制约。就影响公务人员工资水平的地区差异而言，经济因素的影响主要体现在为各地区"设定"了一定的经济基本面，并以此制约着政府行为。首先是经济发展水平。作为最主要的财政供养人口，公务人员工资归根到底来自于不断变动中的经济体，政府从中汲取财政收入以维持基本运转；可以预期的是，经济发展水平越高，经济总量增长越快，则对于政府增加公务人员工资收入的制约就相对越小。同时，经济发展水平增加了对劳动力数量与技能的需求，其中也理应包含公共事务劳动者的增加，从而推高公务人员的工资水平。其次则是与经济发展水平紧密相关的生活成本。通常情况下，劳动人员的雇佣合同、养老金以及政府津贴等均会于地区差异明显地生活成本指数（cost-of-living index）挂钩（比如最为普遍的消费者价格指数等）（Boskin，etc.，1998；Boskin，2008）。实际上，根据各地区的生活成本指数，相应的生活成本津补贴每年都在调整各类群体的工资水平，这对于公务人员也不例外。此外，在市场经济条件下，如果将蒂伯特（Tiebout，1956）"用脚投票"的理论由"选民"推广到"资本"，则相对自由流动的资本会挑选的是那些能够满足自身需求的环境，这反过来会影响着政府的绩效。而各地区公务人员的工资实则构成政府运行成本的主体，最终由来自社会的税收买单，因此其运营成本的高低与效率也需要回应对于资本的竞争。当然，由于城镇化水平以及产业结构等"内嵌"于各地区的经济生态之中，也可能是各地区工资水平的潜在影响因素。

相对于经济因素而言，政治因素对于地区间公务人员工资水平的影响则更为直接，其中又以政府间关系最为重要。为简化推理起见，我们设想只存在中央和地方两级政府。理论上看，一国各地的公务人员工资水平决定机制无非有三种模式：（1）完全由中央政府决定；（2）完全由各地方政府自行决定；（3）中央政府和地方政府共同决定。实行中央计划经济的国家（如苏联和改革开放前的中国）接近于第一种模式，高度分权的联邦制国家（如美国）接近于第三种模式。然而，毫无疑问，大多数国家，包括改革开放后的中国都属于第二种模式。中央政府对各地工资水平的控制可以有政策规制和财政拨款两大类手段。在高度中央集权的计划经济条件下，中央政府不仅规定公务人员（通常还有企业职工）的工资级别和地区分类（生活成本较高的地方享受较高待遇的地区补贴系数），而且各地公务人员的工资悉数来自中央政府的财政拨款。在中央政府和地方政府共同决定的模式那里，前者仍然可以采用政策规制和财政拨款两个手段来影响公务人员的工资水平及其地区差异（这里的财政拨款通常被称作转移支付）。同理，在第二种和第三种模式下，地方政府用于影响其雇员的工资水平的手段也有政策规制和财政拨款两类，但毫无疑问以后者更为重要。一般而言，地方掌握的财力越大（而这又可能取决于地方经济发展水平和地方政府的税收能力），其公务人员的工资水平越高。

综上所述，一国内部各地公务人员的工资水平及其差异，就是在政治（从政府间关系角度看就是中央和地方政府）和该国各地的经济基本面的制约和回应的互动过程中，在中央与地方政府使用政策规制、财政拨款（包括转移支付）等手段博弈互动过程中实现的。图1展现了这些要素之间的互动关系。

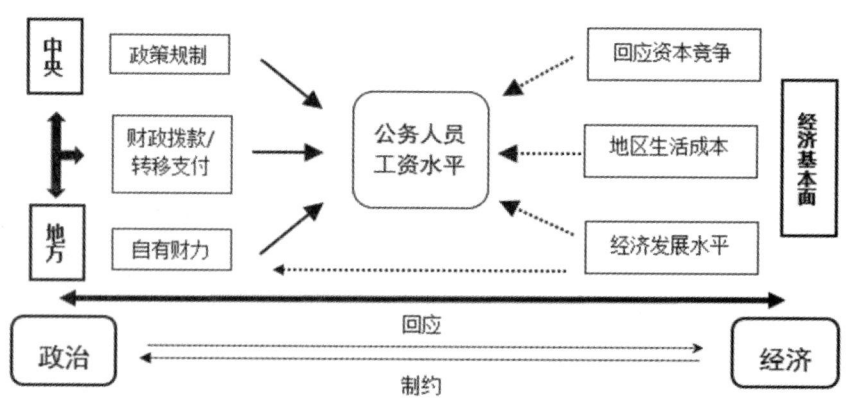

图1　公务人员工资水平地区差异：理论框架

注：实线箭头表示直接影响，虚线箭头表示间接影响。
资料来源：作者自制。

三、中国公务人员的工资水平：政策变迁概述

新中国成立以来，中国始终是一个单一制国家。各级国家公务人员工资定级和政策调整的大权，一直由中央政府牢牢地把握着。但改革开放之前和之后有极大的区别。改革开放之前，中国的经济基本面是一个计划经济体制，地方政府完全是中央的执行者。中央制定全国统一的工资级别，并在高度平均主义的观念之下划定同级工资的地区差异，并依靠统收统支的财政体制，向各地的工资支出提供财政拨款。

具体来看，新中国成立初期到1956年，中国曾短期实行了"供给制"与"工资制"的双轨制度。1955年8月正式颁布的《国家机关工作人员全部实行工资制和改行货币工资制的命令》决定废除供给制，推行工资制改革（国务院，1955）。这一改革于次年正式实施。行政干部工资分为30级；并基于生活水平和成本差异等因素把

全国分为11类地区，1类地区多位于西南省份，11类则多在西北地区，同级官员的工资在第11类地区比第1类地区高30%（石剑、吴质，1993；Wu，2010）。行政干部的升级，按照1956年的政策规定，有定期和不定期两种。前者每年定期评级一次，且因职务提升后做相应的调整。然而，1956年制定的工资制度，因国家政治动荡未能实施。每年定期评级升级的规定完全落空。而不定期升级从1957到1977年于全国职工总共只有四次，升级面累计只有90%左右，平均每名职工不到一级。而在同一时期，国家机关工作人员的升级只有三次（石剑、吴质，1993：213）。改革前中国公务人员的工资水平不但长期保持低水平，而且地区差异极小，几乎完全由中央决定的工资地区类别决定。

改革开放后，中国在经济基本面逐步引入了市场经济体制，在政府间关系上引入地方分权要素，形成了公务人员的工资水平及其地区差距由中央政府、地方政府和市场经济因素共同决定的局面。但同其他大多数行业相比，公务人员的工资水平是受到国家特别是中央政府控制最严的部门。这一点，最清晰地表现为中央政府始终是全国统一的公务人员工资制度的制定者和决定者。同改革开放前一样，中央政府决定所有公务人员的工资职务级别分类，决定全国性的调资升级时间。然而，同改革开放前不一样的是改革后中央政府引入结构工资制度，逐渐给予各地方政府决定本地公务人员工资水平的部分权力。1985年颁布的《国家机关和事业单位工作人员工资制度改革方案》（国务院，1985），首次引入了以职务工资为主要内容的结构工资制。结构工资分为基础工资、职务工资、工龄工资和奖励工资四个部分。在这四个部分中，除了少数的例外（如经济特区），前三者基本没地区差别，而奖励工资部分，原则上是用于奖励工作绩效较好的员工，其资金来自于所在单位行政经费的节余。因此，这部分的工资收入可以因公务人员所在单位和地区的不同而不同，尽管差异不可能很大。此外，1985年的工资改革仍然沿用了之前的工资地区分类方法。同改革前相比，这次工资改革所造成的公务人员工资地区差异仍然是很有限的（见图2）。

1993年颁布的《国家公务员暂行条例》对公务人员工资结构做了重大的改变。除了全国统一的职务工资、级别工资、基础工资和工龄工资外，增加了地区津贴和其他津贴的内容。2006年实施的《国家公务员法》在第七十四条"公务员工资结构"中重申，"公务员工资包括基本工资、津贴、补贴和奖金"。津贴包括"地区附加津贴、艰苦边远地区津贴、岗位津贴等"，补贴则包括"住房、医疗等补贴、补助"。从1993年起，每个公务人员工资包含了全国统一的基本工资和因地而异的津补贴。公务人员工资从此进入了地区差异不断扩张的时代（见图2）。

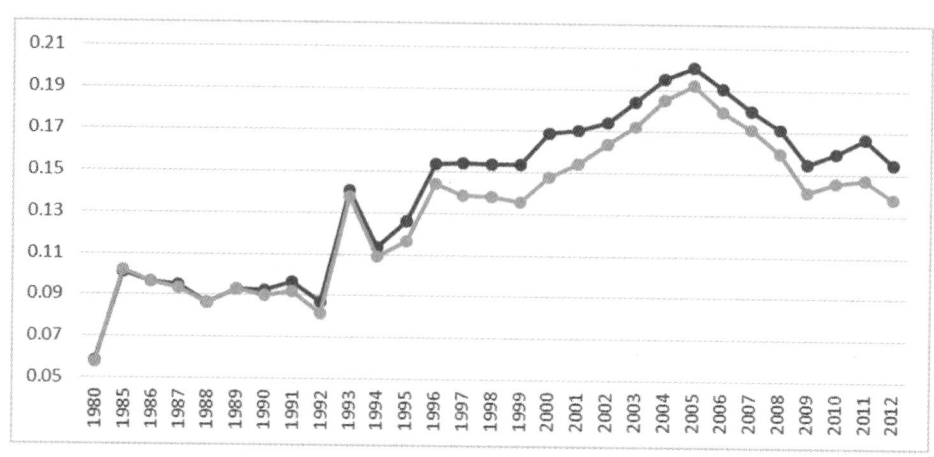

图2 各地区公务人员平均工资基尼系数（1980—2012）

注：1980—2008年数据根据公务人员职工平均工资计算，2008年之后数据根据公务员就业人员平均工资计算，这不影响地区之间公务人员收入差距的比较；基尼系数根据 Wessa（2014）计算。由于海南省与重庆市没有成为省级行政单位，1980—1987年的分组为29组；1988—1996则未包括重庆，故相应分为30组，其中1993年云南的数据缺失，1997年及其后的数据均分为31组。

资料来源：国家统计局（1987）；国家统计局（1989—2013）。

上述公务人员工资结构变化，工资水平地区差异扩大，是在改革开放后经济基本面逐步市场化、地方分权渐成气候的大背景下发生的。20世纪80年代的经济改革是按照增量先动存量后动、做大前者冻结后者的渐进主义方式进行的，学者诺顿（Naughton，1996）把这一过程形象地概括为"通过增长走出计划"（growing out of the plan）。经济改革大大地改善了受计划经济约束较少的非公有制部门的收入水平。到了80年代末期，出现了"造导弹不如卖茶叶蛋、拿手术刀不如拿剃头刀"的现象。而被赋予一定的经营自主权的国有企业部门的职工平均工资，到80年代后期，大体上比国家机关人员高10%左右，而在1977年机关职工平均工资为全民所有制职工平均工资的105.5%（石剑、吴质，1993：301）。在1985年之前，中央对公务人员的调资政策通常是作为对全国职工的统一调资政策的一部分做出的，而从这一年开始，中央开始不定期地出台并实施专门针对调整公务人员以及事业单位人员工资结构和普调工资水平的政策。1993年的《国家公务员暂行条例》确定"国家根据国民经济的发展和生活费用价格指数的变动，有计划地提高国家公务员的工资标准，使国家公务员的实际工资水平不断提高"（第十七条）；"国家公务员工资水平与国有企业相当人员的平均工资水平大体持平"（第十六条）。2004年《中共中央国务院关于进一步加强人才工作的决定》再次指出，要"建立公务员工资与国民经济发展相协调、与社会进步相适应、与企业相当人员平均工资大体持平的工资水平决定机制"（参见表1）。

表1 改革开放以来历次公务员以及事业单位人员工资结构与工资普调政策

调整时间	内 容	中央补贴地方方式
1985年6月	国务院颁布《国家机关和事业单位工作人员工资制度改革方案》,开始实施以职务工资为主要内容的结构工资制。结构工资分为基础工资、职务工资、工龄工资和奖励工资四个部分。此次改革使公务人员工资普遍有所增加。	不详
1989年	国家机关和事业单位工作人员普调一级工资。	不详
1993年10月1日	《国家公务员暂行条例》正式实施,公务员工资分为四个部分:职务工资、级别工资、基础工资、工龄工资,这次工资制度改革同时确定机关与企业、事业单位实行不同的工资制度。机关工作人员的平均工资水平与企业相当人员的平均工资水平大体持平。	不详
1997年7月1日	机关行政人员基础工资标准由每人每月90元提高到110元。机关新录用人员的试用工资相应提高:大学本科生由每月70元提高到225元;硕士生由每月97元提高到260元;博士生由每月105元提高到290元。	不详
1999年7月	将基础工资标准由每人每月110元提高到180元,级别工资标准由15级至1级每月55元至470元提高到85元至720元。 调资标准:在职,120元/人/月;离休,165元/人/月;退休,96元/人/月。	根据人员经费和公用经费占可支配财力的比重在60%—100%之间的地区分四个档,补助系数分别为0.6、0.65、0.7、0.75;民族地区调增5个百分点;天津市、辽宁省属于财政困难的老工业基地,云南省属于中西部地区和民族地区,参照其人均GDP水平确定三地补助系数分别为0.3、0.4、0.5。
2001年1月1日	基础工资标准由每人每月180元提高到230元,级别工资标准由15级至1级每人月85元至720元,提高到115元至1166元。 调资标准:在职,100元/人/月;离休,128元/人/月;退休,100元/人/月。	沿用1999年调整工资系数。
2001年10月1日	再次提高机关、事业单位工作人员工资标准,人均月工资增加80元,增幅为15%。主要体现在"职务工资"上,由原来的50元至480元提高到100元至850元。 调资标准:在职,80元/人/月;离休,120元/人/月;退休,80元/人/月。	除北京市、天津市、辽宁省、上海市、江苏省、浙江省、福建省、山东省、广东省外,其余予以全额补助。2002年起辽宁省(不含沈阳市、大连市)、山东省(不含济南市、青岛市)按照20%予以补助。

(续表)

调整时间	内容	中央补贴地方方式
2003年7月	颁布实施《关于调整机关工作人员工资标准的实施方案》《关于调整事业单位工作人员工资标准的实施方案》《关于增加机关事业单位离退休人员离退休费的实施方案》，将职务工资由原来的100元至850元提高到130元至1150元。 调资标准：在职，50元/人/月；离休，80元/人/月；退休，50元/人/月。	除北京市、天津市、上海市、江苏省、浙江省、福建省、广东省、沈阳市、大连市、济南市、青岛市自行负担，辽宁省（不含沈阳市、大连市）、山东省（不含济南市、青岛市）补助40%外，其余地区全额补助。
2006年7月1日	《国务院关于改革公务员工资制度的通知》出台，基础工资和工龄工资不再保留，级别工资的权重有所加大。公务员工资级别从原来的15级调整为27级。公务员考核称职，每两年可在所任职务对应的级别内升一个工资档，每五年升一个工资级别。 调资标准：在职，300元/人/月；离休，450元/人/月；退休，270元/人/月。	除北京市、天津市、上海市、江苏省、浙江省、福建省、广东省、沈阳市、大连市、济南市、青岛市、福州市、厦门市自行负担，辽宁省（不含沈阳市、大连市）、山东省（不含济南市、青岛市）、福建省（不含福州市、厦门市）补助40%外，其余地区全额补助。

资料来源：李萍（2010）；石剑、吴质（1993）；吴木銮（2009）；易强、郭威（2006）；贺军（2011）。

改革开放以来的央地关系调整特别是地方财政分权的进展，对公务人员工资结构和水平调整，尤其是工资水平的地区差异，产生了深刻的影响。改革开放前的统收统支体制，决定地方政府没有任何制度化的财政和经济政策自主权，完全是中央政府的代理人，尽管当时地方政府承担了征收大部分国家税收和公共支出（如教育、卫生和行政管理）的职责。黄佩华对这个体制的中央集权本质做了准确的刻画（Wong, 2007：21）：

收入由地方征收，然后上解。收入分配完全是事后决定的，年年谈判而定，以完成中央布置的支出功能。在这个体制下，转移支付和收入分配之间并无一条清晰的界线，在西方体系中被视作"转移支付"的东西，在这里却隐而不见：严格地说，所有的地方支出都是由中央转移支付融资的。

地方公务人员的工资支出也属于中央分配的支出任务，是使用中央"转移支付"或财政拨款完成的。在这个体制下，公务人员工资的地区差别完全是由中央规定的地区分类决定的，非常小。如图2所示，1980年，公务人员平均工资地区差异基尼指数不到0.06。

中国的改革开放，在财政上，是从放弃统收统支的体制，而采用财政包干体制开始的。在这个体制下，地方政府仍旧承担着征收大多数国内税收的任务。但是，与统收统支体制下地方征收的每一分钱都是国家的、花费的每一分钱都是中央"拨款"不同，财政包干制对地方和中央在财政收入上的分配关系，以合同的形式加以规范。合同期一般为五年，合同期内每年的收入在中央和地方之间、乃至各级政府之间的分配按照事先约定的规则进行。例如，在财政包干制成熟期（1988—1993），中央和各地方的财政关系首先可以按是否为中央定额补助对象分为两大类。在与中央直接发生财政关系的30个省级行政区和5个计划单列市中，有14个为中央定额补助地区。这些地区在合同期内，每年从中央获得合同规定的定额补助，而它们自己在本地征收的收入，除了少数按规定上解中央外，均由自己留用。非定额补助地区则根据不同的分成方式，从本地征收的税收收入中，向中央上缴部分收入，其余均归地方自由支配。

按理说，在财政包干体制下，各地公务人员工资水平，势必受到本地财政能力的影响，从而加大工资水平的地区不平等。然而，如图2所示，公务人员平均工资地区分布基尼指数在1985年有较大幅度的上升后，直到1992年，一直保持在低于1985年的水平，0.10左右。我们认为，导致这一局面的原因可能有三。其一，直到1992年邓小平南行、中国全面进入市场经济之前，中国经济的地区间的差距仍旧是很有限的。其二，1985年颁布实施并沿用至1992年的《国家机关和事业单位工作人员工资制度改革方案》规定的结构工资要素中，没有地方津贴补贴一项，地方政府在正式工资发放上没有多少操作的空间。其三，财政包干时期规模逐年增大的预算外收入中，有相当大的份额被用于福利奖励支出和行政事业支出（Wedeman，2000；马元燕，2005；李学文等，2012），而按中国的统计口径，职工获得的福利收入是不被计入工资收入之中的。

1994年的分税制改革，既是中央集权又是地方分权的改革。之所以集权是因为它一改中央政府依靠地方政府征收国内税收的传统做法，成立国税局征收国税和央地共享税，并在国税、地税和共享税收入划分上让中央占有远远多出其支出责任所需要的份额。因此，中央必须使用政府间财政转移支付来消化它所有的巨额财政"剩余"，从而使它能够系统地使用财政转移支付政策工具来影响地方行为。另一方面，分税制对中央和地方收入划分，达到了财政包干制所不可比拟的制度化水平。国家税收被明确地划分为国税、地税和共享税，且共享税按照事先约定的规则在中央与地方之间分配，部分中央转移支付按公式化方式分配，这些制度使地方财政行为具有更大的自主性。

因此，分税制改革后各地公务人员的工资水平，乃是地方财政收入及其获得的转移支付收入的函数。如财政部官员李萍（2006：63）所言，普通转移支付的目的是

"保障机关事业职工工资发放和机构正常运转等基本公共支出需要"。除了常规的一般性转移支付外，朱镕基担任总理期间，为了缓解亚洲金融危机后国内有效需求不足的矛盾，中央分别于1999年7月、2001年1月和10月、2003年7月四度调高机关事业单位职工工资和离退休人员离退休费。最近的一次调整工资发生于2006年7月（表1）。地方因调资而增加的支出，沿海经济发达地区自行解决；对财政困难的老工业基地和中西部地区，中央政府给予不同程度的补助，民族地区给予特别的照顾。为此，中央财政专门设立了调整工资转移支付，每次补助地方的调整工资转移支付数额确定后，以后年度均作为基数定额补助地方（见图3）。

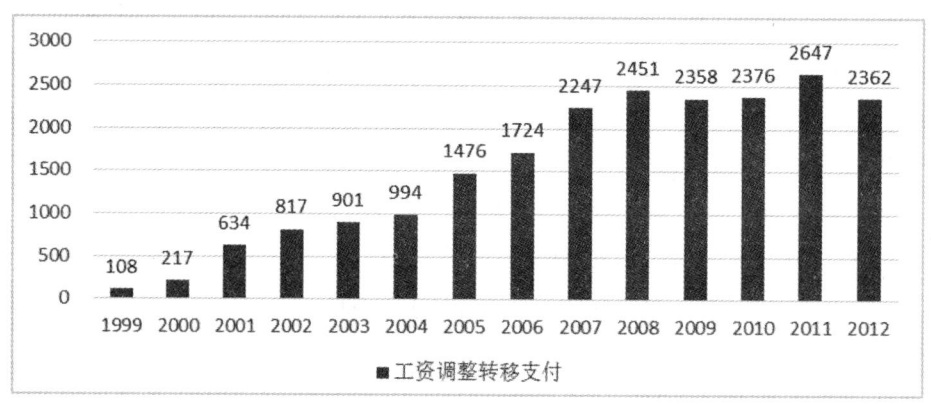

图3 历年中央工资调整转移支付（1999—2012）（单位：亿元）

资料来源：国家财政部（历年）；李萍（2010）。

分税制改革以来的数度工资调整大大地提升了公务人员的工资水平且加剧了地区差距（见表2和图2）。如表2所示，国家机关职工的平均工资对全国职工平均工资的比例，从1993年的1.0上升至2008年的1.15，而在同期，企业职工平均工资对全国职工平均工资比从1.0下降至0.97，事业单位工资除了在2000年代初一度上升至1.06左右的水平外，到2008年回落至1.01的平均水平。由于《中国统计年鉴》不再提供2008年之后按企业、机关和事业分的平均工资数据，我们无从了解2008年之后的全国一般情况。好在许多省级统计年鉴在2008年之后仍旧按照这一分类提供数据。表2提供了广东和河南两个人口大省的数据。从中我们看到，机关平均工资对全国平均比，在广东省从1993年的0.99逐年增至2008年的1.38；2008年之后虽有回落，但到2012年仍旧保持1.25的水平。然而，在河南，这一比例仅在2000年前后上升到1.10左右的水平，2003年之后，除了2007、2008和2009三年超过1.0之外，其余各年均低于1.0。2012年竟然低至0.92。广东和河南公务人员的工资水平，无论是相对于当地其他人群而言，还是两者之间（如2012年广东国家机关公务人员平均工资为63066元，是河南省的34439元的1.83倍），都判若两样。那么,究竟是什么因素决定广东的公务人员工资水平大大高于河南呢?更一般地说,是什么因素决定中国公务人员工资水平的地区差异呢?我们将建立多年度跨地区模型来回答这个问题。

表2 广东河南企业、事业和机关职工平均工资与全国平均水平的比例(1993—2012)

年	全国			广东			河南		
	企业	事业	机关	企业	事业	机关	企业	事业	机关
1993	1.00	1.00	1.00	1.01	0.94	0.99			
1994	0.97	1.09	1.09	0.98	1.06	1.05			
1995	0.97	1.00	1.01	0.96	1.00	1.01	0.99	1.03	1.07
1996	0.95	1.00	1.02	0.99	1.04	1.08	1.00	1.00	1.03
1997	0.98	1.06	1.08	0.98	1.04	1.10	0.98	1.04	1.05
1998	0.99	1.02	1.03	0.98	1.05	1.13			
1999	0.98	1.04	1.07	0.95	1.03	1.14	0.97	1.03	1.10
2000	0.98	1.03	1.07	0.97	1.05	1.17	1.00	0.98	1.05
2001	0.96	1.06	1.12	0.95	1.07	1.23	0.96	1.06	1.12
2002	0.96	1.07	1.13	0.94	1.11	1.29	0.97	1.04	1.07
2003	0.97	1.04	1.12	0.94	1.07	1.28	1.00	1.00	1.03
2004	0.97	1.03	1.12	0.92	1.12	1.37	1.01	0.98	0.97
2005	0.97	1.02	1.13	0.92	1.12	1.41	1.02	0.97	0.95
2006	0.98	1.01	1.11	0.94	1.09	1.34	1.02	0.99	0.96
2007	0.97	1.03	1.15	0.93	1.13	1.36	0.98	1.03	1.06
2008	0.97	1.01	1.15	0.97	1.13	1.38	0.98	1.02	1.04
2009				0.93	1.12	1.38	0.98	1.03	1.02
2010				0.93	1.13	1.32	1.00	1.03	0.99
2011				0.94	1.13	1.28	1.01	1.00	0.94
2012				0.95	1.14	1.25	1.01	1.00	0.92

资料来源:国家统计局,历年;广东省统计局,历年;河南省统计局,历年。

四、数据与方法

最完整的按省级行政区分中国公务人员工资数据,见于《中国统计年鉴》报告的按行业和地区分的工资数据。在那里,公务人员的工资总额和平均工资在"公共管理和社会组织"(2004年以来)或"国家机关、政党机关和社会团体"(2004年之前)

的名目下加以报告。该年鉴使用两个口径来报告工资数据：城镇单位职工和就业人员，后者的口径略大于前者。《中国统计年鉴》自2009年起不再报告城镇单位职工工资数据，而城镇单位就业人员数据则是2005年之后才开始报告的。为统计口径统一起见，我们使用1997—2008年的城镇单位职工数据建立面板数据模型。模型使用的数据主要来自《中国统计年鉴》《中国财政年鉴》与《中国人口与就业统计年鉴》。

本文采用如下回归模型：

$$Y_{ij} = \alpha + \beta_1 Y_{it-2} + \beta_2 X_{ij} + \beta_3 Z_{it} + K_i + F_j + \varepsilon$$

其中 i 表示省份，j 表示年。Y_{it} 为模型的被解释变量，即公务人员平均工资水平（取对数）；Y_{it-1} 则为解释变量的一阶滞后，X_{it} 为一系列政治和行政因素；Z_{it} 表示一系列经济和市场因素。K_i 是不随年份变化的省份效用，F_j 表示不随省份变化的年份效应，ε 为残差，即其他可能起作用但未在模型中体现的因素。

在经济因素上，我们以人均GDP来衡量各地区的经济发展水平，经济发展水平越高意味着财税资源约丰厚，从而可能对公务人员付出更高的工资。以商品房均价来衡量各地区的生活成本：高房价通常意味着高租金，而租金上涨则意味着成本的提高从而带来大部分基础产品的价格上涨，因此也提高了地区内的生活成本，这在中国表现的尤其明显（Chen，1996）。我们预期，这两个变量越大，公务员工资水平越高。基于同样的理由，我们对城镇化（按城镇人口占总人口比重测量）和产业结构（按第二产业和第三产业产值占GDP测量）这几个变量与公务人员工资的关系也做同样的期待。外商直接投资（FDI）用来衡量资本"用脚投票"的倾向。在其他条件相等的情况下，外商将选择政府运行成本低的地方经营。对以招商引资为要务的中国地方政府而言，对此必须做出反应。我们期待，在其他条件相同的情况下，一个地方吸引的外资规模越多，其政府人员的工资水平相对较低。

经济因素显然无法解释公务人员工资水平地区差距的全部，中央的政策规制与政府间财政关系扮演同等甚至更加重要的角色。我们可以用各地区公务人员工资水平与人均GDP的关系散点图来说明这一点（见图4）：首先，四个散点图的 R^2 在0.54到0.68之间，说明尚有32%到46%的地区差异无法用各地的经济发展水平差异加以解释。其次，四个散点图都有若干偏离最优"回归线"的异常点（如西藏、新疆、甘肃等）。再次，比较四个散点图的拟合优度，可看到经济基本盘的解释能力，在进行普调工资的1997和2003年那里要显著低于非调资年2009和2012年，这显示出政治因素的影响力。

在政治因素上，我们运用各地人均预算内收入来衡量各地的自有财力：作为公务人员非基本工资的主要来源，各地区的自有财力越雄厚，其公务人员工资水平也应当越高。同时，我们把各地区人均转移支付净收入（即地方的中央补助收入减去地方上解中央支出部分)与地方转移支付依赖度(即转移支付净收入与一般预算内支出的比值)变量引入模型,其方向也预期为"正"。理想地说,我们应当把用于支持地方发放工资的财力性转移支付和用于项目的专项转移支付区分开来。但是,相关数据的缺乏使我们无法做到这一点。不过,即便是专项转移支付也可能对地方公务人员的工资产生影响:它们可能被挪用来发工资,也可能因为地方需要为专项补助配套而拖欠工资(王蓉,2004;吴木銮,2009,2011;Wu,2010)。我们还使用"官民比"(即公务人员与常住人口的比值)来衡量各地区的政府规模。考虑到公共行政部门实为劳动密集型部门,人员工资开销是公共行政部门最大的成本驱动因素。因此,雇佣规模越大,补偿水平越低;反之亦然(Schiavo-Campo and McFerson,2008)。我们使用虚拟变量来操作工资普调政策,把实施工资普调政策的次年设为1,其余为0(中央在2001年1月与10月实施两次普调,因此2001年与2002年均为1)。

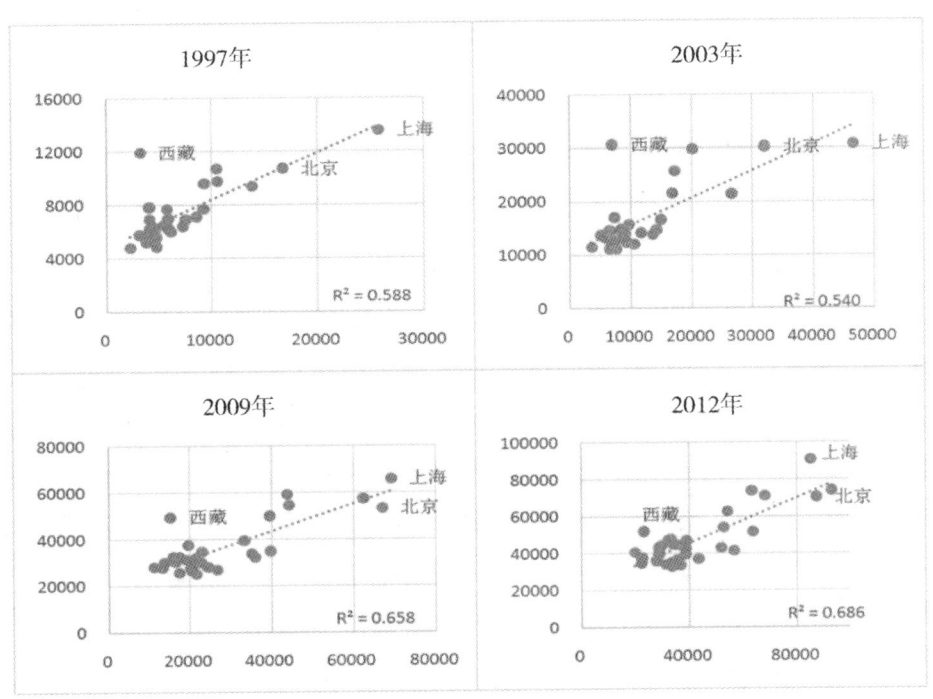

图4 各地区公务人员平均工资与人均 GDP 相关性

注:纵轴表示公务人员平均工资,横轴表示人均 GDP,单位均为元。2003—2008年根据公务人员职工平均工资计算,2008年之后根据公务员就业人员平均工资计算。

资料来源:国家统计局(历年)。

模型使用的所有货币单位数据都按照2005年 CPI 为基数进行调整。除了转移支付依赖度、城镇化、产业结构和政策虚拟变量外,其余变量数据均取对数进入模型。我们考虑使用的估计方法有系统广义矩估计法(SYS-GMM)或固定效应模型

(FE)。相对差分广义矩估计（DIF – GMM）为克服易受弱工具变量而产生的有限样本偏误（finite-ample bias）(Arellano and Bover, 1995; Blundell and Bond, 1998); 经过一阶自相关检验后，在此主要使用系统广义矩估计的两布估计（two-step）。而系统广义矩估计法要求误差项的一阶差分在一阶序列相关上显著，且在二阶序列相关上不显著（Bond, 2002），表3中的 Arellano-Bond test 结果显示系统广义矩估计法是满足上述条件 [即 AR (1) 显著而 AR (2) 不显著]；同时，Sargan test 结果则表明模型的工具变量外生性条件得到满足（模型2与模型4 – 6）。然而，很可能由于工资调整政策模型包含了过多虚拟变量等原因，其无法满足广义矩估计的相关估计要求，所以本文使用固定效应模型对其进行分析。

五、实证结果与讨论

表3和表4报告了我们建模分析的结果。前者报告的模型考察了除中央调资政策之外的政治因素与相关市场因素对于地区间公务人员工资水平的影响，后者考察中央工资政策对各地区工资水平的影响。两个表报告的模型 R^2 等判断系数表明，我们引入的自变量对公务人员工资水平的地区差异具有非常好的解释能力。

我们首先观察并分析市场因素对公务人员工资水平的影响。人均 GDP、城镇化、工业产值占 GDP 比重、服务业产值比重、商品房价格和外商直接投资等市场因素变量，在表3和表4报告的多个甚至所有的模型中，都以我们所预期的方向通过了显著性检验。具体而言，除了外商直接投资为负向外，其余均为正向。这说明，各地区公务人员工资水平的差异反映了它们在经济发展、城镇化水平、工业化水平和服务业发展水平上的差异。在表3和表4报告的7个模型中，商品房价格变量的系数在6个模型以正的方向通过5%或10%水平的显著性检验，说明生活成本确实影响到各地公务人员不同的工资水平。外商直接投资在表3报告的两个含有因变量一阶滞后变量的模型中在1%的显著水平上以负的方向通过检验，说明在其他条件的情况下，资本的流向成为制约地方公务人员工资的因素。

我们用来操作政治因素的诸变量也都在我们预期的方向上通过了显著性检验。统计分析结果表明，各省的自有财政收入和转移支付收入均以1%的信心水平在正的方向通过检验。二者对于各地工资的涨幅程度影响大致相同：二者每上升1%，各省工资水平会相应上升0.2%左右（前者比后者略大）。转移支付依赖度对各省公务人员工资水平的影响也是正向的。表4报告的模型表明，公务人员工资增长的幅度，在中央政府调整工资的年份要比其他年份平均多3.5%到5.8%。政策调整年变量和东中西部以及少数民族地区合成的交互项变量的回归系数表明，在政策调整年，西部省份的工资增长幅度平均而言比东部高了3.0%，比中部高了2.8%。少数民族地区的平均增幅比非少数民族地区高3.8%。官民比变量的回归系数表明，一个地区的官员规模越大，其人均工资水平越低。最后，人均工资滞后变量的回归系数为正且通过显著性检验，表明各地区的工资增长水平与前一年显著相关，公务人员工资水平有着强烈的"路径依赖"。

通过比较模型中各变量的回归系数的 t 值的大小，我们可以获知它们对公务人员工资水平及其增长幅度的地区差异的解释力。人均工资滞后变量的 t 值远远大于其他变量的 t 值，说明"路径依赖"具有最强的解释能力。各省的人均净转移支付收入变量的 t 检验值显著大于出滞后变量之外的所有其他变量的 t 值，这说明在模型中引入的变量中，转移支付是决定公务人员工资的省际边际差异的最重要的因素。这一发现说明尽管中国的经济基本面已经达到较高的市场化水平，尽管财政分权下"一级政府，一级预算"，中央政府仍旧对决定各地公务人员的相对工资水平持有重大的影响力。这一影响力一方面是通过中央规制实现的，另一方面则是依靠中央手中掌握的转移支付予以实现的。分税制改革以来，中央预算内财政收入占全国财政收入的比重在50%—55%之间波动，而其支出占全国财政支出的比重则从1994年的30%逐渐降至2008年的21%和2012年的15%。这就意味着，中央政府必须使用转移支付工具来消化它所占有的大量财政收入，而地方政府则必须依靠来自中央政府的巨额转移支付资金来填补它们的收支缺口。例如，2008年在中央政府的36511.92亿元收入中，有22945.61亿元被用于对地方政府的税收返还和转移支付，占62.84%。地方政府的总收入51590.52亿元中，有22945.61亿元来自中央的税收返还和转移支付，占44.48%。如此巨大的转移支付资金成为塑造中国公务人员工资水平地方分配格局的最重要的因素。毫无疑问，转移支付特别是调整工资转移支付的分布是向落后地区倾斜的（见表1）。

表3 公务人员工资水平地区差异的影响因素（1997—2008）

	模型（1）	模型（2）	模型（3）	模型（4）
人均财政收入（ln）	0.235*** (5.82)	0.203*** (4.10)	0.308*** (6.85)	0.243*** (6.54)
人均净转移支付收入（ln）	0.197*** (9.64)	0.185*** (15.55)		

（续表）

	模型（1）	模型（2）	模型（3）	模型（4）
转移支付依赖度			0.0623** (2.28)	0.0238** (2.05)
因变量一阶滞后		0.537*** (23.92)		0.734*** (36.45)
官民比	-42.32*** (-7.73)	-25.76*** (-6.01)	-41.74*** (-6.79)	-27.01*** (-6.40)
商品房均价（ln）	0.056* (1.91)	0.049* (1.90)	0.035 (1.08)	0.052** (2.13)
人均GDP（ln）	0.400*** (7.47)	0.0628 (1.10)	0.557*** (9.77)	0.118** (2.37)
FDI（ln）	0.00447 (0.29)	-0.0549*** (-4.96)	-0.0260 (-1.52)	-0.124*** (-11.67)
城镇化	0.856*** (4.74)	-0.0305 (-0.21)	0.863*** (4.26)	-0.300*** (-3.01)
工业产值比重	0.311 (1.05)	0.0993 (0.36)	1.379*** (4.47)	0.857*** (3.39)
服务业比重	1.562*** (5.68)	0.624*** (3.91)	2.536*** (8.85)	0.822*** (4.37)
Constant	2.064*** (7.76)	1.380*** (5.42)	0.849*** (3.26)	0.00292 (0.01)
N	372	341	372	341
估计方法	FE	SYS-GMM	FE	SYS-GMM
省份个数	31	31	31	31
R^2	0.956		0.934	
AR(1)		0.001		0.001
AR(2)		0.550		0.814
Sargan test		0.998		0.998

注：1. * $p<0.05$，** $p<0.01$，*** $p<0.001$，括号内是 t 值。

2. 经过 Hausman 检验，本文选取固定效应模型，且经过检验不存在异方差。

资料来源：国家统计局，历年。

表4　公务人员工资水平与工资调整政策（1997—2008）

变量	公务人员平均工资（ln）		
	模型（7）	模型（8）	模型（9）
因变量一阶滞后	0.829*** (23.93)	0.824*** (23.78)	0.827*** (24.01)
商品房均价（ln）	0.0605** (2.20)	0.0526* (1.90)	0.0551** (2.01)
人均GDP（ln）	0.195*** (5.74)	0.205*** (5.98)	0.200*** (5.90)
城镇化	0.00280 (0.02)	-0.0226 (-0.16)	0.00321 (0.02)
工业化比重	0.0946 (0.44)	0.128 (0.60)	0.115 (0.54)
服务业比重	0.268 (1.21)	0.317 (1.42)	0.297 (1.35)
工资调整政策	0.0408*** (5.92)	0.0584*** (5.45)	0.0347*** (4.70)
政策*中部地区		-0.0276* (-1.69)	
政策*东部地区		-0.0296* (-1.92)	
政策*少数民族			0.0381** (2.19)
常数	-0.659*** (-5.98)	-0.667*** (-6.07)	-0.661*** (-6.03)
N	341	341	341
R^2	0.936	0.946	0.947
省份个数	31	31	31

注：1. $*\ p<0.05$，$**\ p<0.01$，$***\ p<0.001$，括号内是t值。2. 经过Hausman检验，本文选取固定效应模型，且经过异方差检验。

资料来源：作者自制。

各省的人均自有财政收入和人均GDP等变量，若单独观察，其t值大都显著小于人均转移支付变量。这说明各地的经济发展水平和自有财政收入水平对它们的公务人员的工资水平的影响，应当不会高于转移支付。最后，外商直接投资的边际影响力几乎接近于经济发展水平，而各地的房价差异对它们的公务人员工资的边际差异的影响，在我们考察的变量中是最小的。

六、结论

本文在省级层面分析了公务人员工资水平的地区差异及其原因。总体来看，公务人员工资水平的地区差异实际上是一个"投射"了我国政府间关系、政府财政行为以及各地经济生态等多方面因素的政治经济学命题。

基于此，我们建立了一般性的理论框架，并简要地将影响因素分为相互作用的两大类：政治因素与经济因素。在前者一端，对各地区政府公务人员工资水平差异影响最大的政治因素是政府间关系制度安排以及中央与地方的财政能力。就中国而言，中央主要通过"编制"与工资政策以管控各地区的公务人员规模及其基本工资水平。在分税制后形成的中央财政收入集权与地方财政支出分权的格局之下，地方的预算内收入与中央对于地方的转移支付实际成为各地公务人员工资的两大核心来源——其中地方自有财力则又间接受到各地区经济发展水平的影响，而中央的转移支付则主要在于实现中央的政治考量与调控地区工资差距。而经济因素则在多个层面制约着政府的工资政策与财政行为：从长期来看，这些市场或经济因素则为各地区公务人员工资水平起到了奠定工资"基数"的作用，同时也在短期内直接影响了中央工资调控政策的倾向与力度（如对于落后地区更大的财政转移支付数量等）。总之，在分税制之后，我国公务人员工资水平的地区差异主要是在经济基本面对于政府的制约与政府对于各类经济因素的回应中波动。实证结果也支持本文的理论框架。

具体来看，在经济发展水平与地区生活成本的基础上，影响公务人员工资水平地区差异的政治因素主要体现在四个方面。首先是地区自有财力与获取的中央转移支付力度，这实际也是公务人员工资的最主要资金来源，二者在不同地区间的不同程度的"搭配"构成了这一群体工资收入的稳步增长，而且后者在决定工资水平的省际差异上的作用大于前者。其次，在受到严格规制并在前期基数上增长或调涨的制度背景下，公务人员的工资水平存在着较强的"路径依赖"。再次，在政府规模受到"编制"限制、经济发展水平以及各地财力等因素影响的情况下，公务员工资水平也与其人员数量保持着较强的边际弹性，即在相关预算变动不大的前提下，公务员规模的细微扩张很可能在短期内拉低其平均工资水平。最后则是中央的工资调控政策，这一调控政策具有显著的区域间再分配倾向。

同时，各地区的经济基本面在一定程度上制约着政府的工资政策行为，后者的跨地区差异是地方政府回应各地区经济因素的结果。一方面,"供养"政府的各类税收直接来源于因经济增长而不断扩张的经济总量之中,这成为政府雇员工资的主要来源。另一方面,各地区差异巨大的生活成本也为巨大的地区间公务人员工资水平差距提供了"合法性";中央则要考虑的是如何将这一差距控制在合理范围之内(这是2006年工资改革的主要目标之一)。同时,在多重因素共同作用之下,"行政干预"与"市场调控"的作用机制在区域间也很可能呈现非均衡的"传递":西部可能更多地受惠于计划性再分配,而东部则更多地借助于了"看不见之手"的推力。

至此可以看出,如果我们简单地将影响各行业工资或收入水平的因素描绘成"计划与市场"光谱的话,则整体上公务人员将明显地处于靠近"计划"一端。因此,本文的研究实际上处于这一较为宏大的理论命题之中:在中国这样一个计划与市场如此分明的混合经济体之中,各行业或各部门间的工资收入如何受制于国家的计划调控,又是如何对市场规律以及市场化程度做出回应,理当是一个重要的政治经济学研究课题。本文的理论框架可以在多大程度和范围上扩展其解释力也同样值得讨论。由此出发,本文实则是选取了其中比较具代表性的群体在这一理论框架内进行了具体分析。然而,就"各行业间工资水平的地区分布差异决定因素的政治经济学"研究而言,本文仅仅是一个开始。

---

[1] Arellano, M. and Bover, O., "Another Look at the Instrumental Variable Estimation of Error-components Models", *Journal of Econometrics*, 68 (1), 1995, pp. 29 – 51.

[2] Beramendi, P. and Cusack, T. R., "Diverse Disparities: The Politics and Economics of Wage, Market, and Disposable Income Inequalities", *Political Research Quarterly*, 62 (2), 2009, pp. 257 – 275.

[3] Blundell, R. and Bond, S., "Initial Conditions and Moment Restrictions in Dynamic Panel Data Models", *Journal of econometrics*, 87 (1), 1998, pp. 115 – 143.

[4] Bond, S. R., "Dynamic Panel Data Models: A Guide to Micro Data Methods and Practice", *Portuguese Economic Journal*, 1 (2), 2002, pp. 141 – 162.

[5] Boskin, M. J., "Consumer Price Indexes", in David R. Henderson (ed.), *Concise Encyclopedia of Economics* (2nd ed.), Indianapolis: Library of Economics and Liberty, 2008.

[6] Boskin, M. J., Dulberger, E. R., Gordon, R. J., Griliches, Z. and Jorgenson, D. W., "Consumer Prices, the Consumer Price Index, and the Cost of Living", *Journal of Economic Perspectives*, 12, 1998, pp. 3 – 26.

[7] Brennan, G. and Buchanan, J. M., "The Power to Tax: Analytic Foundations of a Fiscal Constitution", Cambridge University Press, 1980.

[8] Brødsgaard, K. E., "Institutional Reform and the Bianzhi System in China", *The China Quarterly*, 170, 2002, pp. 361 – 386.

[9] Chan, H. S. and Ma, J., "How Are They Paid? A study of Civil Service Pay in China", *International Review of Administrative Sciences*, 77 (2), 2011, pp. 294 – 321.

[10] Chan, H. S. and Suizhou, E. L., "Civil Service Law in the People's Republic of China: A Return to Cadre Personnel Management", *Public Administration Review*, 67 (3), 2007, pp. 383 – 398.

[11] Chen, A., "China's Urban Housing Reform: Price-rent Ratio and Market Equilibrium", *Urban Studies*, 33 (7), 1996, pp. 1077 – 1092.

[12] Chew, D. C., "Recent Developments in Civil Service Pay in China", *Int' l Lab. Rev.*, 129, 1990a, p. 773.

[13] Chew, D. C., "Civil Service Pay in China, 1955 to 1989: Overview and Assessment", *International Review of Administrative Sciences*, 56 (2), 1990b, pp. 345 – 364.

[14] Child, J., "Changes in the Structure and Prediction of Earnings in Chinese State Enterprises During the Economic Reform", *International Journal of Human Resource Management*, 6 (1), 1995, pp. 1 – 30.

[15] Cooke, F. L., "Public-sector Pay in China: 1949 – 2001", *The International Journal of Human Resource Management*, 15 (4 – 5), 2004, pp. 895 – 916.

[16] Erickson, C. and Ichino, A., "Wage Differentials in Italy: Market Forces, Institutions, and Inflation", in *Differences and Changes in Wage Structures*, University of Chicago Press, 1995, pp. 265 – 306.

[17] Gabriella M., Qian Y. and Weingast B., "Federalism, Chinese Style: The Political Basis for Economic Success in China", *World Politics*, 48, 1995, pp. 50 – 81.

[18] Gong, T., and Wu, A. M., "Does Increased Civil Service Pay Deter Corruption? Evidence from China", *Review of Public Personnel Administration*, 32 (2), 2012, pp. 192 – 204.

[19] Hering, L. and Poncet, S., "Market Access and Individual Wages: Evidence from China", *The Review of Economics and Statistics*, 92 (1), 2010, pp. 145 – 159.

[20] Lasswell, H. D., *Politics: Who Gets What, When, How*, New York: P. Smith, 1950.

[21] Ma, J., "'If You Can't Budget, How Can You Govern?' —A Study of China's State Capacity", *Public Administration and Development*, 29 (1), 2009, pp. 9 – 20.

[22] Niskanen, W. A., *Bureaucracy and Representative Government*, Chicago: Aldine-Atherton, 1971.

[23] Naughton, Barry, *Growing Out of the Plan: Chinese Economic Reform*, 1978 – 1993, Cambridge University Press, 1996.

[24] Qian Y. and Weingast B., "Federalism as a Commitment to Preserving Market Incentives", *Journal of Economic Perspectives*, 11 (4), 1997, pp. 83 – 92.

[25] Schiavo – Campo, S. and McFerson, H. M., *Public Management in Global Perspective*, ME Sharpe, 2008.

[26] Shue, Vivienne and Christine Wong (eds.), *Paying for Progress: Public Finance, Human Wel-*

fare and Inequality in China, Routledge, 2007.

[27] Soskice, D., "Wage Determination: The Changing Role of Institutions in Advanced Industrialized Countries", *Oxford Review of Economic Policy*, 6 (4), 1990, pp. 36 – 61.

[28] Tiebout, C., "A Pure Theory of Local Expenditures", *The Journal of Political Economy*, 64 (5), 1956, pp. 416 – 424.

[29] Wedeman, A., "Budgets, Extra-budgets, and Small Treasuries: Illegal Monies and Local Autonomy in China", *Journal of Contemporary China*, 9 (25), 2000, pp. 489 – 511.

[30] Wessa, P., "Free Statistics Software, Office for Research Development and Education", version 1.1.23-r7, URL http://www.wessa.net/, 2014.

[31] Whittaker, D. H., Zhu, T., Sturgeon, T., Tsai, M. H. and Okita, T., "Compressed Development", *Studies in Comparative International Development*, 45 (4), 2010, pp. 439 – 467.

[32] Wong, C., "Can the Retreat from Equality Be Reversed? Assessing Fiscal Policies toward Redistribution from Deng Xiaoping to Wen Jiabao", in Shue, Vivienne and Christine Wong (eds.), *Paying for Progress: Public Finance, Human Welfare and Inequality in China*, Routledge, 2007, pp. 12 – 28.

[33] Wu, M., "Civil Service Pay Arrears at CountyLevel in China: Causes and Implications (Doctor Thesis)", HK: CityUniversity of Hong Kong, 2010.

[34] 广东省统计局：《广东省统计年鉴》，中国统计出版社，历年。

[35] 国家财政部：《中国财政年鉴》，中国财政杂志社，历年。

[36] 国家统计局：《中国统计年鉴》，中国统计出版社，历年。

[37] 国家统计局：《中国劳动工资统计资料，1978—1987》，中国统计出版社1987年版。

[38] 国家统计局人口与就业统计司：《中国人口与就业统计年鉴》，中国统计出版社，历年。

[39] 公婷、吴木銮：《关于以薪养廉有效性的探讨：基于中国的经验》，《经济社会体制比较》2012年第5期。

[40] 国务院：《关于国家机关工作人员全部实行工资制和改行货币工资制的命令》，〔55〕国秘字第171号文。

[41] 国务院：《关于国家机关和事业单位工作人员工资制度改革问题的通知》，中发〔1985〕第9号文。

[42] 国务院：《关于调整机关工作人员工资标准的实施方案》，国办发第93号文。

[43] 国务院：《国务院关于改革公务员工资制度的通知》，国发〔2006〕第22号文。

[44] 贺军：《中美公务员工资制度比较》，FT中文网，2011年8月19日。

[45] 河南省统计局：《河南省统计年鉴》，中国统计出版社，历年。

[46] 黄佩华：《中国：国家发展与地方财政》，中信出版社2003年版。

[47] 李萍：《财政体制简明图解》，中国财政经济出版社2010年版。

[48] 李学文、卢新海、张蔚文：《地方政府与预算外收入：中国经济增长模式问题》，《世界经济》2012年第8期。

[49] 马元燕：《分税制改革后省级预算外收入膨胀的原因分析》，《公共管理学报》2005年第

1期。

[50]石剑、吴质:《中国官员的工资》,改革出版社1993年版。

[51]王绍光:《中国财政转移支付的政治逻辑》,《战略与管理》2002年第3期。

[52]吴木銮:《我国政策执行中的目标扭曲研究——对我国四次公务员工资改革的考察》,《公共管理学报》2009年第3期。

[53]吴木銮:《分权下集权是否有效:一个公务员工资执行的视角》,《开放时代》2011年第6期。

[54]新华社:《公务员住房补贴政策》,网址:http://house.shangdu.com/news/2013-07-16/81628.html,访问日期:2013年7月16日。

[55]易强、郭威:《公务员工资改革调查:三大争议阻碍调薪》,《财经时报》,2006-6-17http://www.ce.cn/cysc/cysczh/200606/17/t20060617_7391691.shtml。

[56]张光:《"官民比"省际差异原因研究》,《公共行政评论》2008年第1期。

[57]张光:《财政规模、编制改革和公务员规模的变动:基于对1978—2006年的实证分析》,《政治学研究》2008年第4期。

Modeling Voluntary Compliance: The Roles of Service Satisfaction, Policy Knowledge, and Trust in Government

Jesse Campbell Jungho Park Tobin Im[*]

Abstract

Enhancing trust in government via improved performance and transparency are central themes of the contemporary public administration reform agenda. However, little empirical work has examined whether this strategy may also facilitate an enhanced policy implementation context by increasing citizen's willingness to comply with difficult policy choices. This study addresses this question empirically using survey data collected in 2011 from 884 citizens of Seoul, South Korea. The results of structural equation modeling suggest that both service satisfaction and knowledge of public policy enhance voluntary compliance, but that their effects are mediated by increased trust in government. This study makes a contribution to the public management literature by identifying a potentially important outcome of government performance and transparency and developing a theoretical model linking these constructs together. Both the theoretical and practical implications of this topic are discussed following a presentation of the empirical analysis.

Introduction

Implementing controversial policy decisions is a challenging but necessary component of effective governance. While successful policy implementation depends on a variety of factors, scholars have argued that the voluntary compliance of citizens is critical (Baer,

---

[*] Jesse Campbell, Higher School of Economics, Moscow, Russia. Jungho Park, Korea Institute of Public Administration Seoul, South Korea. Tobin Im, Seoul National University Seoul, South Korea.

Simmons, and Flexer, 1996; Bali, 2003; Torgler, 2002; Ulli-Beer, 2003). The foundations of citizen compliance with government policy are often sought in a rational choice model of decision-making where citizens play the role of utility maximizers willing to disregard rules and regulations when they perceive the benefits for doing so to outweigh the risks (Braithwaite & Makkai, 1994; Slemrod, 1998). In this framework, coercion is the natural tool by which the government can secure the cooperation of citizens. However, in democratic societies, coercive mechanisms may both lack legitimacy and have important limitations and inefficiencies associated with them. As such, some scholars have suggested that enhancing the normative foundations of citizenship can provide an alternative strategy by which to secure citizen compliance and make coercive methods less necessary (Scholz, 1998; Tyler, 1997). According to this view, voluntary compliance may result from the perceived legitimacy of government policy and institutions, rather than a self-interested risk analysis on the part of citizens.

A better understanding the factors that underpin voluntary compliance can have important implications for public policy and management. This study examines the roles of public policy knowledge, service satisfaction, and trust in government as factors underlying the voluntary policy compliance of citizens. Public management scholarship has emphasized the creation of more results-oriented, citizen-centered, and open public sectors, viewing government performance and transparency as important foundations of government legitimacy (Moynihan and Pandey, 2005; Jin, 2013). While such initiatives are assumed to positively impact citizen attitudes toward their governments, little research has addressed the question of whether citizen satisfaction and knowledge of policy initiatives can positively impact policy implementation. This study aims to address this question by linking information and service satisfaction to voluntary policy compliance. Secondly, trust in government is an important attitude underpinning a range of positive dispositions and behaviors (Gilmour, 2008; Murphy, 2004), and moreover the links between increased service performance and trust are well known (Welch, et al. 2005; Van Ryzin, 2006, 2011). Accordingly, this study asks whether high levels of trust may function as a non-coercive antecedent to compliance by reducing perceived risk as well as enhancing the view of government as competent and benevolent.

This study uses survey data gathered from across South Korea in order to test a number of empirical hypotheses related to the above constructs. The study is organized as follows. Literature relevant to compliance and its antecedents is reviewed and discussed, and empirical hypotheses are proposed. Next, the data, measurements, and methodology used to test these hypotheses are described in detail. Relevant features of the South Korean context, and why it makes for an interesting venue for this study, are highlighted in this section. Following a presentation of the principle findings, the results of the analysis are discussed, with particular attention given to the practical implications of this study for public management. Finally, this study's contributions to the literature are summarized, and some directions for further study are proposed.

Literature review

Modeling voluntary compliance: Citizen satisfaction and knowledge

Policy studies have long recognized that citizen cooperation and involvement in the policy implementation process is a critical factor in its success. Pressman and Wildavsky (1984), for example, argued that citizen resistance to policy tends to be a critical barrier to effective policy implementation, and that resistance to the implementation process can ultimately lead to policy failure (p. 213). Much literature focusing on the issue of citizen compliance has taken a rational choice approach, understanding citizen compliance as the outcome of a calculative process focusing on the risks and payoffs of different courses of action. This perspective posits that citizens are economically rational actors who tend to comply with public policies or regulations only when those policies align with their self-interest (Braithwaite & Makkai, 1991; Sholz, 1998). Accordingly, the issue of policy compliance from an administrative perspective has been depicted as a matter of effective deterrence (i.e., detection of violations, auditing, sanctions, penalties, and incentives). This stream of research suggests that citizen compliance depends on citizens' passive conformity to public policy and regulations, rather than their active involvement (Murphy, 2004; Tyler, 1997).

While this rational choice perspective is compelling in its straightforwardness, a separate vein of research has pointed out the limitations of deterrence-based approaches to compliance, observing that various domains of policy necessitate voluntary compliance and involvement in order to achieve desirable policy outcomes (Slemrod, 1998; Sholz, 1998; Sholz & Lubell 1998; Murphy, 2004; Tyler, 1997; Winter & May, 2001). This perspective emphasizes the shared norms of civic cooperation among constituents of a political and social system, with citizens willing to comply with public policies when they are determined through a democrat, consensus building process, which heightens the normative sense of citizenship (Scholz and Lubell, 1998; Scholz, 1998; Slemrod, 1998; Winter and May, 2001). This civic duty model emphasizes citizens' moral duty and sense of responsibility as the underlying motive for complying with public policies (Tyler, 1997). As such, compliance outcomes are here dependent on views that citizens hold of government, rather than their pure self-interest.

Empirical evidence tends to support this latter view. For example, Baer and Flexer (1996), examining education outcomes, suggest that citizens' voluntary compliance and involvement throughout the policy implementation process is critical for policy effectiveness. Specifically, they argue that policy outcomes "may not be achieved by laws alone, since enforceable rules and regulations cannot compel" (p. 61) vastly different policy actors to behave according to the contents of policy. Similarly, Ulli-Beer (2003), who examined environmental policies in Switzerland, states that "the success of a national policy depends on a farsighted development of local strategies to motivate citizens to comply with public policy initiatives" (p. 2). Bali (2003) also explores why popular educational initiatives fail in the state of California, and emphasizes the importance of "publicized endeavors" (p. 1134) for the success of policy. Each of these studies has in common the view that compliance is closely linked to a broader type of engagement with government.

One concept at the heart of this vein of compliance literature is citizens' perception of government legitimacy. Put simply, citizens tend to exhibit high levels of noncompliance when they question the legitimacy of government and its actions (Coombs, 1980). Although there are various types of and antecedents to perceived legitimacy (Jin, 2013; Tyler, 1997; Baimyrzaeva, 2007), one factor that has particular relevance in democratic societies is citizens' perceptions of how well public organizations are performing when providing public services. Citizens' satisfaction with public services can be explained as the difference between citizens' perceptions on the quality of public service and their expectations imposed on public service (Bouckaert and Van de Walle, 2003, Van Ryzin, 2004, Kampen et al., 2006). Implied by this definition is the notion that citizens' satisfaction with has both a subjective and objective component. For example, citizens' own experiences with public services are considered to be an important determinant of their expectations and service satisfaction, which together are said to relate to general perceptions of government performance (Goodsell, 2003; Van de Walle, 2003). In accord with this, in the public sector the most prominent method of improving citizen satisfaction is targeting objective features of performance by attempting to improve actual performance (cf. Bouckaert and Van de Walle, 2003).

The perception of poor performance based on low levels of satisfaction may contribute to resistant attitudes towards new government initiatives in a number of ways. Firstly, new laws and public policies can be understood to entail a level of risk for citizens in the sense that there is a chance of policy failure. As such, to the extent that citizens perceive that the government is performing poorly in the delivery of public services, there is a chance that they will doubt the competence of government to achieve future success. In other words, the perception of poor performance may reduce expectations of good policy outcomes, and thereby in turn reduce the perceived legitimacy of government policy making, which has long been connected to voluntary compliance (Coombs, 1980). More broadly, however, low satisfaction with public services may lead to a "performance challenge" as described by Hirsch and Andrews (1984). As the delivery of public services may be understood as one of the core purposes of government, failure to meet expectations in this domain can result in the inability to gain support for new initiatives and increased scrutiny of government action.

As a core function, how well government performs at delivering services to the public may affect the readiness of citizens to voluntary comply with new policy initiatives. However, as an evaluation of government performance may also be based on an understanding of the factors that influence performance (Bouckaert, 2011), citizen's understanding of public policy processes should also contribute to their evaluation of government legitimacy and, therefore, their compliant attitude. Several scholars have suggested that awareness and knowledge of public policy may be linked directly to citizen compliance. Coombs (1980), for example, argued that ambiguity about policy goals resulting from a lack of communication and information about policy could result in citizens resisting government. Again, this lack of knowledge of public policy is directly tied to the government's legitimacy. Winter and May (2004) argue that in addition to citizens' ability to comply, an understanding of the content of policy may also contribute directly to compliance. These ideas suggest that, the less citizens understand government policy, the less willing they may be to act in such a way that policy implementation can proceed smoothly.

The relationship between citizen satisfaction with government performance and knowledge of government policy initiatives have an intuitive link with compliant attitudes. Perceived performance and knowledge may suggest to citizens that government is competent, thereby lowering the perceived risk of failure associated with new policy initiatives. Knowledge of pubic policy initiatives also may help citizens to understand the inherent complexity of a given governance situation, as well as the trade offs involved in making difficult policy decisions. These considerations lead to two hypotheses regarding the relationship between citizen satisfaction with public services and knowledge of public policy and their probability of voluntary compliance with government policy implementation.

Hypothesis 1: Citizen satisfaction with public services is positively related to voluntary compliance with public policy implementation.

Hypothesis 2: Citizen knowledge of public policy is positively related to voluntary compliance with public policy implementation.

The role of trust in voluntary compliance

While citizen satisfaction with public services and knowledge of government policy may reduce resistance to policy through enhancing confidence in public institutions and reducing perceived risk, others have suggested that trust in government plays an important role in producing cooperation with government policy (Murphy, 2004; Scholz and Lubell, 1998; Tyler, 1997; Braithwaitea and Makkaia, 1997). Murphy (2004), for example, demonstrates that taxpayers' trust in the collection institutions is related to their resistance to changes in tax policies. Although Murphy does not disregard the effectiveness of regulatory approaches (e. g., inspection, punishment) as a way of assuring the tax payers' compliance, trust in public institutions still plays a substantial role in fostering compliant attitudes. Tyler (1997) also notes that individuals' perceptions of the legitimacy of authority (e. g., local and national government) can affect individuals' compliance with "social rules... irrespective of the likelihood of reward or punishment" (p. 323). In particular, Tyler's (1997) study illustrates that citizens' perception of the competence and fairness of government authority, critical components of trust, affects their "willingness to voluntarily accept decisions" (p. 335).

In a popular definition, trust is understood as "a psychological state comprising the intention to accept vulnerability based upon positive expectations of the intentions or behavior of another" (Rousseau et al., 1998:395). From a rational choice perspective, citizens may resist policies to the extent that the perceived outcomes of compliance are not in line with their self interest. As such, to the extent that citizens attribute benevolence, integrity, and competence to government (Mayer, Davis, and Schoorman, 1995), the more likely they may be to accept vulnerability based on the belief that a given policy is in their best interests. From an institutional perspective, moreover, trust has been linked to voluntary compliance and therefore reduced need for external mechanisms to enforce contracts (North, 1990). Conversely, it is when compliance is non-voluntary when such mechanisms are necessitated. In addition to satisfaction with government service provision and knowledge of public policy, therefore, it may be the case that trust also plays an important role in voluntary compliance. As such, the following hypothesis is proposed.

Hypothesis 3: Trust in government is positively related to voluntary compliance with public policy implementation.

At the same time, however, as trust is understood be closely connected to positive expectations regarding the future behavior of another (Misztal, 1996; Mollering, 2001; Kramer and Lewicki, 2010), trust should not be entirely independent of the antecedents of voluntary compliance described in the previous section. For example, lower levels of citizen trust are frequently attributed to a poorly performing public sector, which in turn negatively influence citizens' perceptions of the legitimacy government organizations (Braithwaite and Makkai, 1994; Jin, 2012; Im et al., forthcoming). As such, levels of satisfaction with government performance may have a direct impact on citizens' trust in government, a relationship which has been supported by previous literature (Meier and Morgan, 1982; Braithwaite, 1998; Scholz, 1998; Rudolph and Evans, 2005; Kim, 2005).

Knowledge of government behavior and public policy initiatives is also likely connected to trust in government. For example, higher levels of understanding of public policy is likely to impact citizens' levels of trust and satisfaction via expectations, which play a key role in influencing citizens' trust in and satisfaction with their government (Bouckaert, 2011). Because public policy actually guides the performance of the entire public sector, the expectations of citizens who are more aware of public policy are likely to better understand the actual capabilities of the government, thereby having more reasonable expectations for its performance (James, 2011; Bouckaert and Van de Walle, 2003). Moreover, access to sufficient information, on which a reasonable understanding of public sector phenomena is based, can directly impact the perception of risk (Lewis and Weigert, 1985).

Based on these considerations, the following two hypotheses are proposed.

Hypothesis 4: Citizen satisfaction with public services is positively related to trust in government.

Hypothesis 5: Citizen knowledge of public policy is positively related to trust in government.

The Korean case

An equally impressive democratic transformation beginning in the late 1980s followed South Korea's economic transformation beginning in the 1960s. However, despite having established a representative democracy and achieved rapidly improved public service performance, Korean society has recently begun to face social turmoil due to citizens' noncompliance with public policies. Over the last decade, the Korean government has to cope with a series of mass demonstrations against major policies such as the expansion of free trade agreements, labor reforms, as well as the location of various undesirable facilities, such as waste disposal facilities or high voltage power transmission lines. In these demonstrations, the Korean government failed to legitimize the primary goals of policies and anticipated benefits to the overall society. Even with efforts to enhance the quality of communication and consultation, distrust in the government continues, with many citizens flatly rejecting as lies the information provided by government and suggesting that government is in collusion with interest groups (such as the Korean conglomerates). Korea's highly developed online culture, moreover, facilitates the rapid dissemination of counter-government information, and in turn high levels of mobilization by citizens (Park, 2014).

These conditions make the Korean context an interesting venue in which to explore propositions related to trust, information, satisfaction, and compliance. However, they may also affect the generalizability of the findings of the study.

Data and methodology

Research framework

The previous section outlined the proposed relationships between citizen satisfaction with public services, knowledge of public policy, trust in government, and voluntary compliance. The causal ordering of implied by these hypotheses suggests that trust in government may play an important mediating role linking satisfaction and knowledge to voluntary compliance. Figure 1 presents a schematic illustration of these relationships, with trust in government situated in this mediating role.

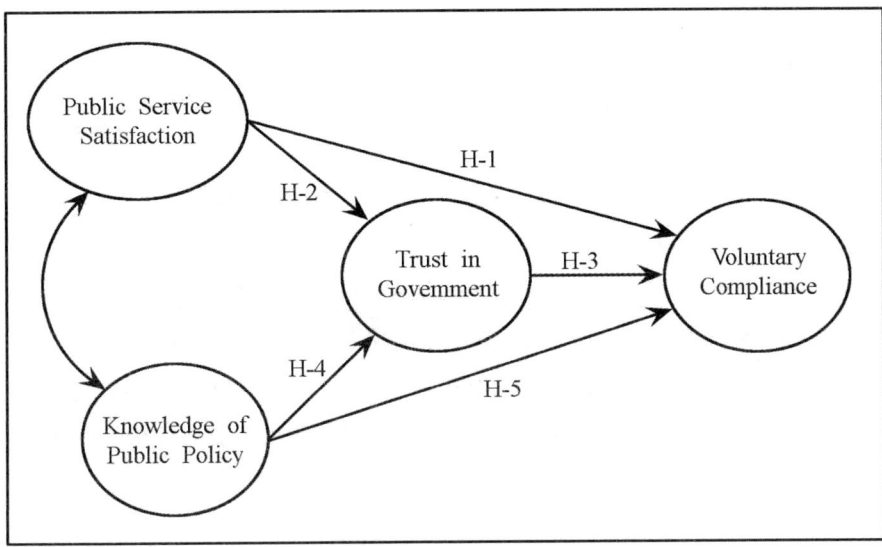

Figure 1 Model 1: Schematic Illustration of This Study's Hypotheses

In order to test the reliability of the model, an alternative framework is proposed in which other relevant variables, such as demographic characteristics and perceived economic well-being, are included. This model can be considered a post-hoc analysis reexamining whether the base conceptual model (Figure 1) is reliable even after controlling for various relevant variables.

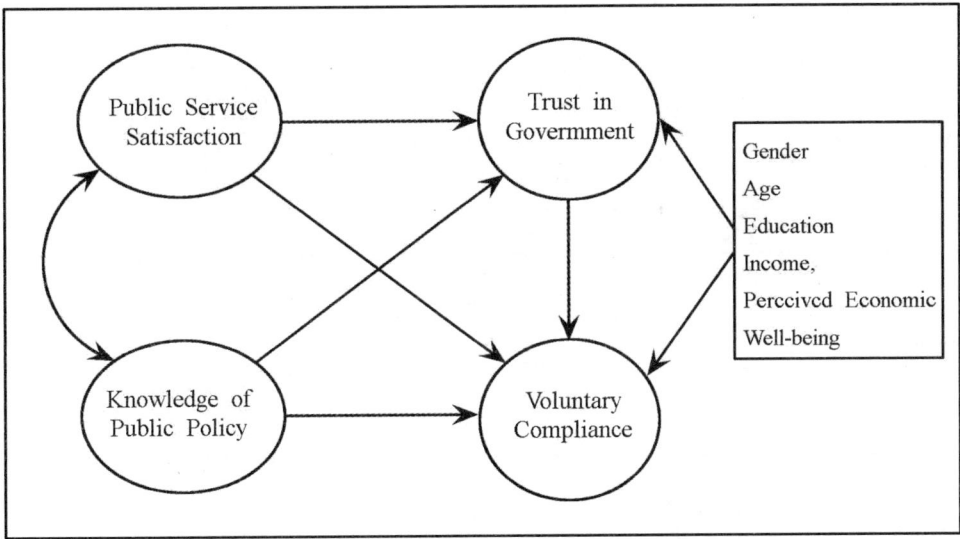

Figure 2 Model 2: Post-hoc Analysis of Model Reliability

Data

This study uses data from the 2011 Knowledge Center for Public Administration and Policy (KCPAP) survey, which was conducted by Gallup Korea and Seoul National University. Respondents to the survey were selected using both proportional stratified sampling and multistage cluster sampling methods to ensure representativeness; the sample was stratified by eight geographic areas and then a multistage cluster method was used within the eight areas. The data was collected from March 12th to 31st, 2011, using face-to-face interviews and structured questionnaires. Table 1 provides the description of the sample sorted by various group classifications. The sample is consistent with the key demographics of the entire Korean population.

Table 1 Characteristics of Respondents

Classification		Responses (%)	Classification		Responses (%)
Gender	Female	50.9	Metropolitan Status	Central	44.7
	Male	49.1		Suburban	44.1
Age	19-29	21.2		Rural	11.2
	30-39	21	Region	*Seoul*	18.9
	40-49	22.6		*Gyunggi*	22.9
	50-59	16.2		*Gyungnam*	14.8
	60 or More	19		*Gyungbuk*	10.9
Income (USD/a Month)	Below 938	6.4		*Jeolla*	13.8
	837-2950	46.7		*Chungcheong*	13.8
	2951 more	46.8		*Kangwon*	4.2
Education (graduation)	Elementary school	7.7		*Jeju*	3.7
	Middle school	9.6			
	High school	48.8			
	College	34			

Measurements

The rational model and civic duty model present theoretical perspectives on why citizens tend to comply with certain policies. In this study, we focus on aspects of citizens' civic duty, which can be thought of as citizens' willingness to risk their own self interest, if they perceive doing so as beneficial to society as a whole. To test the effects of the various proposed antecedents on voluntary compliance, respondents are presented with a hypothetical situation where their willingness to risk their own self interest is assessed according to their willingness to comply with the demands associated with the construction of unpleasant facilities, such as an incinerating plant or crematory, which could be constructed nearby their homes. Respondents' voluntary compliance with this hypothetical policy was measured by three items: "I am willing to comply with government policies even if those policies conflict with my own interest", "If it is necessary for the good of our society I would not oppose government decisions to build some unpleasant facilities such as incinerating plant or crematories in my community", and "I am quite cooperative with what public policy requires me to do." These measures are with 5-point Likert scale ranging from 1, "not at all", to 5, "very much." The construct showed sufficient internal consistency, with an alpha level of .674.

Citizens' trust in government was measured by employing the standardized questionnaire developed by the Institute for Social Research (ISR) at the University of Michigan, which has been used by most research on the subject of trust in government and has been shown to ensure consistency and stability of results (Brewer, 2003; Im et al., forthcoming). Six questions were asked, each with possible responses ranging from 1, "not at all", to 5, "very much". Some example questions are as follows: "Do you think that the government generally makes the right decisions?"; "Do you think that people in government waste a lot of the money we pay in taxes?"; "Would you say that the government is pretty much run for the benefit of all the people, as opposed to being run by a few big interests looking out for themselves?" (The appendix lists the full scales used.) Based on a principal component and reliability analysis, the construct was found to be both unidimensional and internally consistent, with an Cronbach's alpha of. 810.

Citizens' global satisfaction with public service is measured by inquiring about satisfaction with eight distinct and representative areas of public services, including public libraries, road conditions, and emergency services. The questions were answered using a 5-point Likert scale ranging from 1, "not satisfied at all", to 5, "very satisfied". A single component accounted for the variation among the items subjective satisfaction items. The Cronbach's alpha was .858.

As this study is interested in measuring citizens to be internally consistent, with an action with eight ather than their objective knowledge, policy understanding was measured by asking about respondents perceived understanding of recent debates related to a variety of policy issues. Questions inquired as to perceived levels of understanding about areas including economic policy, welfare policy, and, particular to Korea, unification policy, among other areas (see appendix). Questions were answered on a 5-point scale ranging from "very poor understanding" to "very good understanding". Internal consistency was found to be acceptable across policy understanding questions, with a Cronbach's alpha of .883.

The control variables added in model 2 were measured as follows. Demographic factors measured included gender (female = 1), age (years), education level (a 5 point scale ranging from g to "very good understanding". Internal consistency was found to be conomic wellbeing (measured on a 5-point scale). Marital status was measured using a dummy variable with 1 representing married.

Findings[①]

Measurement model

As the relationships between social phenomena often possess direct and indirect relations that are transmitted via diverse paths, structural equation modeling (SME) is frequently considered an appropriate approach to examine complex relationships (Kline, 2005; Bollen, 1989). When analyzing the relationships among variables, we use Satora-Benlter scaled chi-square, which is robust to violations of multivariate normality (Satora and Bentler, 1988, 1994). Before analyzing the structural model, the overall model fit was evaluated by four fit indices: the Comparative Fit Index (CFI), the Tucker Lewis Index (TLI), the Root Mean Square Error of Approximation (RMSEA), and the Standardized Root Mean Square Residual (SRMR).

As can be seen in Table 3, for Model 1 both CFI and NFI values are above 0.95; the RMSEA value is less than 0.05; and the SRMS is less than 0.08. These statistics indicate that model 1 is a good fit for the data and well specified. Model 2, which incorporates the control variables, shows a slightly worse model fit when compared to those of Model 1. Nevertheless, the model fit statistics for Model 2 still indicate acceptable levels of model fit, with all indices exceeding the relevant thresholds of acceptance.

[①] Descriptive statistics and zero-order correlations are available in the appendix.

Table 2 Evaluation of Models

Model Fit Indices	Model 1 Without Control Variables	Mode 2 Inclusion of Control Variables
S-B Adjusted X^2	323.967	644.130
Scaling Correction	1.140	1.058
df	300	375
CFI	0.986	0.967
TLI	0.982	0.960
RMSEA	0.022	0.028
SRMR	0.031	0.034
Sample Size	884	884

Principle findings of structural equation modeling

Figure 3 reports the results of the structural analysis. Although hypotheses 1 through 3 stated respectively that citizen satisfaction with public services, knowledge of public policy, and trust in government would be positively related to voluntary compliance, only trust in government shows a statistically significant regression coefficient (.481, p < .001), with both satisfaction and knowledge having no significant direct effect. This result indicates that improved public service and citizens' awareness of public policies are not directly related to citizens' attitudes toward the public policies after taking into account the effects of trust in government. However, both public service satisfaction and knowledge of public policy have a positive relationship with trust in government (.391 and .117, respectively, p < .001). This suggests that, as hypothesized, trust in government mediates the effects of the independent variables on voluntary compliance.

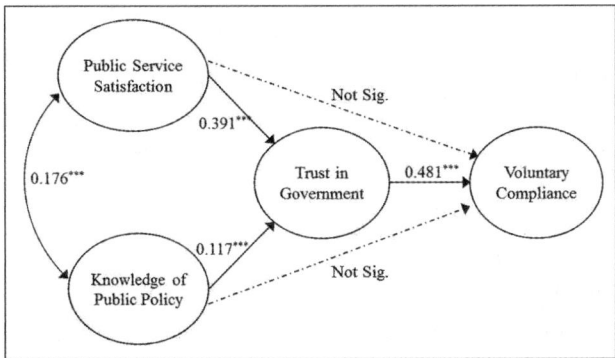

Figure 3 Important Mediating Effect of Trust in Government

Table 4 reports both direct and indirect effects of citizens' service satisfaction and knowledge of public policy on compliant attitudes. As is shown, despite the insignificant direct effects, service satisfaction and knowledge of public policy have significant total effects that are mediated by trust in government. As such, even though hypotheses 1 and 2 are rejected based on the results of model 1, it can be seen that both public service satisfaction and knowledge of public policy impact voluntary compliance through their relationship with trust in government.

Table 3　Direct and Indirect Effects on Voluntary Compliance

	Direct Effect (on Voluntary Compliance)	Indirect Effect (Mediated via Trust in Government)	Total Effect (on Voluntary Compliance)
Public Service Satisfaction	-0.038 (0.043)	0.188*** (0.031)	0.150*** (0.039)
Knowledge of Public Policy	0.051 (0.033)	0.056*** (0.021)	0.108*** (0.038)

As a follow-up analysis, the antecedents reviewed in literature review were also included in the model to examine whether the conceptual models show reliable results with the influences of citizens' socio-demographic characteristics and political orientation. As shown in Table 5, there was no qualitative difference between Model 1 and Model 2 for the main variables, which indicates that the findings of Model 1 (i.e., structural model) are stable even after the inclusion of control variables.

Table 4　Consistent Pattern After Controlling Numerous Types of Variables

		Trust in Government	Voluntary Compliance
Model 1	Satisfaction with Public Service	0.391***	-0.038
	Knowledge of Public Policy	0.117***	0.051
	Trust in Government	-	0.481***
Model 2	Satisfaction with Public Service	0.349***	-0.040
	Knowledge of Public Policy	0.114***	0.025
	Trust in Government	-	0.474***

Table 5 shows the effects of the control variables on trust in government and voluntary compliance. The table shows that age is positively related to both trust and compliance as statistically significant levels, while education is associated with higher levels of policy compliance.

Table 5 Effects of all Covariates on Trust in Government and Voluntary Compliance

Variables		Influence of Control Variables	
		Trust in Government	Voluntary Compliance
	Control Variables	Standardized Estimate (S.E)	Standardized Estimate (S.E)
SES Variables	Gender	-0.006 (0.036)	0.020 (0.031)
	Age	0.193*** (0.052)	0.138*** (0.049)
	Marital Status	-0.038 (0.047)	-0.028 (0.042)
	Education	-0.033 (0.043)	0.079** (0.037)
	Income	-0.031 (0.040)	0.029 (0.034)
	Perceived Economic Well-being	0.045 (0.037)	-0.008 (0.035)

Discussion

Successful policy implementation, particularly for controversial policy, is difficult to achieve without voluntary compliance on the part of citizens (Scholz, 1998; Braithwaite and Makkai, 1994; Gilmour, 2008; Slemrod, 1998). As such, this study looked at the relationships between citizen satisfaction with public service delivery, perceived knowledge of public policy, trust in government, and voluntary compliance. Before discussing in more detail the results of this study and their implications, we will stay here a few words about the limitations of this study. First and foremost, our analysis is based on cross-sectional data and as such, while the causal relationships we proposed between the various constructs of interest are theoretically plausible and consistent with existing research, causality cannot be shown conclusively based on this data set. For example, it could be suggested that trust in government, insofar as it impacts public service expectations, is actually an antecedent of service satisfaction, or at least that the two variables have a mutually reinforcing relationship (Van de Walle and Bouckaert 2003). Again, unfortunately, such questions are beyond the scope of this research, and moreover cannot be conclusively answered using this data set. Future studies can address this limitation through the use of a more sophisticated research design that incorporates a temporal element.

The results of the analysis strongly suggest that trust in government is an important antecedent of citizen compliance. While many scholars have argued from a rational choice perspective that externally imposed laws and regulations which increase the cost of noncompliance are an important driver of whether or not citizens behave in accordance with the law, the results of this study's analysis suggest that the cognitive evaluation of government itself may play a fundamental role as well. This finding is very much in line with existing theory (Tyler, 1993; Barithwaite and Makkai, 1994). Citizens who trust their government attribute to it sufficiently high levels of competence, integrity, and benevolence towards them. In particular, especially in situations where outcomes are unclear, which is very much the case for high risk projects such as the building of incineration plants, citizen trust may act as a lubricant facilitating effective policy implementation. This result has important practical implications. Particularly as it may be the case that when risks are perceived to be great, it is unclear extent to which external regulation will be successful in compelling citizens to comply with policy. As scholars have noted the limitations of the rational choice approach, this study makes a contribution by helping to establish an alternative approach to voluntary compliance with public policy.

Demonstrating the strong link between citizen compliance and trusting government represents the primary contribution of this study. In addition to this finding, however, the relationship between trust in government and voluntary compliance is further underscored by its important mediating relationship to voluntary compliance with regard to both public service satisfaction and public policy knowledge. Despite a plethora of arguments related to the direction of government reforms and the importance of trust in government, few questions have been raised about whether efforts for better performance and higher trust can contribute to increasing citizens' policy compliance. The study argued that both satisfaction and knowledge could affect voluntary compliance by impacting levels of confidence in government competency, evaluations of risk, and, ultimately, the perceived legitimacy of government action. After taking into account trusting government, however, both of these factors were found to be have insignificant direct effects with compliance. However, mediation analysis uncovered that both satisfaction and knowledge had statistically significant indirect effects with voluntary compliance via their effect on trusting government. Theoretically, then, recent scholarship on the importance of trust in government is supported by this study.

On the other hand, this indirect relationship suggests important practical implications for government faced with implementing difficult but necessary public policies. In line with the recent performance turn in public administration theory (Moynihan and Pandey, 2005), better management of public service is shown by this study to be important for cultivating positive attitudes towards government in general, and particularly future government endeavors through enhancing trust in government. Also importantly, the indirect effect of policy knowledge suggests that an important action that government can take in order to cultivate trust and voluntary compliance may be found in the enhancing the transparency of the policymaking process and perhaps involving citizens in meaningful ways. This is particularly important given that enhancing the performance of government service provision is challenging, however, enhancing the transparency of government behavior and policymaking represents a relatively straightforward way by which to boost confidence in new government initiatives and overcome collective action problems. In addition to the public performance literature, therefore, the study's results also directly contribute to discussions of the importance of transparency in policymaking as well as improved communications and public relations efforts on behalf of government.

This study tested a number of empirical hypotheses related to predicting voluntary policy compliance. Using large data set collected from citizens of South Korea, the results of the analysis the results of structural equation modeling suggest that trusting government plays an important mediating role in the relationship between satisfaction with public services, and knowledge of public policy, on the one hand, and the voluntary compliance of citizens with public policy. The study's finding underscores the practical importance of facilitating trustful attitudes in government, particularly when it is necessary to implement controversial public policy, a situation which is not uncommon and represents a fundamental challenge for effective governance. Cultivating trust in government is an important task for public administrators and the results of this analysis of this study demonstrates the importance of trusting government as a means to address fundamental concepts in public administration.

Measurement Items

Trust in Government ($\alpha = 0.810$)

1. Do you think that government generally makes rightdecisions?

2. Do you think that people in government waste a lot of the money we pay in taxes? (R)

3. Would you say that the government is pretty much run for the benefit of all the people, as opposed to being run by a few big interests looking out for themselves being?

4. Do you think that quite a few of the people running the government are crooked?

5. Do think that the voice of the public well penetrated into the policy making process?

6. Government does not lie.

Satisfaction with Public Service ($\alpha = 0.858$)

1. Cleanliness of pedestrian sidewalks

2. Quality of public transportation (e.g, subway and bus services)

3. Overall maintenance of city streets

4. Quality of Public libraries

5. Quality of Recreation and City Park

6. Fire & ambulance services

7. Quality of public education

8. Police servicesreducing crimes

Voluntary PolicyCompliance ($\alpha = 0.674$)

1. I am willing to comply with government policies even if those policies conflict with my own interest.

2. I would not oppose government decisions to build some unpleasant facilities such as incinerating plant or crematories in my community if it is necessary to our society.

3. I am quite cooperative with what public polices expect me to do.

Knowledge of Public Policy ($\alpha = 0.883$)

How much do you think that you understand following areas of recent policy issues?

1. Economic policy

2. Education policy

3. Health policy

4. Welfare policy

5. Environmental policy

6. Land use policy

7. Reunification policy

8. Energy policy

SES Variables

1. What is you gender? (1) Male (2) Female
2. What is your age?
3. What is you education level?
4. What is your approximate annual income?
5. What do you think your economic status?

Appendix

	(1)	(2)	(3)	(4)	(5)	(6)	(7)	(8)	(9)	(10)
(1) COMPLF	1.00									
(2) TRUSTF	0.48	1.00								
(3) SATISF	0.17	0.41	1.00							
(4) KNOWLEDGE	0.13	0.19	0.18	1.00						
(5) GENDER	0.03	-0.01	-0.02	0.09	1.00					
(6) AGE	0.20	0.26	0.19	0.08	-0.05	1.00				
(7) MAR	0.11	0.15	0.12	0.08	-0.13	0.67	1.00			
(8) EDUCAT	-0.02	-0.14	-0.10	0.16	0.20	-0.46	-0.20	1.00		
(9) INCOME	-0.01	-0.08	-0.08	0.15	-0.02	-0.24	-0.11	0.33	1.00	
(10) ECON WELL-BEING	0.04	0.07	0.08	0.17	-0.04	-0.05	-0.01	0.17	0.32	1.00

Variable	Mean	Std. Deviation
Voluntary Compliance	3.031	0.627
Trust in Government	2.678	0.593
Service Satisfaction	3.109	0.650
Gender	0.4910	0.500
Age	43.399	14.377
Education	3.302	1.136
Income	5.314	2.673
Perceive Economic Well-being	2.968	0.833

[1] Baer, R., Simmons, T. and Flexer, R., "Transition Practice and Policy Compliance in Ohio: A Survey of Secondary Special Educators", *Career Development for Exceptional Individuals*, 19 (1), 1996, p. 61.

[2] Bali, V. A., "Implementing Popular Initiatives: What Matters for Compliance?", *Journal of Politics*, 65 (4), 2003, pp. 1130 – 1146.

[3] Baimyrzaeva, M., "Corruption and Legitimacy Problems in Postcommunist States", *Public Administration Review*, 67 (3), 2007, pp. 594 – 596 (doi: 10.1111/j.1540 – 6210.2007.00741_5.x).

[4] Bollen, K. A., *Structural Equations with Latent Variables*, New York: Wiley, 1989.

[5] Bouckaert, Geert and Steven Van de Walle, "Comparing Measures of Citizen Trust and User Satisfaction as Indicators of 'Good Governance': Difficulties in Linking Trust and Satisfaction Indicators", *International Review of Administrative Sciences* 69 (3), 2003, pp. 329 – 343.

[6] Brewer, G. A., "Building Social Capital: Civic Attitudes and Behavior of Public Servants", *Journal of Public Administration Research and Theory: J-PART*, 13 (1), 2003, pp. 5 – 25.

[7] Braithwaite, John and Toni Makkai, "Trust and Compliance", *Policing & Society*, 4 (1), 1994, pp. 1 – 12.

[8] Coombs, F. S., "The Bases of Noncompliance with a Policy", *Policy Studies Journal*, 8 (6), 1980, pp. 885 – 892.

[9] Gilmour, S., "Why We Trust the Police: Police Governance and the Problem of Trust", *International Journal of Police Science & Management*, 10 (1), 2008, pp. 51 – 64.

[10] Goodsell, C. T., *The Case for Bureaucracy: A Public Administration Polemic* (4th ed.), Washington DC.: CQ Press, 2003.

Jin, M., "Citizen Participation, Trust, and Literacy on Government Legitimacy: The Case of Environmental Governance", *Journal of Social Change*, 5 (1), 2013, pp. 11 – 25.

[11] James, O., "Performance Measures and Democracy: Information Effects on Citizens in Field and Laboratory Experiments", *Journal of Public Administration Research and Theory*, 21 (3), 2011, pp. 399 – 418 (doi: 10.1093/jopart/muq057).

[12] Lewis, J. David and Weigert, Andrew, "Trust as a Social Reality", *Social Forces*, 64 (3), 1985, pp. 967 – 985.

[13] Kim, Y. C. and Yoon, S., "The Influence of the Internet on the Electoral Concern and Voting Participation in the 17th National Assembly Election", *Korean Political Science Review*, 38 (5), 2004, pp. 197 – 216.

[14] Kline, R. B., *Principles and Practice of Structural Equation Modeling* (2nd ed.), New York: Guilford Press, 2005.

[15] Lee, Aie Rie, "Down and Down We Go: Trust and Compliance in South Korea", *Social Science Quarterly*, 84 (2), 2003, pp. 329 – 343.

[16] Moynihan, D. P. and Pandey, S. K., "Testing How Management Matters in an Era of Government by Performance Management", *Journal of Public Administration Research and Theory*, 15 (3), 2005, pp. 421-439.

[17] Murphy, K., "The Role of Trust in Nurturing Compliance: A Study of Accused Tax Avoiders", *Law and Human Behavior*, 28 (2), 2004, pp. 187-209.

[18] Murphy, K., "Procedural Justice and the Australian Taxation Office: A Study of Scheme Investors", Centre for Tax System Integrity, Research School of Social Sciences, Australia National University Working Paper, No. 35, 2002.

[19] Nevitte, Neil., *The Decline of Deference: Canadian value Change in Cross - National Perspective*, Peterborough, On: Broadview, 1996.

[20] Park. J., "The Effects of Government's Information-Providing on Trust in Government and Service Satisfaction: Seoul Metropolitan Case", *The Korean Journal of Local Government Studies*, 18 (1), 2014, pp. 291-313.

[21] Pressman, J. L. and Wildavsky, A., "Implementation: How Great Expectations in Washington Are Dashed in Oakland"; or, "Why It's Amazing That Federal Programs Work at all", this being a saga of the Economic Development Administration as told by two sympathetic observers who seek to build morals on a foundation of ruined hopes: Univ of California Pr., 1984.

[22] Satorra, A. and Bentler, P. M., "Scaling Corrections for Chi-square Statistics in Covariance Structure Analysis", Proceedings of the Business and Economic Statistics Section, American Statistical Association (308-313), 1988.

[23] Satorra, A. and Bentler, P. M., "Corrections to Test Statistics and Standard Errors in Covariance Structure Analysis", in A. V. Eye and C. C. Clogg (eds.), *Latent Variables Analysis: Applications for Developmental Research*, Thousand Oak, CA: SAGE, 1994, pp. 399-419.

[24] Slemrod, J., "On Voluntary Vompliance, Voluntary Taxes, and Social Capital", *National Tax Journal*, 51, 1998, pp. 485-492.

[25] Scholz, John T., "Trust, Taxes, and Compliance", in V. Braithwaite and M. Levi (eds.), *Trust and Governance*, New York: Russell Sage Foundation, 1998, pp. 135-166.

[26] Scholz, J. T. and Lubell, M., "Adaptive Political Attitudes: Duty, Trust, and Fear as Monitors of Tax Policy", *American Journal of Political Science*, 42 (3), 1998, pp. 903-920.

[27] Suk, G., "KEPCO Forges Ahead with Miryang Project Despite Protests", *The Korean Herald*, Seoul, South Korea, The Korea Herald, 2013/10/02.

Tolbert, C. J. and Mossberger, K., "The Effects of E Government on Trust and Confidence in Government", *Public Administration Review*, 66 (3), 2006, pp. 354-369.

[28] Torgler, B., "Speaking to Theorists and Searching for Facts: Tax Morale and Tax Compliance in Experiments", *Journal of Economic Surveys*, 16 (5), 2002, pp. 657-683.

[29] Tyler, T. R., "The Psychology of Legitimacy: A Relational Perspective on Voluntary Defer-

ence to Authorities", *Personality and Social Psychology Review*, 1 (4), 1997, pp. 323 – 345.

[30] Ulli – Beer, S., "Dynamic Interactions Between Citizen Choice and Preferences and Public Policy Initiatives-A System Dynamics Model of Recycling Dynamics in A typical Swiss Locality", 2003.

[31] Van de Walle, Steven and Geert Bouckaert, "Public Service Performance and Trust in Government: The Problem of Causality", *International Journal of Public Administration* 26 (8, 9), 2003, pp. 891 – 913.

[32] Van Ryzin, G. G., "Testing the Expectancy Disconfirmation Model of Citizen Satisfaction with Local Government", *Journal of Public Administration Research & Theory*, 16 (4), 2006, pp. 599 – 611.

[33] Van Ryzin, G. G., "Outcomes, Process, and Trust of Civil Servants", *Journal of Public Administration Research and Theory*, 2011 (doi: 10.1093/jopart/muq092).

[34] Welch, E. W., Hinnant, C. C. and Moon, M. J., "Linking Citizen Satisfaction with E – Government and Trust in Government", *Journal of Public Administration Research and Theory*, 15 (3), 2005, pp. 371 – 391.

[35] Winter, S. C. and May, P. J., "Motivation for Compliance with Environmental Regulations", *Journal of Policy Analysis and Management*, 20 (4), 2001, pp. 675 – 698.

参与式预算的模式：云南盐津分析

贾西津[*]

"参与式预算"通常被认为是1989年巴西南部城市阿雷格里港（Porto Alegre）的民主试验创新。它的背景是巴西工党在选举胜利后提出以"全民管理"的方式参与政府管理，而不仅仅是在四年一度的选举之中才体现公民的权力。

在"协商民主""参与式民主"兴起的时代环境下，巴西的这项创新得到了广泛的扩展。2000年前，巴西的参与式预算约涉及了3万人，其后被推广至整个南里奥格里德州，在2002年参与人数迅速达到30万（张梅，2005），同时这一做法开始传播到全球范围。目前巴西已有80%的城市采用了此种做法，而截至2008年，世界各地有2000个城市引进了参与式预算（何包钢，2011），涉及美国、加拿大，欧洲的德国、法国、意大利、西班牙、瑞典，拉美的秘鲁、厄瓜多尔、玻利维亚、哥伦比亚、阿根廷、巴拉圭、乌拉圭、智利、多米尼加共和国、尼加拉瓜、萨尔瓦多和墨西哥，以及印度、韩国、日本、印尼、喀麦隆、斯里兰卡、南非等亚非国家（徐娟娟，2011）。

如果考察公共预算中公民直接参与的权力，巴西阿雷格里港的做法并不是空前的，比如美国俄亥俄州1975年就有"公民优先顺序小组"（citizen priority board）（董晓辉，2011），作为公民的公共预算参与形式；另外英美各州普遍保留的公民创制（citizen initiative）传统中，经常包含对财税问题的直接投票，当然它涉及的不是整体公共预算，而是具体的某项引发公民普遍关注的问题。

"参与式预算"在明确提出后之所以吸引了广泛关注，代表了这个时代的一种思潮，即重新拥抱直接民主，它反映了人群对代议制民主的间接权力控制、间断性公民权力行使的不满足，期求有更全面的、持续的、更深入的公民权力的参与过程。古希腊"公民大会"式的直接民主再次激起了人们的热情。其中，公共预算显然是重要而适宜参与的切入点。基于此，参与式预算的制度含义在于实践直接民主，试图增进普

---

[*] 贾西津，清华大学公共管理学院NGO研究所、清华大学公益慈善研究院副教授。

遍的、全过程的、直接的公民参与控制国家的过程。

公民参与理论的一位代表人物 Sherry Arnstein 在 1969 年基于对美国参与实践的实证分析，提出以公民权力来划分参与类型的理论，从而将公民参与依程度分为三个层次八种模式。①在"公民权力"的理论框架下，可以看出参与式预算创新的目的，在于试图让"代表权"走向"公民控制"的层次，在制度含义上即以直接民主补充代议民主。但是对现实实践的观察发现了新的问题："参与式预算"是不是能够体现"公民控制"？具体做法在多大程度上体现了公民权力？由于参与的范畴不同、参与主体不同、程序安排不同、决策方案设计不同等等，在不同实践、不同模式中，公民权力体现的程度是差异非常大的。尤其对于中国这样的转型国家，参与式预算并不是在代议制民主作为正式制度的基础上演进的，而在很大程度上，参与式预算本身是作为选举民主程度不足的弥补性改革以及制度创新路径。相应的问题是：中国的参与式预算在大多程度上体现了公民权力？"公民控制"的实现程度与参与过程中的哪些要素安排有关？这些要素安排的前提条件是什么？在不同要素安排下相应的参与效果是什么样？进一步，站在更宏观的制度改革层次，公民权力由低水平向高水平的发展有没有逐级递进关系？或者说，"公民控制"的实现与"代表权"之间有没有什么关系？

本文回顾了国外较成熟的参与式预算试验，总结参与式预算模式的关键要素。并结合中国云南省盐津县的群众参与预算改革案例，比较国内外不同模式中的要素差异及其影响，分析参与式预算模式的关键环节制度安排，如何影响了公民权力的实现程度。

一、参与式预算的模式要素

参与式预算目前在世界各地的实践，其模式却是千差万别，做法各式各样；即使在巴西的不同城市之中，开展的形式也是不一样的；纵便作为参与式预算首创城市的阿雷格里港，1989 年第一次实践参与式预算二十余年来，程序也在不断发生着变化。可以说，参与式预算很难找出一个确切的固定模式，我们只能从各地不同的

---

① Arnstein, Sherry R., "A Ladder of Citizen Participation", JAIP, Vol. 35, No. 4, July 1969, pp. 216 – 224. Arstein 教授的框架中，参与的最高级别是"公民控制"（Citizen Control），它与次之的"代表权"（Delegated Power）和共享权力的"伙伴关系"（Partnership）构成第一个层次的参与，即"公民权力"（Citizen Power）；第二个层次的参与被称作"象征"（Tokenism），它又包含了"纳谏"（Placation）、"咨询"（Consultation）和"知情"（Informing）三个等级，它们均有公民的参与，但是最后的选择和决策权仍然在于政府；第三个层次是形式上的而不具有真实公民权力意义的"非参与"（Nonparticipation），包括"训练"（Therapy）和"操纵"（Manipulation）两种形式，指政府通过让公民参加的形式达到训导公民的目的或者摆样子看的。

实践中，寻找出参与式预算所体现的基本理念，以及哪些关键要素会如何影响参与的效果。

以巴西阿雷格里港为例，整个参与式预算过程依参与性质可以被分为两个阶段，第一个阶段以直接民主为落脚点，开放公民参与，并引向议题汇集和代表产生；第二个阶段以代议民主形成最终决策，但过程是向普通公民开放的。通过直接民主和代议民主两个交错融合的过程，力图最大限度地将公民的普遍直接参与纳入现代公共预算体系。对阿雷格里港参与式预算的研究非常多（Marquetti, 2012；Celina, 2001；Boaventura, 1998；刘邦驰, 2009；王逸帅, 2009），下面将其模式中几个关键要素的特点概要阐述如下：

首先，参与的组织结构，包括市政方、公民方和中间结构三类。在市政管理方，包括规划办公室（GAPLAN），社区关系协调机构（CRC）及其片区协调者（CROPs）、主题协调者（CTs）、社区顾问论坛（FASCOM）等一系列参与式预算管理机构；在公民方面，主要基于各片区内公民既有的自治结构，如大众委员会、乡镇联盟、区域联合等；同时在两类机构之间设计有中介互动性架构，主要是参与式预算委员会（COP）、片区全体大会、预算片区论坛、主题全体大会、预算主题论坛。（Boaventura, 1998）

其次，参与的过程，时间跨度在七个月以上，多轮讨论、多层次会议、多种投票、复合选举，不是一个单一线性的过程。为开展参与式预算，阿雷格里港被分为十六个片区。第一个阶段直接民主，公民片区会议分为两轮，分别约在3—4月和6—7月，在第一轮会议之前由片区公民自主筹备、收集需求和代表意向，在两轮之间则是片区内各种小社区的预备会议。这一阶段会议除审计上一年预算外，最主要达到两个目的：确定片区议题优先性，以及选出市预算委员会（COP）代表进入市级代议民主。片区会议之所以分为间隔的两轮，是为了通过集合讨论—分散讨论—集合讨论、选定议题优先性和代表的过程，容留给公民充分的参与、表达、相互影响、妥协、修正等的空间和时间。在第一阶段系列会议结束之后，大约在6月进入第二个阶段的代议民主，被选出的COP委员在市级讨论预算，并最终确立预算的分配标准、评定出每个项目获得的预算资源。这样整个参与式预算过程便形成一个年度循环：公民片区筹备（3月）—第一轮公民片区会议（3—4月）—片区各种公民预备会议（3—6月）—第二轮公民片区会议（6—7月）—新一届COP委员就任、在市级召开定期会议（7—8月）—政府起草预算、COP确定预算分配（8—9月）—预算方案提交市长、COP与政府一起于月底前提交议会（9月底前）—议会批准预算（11月底前）—COP准备详细投资计划（9—12月）—委员在预算执行中监督、调整、争议解决和反馈（12月—次年7月新COP就任）。（Boaventura, 1998；Marquetti, 2012）

程序中有两个最值得注意的发展变化。一是公民大会的单元增加。1994年以后，与片区会议并行地引入了另一种公民会议形式——市级主题大会，分别包括流通、运输和城市流动，教育、休闲和文化，健康和社会福利，经济发展、税收、旅游，以及城市组织、城市和环境发展等五个主题，目的是增加讨论城市的一般利益，提升公民参与预算的能力。(Marquetti, 2012) 每个市级主题大会在程序上与一个片区会议等同看待，这样第一阶段就变为片区会议和市级主题会议两种参与式会议并行开展，相当于16个片区加5个主题共21个公民参与式会议单元，相应地，优先性选择、代表产生也变成了21个单元。

另一个方面是公民代表比例和产生方式的变化。公民代表是在参与公民中按比例选出的，最初每5人一名代表，1990年代初每10人一名代表，到1996年每20人一名代表，1997年改为按各单元中参与人数的浮动比例制，从100人以下的片区每10人一个代表，到1000人以上的片区每80人一名代表。(Boaventura, 1998) 代表的人口比不断增加，显示参与式预算吸引了越来越多的人参与进来。2001年以后，公民代表不再简单按比例选举产生，而分成两部分，其中一半依旧按照片区选举，另一半改由社区组织指派，其主要的考量是避免代表只为地区利益考虑。(刘邦驰，2009)

最后，预算的决策权安排是复合结构分享的，其中，公民的参与可以体现为作为个体公民及公民组织成员、作为公民代表、作为市预算委员会(COP)委员三种逐级递进的参与形式。最后的预算分配决定是COP制定标准并评定做出的，评定的基本标准主要是：片区确定的该议题优先度、该片区人口占城市总人口的比例、片区贫穷或基本建设缺少的程度。COP对之赋予不同权重，最终计算出的分值在全市总分值中的比例，即为该片区在该议题中所分得的资源比例。1991年COP打破片区的平衡，决定将70%的资源分配向五个优先片区，这几个片区由公众动员、片区对城市的组织重要性、基础设施缺少、公共服务和设施的人口绝对贫困等五个要素决定。(Boaventura, 1998)

公民代表与COP委员的产生和参与权不同。前者在第一轮片区会议及其后的预备会议期间产生，是咨询、控制和动员机构，选出后每个月开一次会，主要功能是监督预算过程，以及作为COP与片区公民之间的中介；COP则是预算参与机构，委员在第二轮片区会议中选出，每个片区(主题)单元2名，另有2名候补，委员任期一年，只能连任一次，在7—8月COP就任后，委员每周开一次例会，对预算进行讨论。公民的比例代表对COP具有一定的控制权，半数以上代表参加，2/3投票就可以临时召集COP会议。

作为普通公民，参与到片区会议之中，可以在两个方面体现决策权：一是直接决定片区议题优先性，这一优先性继而以权重方式体现在最终的预算分配中；二是对代表和COP委员的选择与控制。参与式预算中的会议全程是向任何公民开放的，不过片区会议中的投票权只有在该片区的登记住户才享有。另外，在当地公民社会组织中的活跃参与会增加其作为代表的机会，因为有一部分公民代表是在两轮片区大会之间选出的，而这些代表主要通过社会组织推举出来，所以没有参加任何社会组织的人当选代表的机会就低多了。(Boaventura，1998)

政府在预算中的权力及其局限主要体现在：市政厅是制定参与式预算方法和提出可分配资金额度的主体，巴西的参与涉及的不是全部公共预算，而是投资建设的部分预算，一般大约为30%的总预算额度；两轮片区会议的主持召开由市政厅负责，但日程要由片区内的公民领袖和市政共同议定；预算方案的起草，由市规划办公室（GAPLAN）具体负责，并交相关部门讨论；预算分配的决定过程，COP决定基本标准及其权重，市政厅也参与其中，可以提出建议，以及细化技术标准，但不参与投票；最后对预算分配方案，市长具有否决权，提交议会后议会依然可以选择拒绝，但是由于参与过程达成的社区需求和形成的公众压力，否决权基本没有被行使过。

巴西的参与式预算在世界其他地区的扩展和操作模式各有特色。比如德国1998年引入参与式预算制度，目前是欧洲参与式预算改革持续时间最长、参与城市最多、多党支持的国家，波恩、科隆、索林根、柏林等许多市区均有开展。德国参与式预算的特点是重视信息的公开、互动、回馈过程，公民提议渠道多样，但最后的预算决策权由行政区中心会议负责。德国参与式预算三阶段及其特点是：信息公开阶段，公民获得市政预算收支信息；公民咨询阶段，公民通过分区会议、市政在线对话、写信给公民服务办公室、参与市政府的市民问卷等多种形式，表达议题优先性倾向和提出建议；预算审议阶段，政府将每个分区会议讨论选出的前五项优先提议，连同网络等汇集的前十条提议，汇总列表，在公民中随机抽样对这些提议进行投票，决定提议优先顺序，改汇总表最终提交本行政区中心会议，做出预算安排，若提议不被采纳，亦须对之做出反馈解释。(袁方成，2009) 这种形式与20世纪70年代迪内尔（Dienel）教授首提的公民陪审团性质的"规划小组"传统有关，后者是公民中随机抽选的、每个议题更换的公民小组，深入参与城市规划的议题讨论中，他们更注重冲突解决而不是产生开放意见的功能。(朱圣明，2014)

法国的特色是公民的预算参与得到法律保障。法国2002年颁布的《勇士法案》强制在人口超过8万的城市都必须建立城市委员会，开展公共咨询。(胡肖华，2014) 市镇人口3500人以上的地区，在市长编制预算和议会审议预算之前，必须先在市镇会议进行讨论。(张晓然，2011) 街区议事会设有预算专题工作室。不过，由于各街区的资金是平均分配的，公民参与讨论权只是固定金额内项目安排，加之街区会议和市镇大会两个层次公民会议，每年数次，法国的公民参与率很低，上万人的街区参加街区会议的通常只有十几人。

西班牙塞维利亚作为欧洲采纳参与式预算城市中规模最大的一个，起步于2004年，公民会议按照街坊、区、市三个层次展开，其中街坊会议提出议题并选举区、市级代表，区级代表产生优先性排序，市级代表讨论涉及市级的议题。这个参与只涉及公民活动、体育、城市风尚三个领域。（朱圣明，2014）

美国的城市预算中公民本来有参与影响的途径，如在预算决定前必须召开公开的听证会是法律规定的。2009年芝加哥第49街区开始进行公民直接参与预算的改革试验，是美国最早推行参与式预算的地区。试验由该区的市议员乔·摩尔（Joe Moore）发起，并邀请布朗大学沃森研究所的白奥奇（Baiocchi）教授共同设计过程，参与内容是分配Moore可自行支配的130万美元预算经费。芝加哥的参与特点是充分发挥公民自治，由社区邻里会议酝酿议题（10—11月），社区代表大会准备项目（11月至次年2月）、最后一轮社区代表大会（4月）后通过平等投票确定优先支持的项目及其资金分配。（王钰清，2013）在这个过程中，白奥奇邀请成立了由40名社区代表参加的督导委员会，监督程序，并指导六个专题委员会工作。

印度公共预算参与的特色是公民预算组织的角色。印度最早在1994年中南部城市班加罗尔市（Bangalore）开展公民预算参与，公民组织于1995年在古吉拉特（Gugarat）邦推行"公民报告卡"，主要是在预算分析、绩效追踪和监督过程中，让公民知情，反馈服务意见，促进城市公共服务，并提升弱势群体声音。（王逸帅，2009）希腊比雷埃夫斯（Piraeus）也有类似的"市政核对表"，由公民对市政预算提出问题和进行监督。

韩国蔚山市东区的参与式预算始于2004年，最大特点是"联合决策"形式，即由公民通过联合平台与政府官员就全部预算多次往复地进行讨论，一起工作。这些联合平台包括参与式预算公民委员会、专题委员会、顾问委员会、理事会、片区会议和全体会议。

日本自2000年以来开始参与式预算，其重点是预算的编制阶段。具体做法有：各地预算编制过程公开透明化、市民直接编制预算方案（名张市）、市民与政府分别编制预算方案进行对照（志木市）、社会组织提议预算项目建议再编制预算方案（千叶县）、将1%居民税交给社会组织并由其安排公民投票决定税的最终资助用途（市川市）等。（朱圣明，2014）

还有一些特定领域的参与，如南非成立"妇女预算提案小组"（The Women's Budget Initiative），专门针对性别因素进行预算参与；波兰普沃茨克（Ptock）2002年执行联合国开发计划署的一项动议，由市政和企业共同出资设立对社会组织的"小额资助基金"，由公民、专家和出资方代表共同评审项目的资助申请。

纵观世界各地的实践，参与式预算的范畴、程序、公民参与的形式、广度、深度等各不相同，总是与当地的治理结构和预算条件相关联的。Dahl（1989）认为参与式预算可被称为民主的条件包括：有效参与，即每个公民对偏好的平等表达权；决策阶段的平等（等权重）投票；充分理解，即每个公民有平等的机会了解要决策的事务；公民控制要决定的事项；民主过程涵纳全体公民。Cabannes（2004）则列出参与式模式的七个要素：直接民主而不只是在社区层次的代议民主；参与式决策层级在市级而不是区级；谁主导参与式的决定；多少预算纳入参与式过程；谁做最后的决定；预算批准后的社会控制与监督；规范化和制度化的程度。Marquetti（2012）归结参与式预算设计中的三个主要方面是：城市偏好如何定义，包括谁是参与者，参与如何组织，什么话题被展示；决策过程如何运作，设计预算怎么制定以及谁来制定；监督过程如何组织。

为分析公民权力在参与式预算模式中的实现程度和实现特点，本文将观察分析参与式预算的模式归纳为以下三个维度共十个要素：第一个维度，参与的组织结构。谁发起？谁是过程的控制者？政府和公民社会方面各自有哪些组织机构或参与平台？第二个维度，参与的过程，其中体现公民权力的有七个关键要素。其一，预算开放权限。哪部分预算进入公民参与，是什么政府层级的预算？是其全部还是部分预算？如果是部分，是哪一部分，谁来定义？其二，公民的参与权重。谁有参与资格？是平等资格吗？如果有代表是如何产生的，有几个权力层次的代表，其各自的权限是什么？代表产生有没有选举过程，选举程序是什么样的？最后实际实现的权力结构是什么样的、与制度设计的权力结构是否一致？有没有人被排除在参与之外，因为什么？其三，预算的最终决策权配置。最终预算分配决策由谁做出，如何做出，是投票还是协商，有没有计算标准，谁掌握标准制定权，决策者有多大自由裁量权？有没有全体公民对于预算的投票，全民投票决定的是什么，投票的权重如何？公民、不同代表和政府在预算决策权配置中是什么关系？其四，除预算最终决定权外公民的其他预算权力。包括信息权、议题提出权、预算编制权、预算修正权等，有没有制度安排？其五，规则制定权。参与的规则由谁决定？会议谁来召集主持，谁来安排议程，对规则的解释权在谁，参与过程中对规则有异议如何解决？有没有专门的安排规则和程序的机构？在规则和程序的安排中有没有第三方的介入？其六，公民参与的权程。参与式预算的一次完整过程时间是多长？公民是一次性参与还是在公共预算过程中反复地参与？公民的参与是涉及预算的提出、编制、决议、执行、监督及调整的全流程，或是体现在其中的哪些部分？预算决议后的阶段有没有持续参与的机制和组织结构？有没有决算的参与、在决算中有无体现向公民反馈的责任机制？其七，公民组织的参与及其权力。预算参与过程有没有社会组织的角色？是自发参与还是制度安排？第三个维度，参与的制度属性。包括两个方面，其一，参与式预算的制度安排在现行正式预算制度之中，是有所冲突的、相对独立的，还是能够衔接的？该参与式改革有没有改进正式制度并成为其一部分的趋势？其二，参与式预算有没有得到法律保障？与前一个问题相关，这种改革做法在多大程度上依赖于改革者的个人偏好？还是发展出了法律制度的保障，有多大持续性？

二、中国参与式预算：云南盐津的案例

中国参与式预算的试验主要在 2004 年以来，虽然有些学者认为若看到"村务公开"和"村务民主管理"，中国农村的参与式预算实践在 20 世纪 90 年代就开始了。（何包钢，2011）2004 年，上海惠南镇将民生预算交由镇人大代表及公众协商，以"点菜"方式决定"实事工程"。同年，广东省在人大会议中创新"预算草案座谈会"，开始不断深化人大对预算的介入以及向社会的预算公开。2005 年，浙江省温岭市在七年"民主恳谈"的创新基础上，选择新河镇和泽国镇尝试了两种不同的参与式预算改革，其中，新河模式在开放公众"恳谈"参与的基础上，与镇人代会制度结合，通过改革人大会议议程力图将预算权实赋予人大代表；泽国则采用"协商民主恳谈"，以随机抽样发放公民问卷，确定公共项目的偏好优先性，直接决定预算安排。2007 年，上海市闵行区探索公共财政体制改革，在人大预算审议中进行了细化预算、充实审议权、人大进行公共预算听证、信息开放公众参与质询等一系列制度创新，加强人大对政府预算的审议监督和公众参与，2009 年闵行区人大讨论公共预算的时间是两天半，在中国类似改革实践中达到最长时间。中国发展研究基金会相继在江苏省无锡市和黑龙江省哈尔滨市推进了大规模的"参与式预算"改革试验，2006 年 3—4 月，无锡市北塘区北大街街道和滨湖区河埒街道实施参与式预算，2008 年哈尔滨市阿城区和平街道、胜利街道，道里区安静街道、工程街道、太平镇推出参与式预算，两地市政府先后开展十多项参与式预算项目，是试点规模比较大的地区，参与模式主要是政府拟定项目方案，交由公众投票选择优先性。2007 年河南省焦作市在财政体制中开展决策、执行、监督、评价"四权分离"的改革，包括预算信息公开、向公众征询意见、公众听证等制度。2010 年 1 月四川省巴中市巴中区白庙乡启动"财政预算公开及民主议事会"，是中西部地区第一个参与式预算改革案例，包括公众参与和人大参与，其参与流程和参与方式都是比较复合的。2012 年北京朝阳区麦子店街道从"问政"升格为预算参与，类似形式继而在其他街道出现改革苗头。同年，广东顺德试点参与式预算，选取两个项目邀请公众参与，并依据参与结果调整了预算编制。也是 2012 年，云南省在盐津县试点群众参与预算改革，形成庙坝镇和豆沙镇两种模式，

2013 年扩大至中和镇、牛寨乡共四个试点乡镇。此外，广西、甘肃、安徽等地也有参与式预算的项目，目前全国大约有十几处在乡镇或街道级别的案例，区或市级的则很少。有些改革具有相当持续性，如温岭的"民主恳谈"，更多地表现为阶段性，如无锡、黑龙江的项目，北京麦子店的改革等。

云南省盐津县的参与式预算试点，开展时间较新近，借鉴了国内外经验，同时，盐津县的改革作为云南省财政体制改革的试点，是在国内类似改革中最具有推广平台的案例，目前盐津县改革已经两年，模式较为成熟，而专门的研究介绍尚不多。本文在对 2014 年 4 月盐津县豆沙镇、中和镇等群众参与预算改革会议实地观察的基础上，总结盐津县的制度特点，并与国内外其他模式相比较，探讨参与式预算模式关键环节的制度安排对公民参与权力的影响和意义。

（一）谁的改革？

盐津县的乡镇参与式预算改革是云南省财政厅在财政体制改革总体构思中的试点，所以虽然改革实在县级实施，在乡镇级预算参与，这一创新模式实际具有更为宏观的支持平台，和潜在的广泛扩展前景。在创新启动方面，盐津县的改革是在国内目前参与式改革中最具备"上下结合"、省内推广条件的案例。

相比而言，在国内时间最持久、演化最丰富的温岭模式，创新发起于温岭市的宣传部门，在创新层级上启动于县级市，在部门系统中依托于宣传部，从而带来路径中不一样的特点。而无锡和哈尔滨的创新，是外来项目的支持与促动，虽然一度做到十几个街道的规模，但项目结束，做法也就复归原位了。上海闵行和广东省的改革，创新层次比较高，分别在直辖市的区和省级，但主要是人大审议公共预算的深化，重点非直接的公众参与。改革的启动层级对模式演进和扩展前景具有重要影响。巴西阿雷格里港参与式预算成为国际上的典范，并扩展到本国大多数城市，便与其国家 1989 年从军政府回归民主化后，左翼执政党执政思路相应。

盐津模式是省县互动、财政厅试点的，直接公众参与预算的改革。盐津县财政改革 2012 年启动，是一个综合性改革，包括三项内容：县乡财政体制改革、县直部门"比例—绩效预算"改革、乡镇群众参与式预算改革。改革的方向是将现行"乡财县管"、乡镇作为一个部门预算管理的体制，还归《中华人民共和国预算法》规定的"一级政府一级预算"、乡镇作为一级政府预算单位的地位。这一改革对于云南而言有更加切实的意义，即云南多交通不便的山区农业县，乡财县管的每月审批工资、请拨、报账，往返乡县成本和效率都凸显问题。县乡财政体制改革，实行了县和乡镇的收入划分，下放乡镇财权，而乡镇获得财权后怎么管？乡镇"参与式"预算改革即是针对相应的管理环节的改革。

(二) 哪级预算？

盐津县参与式改革预算参与的层次是乡镇预算。农村的乡镇和城市的街道也是目前国内参与式预算试验比较普遍的参与层级。① 开展于市区或省级的预算改革，如上海市闵行区、广东省级的预算改革，侧重于人大制度层面，直接针对民众的开放参与度局限于信息公开。20 世纪 90 年代即开始的农村"村务公开""村务民主管理"，参与程度直接关涉每一个村民，但由于不是一级财政预算单元，这种参与构不成"参与式预算"。

预算参与层次和参与深度的关系是，预算层级较低，参与程度越可能普遍直接；预算层级越高，涉及人口越多，直接民主越难，参与程度越弱，越间接。从国际经验看，参与式预算的典型层级是市级预算，如巴西阿雷格里港 1989 年开始参与式预算试验时城市人口 2.8 万人，后期已达到 27 万人；同样进行了参与式预算的西班牙塞维利亚市都市人口 70 万，日本公民投票决定居民税给予的市川市人口 47 万。云南盐津县人口 39.6 万，开展参与式预算的豆沙镇、庙坝镇、中和镇、牛寨乡人口分别为 2.36 万、4.88 万、3.63 万、3.3 万；浙江温岭模式中，温岭市人口 136.7 万，最早进行参与式预算的新河镇、泽国镇人口分别为 4.6 万、12 万。可见，中国乡镇是一个适宜的、但仍然是较小的参与范畴，在具有条件的地区可以尝试县级预算。

(三) 参与预算中的什么？

盐津县《群众参与预算试点方案》明确规定，乡镇政府测算参与式预算的资金总量，是当年财力减去基本支出和政策性规定必保刚性支出后的财力余额，对上级专款未指定具体项目的资金，由县财政测算预计，按比例下达到各乡镇，乡镇应一并纳入群众参与预算的项目资金安排。其中，基本支出主要是人员经费和办公（公用）经费，必保支出主要是依上级政策要求的本级支出。

例如 2014 年群众参与预算中，庙坝镇全年预计可用收入总计 2414.83 万元②，财政预算支出预计完成 1598.73 万元③，其中基本支出 624.47 万元（有详细明细）、政策必保项目支出 415.86 万元（包括各种本级活动经费）、拨付欠拨工程款 133.4 万元、年初预留 70 万元、总预备费 3% 即 45 万元④，当年用于群众预算参与资金 310 万元。

---

① 街道作为区的派出机构，严格在法律意义上不是一级预算单位。
② 包括地方财政预算收入 1289.57 万元、专项转移补助收入 80 万元、上年结余 1045.26 万元。
③ 滚存结余 816.1 万元结转下年使用。
④ 《中华人民共和国预算法》规定总预备费用于当年财政预算执行中不可预测自然灾害等特大事件支出，按预算总支出 1%—3% 提取。

豆沙镇全年预计财政可用收入总计1142.65万元①，财政支出预算基本支出473.23万元（包括人员经费369.97万元、公用经费103.26万元），按照上级政策安排本级支出15万元、上年未拨专款支出345.42万元，另预留总财力的3%即30万元预备费，余额全部纳入参与式预算，共279万元。2014年四个参与试点的乡镇，纳入参与式预算的资金总额均在270万—340万元，占该乡镇全年预计可用收入总额的9%（牛寨乡）—30%（中和镇）。②

国内大多数试点参与预算的资金是政府专门拨出一笔用于民生建设的资金，比如几十万，参与式预算更类似于在方法上的探索，而其结果无论如何都不会影响到整体预算的支出结构。温岭的新河模式由于紧密嵌入人大会议制度中，纳入参与额度是全部可支配预算。国际上如巴西的参与式预算也是部分预算，主要涉及投资建设部分，不超过30%。云南盐津的试点，在制度设计上是全部"财力余额"，即政府基本运转以外的所有非指定的公共财力，在纳入的预算范畴上力度较大的。实际运作中地方公共财政预算收入较低，主要依靠转移支付的豆沙镇和中和镇，基本是全部财力余额参与预算；地方公共财政预算收入较高、财政收入较为自给的庙坝镇和牛寨乡，会将常规的各类活动、人代会已通过的项目，或政府已承诺的实事工程等事先安排，并提取足够预备费和留出较大结转空间。以盐津全县情况看，盐津是国家级贫困县，地方公共财政预算支出中上级补助比重达90%，财政自给率不足10%；在公共预算支出中，全县人员经费、公用经费、上级专款支出、项目经费分别占总预算支出的31.8%、3.5%、32.1%、32.7%。可见在豆沙镇和中和镇纳入参与的预算比例基本达到县平均"财力总余额"比例。这样看，参与式预算在越是"保工资、保运作"的地区可能带来更显著的公共事业绩效。

（四）参与的组织结构

盐津县的改革试点由县委、县人民政府领导实施。在县、试点乡镇，乃至有些村/社区（如中和镇），均成立了改革的专门责任机构。在县级，县人民政府成立三个宏观组织机构和一个具体评审机构。三个宏观组织机构包括：第一，"盐津县乡镇群众参与预算改革领导小组"（以下简称"县领导小组"），县长为组长，县15个部门的负责人和试点乡镇的乡镇长参与其中，下设办公室在县财政局，负责群众参与预算工作的统一领导、统一部署、统一安排；第二，"盐津县乡镇群众参与预算改革监督委员会"（以下简称"县监督委员会"），主任为县人大常委会主任，其他参与者包括6

---

① 包括地方财政预算收入123.93万元、上级补助收入797.31万元、上年结转结余221.41万元。

② 如果扣除预计结转金额，安排的参与式预算资金量占当年预计完成预算支出的比例则在16%（牛寨乡）到30%（中和镇）。

名县人大常委会相关负责人员，以及试点乡镇的人大主席，下设办公室在县人大，办公室主任为人大常委会财经委主任，县监督委员会负责改革的全程监督包括民主议事会的监督；第三，"盐津县乡镇群众参与预算改革专家咨询小组"，成员全部是相关的专家学者，负责改革方案的整体设计、项目库管理等过程控制、绩效评价和群众议事员培训等工作指导。一个具体评审机构是盐津县财政局成立"项目评审领导小组"，负责从申报项目库到正式项目库的审查环节的具体组织工作。

相应的，试点乡镇也成立改革领导机构，其中，牛寨乡以党委书记为组长、乡长为常务副组长、各村联系人为村总支书记，其他三个试点乡镇均是镇长作为领导（小）组组长、村联系人为各村村长。具体组织结构各乡镇有细微差异，如豆沙镇是改革领导小组、改革工作组、改革宣传组、预算监督委员会四个机构并列；庙坝镇和中和镇则在改革领导组下设办公室、宣传组、资金额度测算组、群众议事员推选组、项目编制审查组、项目实施审查组、项目绩效评价组七个部门。牛寨乡组织结构比较简单，成立群众参与预算试点工作领导小组，下设办公室和工作组。

预算参与的主要平台是乡镇民主议事会，议事的主体是各村推选来的群众议事员。

盐津县的乡镇参与式预算组织结构特点是：在政府方面，县、乡两个层级成立专门机构，起到领导作用，其中，试图在县级搭建起政府领导、人大监督、专家技术支持的架构。人大在这个组织架构中主要体现的是监督权，而不是预算审议权；人大的监督权又是通过县级委派监督员实现对各乡镇预算过程的监督，而主要不是乡镇人大对同级政府的监督。在公众参与方面，主要依托于村民小组、行政村的现有制度架构，产生代表（群众议事员）参与到预算决策过程，没有民众自发组织或社会组织的参与。参与式预算最后通过群众议事员在乡镇"民主议事会"中实现，是在人大制度之外的代议权力结构，群众不直接参与预算决策。

国际上参与式预算的典型案例，均有政府方、公民方和中间结构三方面形成组织架构，其中公民方面的活跃自组织系统是参与必不可少的组织主体，国内创新中政府的单方主导性均为突出；同时，国际案例中均有公民直接决策的制度设计，比如议题优先性的直接民主会议，国内实践目前没有公民直接投票的案例。

（五）参与的流程

盐津县的乡镇参与式预算核心机制是"民主议事会"。

在"民主议事会"之前的准备工作有三方面：群众议事员的推选、乡镇政府测定参与式预算资金总量、项目库的准备。其中，项目库建立的程序是：第一，申报项目库，群众议事员和政府分别提出项目，全部汇总形成项目库，一般每个议事员提一个项目，最多不超过两个。第二，项目审查，项目汇总后，由乡镇改革领导小组上报县改革领导小组，后者组织相关部门人员或委托专业机构进行独立审查，审查标准包括技术性审查和政策性审查，具体包括，其一资格审查，即项目是否属于乡镇财政支持范畴，其二形式审查，即材料是否规范齐备，其三内容审查，即是否立项真实，预算合理，没有重漏等，审查结果在民主议事会召开十天前提交群众议事员，无论项目是否通过，审查意见均在民主议事会上通报。第三，通过审查的项目构成民主议事会竞争环节的正式项目库。

在上述准备齐备之后，乡镇工作小组组织召开"民主议事会"，民主议事会每年两次，分别于2月和11月召开，分别决定年初预算编制和预算调整方案。遇紧急新增项目或执行过程的重大问题，工作小组可召集临时会议。县群众参与预算监督委员会向各乡镇民主议事会派监督员对议事会进行全程监督。

民主议事会决定投资项目之后，进入其后预算过程：乡镇财政依表决结果编制预算草案，经乡镇政府批准，报乡镇人代会或人大主席团会议审议通过后批复预算，乡镇人民政府依次执行，调整预算也须经民主议事会表决，乡镇人大主席团审议批复，财政年度结束后，乡镇财政所组织决算，县财政局牵头组织项目绩效评价和问责，在次年民主议事会上公布。

2014年豆沙镇7个村（社区）26个议事员，共有项目申报40个，通过审查的正式项目库项目16个（含2个镇政府项目）；中和镇9个村（社区）37名议事员，共有项目申报37个，通过审查的正式项目库项目18个（含4个镇政府项目）；庙坝镇12个村（社区）48个议事员，共有项目申报81个，通过审查的正式项目库项目27个（含两个政府项目）。项目审查环节被剔除资格的项目比例在51%—67%，一多半项目在资格审查环节被剔除，其中内容审查也是重要一部分。政府审查是形式合法性还是包括内容合理性，可以考虑逐步放开，将后者交由议事员投票判定。

（六）代表怎么产生？

盐津县的乡镇预算参与最后的项目决策是群众代表做出的，这些代表称为"群众议事员"。群众议事员以行政村为单位产生，由两部分人构成：第一，定额推荐，即每行政村（社区）两名，村两委召开会议提名推选；第二，随机抽选，即每个行政村（社区）人口0.5‰的名额，各村民小组推荐1人进入抽选库，然后村（社区）两委召开群众会议，从抽取库中随机抽取出与名额相应的议事员。2012年议事员产生模式，豆沙镇采取与人大代表推选类似的过程，以村（居）民代表提名、镇政府批准确认、村（居）民代表会议无记名投票方式产生，每村2—3个名额；庙坝镇采取以户代表选举的方式，由村（社区）党总支主持，以户代表无记名投票方式选举产生。

2014年四个试点乡镇群众议事员一共是：庙坝镇48名（24定额、24抽选），豆沙镇26名（14定额、12抽选），中和镇37名（18定额、19抽选），牛寨乡32名（16定额、16抽选）。以中和镇为例，37名议事员中村干部18名，群众19名，村两委以外的代表大概占到一半。

议事员资格上必须是年满18岁的户籍或常住人口，一般应具备初中以上文化程度。一旦当选，任期三年。议事员资格撤销有七种情况，除一些不能继续履职原因外，所提出并参与实施的项目累计两次绩效评价不合格，也将被撤销议事员资格。

由于预算是通过代表，即"群众议事员"，做出表决，因而代表的产生规则就会相应影响代表权的配置。盐津县对议事员的名额规定兼顾了村和人口量两方面的权重，产生方式一是推选，二是随机抽选，没有明确的投票规则。其中推选相应体现村两委的权力，随机抽选的单位决定代表权的范畴。以村民小组为单位的随机抽选，由于每个议事员代表范畴为村民小组，会造成两个相应后果：一是抽样参会造成部分人群有代表、部分人群没有代表；二是议事员所提议题范畴局限于村民小组单元内，不太可能提出较大受益范畴的议题。国际上的做法一般是公民投票产生议事员，如巴西阿雷格里港的参与式预算划分十六片区，片区即是投票单元。温岭的新河模式直接嫁接于人大代表机制，没有单独的代表产生机制；其泽国模式则采取全镇人口为抽样库的随机抽样，是个人代表意见汇集的模式。盐津模式如果使代表权具有普遍覆盖性，每个村（居）民、或每个户代表直接投票产生村（社区）议事员，是一个可行的方案；另一种可能是在村内按议事员名额划分为几个较大片区（如几个自然村为一个片区），每个片区以村民、或户代表直接投票产生一名议事员。直接投票选出符合名额的议事员，才可能使议事员的代表权具有覆盖性，同时扩大议题的受益范畴。

（七）预算如何投票？决策什么？

盐津县的乡镇参与式预算决策机制为"民主议事会"。民主议事会的决策主体是群众议事员，政府其他人员经登记后可参加、经主持人同意可发言，但没有表决权。庙坝镇特意适当邀请党代表、人大代表、政协委员和知名人士列席。

民主议事会的主持人有专门的产生机制。第一步，乡镇群众议事员和乡镇政府共同推荐4—5名候选人，报县领导小组审定后形成主持人备选库；第二步，备选主持人需参加县的培训，具备一定会议支持技能；第三步，民主议事会前三天，从主持人备选库中随机抽取出本次会议的主持人。庙坝镇采用的是乒乓球抽取箱的方法，在乒乓球上写上主持人号码，由乡镇改革领导组指定人员，在镇人大、纪委等监督下，从抽取箱随机抽取号码，确定主持人。主持人负责会议进程，控制时间，维持会场秩序。2014年豆沙镇和中和镇的民主议事会主持人分别是一名中学教师和一名政府机关的普通工作人员。

到会议事员不低于本届登记议事员85%为会议有效，豆沙镇的这一比例是2/3到会。会议议程依次是：第一，主持人统计议事员实到人数，宣布大会开始，议程和议事规则；第二，议事员中推选监票员、唱票员、计票员；第三，乡镇工作小组通报上年项目执行、绩效评价与问责情况，乡镇财政所负责人（或乡镇改革领导组）通报本年度财力测算，项目库项目、未通过审查项目逐一说明审查意见；第四，逐一进行项目陈述①，每个陈述5分钟，提问、讨论，每次发言不超过3分钟；第五，议事员投票表决，投票规则采取一人一票，超过（含）1/2票数（如豆沙镇）或2/3票数（如庙坝镇、中和镇）为通过；第六，公开唱票、监票、计票，监督员复核无违规后，乡镇工作小组现场宣布投票结果；第七，表决通过的项目，按照得票顺序确定实施项目，直到可分配资金总额分配完为止。超出预算总额时，表决通过的项目可在下半年预算调整环节顺序安排，当年仍无法安排，直接进入下一年项目库（如豆沙镇）或取消当年资格（如庙坝镇）。

2014年豆沙镇正式项目库项目16个（含2个镇政府项目），议事会表决票数过半通过项目12个，申请政府资金共344.19万元，本期可安排预算经费279万元。中和镇正式项目库项目18个（含4个镇政府项目），议事会表决票数过2/3通过项目13个，申请政府资金共275万，小于可安排预算经费315万的总额，剩余资金留待预算调整接受新申请项目。

镇政府项目会否在表决中通过？结果显示，豆沙镇政府2个项目，环卫基础维护和集镇基础设施维护，全部以满票通过，也是仅有两个获得满票的项目；中和镇没有满票项目，镇政府4个项目中，集镇及环卫基础维护、便民服务中心改造、教育奖补基金，以较高票通过，但小米辣产业发展仅获得3票而落选。在议事会讨论中议事员提出了一系列问题，如土地适合性、市场问题、效益一直不好、受益人群为何选择两个特定村等，镇政府提出了自己的效益计算理由，但对部分问题无法给出解答。以全部"财力余额"纳入参与式预算，政府非常担心的一个问题是各议事员只关心自己村的项目利益，诸如环卫等基本公共维护费得不到通过，使乡镇基本公共服务无法维系。在盐津至今为之的试验中，尚没有出现过这类问题。浙江温岭的长时间以来实践同样表明，代表对乡镇的基本公共服务，包括乡镇政府的办公、运行经费，表现出相当的理性和理解。可见将乡镇本级的公共服务纳入参与式预算，是可行的。

---

① 中和镇为保证项目陈述顺序的公正性，对陈述顺序也采取了乒乓球抽序号的方式，按照现场随机抽取的顺序安排项目陈述。

参与式预算能不能决策乡镇本级的公共服务，是参与模式的一个重要维度。预算决策什么？实践中实际有三种情况。第一是代表共同参与整个乡镇的公共事务决策，第二是代表协商表决、决定资源在各自代表区的投入分配，第三是政府将资金平均分配给各村（社区），各村（社区）决定资金的具体使用项目。最后一种形式实质已经不是公共预算资金配置的参与了。盐津模式是前两种形式的结合，以第二种形式为主。进一步的改革可以尝试扩大项目的覆盖人群范畴，不仅是村民小组级别的小项目竞争，而且纳入联合项目机制、扩大受益人群覆盖面，及至乡镇层级公共事务的决策。

产生覆盖面更大的项目，在制度安排上与代表产生机制相关，需要有广泛代表权或联合代表权的发生机制，如大片区直选代表机制，或者联名提议项目的权重安排。如庙坝镇的改革方案中规定，50名民众代表中7人以上联名提出建议案或会议期间7名以上代表提出建议案，政府应纳入预算草案并一并提交议事会讨论，单个建议案项目不得超过参与预算总额的25%。这是一种非常值得探索的方向。另一方面，乡镇政府能不能代表乡镇整体利益加入参与式预算决策流程，在议事会中政府能不能有投票权？豆沙镇规定若投票议事员为偶数，则政府参加投票。在巴西模式中，市政厅不参加投票。北京麦子店的模式则是政府代表和群众代表的混合议事会，政府代表街道的总体利益，有一定的票数比例。2012年豆沙镇的试点以"政府主导"拟定建设项目，群众议事员只是表决优先性。温岭泽国模式类似，也是政府拟定项目，民众抽样代表只表达对每个项目的倾向顺序。政府拟定项目，议题开放性受局限；小单元的代表提议题，议题覆盖面有局限，多层次的议题提出单元，包括联合议题和政府提出议题，是一种结合。

（八）谁控制过程？

规则本身也是一种权力。在中国参与式预算改革中，政府的主导角色是明显的。盐津县的改革方案是县领导小组总体部署的，包括基本组织结构的建立、群众议事员选取方案、培训方案、民主议事会实施办法、项目库管理办法、项目支出管理办法、项目预算执行情况监督办法、项目预算执行绩效评估办法等，县领导小组给出了基本规则。乡镇改革领导小组扮演了对规则具体实施的角色，包括"群众议事员"的推选组织过程，决策预算的"民主议事会"则在县乡两级改革领导小组领导下进行。

不过，盐津县乡政府避免了直接介入决策过程，最重要一个制度安排是民主议事会的主持人角色。主持人是非利益相关者的中立角色，经过专业培训，他们良好地保持了议事会民主决策机制的独立性，避免了党政一把手主持会议对决策带来的倾向性影响。

改革咨询小组设置也是盐津县的制度特色，改革方案中的规则设计，在很大程度上体现了专家的意见，这也是盐津的改革尽管实践时间不长，模式却比较成熟，且具有一定多样性、试验性的一个因素。

（九）公民做什么？

参与式预算的目的是实现公民的直接参与。以巴西为代表的国际经典模式，均分为直接民主和间接民主两个参与阶段，其中前一个阶段是公民的直接投票，确定议题优先性和选举代表。在最后的决策结果中，直接民主和间接民主的结果均体现出一定权重。中国各创新模式中公民直接投票参与的环节一般较弱，没有明确的投票议题和投票程序。

公民直接参与不足，其中很核心的原因是中国创新模式中，几乎都没有公民组织的身影。国外模式中，在直接参与阶段，公民自组织，特别是联合性组织，是公民参与的主要组织途径。

（十）参与的时间

时间本身是预算权力配置的一个重要因素。民主国家的预算编制周期通常在数月甚至一年以上，也就是提前一年时间要进入下一财年的预算过程，预算在议会与政府之间往复地讨论修改，历经多个回合，才进入最后的表决过程。同样，参与式预算改革介入预算的时间周期也是相当长的，巴西一个参与式预算的流程是七个月，而参与式组织机构介入整个预算编制、执行、修订评估的周期则是全过程的。

中国预算参与的流程时间均不长，核心决策往往在一天会议议程做出。盐津县的参与式预算，一次预算参与的流程，主要经历选群众议事员、准备项目库到民主议事会表决预算项目，其中主要决策环节民主议事会为一天时间。浙江温岭的改革在人大会议期间适当延长了讨论预算环节的时间，并试图在人大闭幕期间建立监督机构，跟进预算执行，但是这种制度创新无法得到正式制度的支持。

在预算周期中，包括预算参与的制度设计，是仅有"是"或"否"的一次性决策，还是有预算修订环节，会对参与权有不同影响。中国人大会议表决预算通常是某半天会议中的一个环节，简单"同意"或"反对"的选择，预算被人大否定的可能性几乎是不存在的，以至于人大的决议成为"走形式"。在温岭新河模式中，人大预算讨论延长了讨论时间，增设了讨论、意见反馈、政府修改预算、再交由代表讨论的循环过程，如此反复，"三上三下"，最后针对修订案再表决，修订权赋予了人大一个可实现性的参与权力。盐津县制定的民主议事规则中提出了修改预算，但由于实际会议议程时间较短，每个项目在陈述、讨论后，就进入了直接表决，没有预算修订环节。在试点的参与预算进入常态化后,可以适当提前参与的时间,容留更宽裕的时间量,增加民主议事会之前的准备过程,在民主议事会上增设预算调整修改的环节等。

(十一) 与正式制度衔接

参与式预算是一种试验,民众和代表的参与权与现行公共预算决策体制之间是什么关系?大概有两种情况:第一,直接通过人大代表参与,没有其他的代表产生途径,如温岭的新河模式。新河模式的预算参与分两个阶段:一是民主恳谈会,开放公民参与,人大代表听取民众意见;二是人大代表会议,实化和细化人大的预算权,实现人大代表对公共预算的参与。这对于现行体制中人大"走形式"的预算模式是一个切实的制度化的民主发展。第二,不改变人大的制度安排,在人大代表之外,单独设置公共预算的代表机制,通过预算代表参与到预算过程中。预算代表的产生方式一种是随机抽样代表,即在整个有参与资格的人群中随机抽取代表,参加预算决策,他们的代表性是通过科学抽样方法来体现的,如温岭泽国模式;另一种是选举代表,在一定范围内,投票产生代表参与预算决策,从而代表权是通过民主赋权过程实现的,巴西模式及国外大多数参与式预算都是议会外的民选代表。盐津模式是在不介入人大正式制度的情况下,推选和抽样结合产生专门的预算代表(群众议事员),设立专门的预算参与机制(民主议事会)。

单独设立预算参与机制,优点是改革阻力小,可行性较普遍,但必然面对与正式预算制度之间的关系问题。盐津的改革定位在政府编制预算阶段的民主参与。因而它对时间要求的提前量是比较长的。

(十二) 法律制度保障

2012年3月《盐津县人民政府关于乡镇财政管理体制改革的实施意见》,提出探索"参与式"预算管理的路子,《实施细则》提出选择相对成熟乡镇试点。在财政体制改革的大背景下,盐津县人民政府2014年1月印发了《盐津县群众参与预算改革试点方案》《盐津县群众参与预算群众议事员推选办法(暂行)》《盐津县群众参与预算民主议事会议事规则》《盐津县群众参与预算项目支出管理办法(暂行)》,各试点镇相应发布了《改革实施细则》。

表1总结了参与式预算盐津模式在各关键要素上的特点,及其与国内外参与式预算试点相比较,所体现出的公民参与权力的程度。

表 1 盐津参与式预算模式关键要素总结

	关键要素	盐津模式	其他模式	盐津模式公民权程度
1	启动层级	省财政改革试点	市、区；巴西全国性	+++
2	预算层级	乡镇	乡镇、街道；广东省以及河南焦作市、上海闵行区的预算参与指体制内人大参与和听证	++
3	预算范畴	除去基本支出和必保刚性支出后的全部"财力余额"，含转移支付	一笔定额公共投资；全部预算（温岭新河模式）	++
4	组织结构	县委、县人民政府领导实施，试点乡镇领导小组负责组织；政府领导、人大监督、专家咨询三方架构 预算决策机制为乡镇民主议事会、群众议事员 没有社会自组织	巴西有政府、居民、中间结构三方面组织架构，居民主要依托自组织体系	++
5	参与程序	推选群众议事员、测定资金、准备项目库—民主议事会投票表决—政府依据表决结果编制预算，人大审议通过预算—预算执行、调整 项目库的建立由各群众议事员和政府分别提出项目，经县改革领导小组组织审查产生正式项目库	巴西模式：第一个阶段直接民主，片区筹备—第一次片区会议—各种预备会—第二次片区会议，投票确定片区议题优先性，选出市预算委员会委员；第二个阶段代议民主，委员定期会议、表决议题权重、计算预算分配、政府起草预算—预算方案提交会、批准—委员准备详细投资计划—委员在预算执行中监督、调整、争议解决和反馈	++
6	代表产生	定额推荐，每行政村（社区）两名，村两委召开会议提名推选；随机抽选，每行政村（社区）人口 0.5‰，村民小组推荐或户代表投票，抽选库随机抽取	人大代表； 随机代表； 推选代表	++

（续表）

	关键要素	盐津模式	其他模式	盐津模式公民权程度
7	预算投票	正式项目库来自议事员和政府提出项目；群众议事员在民主议事会投票表决，85%或2/3议事员到会，过1/2或过2/3得票为通过；表决通过的项目按照得票顺序依次获得投资，直至完成总金额 政府没有投票权； 有中立主持人； 县乡人大监督	政府提出项目，代表投票选择出项目优先性顺序（温岭泽国）； 政府和代表各占一定投票权重（麦子店）； 人大代表会议表决预算修正提案和修改的预算方案（温岭新河）； 巴西参与预算委员表决要素计算权重，预算决策是公民投票权（议题优先性）和委员权力（权重安排）的结合	++
8	规则控制	县领导小组负责领导、部署、方案规则制定、议事员和主持人培训，组织项目库评审，流程监督 有专家咨询组； 乡镇工作小组组织群众议事员推选； 民主议事会在县乡改革领导小组领导下进行	党委主导； 第三方倡导（无锡、黑龙江）； 人大主导（广东、闵行）； 巴西是公民选举的参与预算委员主导标准，政府制定技术标准，公民与政府两方面密切互动	/
9	村民参与	在议事员调研或村民大会中提议项目，在村民小组中推选议事员	温岭模式：广泛的民主恳谈； 巴西模式：活跃的社会自组织	+
10	参与时间	群众参与预算草案编制，以及预算调整决策，准备过程在一个月内，民主议事会一天，一年两次 单次决策	群众参与预算草案编制，单次决策； 温岭新河及上海闵行人大会议预算讨论最长延长到1.5—2.5天，往复讨论，有组织结构延伸入预算执行、监督、反馈环节； 巴西：一次预算参与过程七个月，并在预算编制、执行、调整监督等全过程跟进	++
11	制度衔接	人大审议预算之前的参与，并赋予人大监督职能，但不介入人大预算审议制度	温岭新河与人大制度改革结合； 巴西提前于议会审议的独立参与机制	+

（续表）

	关键要素	盐津模式	其他模式	盐津模式公民权程度
12	法律保障	县人民政府制定改革试点方案、群众议事员推选办法民主议事会议事规则等，乡镇相应制定实施细则	不同细化程度的方案	++

三、盐津模式及参与式预算的问题讨论

参与式预算是公民和公民组织直接参与预算决策权的民主形式。这种参与形式在多大程度上体现公民权力，是分析参与模式的重要指标。云南盐津模式将乡镇"财力余额"全部放到参与的方式决定，包括了财政资金在各村（社区）之间的配置，以及乡镇本级的公共事务预算，采用项目竞争的方式，全部由群众议事员通过民主议事会独立做出投票表决，政府依据表决结果编制预算，并在预算调整阶段同样采用民主议事会的方式做出决策，整个过程公民参与权力的体现程度是比较高的。盐津作为云南省参与式预算改革的试点，自2012年以来，一直在各项具体制度环节尝试不同的制度安排，比如代表产生方式、投票规则、项目入选标准等等，进行多元化的试验，为试点的进一步扩展累积了实践经验。

比较国内外经验，改革可以进一步深化的几个关键环节包括：

第一，扩展参与的时间，特别是村（居）民直接参与的阶段，更多体现群众的需求表达，并依此提出预算额度高低不等的项目方案，进而在民主议事会上加入权重计算，增加修正案等方法，不仅是"是"或"否"的单次表决；并使参与贯穿编制、执行、监督的预算环节，规范决算责任。

第二，代表选择方式，除村（居）两委推选的定额代表外，可以将按人口比例配置的代表名额开放竞选，由全体村（居）民或户代表直接投票选出相应数量的议事员，或者按照名额划分片区，每个片区全体就村（居）民直接投票选出一个议事员。这样通过增大议事员代表范围，可以避免部分人群有代表、部分人群没有代表，以及代表只能提出小受益面项目的问题。

第三，乡镇层次公共事务的参与决策机制，除政府提项目进入项目库外，可以设立议事员联名提案制度，对联合提案作为额外名额，鼓励跨越片区或者行政村的项目提案，这样使得乡镇预算参与不仅是讨论"分钱"，决定各村之间的资源配置，而且可以使议事会成为共同的公共事务讨论平台。

第四，激励村（居）民自组织的作用，包括开放一定的规则制定权，激发社会活力。

第五，在适宜的条件下，探索参与式预算与人大制度改革的结合。

第六，国际比较显示，县级规模也是适宜的参与规模。目前国内直接的公共预算参与均止于乡镇、街道层级，探索县级参与式预算，是未来的制度创新方向。

中共十八届三中全会提出构建现代国家治理体系，促进社会改革和协商民主的发展，并将财政定位为国家治理的基础和重要支柱。参与式公共预算的试点，是现代国家财政体系改革道路上非常有意义的探索，它的多元化制度尝试正在为改革提供宝贵的经验。

---

[1] Arnstein, Sherry R., "A Ladder of Citizen Participation", *Jaip*, Vol. 35, No. 4, July 1969, pp. 216 – 224.

[2] Arthur C. Brooks, "Can Nonprofit Management Help Answer Public Management's 'Big Questions'?", *Administration Review*, 2002, Vol. 62, No. 3, pp. 259 – 266.

[3] Baiocchi, G., "Emergent Public Spheres: Talking Politics in Participatory Governance", *American Sociological Review*, 2003, Vol. 68 (1), pp. 52 – 74.

[4] Baiocchi, Gianpaolo and Ganuza, Ernesto, "Participatory Budgeting as if Emancipation Mattered", *Politics & Society*, 2014, Vol. 42 (1), pp. 29 – 50.

[5] Bherer, Laurence, "Successful and Unsuccessful Participatory Arrangements: Why Is There a Participatory Movement at the Local Level", *Journal of Urban Affairs*, 2010, Vol. 32 (3), pp. 287 – 303.

[6] Bingham, L. B., Nabatchi, T. and O'Leary, R., "The New Governance: Practices and Processes for Stakeholder and Citizen Participation in the Work of Government", *Public Administration Review*, 2005, Vol. 65, pp. 547 – 558.

[7] Cabannes, Y., "Participatory Budgeting: A Significant Contribution to Participatory Democracy", *Environment and Urbanization*, 2004, Vol. 16 (1), pp. 27 – 46.

Dahl, R., *Democracy and Its Critics*, New Haven, C. T.: Yale University Press, 1989.

[8] Ernesto Ganuza, Héloïse Nez and Ernesto Morales, "The Struggle for a Voice: Tensions between Associations and Citizens in Participatory Budgeting", *International Journal of Urban and Regional Research*, 2013, pp. 1 – 18.

[9] Fung, A. and Wright, E. O., "Deepening Democracy: Innovations in Empowered Participatory Governance", *Politics & Society*, 2001, Vol. 29, No. 1, pp. 5 – 41.

[10] Marquetti, Adalmir, Schonerwald da Silva, Carlos E. and Campbell, Al., "Participatory Economic Democracy in Action: Participatory Budgeting in Porto Alegre, 1989 – 2004", *Revies of Radical*

Political Economics, 2012, Vol. 44 (1), SI, pp. 62 – 81.

[11] Patsias, Caroline, Latendresse, Anne and Bherer, Laurence, "Participatory Democracy, Decentralization and Local Governance: The Montreal Participatory Budget in the Light of 'Empowered Participatory Governance'", *International Journal of Urban and Regional Research*, 2013, Vol. 37 (6), pp. 2214 – 2230.

[12] Renée A. Irvin and John Stansbury, "Citizen Participation in Decision Making: Is It Worth the Effort?", *Public Administration Review*, 2004, Vol. 64, No. 1, pp. 55 – 65.

[13] Santos, B. D., "Participatory Budgeting in Porto Alegre: Toward a Redistributive Democracy", *Politics & Society*, 1998, Vol. 26 (4), pp. 461 – 510.

[14] Sintomer, Yves, Herzberg, Carsten and Rocke, Anja, "Participatory Budgeting in Europe: Potentials and Challenges", *International Journal of Urban and Regional Research*, 2008, Vol. 32 (1), pp. 64 – 178.

[15] Souza, C., "Participatory Budgeting in Brazilian Cities: Limits and Possibilities in Building Democratic Institutions", *Environment an Urbanization*, 2001, Vol. 13 (1), pp. 159 – 184.

[16] Wampler, B. and Avritzer, L., "Participatory Publics: Civil Society and New Institutions in Democratic Brazil", *Comparative Politics*, 2004, Vol. 36 (3), pp. 291 – 312.

[17] 董晓辉:《公民参与预算的平台构建和路径设计》,《财经问题研究》2011 年第 2 期, 第 81—84 页。

[18] 何包钢:《近年中国地方政府参与式预算试验评析》,《贵州社会科学》2011 年第 6 期, 第 27—32 页。

[19] 刘邦驰:《试析参与式预算的理论基础与实践: 基于巴西与中国浙江温岭两镇的比较》,《财政研究》2009 年第 9 期, 第 63—66 页。

[20] 王逸帅:《国外参与式预算改革的优化模式与制度逻辑》,《人文杂志》2009 年第 3 期, 第 83—89 页。

[21] 徐娟娟:《巴西与中国的参与式预算比较: 财政选择和制度思考》,《黑龙江对外经贸》2011 年第 10 期, 第 143—144 页。

[22] 袁方成:《地方治理的域外经验: 德国 Berl Lichtenberg 区的参鉴》,《社会主义研究》2009 年第 4 期, 第 48—52 页。

[23] 朱圣明:《国外参与式预算的实践与探索》,《四川行政学院学报》2014 年第 3 期, 第 83—87 页。

中国官员财产公示申报制度——进入立法议程的析论

孔繁斌　杨淑玲[*]

在中国政治体系中，执政党及其政府的治理意图，主要是依赖各级各类官员得以实现的，而按照廉洁治理或道德管理的理念对官员行为的控制，则构成提高执政党对官员可依赖性的机制。在多种控制方式的尝试中，流行于西方民主国家的政府官员财产申报制度日益受到执政党关注，并在制度约束条件下做出了局部的试点。在未来的国家治理设计中，执政党对官员财产申报制度的态度究竟是什么？是否会将其提上立法议程？本文拟选择公共政策分析的途径，对此做出论述，以扩展该议题研究的视野。

一、中国大陆官员财产申报制度演进轨迹

在1987年11月，时任全国人大常委会秘书长、法制工作委员会主任的王汉斌，在六届人大常委会第二十三次会议上说："一些国家规定公务员应当申报财产收入，我国对国家工作人员是否建立申报财产制度问题，需要其他有关法律中研究解决。"1988年，监察部会同国务院法制局对我国财产申报制度进行论证，并起草了《关于国家行政机关工作人员报告财产和收入的规定》草案，后来工作因各种原因停止。1994年经中央同意并转发的全国人大"八五"立法规划中，将《财产收入申报法》列入立法项目，但实质性的立法工作并未启动。

大陆官员财产申报制度建构的局部突破始于1995年，当年4月30日，中办、国办印发《关于党政机关县（处）级以上领导干部收入申报的规定》，明确了申报收入的目的、申报的主体、申报的内容、申报的时间、受理申报的机关、监督惩戒、解释权限等基本内容，这是中国政府第一次要求领导干部登记个人收入的廉政性规定。有

---

[*] 孔繁斌，南京大学政府管理学院教授。杨淑玲，南京大学服务型政府研究所助理研究员。

学者称这是中国初级的"阳光法案",是从政道德领域的一场革命。

根据2000年12月中纪委五次全会精神,2001年6月中纪委、中组部联合发布了《关于省部级现职领导干部报告家庭财产的规定(试行)》,要求省部级领导干部报告本人、配偶以及由其抚养的子女的家庭财产,包括大额现金、存款、有价证券、房产、汽车、债权债务等。这项规定把1995年以来通行的领导干部"收入报告制度"扩展为"财产报告制度"。

2007年中共十七大报告提出"保障人民的知情权、参与权、表达权和监督权","确保权力正确行使,必须让权力在阳光下运行";十七大还第一次把"实行党务公开"写入党章。这些新论断和新要求明确表明了党中央的决心——党政领导干部个人事项报告制度也应走向公开和"阳光",使之发展成为人们期望的官员财产申报制度。

2009年初,官员财产申报制度在西北边陲新疆阿勒泰地区率先实施。2009年1月1日,阿勒泰地区55名新提任的副县级领导干部的财产申报资料在"阿勒泰地区廉政网"进行了公示。同日,阿勒泰地区所有县处级干部的首次财产申报工作正式开始。这一探索迈出了我国官员财产公之于众的第一步。

2010年7月11日,中共中央办公厅、国务院办公厅印发的《关于领导干部报告个人有关事项的规定》(以下简称《规定》)在媒体上公布。这项规定是按照党的十七届四中全会提出的"完善党员领导干部报告个人有关事项制度,把住房、投资、配偶子女从业等情况列入报告内容"的要求,在征求多方意见的基础上,最后经中央政治局会议审议通过的。新《规定》扩大了申报事项的范围,改进了监督环节,加大了问责力度,表明财产申报制度的实践又迈出了新的一步。

上述官员财产申报制度从无到有,契入国家官员治理的实务之中,但执行中仍旧存在制度效率有限的问题,尚未形成更具权威的法律形式。那么,是否应该推进其进入立法议程促进其通过?如何就此问题达成共识呢?

二、大陆官员财产申报立法趋势分析

在经济合作与发展组织编撰的《中国治理》报告中,中国大陆公共部门是廉洁治理被视作完善治国理政的首要任务。该报告分析认为,伴随中国大陆现代化进入制度完善阶段,制定和颁布国家公务员财产申报方面的正式法律,已经成为具有战略意义的重要工作,也是公众期待已久的政府决策。下面本文将依照公共政策预测分析的有关知识,从趋势外推、理论演绎和判断估测三个逻辑角度,对我国公务员财产申报制度的发展趋势展开分析。

(一)"由此及彼":基于实践事实的根据

在公共政策分析中,预测政策发展趋势的趋势外推法,要求基于反映历史和现实变动规律的数据并参照相关影响因素或约束条件来推测未来,可以理解为是"由此及彼"的方法。本文尽管在理论上指认公务员财产申报对我国廉洁政府建设和公共服务品质提升具有积极作用,但尚须提供进一步的论证来说明我国试点基础上的该项制度走向全国性立法是基本趋势。这一论证受资料限制无法在理想状态下展开,但本文尝试选择一种间接的途径进行观察。具体做法是,分析透明国际组织颁布的国家廉洁指数与颁布了公务员财产申报法的国家之间的一致性,如果一致性程度高,则大致可以说明公务员财产申报制度的建构对国家廉洁治理具有积极的促进效应。

"透明国际"(Transparency International)是国际上唯一专门致力于抑制贪污腐败的国际性非政府组织(Non-Government Organization,NGO),由德国人彼得艾根(Peter Eigen)于1993年在德国柏林成立,目前在90多个国家成立分会(Chapters)。该组织的宗旨是激起社会关注、建立反腐联盟、开发反贪工具、设定廉洁标准、监测贪腐活动。自成立以来,研发了贪腐印象指数 Corruption Perception Index(CPI)、行贿指数 Bribe Payer Index(BPI)和全球贪腐趋势指数 Global Corruption Barometer(GCB)。该机构每年每年发布全球绝大多数国家和地区政府的廉洁指数。

根据透明国际2006—2011年发布的全球180个国家和地区的廉洁指数报告[1],我们在大约180个国家和地区中,廉洁指数排名位于前10%的国家和地区几乎都颁布了类似公务员财产申报制度的法律,而排名最后15%的国家和地区几乎都没有类似的法律颁布。通过一致性观察所得的结论(见表1),可以初步得出公务员财产申报制度和一国或地区政府的廉洁程度有着密切的相关性。

当然,这一相关性验证方法并非十分严谨,一个国家和地区的政府的廉洁程度必定受多种因素影响,而并非仅是由公务员财产申报制度决定的。所以,这一观察分析的方法仅是一种间接的归纳,深度的解释还有待搜集更完全的资料做出。

(二)"由理及彼":基于合理的理论假设的根据

通过公认的理论假设对政策未来趋势进行推论,也是政策分析中的常见手段,"它利用某些一般的陈述(公理、规律等)来推断其他具体的陈述(包括预测)的真假"。[2]那么,什么样的公共管理的一般理论假设会影响政府廉洁治理制度选择的趋势呢?

任何社会行动都是约束条件下的实践。一般来说,公共管理面临公共资源有限性、集体行动困境和正义普遍性三个条件的约束,支持和实现公共管理行动的具体制度设计，实际上就是对这约束条件的突破。从这样的理解中我们可以提炼出反映公共管理行动发展趋势的两个理论假设。

表1 部分廉洁排名前列国家的官员财产公示法律法规

时间 国家	2006	2007	2008	2009	2010	2011	法规名称
芬兰	9.6	9.4	9.0	8.9	9.2	9.4	1951年《公务员公开法》
冰岛	9.6	9.2	8.9	8.7	8.5	8.3	1996年《信息法》
新西兰	9.6	9.4	9.3	9.4	9.3	9.5	1993年《隐私权法》、1982年《公务员信息法》
丹麦	9.5	9.4	9.3	9.3	9.3	9.4	1970年《行政文书公众使用法》
新加坡	9.4	9.3	9.2	9.2	9.3	9.2	《防止贪污法》《财产申报法》《公务员纪律条例》
瑞典	9.2	9.3	9.3	9.2	9.2	9.3	《保密法》《储蓄消费实名制》
瑞士	9.1	9	9	9	8.7	8.8	（未查到）
挪威	8.8	8.7	7.9	8.6	8.6	9	《公众使用法》《信息自由法》《公共行政文件公开法》
澳大利亚	8.7	8.6	8.7	8.7	8.7	8.8	《公务人员行为准则》《信息公开法》（1982年）
荷兰	8.7	9	8.9	8.9	8.8	8.9	1978年《政府信息公开法》
奥地利	8.6	8.1	8.1	7.9	7.9	7.8	1987年《联邦行政机关信息公开法》
卢森堡	8.6	8.4	8.3	8.2	8.5	8.5	（未查到）
英国	8.6	8.4	7.7	7.7	7.6	7.8	《净化选举，防止腐败法》
加拿大	8.5	8.7	8.7	8.9	8.9	8.7	《公职人员利益冲突与离职行为法》
香港	8.3	8.3	8.1	8.2	8.4	8.4	《公开资料守则》
德国	8	7.8	7.9	8	7.9	8	《环境信息法》，尚无具体行政人员信息公开
日本	7.6	7.5	7.3	7.7	7.8	8	《为了确立政治伦理的国会议员资产公开法》
法国	7.4	7.3	6.9	6.9	6.8	7	《政治家生活资金透明度法》
爱尔兰	7.4	7.5	7.7	8	8	7.5	（未查到）
比利时	7.3	7.1	7.3	7.1	7.1	7.5	1994年《行政公开法》
美国	7.3	7.2	7.3	7.5	7.1	7.1	《信息自由法》《政府官员行为道德法》《道德改革法》

资料来源：根据透明国际组织官方网站信息及相关文献编制。

假设1：公共福利最大化。这是公共管理适应当今社会发展趋势的最根本的价值原则，一切的公共管理行动和支持其效能提升的制度创新，其正当性的衡量标准在于是否促进公共福利取得最大化结果。当然，公共福利最大化并非仅仅意味着结果的线性增加，更主要的是指向公共福利的成本—利益分布的合理化。按照詹姆斯·Q.威尔逊论证，改善公共政策制定质量的发展方向，在于实现政策成本—利益之间的均衡。就此分析，贪腐不仅有违正义而且严重扭曲了政策的成本—利益均衡性，正如我们所见，我国公共治理中因贪腐而导致的公共福利成本剧增的不乏其例。因此，可以说公共福利最大化假设是值得考虑的依据。

假设2：公务员主观责任最大化。 公共管理的趋势之一，是传统的行政伦理学的向公共管理伦理的发展，是公共管理的重心从一个 E（efficiency）过渡到两个 E（efficiency/ethics）。在公共管理伦理构建中，既注重来自他人期待的客观责任承担的制度设计，更关注基于自我期许的主观责任的承诺。政府体制与及运行机制中包含的伦理追求并不能代替公务员个体对公开、忠诚、良知的认同。在公共管理伦理发展趋势要求下，政府廉洁治理的制度工具转向深化公务员主观责任的承诺，正成为一种"时尚"。

综合这两个反映公共管理发展趋势的理论假设，在两因素收敛推论逻辑中可以提炼这样的一个假设（见图1）：

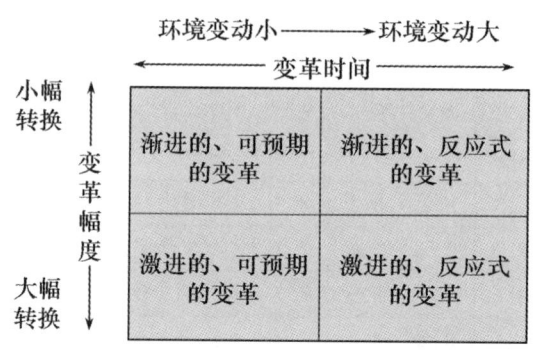

图1 公务员财产申报制度趋势的收敛推论图

按照这一因果推论提供的结果，我们可以获得一个关于理想的政府廉洁治理制度设计的具体假设：我国未来廉洁政府治理的制度绩效，取决于公务员有效自律程度和更充分地保护公共利益的程度。

我们再看公务员财产申报制度作为政府廉洁治理工具的特点。

在民主法治政治框架下，约束公共权力的方式和动力都是丰富而多元的，目的只有一个，就是敦促公职人员廉洁奉公，避免和遏制政治堕入腐败之中，维护正义的价值。在这些方式和动力中，我们可以通过交叉分类获得政府廉洁治理的四种制度形式（如图2），即教育警示制度、财产申报制度、法律追究制度以及道德自省制度。

		动 力	
		他律	自律
方式	预防（事前）	教育警示制度	财产申报制度
	惩处（事后）	法律追究制度	道德自省制度

图 2　政府廉洁治理制度工具分类图

结合上图的因果推论结果，可以发现这四种促进政府廉洁治理的制度工具中，满足公益受损最小化趋势和主观责任增强趋势的制度工具，应该是公务员财产申报制度。者首先是因为公务员财产申报制度具有事前预防贪腐行为的功效，从廉洁治理和反贪腐行动来看，较之于事后追究惩罚来说，能够以更小的损失维护公共利益，实现公共福利最大化。其次公务员财产申报制度是公务员自主行为的体现，是公务员自证清白的最合法方式。总之，这一初步的理论推论的结论，应该能够表明未来我国廉洁政府治理的制度工具选择趋势在于公务员财产申报制度的确立。

（三）"由心及彼"：基于专家判断的根据

是否支持一项政策的根据，还可以来自专家和精英人士基于洞察力的判断。① 在第三章的叙述中我们看到，世界上颁布了官员财产申报制度的国家和地区，一般也都是该国家或地区政治精英竭力推进的结果。在转型以来的中国，也正是执政党在反腐倡廉的历史实践中，逐步探索和在局部试点了我国公务员财产申报制度。在深化改革的现阶段，执政党和一些专家对推动全国范围的公务员财产申报法的关注和阐述也有了发展。

首先，执政党的政治家明确倡导廉洁透明制度的推行。例如，在今年第 8 期《求是》杂志上，中共中央政治局常委、国务院总理温家宝发表了《让权力在阳光下运行》的重要文章。文章指出，"只有在广泛有效的监督之下，政府才不会懈怠，才能有效遏制滥用权力和以权谋私。政府要自觉接受人大监督和人民政协民主监督。加强政府层级监督，加大行政监察和审计监督力度。自觉接受人民群众和社会监督，尊重并依法保护公民、法人和其他组织的监督权。"[4]这实际上表明了执政党高层对包括公务员财产申报制度在内的多项促进公共权力透明化举措的姿态。

---

① 作者曾就大陆公务员财产申报或公示制度问题做过"政策德尔菲法"调查。

其次,国情分析与发展专家的研究提出了战略性提议。经济合作与发展组织、中国科学院和清华大学国情研究中心出版的《中国治理》研究报告,分析了我国改革开放以来社会现代化转型面临的治理挑战,做出了推进治理转型的制度设计和分析,并认为公共管理制度尤其是中国公务员反贪腐制度创新基于基础地位。在分析中该报告还提出中国政府廉洁管理战略应将廉洁措施变成日常管理行为的一个完整部分,包括财产申报制度在内的"预防工具包"从长期来说是一种相对不那么昂贵的制度投资。[5]

最后,公共管理学者比较分析了贪腐治理机制的选择时机。我国有些公共管理学者分析认为,"面对周期性腐败的猖獗以及腐败亡党亡国的教训……只要党和政府继续坚持一手抓经济,一手抓惩治腐败,加强反腐败的制度建设,就能标本兼治"。[6]并且从机制有效性角度判断和认为,随着官员财产申报制度的逐渐发酵和伴随其全国性立法出台,我国公权力的贪腐将进入"衰减期,其一般性标志,一是全社会舆论包括网络、微博、媒体、手机等各种新媒体舆论工具形成了强大的"仇腐"压力;二是腐败成本持续上升。但作为我国公权力贪腐进入衰减期的重要标志,则是建立全国性统一的官员财产申报制度。[7]

综合本节以上三种途径的分析,我国公务员财产申报制度作为政府廉洁治理制度工具选择,应该说是基本的发展趋势。

三、官员财产申报立法的可行性

(一)从政策备选方案类型看可行性

在公共政策分析中,有的学者认为政策方案的可行性应包括四个层次的内容:"适当"(Approriate)、"可能"(Possible)、"可行的"(Feasible)和"可实验的"[8];另一些学者认为,可行性涉及技术可行性、财政可能性、政治可行性和行政可操作性等[9]。此外,我国学者也对公务员财产申报制度发展和完善的可行性有过一些分析。这里我们试图从政策备选方案的类型视角,换个角度再看一看我国公务员财产申报制度改进和完善的可行性问题,当然受经验材料的限制,只能从政策备选方案类型的理论启发中做些初步思考。

政策备选方案的类型理论,是根据政策方案中因果关系的复杂性和政策方案涉及的信息程度两个逻辑划分,形成的一种关于政策方案的交叉分类。根据这一理论框架,政策方案被划分为常规性、条件性、艺术性和创造性四种,每种类型的可行性程度取决于其涉及的因果关系的复杂性和信息的多少,详见图3:

		因果关系的知识	
		高	低
信息	少	☐ 常规性 例如：社会保障政策	☐ 有条件的 例如：失业、通胀政策
	多	☐ 艺术性 例如：国防政策	☐ 创造性的 例如：科技发展政策

图3　政策备选方案的类型

资料来源：盖伊·彼得：《美国的公共政策：承诺与执行》，复旦大学出版社2008年版，第81页。

在图3中，常规性政策方案是指涉及的信息比较单纯、因果关系比较明确的类型，例如社会保障政策；有条件的政策方案涉及的信息不复杂但其因果关系不十分确定，例如失业、通货膨胀；艺术性政策方案反映的是因果关系确定性高但信息量大、复杂，例如国防政策；创造性政策方案是最难确定其可行性的一种类型，因为这种类型的方案因果关系模糊而且涉及的信息复杂。

从这一理论来看，公务员财产申报制度的政策方案，可以认为是常规性的类型，因此我们可以从因果关系确定性和信息复杂性两个维度判断其可行性。

(二) 从政策方案类型的因果关系要求看可行性

在公务员财产申报制度方案中，因果关系的确定性程度应该说是较高的，只要公务员将个人法定范围内的财产状况依程序做出申报，则公务员个体的廉洁状况也就比较清晰地呈现出来，公务员在公职行为中是否存在不轨行为的判断大致也是可以知晓的了。

表2　台湾部分政府官员的财产公示情况

人物	职位	存款	股票证券	房产(建筑)	名车	总资产
马英九	"总统"	7372万	96万	9		2亿
萧万长	"副总统"	1900万	300万			
吴敦义	"副总统"	1300余万		1	1	
陈冲	"行政院长"	1300多万	5000万	2	2	
赖浩敏	"司法院长"	5000万		5		
关中	"考试院长"	2000余万	1600万	20		1亿
王建煊	"监察院长"	1075万	2178万			
王金平	"立法院长"	850万		40		

例如，据台湾地区媒体报道，"'监察院'5日公布最新财产申报资料，马英九夫妇名下的动产与不动产总额破亿，'行政院长'陈冲有1300多万存款，'司法院长'赖浩敏申报存款近五5000万元，吴敦义夫妇有1300余万元存款"。[10]

报道称，台湾这些高官如此富有，却没引来民众质疑。这一例子说明，通过官员所申报的财产状况，公众可以根据验证性信息对其财产获取的正当性做出判断，不仅更深刻了解了政府官员，而且也对政府官员个人和政府施政是否公正廉洁有了合理认识，从而在政府及其官员与公众之间建立起彼此的信任关系。

正因为这一公务员财产申报制度存在显著的因果关系，很多国家和地区在政府廉洁治理和官员贪腐治理中，都选了这一制度作为基础性途径，并由此获得了较好的成效。所以，通过公务员财产申报制度建构促进政府及其官员廉洁，遏制贪腐，是具有很高的可行性的制度设计。

（三）从政策方案类型信息要求看可行性

从政策方案类型理论来看，影响大陆公务员财产申报制度的信息维度是否存在可行性呢？这里所说的信心因素，主要是指作为结果的公务员所申报的个人财产信息，如前所述，这些信息包括个人收入、存款、不动产、高级奢侈品等。应该说，在中国经济逐步发展、人们生活质量不断改善的当今，如何界定公务员个人财产有其复杂一面，但总的来说也是较容易确定其作为申报方位的财产内容的。也就是说，公务员财产申报制度作为廉洁治理的方案，其对信息的需要是"少"而不是"多"，只要获取申报范围中公务员个人财产的数据就可行了。

当然，如何获得这些信息也是影响可行性的因素，伴随我国银行个人资产监管信息化水平的提高和其他必要的配套政策的形成，只要公务员财产申报法颁布，其可行性并不是难题，相反目前的难题是如何促进该法尽早进入立法议程，如何在公务员财产状况的公众认知和评价上形成合理的共识。

四、官员财产申报制度立法的行动建议

中国大陆1995年就提出县处级以上干部申报财产，十几年来公务员申报和公开其财产的制度尚未以国家法律的形式颁布。那么，我国公务员财产申报法进入立法议程的进程，有哪些问题需要加以关注呢？目前，关注公务员财产申报已成为公众舆论关注的重要议题，深入讨论该制度进入立法议程，有其现实意义。

1. "多源流"的因素分析

公共政策议程是十分重要的国家治理平台，也是公共政治活动中充满争执和冲突

的场域。在公共政策议程研究中有较多观察分析模型,这里我们借用目前较有影响的美国政策学者金登的"政策之窗"或"多源流"政策议程分析框架,对我国公务员财产申报制度进入立法议程做简要分析。金登多源流政策议程分析框架的核心思想,是构建了打开"政策之窗"的多因素分析框架,其中"政治流""政策流""问题流"是其关键。[11]金登认为,只有这三流交错汇集,政策之窗才有开启的可能,一项政策问题才会进入决策议程。

第一,政治流分析。

推进我国公务员财产申报制度立法化,是当今我国政府和公务员廉洁治理的重要趋势。从执政党的倡导来看,早于1995年开始的局部处级领导干部层级的试点,就表明一种推进力量。近年来,我国不乏全国和地方人大代表对此议题提请立法机构给予关注,例如,《新民晚报》(2012年3月6日)《连提七年"官员财产公开"的民意价值》一文的报道:

> 全国人大代表、重庆一名叫韩德云的律师,这些年与官员财产申报公开制度结下了"不解之缘",2012年"两会"期间,他将第七次向全国人大递交相关书面建议或议案。……同一议案,连提七年,这股韧劲,或许会让人产生一种感觉,觉得这是愚公移山。……面对这样结果,相信更多人会觉得,这种"愚公移山"式问政,真是值得的。韩德云也说,现在公众对官员财产申报的意愿有增无减,民意既然仍然聚焦在这样的话题上,那么,通过两会平台继续表达相关民意,进一步推进相关制度出台,就是理性务实之举。[12]

伴随网络走进公民生活,特别是在"两会"举行期间,不乏越来越多的公众传递国外官员财产申报和公开的信息,倡议我国加快该法的立法进程。这表明推动此项政策议题进入立法议程的政治流逐步扩大,来自多方面的议程压力正在加强。

第二,政策流分析。

如果仅从我国公务员财产申报政策构建文本来看,也许还显得比较单薄,但是我国针对干部廉洁自律、领导干部财务监督和纪律惩处方面的政策文件,应该说是较多的,例如,2009年出台的《关于实行党政领导干部问责的暂行规定》、2010年出台的《中国共产党党员领导干部廉洁从政若干准则》、2011年颁布的《〈中国共产党党员领导干部廉洁从政若干准则〉实施办法》等,这实际上意味着这一政策议题的发展趋势。同时,推动政府廉洁自律、透明公开的政策法律,也日益增多,例如2011年率先由中央政府部门实行的"三公消费"公开制度、2007年国务院颁布的《政务信息公开条例》,以及廉政风险防控和规范权力运行工作广泛推行,公共资源交易市场建设全面推开等,都表明推进民主行政、促进政府及其公务员廉洁的"政策群"成为治国理政中政策注意力关注的内容。

第三，问题流分析。

一个较为普遍的民意趋势是，我国政府廉洁状况不容乐观，公务员贪腐现象依旧严重，解决贪腐问题是公众反映强烈的突出问题。例如，从2008年至2011年四年间，全国纪检监察机关共立案五十多万件，给予党纪政纪处分五十多万人；在2010年针对工程建设领域腐败现象集中开展专项治理过程中，共排查工程建设项目36.7万个，发现问题15.87万个；在"小金库"治理工作中，清理出"小金库"25738个，涉及金额127.86亿元；2011年1月至11月，新发现"小金库"8202个，涉及金额28.46亿元。

经过三十余年的改革开放，中国大陆已经发展成世界第二大经济体。但是，大陆在转型发展中依旧存在一些"发展的陷阱"，政府机构和公职人员的贪腐就是一个。贪腐的存在，不仅损耗了执政的合法性，降低了公众对公权力及其官员的信任，同时也加剧了经济运行的成本。所以，政府的廉洁治理成为到达问题临界点的重大的公共问题。

2."多源流"的触发机制分析

金登的"政策之窗"中政治流、政策流和问题流的因素解释，只是政策问题进入最终议程的一项条件，究竟能否进入政策议程，还要看是否有"政策企业家"在积极推动，即如何获得进入政策议程的"触发机制"。公共政策中的理性触发机制，是指"政策企业家"通过科学分析论证，基于相应的利益立场，在法定政策议程中推进政策问题进入决策的一种方式。在大陆政策制度结构体系下，执政党，全国人大代表等都是"政策企业家"，按照我国《立法法》的规定，全国人大的委员长会议、国务院、中央军委、最高人民检察院、最高人民法院、全国人大个专门委员会，以及10位以上全国人大常委会组成人员，都是法定的法律案的有权提出者，当然，各机构侧重的法律案领域有所不同。分析这一"政策企业家"群体，我们觉得至少像委员长会议、国务院、最高人民检察院及其他两类委员，都是适宜作为"公务员财产申报法"的立法提出主体。

大陆家治理的领导体制，是执政党居于政策议程把关的最高层，这即是说除了上述《立法法》规定的有权提出立法案的机构和人员外，执政党中央委员会不仅也是当然的立法案提出者，而且是最关键的提出者。因此，如果执政党在自己的相关决议中确立对大陆制定和颁布公务员财产申报法的政策建议，一般来说自然就会进入全国人大立法议程。

按照有些公共政策学者的观察和分析，Roger W. Cobb and Charles D. Elder 认为，一个问题要得到政策制定者的考虑，除了该问题必须是受到广泛关注的问题（范围）

和有相当数量的公众提出必须采取行动的要求（强度）之外，还必须为一个适当的政府机构所重视。从文献涉及的信息来看，中央纪律检查委员会就是这样的一个适当机构，该委员已经对"公务员财产申报法"高度关注并采取过推定其进入立法议程的倡议。在我们前文提到过的《新民晚报》的《连提七年"官员财产公开"的民意价值》报道中，有这样的描述[13]：

> 同一议案，连提七年，这股韧劲，或许会让人产生一种感觉，觉得这是愚公移山，只见愚公奔忙，大山岿然不动。如果这样想，就错了。其实，六年间，每年两会后，韩德云都能收到有关部门答复。韩德云说，"第一次提交该议案时，当时的答复是条件尚不成熟；2007年的答复是存在困难；到了2008年，监察部的负责人亲自打电话给我，说正在积极开展工作；而去年中纪委的答复则是历年来最肯定、最清晰的。"韩德云说，中纪委表示正进一步深入调研，将结合实际对制度设计进行研究论证。由此看，对制度立法的准备已经比较充分了。这些答复显示，官员财产申报的立法准备工作，这些年不断取得进展，足以带给人希望。

这段资料显示，中纪委很可能在推进我国"公务员财产申报法"立法中，是最为合适的"政策企业家"，当然，这需要执政党中央委员将其写进正式决议，才可能通过人大转变为国家立法意志。

3. 政策抉择时机的选择策略

在涉及我国公务员财产申报制度何时能够进入立法议程的问题上，最常见的答案是"时机不成熟"。究竟何时算是时机成熟，这也许不容易分析，因为这既涉及国家治理中对政策议题轻重缓急排序的考虑，也和立法调研、政策方案成熟度等因素密切相关。但这不妨碍我们从理论上对政策抉择时机做出策略性分析。我们先看图4的内容：

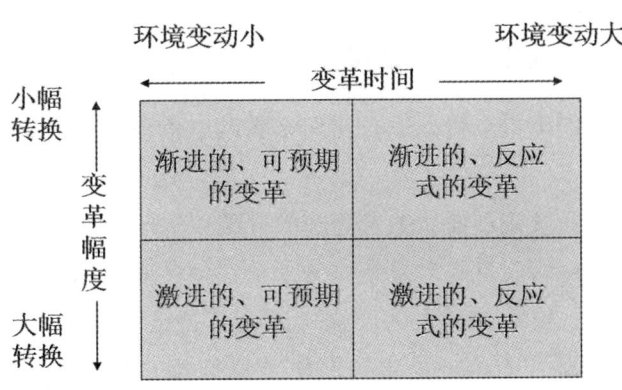

图4 政策抉择时机选择的策略

该图显示的是由变革时间和变革幅度交叉形成的变革策略选择。变革时间主要影响的因素是变革所面临的环境，而变革幅度的主要考虑的是范围大小，由此形成渐进、激进、可预期和反应式四种情形组成的变革策略。

现代国家治理的实践表明，政策议程是指将社会问题提上政策问题议事日程，纳入决策领域的过程并确定政策问题轻重缓急的一项排序，政策问题什么时候进入政策议程。政策议程同时也是"稀缺的资源"，对议程机会做出怎样的分配，始终是现实政治生活中的重大策略难题。从我国公务员财产申报制度进入立法议程来看，其重要性应该说不言而喻，在各公共机构全方位推进，在各类公务员中全范围覆盖也是必需的原则，因此，变革幅度因素是给定的。按照这样的理解，真正影响"进入议程"或"出台"的时机，要到变革时间因素中寻找。换言之，该项政策出台的时机应该具备这样的条件，即政策出台后对行政乃至政治环境不会造成大的或不可控的变动，只要满足这一条件的话，公务员财产申报的时机应该说就具备了。当然，对于是否会造成大的环境变动，并不是说被动等待一个较少波动的机会降临，而是意味着国家应做出相应的安排前瞻性和主动地控制所引发的环境变动。

通过上述策略图的分析，我们觉得我国公务员财产申报制度的立法时机，可选择激进—可预期的策略，这一策略中环境变动较小的条件不是等待其出现而是创造性地获取。当然，如果选择激进—反应式的变革策略，则需要执政当局有强大的控制能力。

五、结束语：需要形成几点共识

尽管中国大陆公务员财产申报制度亟待解决的关键问题是进入立法议程，但从完整的政策分析系统来看，也需要对政策合法化和颁布后的如何提高实施效果提供建议。这里拟从政治文化、技术和管理三个维度，做些思考。

（一）在政治文化进化中改进立法理念

假设我国公务员财产申报法得以颁布，那么有两方面的政治文化将可能对其有效实施产生抵触作用。

一是如何协调和沟通政策利益相关者之间的分歧。

公务员财产申报法尽管规范的对象是公务人员，但实际上这一政策的实施也是与公众的利益密切相关的，作为纳税人的公众一定会对公务员财产申报的范围、方式、信息的真实性等提出质疑；而公务员也会产生类似抱怨、对公共舆论进行抗辩等行为。因此，需要在社会中形成新的政治文化，保持信息的畅通和确立"合法反对"的论辩规则，促进政策利益相关方谋求共识，改善该项政策实施的环境。

二是如何看待立法颁布之前的贪腐行为。

按照法不溯及以往的惯例，一旦公务员财产申报法颁布之后，对公务员法律颁布之前的财产申报如何看待？这可能既是立法颁布后面临的难题，更是目前该制度进入立法议程中的忧虑。这背后涉及一国之政治文化如何对待所谓的"转型正义"问题。我们知道，正义有其抽象的但具有正当性的价值标准和定位准则，但抽象的正义如何与具体的历史情境相勾连呢？某些历史情境下显得具有正义性的行为，可能会与抽象的正义价值产生冲突，对此，政治文化该如何处置呢？

英国考文垂大学宽恕与和解研究中心主任安德鲁·瑞格比，在其政治文化著作《暴力之后的正义与和解》一书中[14]，探讨了这些令人痛苦与困惑的难题，选择了不同的具体分析了不同社会在处理过去创伤问题上所采取的不同方式的优点和缺陷，进而明确指出需要通过建立一种接受过去与展望现在和将来的政治文化，以作为妥善处理暴力创伤后遗症的理念。饱受暴力冲突伤害的社会，在暴力终止之后需要终止复仇的冲动，以对过去的历史采取和解态度的，为一个和平而稳定的未来奠定根基。按照安德鲁·瑞格比不乏深刻的见解，我国应该在公开对话论辩中，形成对待贪腐的一种政治文化心态，即为了未来政府和公职人员的廉洁而对公务员财产申报法的颁布抱最大的支持态度，耽于对过去贪腐的追究而迟缓公务员财产申报法的颁布，只能是将明天的阳光也关进昔日的黑暗中。

（二）在强化信息定量中提高政策公信力

无论从公务员财产申报法规划还是从未来出台后的贯彻执行来看，该项法律或政策唯有赢得政策公信力，才能在廉洁政府治理中产生预期功效。

我们知道，政策公信力的程度，取决于政府政策制定的动机是否公正、规划是否合理、执行是否有效和影响是否能得到控制。但在信息十分发达的当今社会，在越来越注重实证数据的时代，要想改进政策公信力，最值得关注的因素恰恰在于如何尽可能为社会提供反应政策状况的定量化的信息。所以，在我国公务员财产申报法的立法过程中，通过专业化、定量化的方式监测政策信息是不能忽视的措施。同时，一旦出现公务员财产申报法公信力下降的状况，仍旧要通过细致的量化陈述其原因，公布相关的信息，以在相关信息充分公开中，重塑政策法规的公信力，以至该政策因公信力提高而发挥应有的廉洁治理的作用。

（三）在专业化管理中获得政策绩效

一项政策获得合法化和颁布之时，实际上还需要评估该项政策采取什么方式执行最有效。一般来说，从行政管理的角度来看，一项新政策可以采用三种方式执行，即新成立一个机构、交给一个已有的机构，以及交给多个机构。如果我国公务员财产申报法立法通过后，其执法主体需要斟酌。

就我国目前的机构设置来看，一旦公务员财产申报法颁布，与该法执法相关的机构有国家公务员管理机构、行政监察机构等，甚至人民代表大会都可以成为申报管理机构。评估什么机构作为该法的执法机构，是需要在公务员财产申报制度设计、规划和立法过程中审慎考虑和选择的。

今后无论具体的执法机构设置在哪里，提高公务员财产申报管理的专业化水平，则是无可回避的新职能。参照国外的做法，这一专业化的管理应该以履行公务员道德管理为基本职能，申报管理机构需要在申报信息支持下，对公务员道德状况实行监测和分析，采取辅导和帮助，真正实现公务员财产申报所有具有的道德管理功能。

---

[1] 数据来自透明国际官方网站，http://www.transparency.org/。

[2] 邓恩：《公共政策分析》，中国人民大学出版社2001年版，第244页。

[3] 温家宝：《让权力在阳光下运行》，《求实》2012年第8期。

[4] 《中国治理》，第三章第三节相关论述，清华大学出版社2007年版，第68—71页。

[5] 唐任伍、刘立潇：《中国官员腐败将进入衰减期》，《环球时报》2012年4月12日。

[6] 唐任伍、刘立潇：《中国官员腐败将进入衰减期》，《环球时报》2012年4月12日。

[7] 宁骚主编：《公共政策学》，高等教育出版社2003年版，第347页。

[8] 卡尔·怕顿、大卫·沙维奇：《政策分析和规划的初步方法》，华夏出版社2001年版，第205页。

[9] 《财产申报资料公布，台湾高官多富豪》，东南新闻网，网址：http://www.fjsen.com，访问日期：2012年4月6日。

[10] 参见金登：《议程、备选方案与公共政策》，丁煌译，中国人民大学出版社2004年版。

[11] 参见《连提七年"官员财产公开"的民意价值》，《新民晚报》2012年3月6日。因条件限制，我们还无法搜集资料，观察全国究竟有多少人大代表提交过公务员财产申报公开及相关的提案，只能选取这个例子从性质上解释问题，而不能提供量化的证据。

[12] 参见《连提七年"官员财产公开"的民意价值》，《新民晚报》2012年3月6日。

[13] 参见安德鲁·瑞格比：《暴力之后的正义与和解》，刘成译，译林出版社2003年版。

如何发挥公务人员终身学习理念

周和根[*]

一、前言

澳门特区政府成立以来,成功实施了15年免费教育,改善了教育环境,提高了教育成效。而随着社会经济的转型,迈向知识经济型社会的步伐进一步加快,居民对个人素养、技能、知识的需求也随之增加。今天,终身学习已逐渐受到重视和认同。

然而,部分公务人员的学习态度仍较被动,缺乏积极性。那么,如何恰当利用资源,激发公务人员终身学习理念,提升其个人素质,正是特区政府慎重思考的课题。

如何改善上述情况,离不开两大要素:生理和心理的满足。两者互相配合,可使公务人员对所属部门增加归属感及对工作增加积极性。

二、终身学习理念

终身学习的理念与实务发展,自20世纪70年代起,先后得力于联合国教科文组织(UNESCO)、经济合作发展组织(OECD)及欧盟等重要组织的宣扬与推动,而得以全面开展并受到国际社会的重视。在70年代,终身学习的发展已在全球社会中积极进行,同时引起了热烈回响。以整个人类教育发展史观之,90年代无疑是终身学习的重要转折点。而90年代中期之后,全民终身学习的理念更是成为全球教育风潮,此一理念的兴起,也促成了终身学习在许多国家的政府政策中,拥有优先级的发展地位。

当前终身学习的理念与实务,更在国际间被视为21世纪教育的重要发展原则与

---

[*] 周和根,澳门博彩监察协调局顾问督察,澳门终身学习者协会会长。

方向。无可置疑，终身学习的重要性已日益增加。各地学者对终身学习的说法各有不同，但仍可从中归纳出共同的特性：

1. 终身持续性：学习发生于摇篮到坟墓的每一个历程，随着每个历程的发展，个体依其不同的学习需求而持续学习。
2. 全民普遍性：学习是全民所普遍享有的权利与共同期望的机会，不因个体的年龄、性别、职业地位而有任何的差别。
3. 学习自主性：终身学习强调自主的精神，透过个人自由意识的决定，主动地安排适合自己的学习方式及内涵。
4. 全面统整性：在直的层面，终身学习希望连接教育的每一个阶段；在横的层面，则要统整正规、非正规、非正式的学习，使学习者便于时时学习、处处学习。
5. 方式弹性化：终身学习的方式、途径因个人需求不同而充满弹性。

终身学习强调的是，人一生都要学习。从幼年、少年、青年、中年直至老年，学习将伴随人的整个生活历程并影响人一生的发展。这是不断发展变化的客观世界对人们提出的要求。简言之，终身学习即是指"一辈子的学习"。

三、马斯洛需求层级理论

心理学家马斯洛需求层级理论指出，人类需求可分为五个需求层次，由低至高，依序为生理需求（physiological needs）、安全需求（security needs）、归属（社会）需求（social needs）、尊重（自尊）的需求（self-esteem needs）和自我实现需求（self-actualization needs）。当人满足了生理、安全和人际关系的需求后，便会想得到被人尊重的感觉，当中包括自我的尊重和得到他人的尊重，最后，追求自我实现，针对自己认定之理想或目标而努力。例如：公务人员应终身学习，自我增值，改善本身不足，提高使命感。

四、终身学习和向上流动的关系

随着知识型经济在全球的深化，终身学习已不仅仅是一种理念，而是生活的一部分。终身学习能使我们克服工作中的困难，解决工作中的新问题；能满足我们生存和发展的需要；能使我们得到更大的发展空间，更好地实现自身价值；能充实我们的精神生活，不断提高生活质量。

学习可以丰富一个人的知识内涵及精神修养，增加向上流动的机会。因此，为免被时代巨轮压碎，被社会淘汰或落后于他人，而持续教育及终身学习，正好符合实际需要。

换言之，终身学习和向上流动犹如兄弟般关系密切，透过学习，其工作技能及个人修为也会随之而提升，且受用一生。

五、加强培训课程

际此知识爆炸年代，社会发展一日千里，公务人员应多阅读和进修，自我增值，透过学习，改善工作。而知识更可改变命运，那是不容置疑的事实。积极进取，掌握适应社会转变的知识、技能，才不致被社会淘汰。

培训课程目的是提升公务人员水平与技能，扩大视野，提高工作责任心，激励奋进，增加其归属感，各人紧守岗位，那才能彼此发挥团队精神，从而提高工作效率。

目前是全面推广公务人员终身学习的大好时机，只有持续进修，方可优化公务人员的素质，培养更多专业人才，这对公务人员及其所属部门都有得益，而提高效率正是公务人员培训的最终目标。

因此，特区政府应检讨相关措施，加大培训力度，刺激公务人员积极性，自我增值，坚持学习的决心，从而达至向上流动的目的。

六、采用各种资助和奖励措施，鼓励优秀人才脱颖而出

为使公务人员更积极地利用工余时间进修，特区政府可考虑设立公务人员持续进修奖励计划，政府部门开办之课程，以及其他获认可的课程，皆纳入持续进修奖励计划网内，公务人员可按其意愿及工余时间，选择报读有关课程。当然，每一项培训课程必须超过20学时，课程完结时，学员要通过严格的考核，课程更以符合职务需要为主，所得分数亦较高。

建议方案如下：普通课程（1分）；语言、计算机课程（2分）；和职务有关等专项课程，例如：变革与承担研习班（3分）；学士或以上课程（7分）。

倘公务人员的培训课程达到10分者，可得奖励，其晋升时间可缩减一年。

而该公务人员晋升之后，仍继续进修，再达到10分者，可再得上述奖励，换言之，其晋升时间可再缩减一年，依此类推。

而且，在公职生涯中，对于坚持进修的公务人员，其培训课程总合计，达到指定分数者，给予奖座或纪念品以资鼓励，并加以表扬，作为其他公务人员的学习榜样，让优良的学习风气能延续下去。

公务人员终身学习奖励如下：金奖（60分）；银奖（40分）；铜奖（20分）。

最后，把公务人员的学习情况存入其个人档案中，作为他日晋升的参考和依据，择优选贤能。

对优异成绩的公务人员进行奖励，不仅使其本人感到鼓舞，对其他公务人员也形成一种无形的激励作用，互相学习和支持。

七、退而不休，活得更精彩

很多公务员朋友即将退休，却好像漏了气的皮球，没精打采的，整天在盘算距离退休尚余多少日子，对于应负的任务爱理不理的，那态度直接或间接影响其他同事的工作情绪，而低落的士气更严重拖慢部门的效率，对后辈也形成坏榜样！及至退休的时刻降临，那思想斗争和矛盾心情互相夹杂，他们又显得手足无措，不知如何是好。该情景使我想起曹操那首《龟虽寿》中的名句："老骥伏枥，志在千里。烈士暮年，壮心不已。"曹操在诗歌中自比一匹上了年纪的千里马，虽然形老体衰，屈居枥下，但胸中仍然激荡着驰骋千里的豪情。他说，有志干一番事业的人，虽然到了晚年，但一颗勃勃雄心永不会消沉，一种对宏伟理想追求永不会停息啊！

其实，即将退休时，应尽心尽力，以其专业知识和经验扶植后辈，薪火相传，发挥优良的公仆精神，无私奉献，更好地服务市民。要知道，退休不是百无聊赖的悠长假期，而像是球赛下半场的开始。在这中场休息的时候，是停下来检讨及计划下半场的好时机。

当然，退休之初由绚丽回到平淡，确实要花一段时间才适应过来。而在退休生活中要做到作息有序，饮食均衡，适量运动，心境开朗，以包容的心去待人处事，积极面对人生。简言之，要做到放下、放松、放平，乐观地处之泰然。

唐代诗人李白《将进酒》有云："黄河之水天上来，奔流到海不复回。"寒来暑往，物换星移；人长而退休，乃无可避免之事，只是如何做到退而不休，尽展夕阳余晖，进而享受天伦，臻于化境，自觉今生无悔，那才不枉此生。

孔子曰："凡事预则立，不预则废。"意思就是说："任何事情，凡是预先准备就能成功；不能预先准备，就会失败。"

因此，退休前，应该做好准备。退休后，也可继续坚持学习，寻找箇中乐趣。而在终身学习旅途上，可认识一些志同道合的朋友，彼此支持和鼓励，共同迈进。其实，退休公务人员享受退休乐逍遥之余，坚持终身学习，继续干有意义的事，对其身心健康也有好处。

八、结论和建议

总而言之，终身学习是一个重要的概念，如果一个社会可以成功令终身学习的风气广泛蔓延，整体社会的进步也比较能够实现，那将是一个大规模的向上流动。在21世纪，本地以及来自邻近地区的竞争持续升温，愿景及威胁同时出现，只有具有良好的装备才能及时把握机会，大展所长。

对于如何更好发挥公务人员终身学习理念，有关当局应加强激励因素，对于有意学习，具良好公仆精神者，不管高级或是低级，使之都有平等的学习机会，而非现在般，只有具有高级技术员职称者，才可前往北京学习，而其他职称者，纵使具有学士、硕士，甚至博士学位，也只能够往广州学习。

有关当局可考虑增设公务人员行政学院，精心策划各类长期、中期和短期课程，专责培训各级公务人员，借以提升积极性、实效性。

再者，为鼓励各级公务人员更积极学习，可以设置一定数额奖学金，如获取录就读硕士或博士课程，给予三分之一的学费资助，而对于该部门有利的课程，更可获得优先申请机会。

当然，公务人员既然选择了其作为终身职业，应尽心尽力服务市民。之后，为做好工作，迎接新挑战，自我增值，利用工余时间进修，吸收新知识。最后，把所学的，应用于工作上，提高效率，更好地服务市民，反馈社会。

---

[1] 刘羡冰：《教书育人再思考》，澳门出版协会，2012年。

[2] 《终身学习资源手册》，教育暨青年局出版，2006年4月。

[3] 《终身学习杂志》，历年各期，教育暨青年局。

[4] 澳门特区政府2013—2014年度施政报告。

[5] 《澳门手册》，澳门日报。

[6] 《退休乐逍遥——安享福禄寿10大准备》，天地图书有限公司2011年版。

[7] 谷歌网站，http://www.google.com.hk。

[8] 雅虎网站，http://hk.yahoo.com/。

[9] 教育暨青年局网站，www.dsej.gov.mo。

[10] 澳门大学网站，www.umac.mo。

[11] 理工学院网站，www.ipm.edu.mo。

[12] 旅游学院网站，www.ift.edu.mo。

[13] 《澳门日报》。

[14] 《华侨报》。

[15] 《市民日报》。

完善中国基本公共服务体系的公众需求分析[*]

姜晓萍　田　昭[**]

基本公共服务需求不仅是政府明确基本公共服务范围和标准，完善基本公共服务供给机制的前提，也是直接影响公民的公共服务选择权与参与权利能否实现、基本公共服务的公平性和可及性能否保障的关键因素。为了及时了解《国家基本公共服务十二五规划》颁发后公众对我国基本公共服务体系的需求，我们对北京、上海、天津、山东、浙江、广东、河南、湖北、四川、陕西等22个省、直辖市进行了公众需求调查，从基本公共服务的范围与标准、资源配置、供给方式、绩效管理、公民参与等方面进行分析。

一、基本公共服务的范围与标准需求

基本公共服务是由政府主导提供，旨在保障全体公民生存和发展基本需求的公共服务。具有广覆盖、普惠及、促均等特质。对基本公共服务内容的界定，主要指如何根据公众的生存与发展需求确定政府提供公共服务的范围与标准，实质就是对公民应该享有的社会福利权的界定，同时也是对政府公共服务供给责任的界定。因此，了解公众对基本公共服务的范围与标准需求，是国家完善基本公共服务体系的前提。

（一）公众对基本公共服务范围的需求

按照《国家基本公共服务十二五规划》的要求，基本公共服务包括"公共教育、劳动就业服务、社会保障、基本社会服务、医疗卫生、人口计生、住房保障、公共文

---

[*] 本文为国家社科基金重大招标项目"城乡基本公共服务均等化的实现机制与监测体系研究"（项目批准号：14ZDA030）阶段性成果。

[**] 姜晓萍，四川大学公共管理学院教授、博士生导师；田昭，四川大学公共管理学院助教。

化等领域的基本公共服务以及基层设施和环境保护的重点任务"。公共服务是一个系统工程,涵盖了公众生存和发展的各个领域和各个阶段,对于公众来说,获取全面完整的公共服务是其自身发展和家庭发展的必然要求。公众对基本公共服务范围的需求,一方面表现为公众对于公共服务的全面性需求,即公众要求政府提供适合自身发展不同阶段和自身生活工作各个方面的需求,且这一需求从来不是单一的、独立的,而是横向上包括了衣食、居住、健康和文体的需求,纵向上涵括出生、教育、劳动和养老的需求,缺失任何一方面的需求都会对公众的正常生活发展产生影响。调查显示,如表1所示,公众对于以下的公共服务皆存在着刚性需求,只是根据不同时期以及自身需求的不同情况而在优先顺序上对这些公关服务需求有所不同。总体来看,在当前情况下,生态环境保护、医疗卫生和保障性住房成为了公众最为迫切的需求,而作为基础保障的其他基本公共服务仍是公众生存和发展必不可少的基础条件。

表1 公众所迫切需要的公共服务

项目	选择人数	所占总人数的百分比（N=1621人）	排序
生态环境保护	983	60.6%	1
医疗卫生	889	54.8%	2
保障性住房	705	43.5%	3
公共文化设施	594	36.6%	4
基础设施	566	34.9%	5
义务教育	532	32.8%	6
社会保障	512	31.6%	7
就业服务	475	29.3%	8
社会治安	287	17.7%	9
其他	55	3.4%	10

另一方面,公众对于基本公共服务需求的范围不断扩大。随着当前公共服务体系的不断完善,原先的教育、社保、医疗等公共服务在供给水平上不断提高,公众对于这些生存发展基本公共服务之外的公共服务需求也在不断增长,特别是对于提高自身工作、生活品质的需求在当前更为迫切,如对公共文化设施的需求已经超过了基础设施建设、义务教育、社会保障等方面的诉求,生态环境保护更成为了公众所认为政府最迫切要提供的公共服务。可以看出,公众所需求的公共服务范围是一个不断扩展的过程,与之相应,政府的公共服务体系也应该是一个在量上不断增加、品质上不断提高、范围上不断扩展的动态体系。

(二) 公众对于公共服务标准的需求

公共服务的标准，主要体现为政府该供给什么公共服务，为谁提供公共服务，提供何种水平的公共服务，以及由谁来承担公共服务的供给责任。当前公众对于公共服务标准的需求主要表现在以下方面：

首先，公众要求明确的公共服务辐射范围。公共服务辐射范围涉及一个该由谁享受的问题，按照基本公共服务的属性，公众理应成为公共服务的最终受众，但是由于资源的有限性，部分基本公共服务仍然需要通过一定的限制条件来保障其效用效果，而现实中一些歧视性的制度设计却大大地削弱了基本公共服务的效用效果，造成了公共服务的辐射"受阻"问题。一是公共服务辐射不足，导致公共服务"被私有化"，部分公共服务在现实中被一部分群体私有化为"内部服务"，造成了其他公众的权益受损和社会不公，以当前的外来务工人员公共服务需求为例，人民日报就曾刊文指出：户籍制度的门槛、用工制度的壁垒、利益呼声的沉没、讨薪历程的艰难、社会歧视的冷眼，有形无形地把"异乡人"推向城市生活的边缘地带，造成了"社会拒人、权利亏人、心理贬人、文化伤人"的"社会排斥"现象。[1] 二是公共服务的辐射过度，导致公共服务"被过量消费"，公共服务虽然存在着非排他性和非竞争性特征，但是过量的需求辐射亦会导致服务的低效甚至无效，以广东地铁为例，实施免费政策大大扩大了公共服务的辐射范围，这导致了地铁运量比之前增加了100%，地铁呈现出"被挤爆"状态，大大降低了公共服务的质量和效果。因此，公众对于公共服务辐射范围需求，一方面体现为公共服务不能因为辐射过小而将公众排除在享受范围之外，另一方面公共服务也不能因为过度消费而导致品质的降低。公众要求公共服务必须具有一定的边界特征，且这种边界不是以某种特定因素（如户口、职业、收入）为条件，而应兼具公共性与竞争性。

其次，公众要求公共服务供给责任有明确的分担，防止公共服务的费用转嫁。公共服务的公共性和外部性特征决定了其成本应该是由政府等社会公共部门承担，而现实中往往存在着公共服务在实际运行中的费用转嫁问题，大大加剧了社会成本。一方面，公共服务的有限性与社会需求之间不协调导致的寻租问题，一些公共服务的供给者以公共服务的有限为条件，要求公众必须付出相应的租金作为公共服务享受的前提。以农村低保为例，部分地方的低保往往异化为"关系户"低保。另一方面，公共服务成为了部分地方的"创收"工具，部分地方政府因为财政压力问题，将国家一些免费的公共服务项目异化为"收费项目"，如一些地方的义务教育，虽然国家早已明文规定了义务教育的免费特征，但部分地方仍变向收取大量的教育费用，严重阻碍了教育这一基本公共服务的社会效用发挥。因此，公众期望国家明确各类基本公共服务的供给责任,明确中央政府、各级地方政府以及部分企业、社会组织和公众在基本公共服务供给中的责任分配,避免公共服务供给的缺位、越位问题。

再次,公众要求公共服务具有明确的质量标准,即公众需要政府提供足质足量的公共服务。目前,政府与公众社会大多都是从量上对公共服务进行评价,包括公共服务的财政支出情况、公共服务的覆盖率等,但对公共服务的品质关注较少,这导致实践中出现了一些以次充好、政绩工程的公共服务项目,浪费了大量社会资源却没有增加社会效益,有些甚至影响了社会的和谐与稳定。如图1,对于公共服务有67%的公众认为自身所享受的公共服务既不足量也不足质,25%的公众认为公共服务足量但不足质。虽然在总体上,我国当前的公共服务仍然处于质量双重不足的阶段,但是公众对于质的关注在进一步增加,高品质的公共服务已经成为了个人和家庭生活与发展的核心内容,公众需要政府和社会加强对公共服务的品质关注和强化。

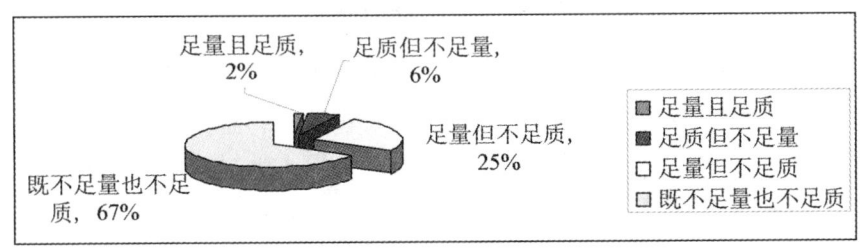

图1 公众对公共服务质量的评价

二、基本公共服务均等化的需求

均等化是基本公共服务的重要特质,从内涵上来看,公共服务均等化包含着三层含义:"全体公民享有的基本公共服务的机会和原则应该均等;全体公民享有基本公共服务的结果应该大体相等;社会在提供大体均等的基本公共服务成果的过程中,尊重某些社会成员的自由选择权。"[2] 从内容上来看,公共服务均等化包括了区域公共服务均等化、城乡公共服务均等化和群体公共服务均等化。公众对于基本公共服务的需求,在根本上体现的是一种公民对于公平权力的诉求。针对公务员的调查显示,有56.3%的公务员认为公共服务均等化是当前公共服务工作的核心内容,其他依次分别为公共服务质量工程(51.7%)、公共服务的全面性(48.5%)、公共服务的满意度(39.6%)、公共服务的可及性(32.1%)和公共服务的效率(30.8%)。公众对公共服务的需求主要表现在以下方面:

(一)区域基本公共服务均等化需求

一是区域基本公共服务政策体系均等化需求。当前我国已经出台了《国家基本公共服务体系"十二五"规划》，针对基本公共服务设置了国家标准，以推进基本公共服务的均等化进程。但基本公共服务均等化，不仅包括了公共服务供给政策，还包括了与公共服务相互配套的政策体系，而政策体系正是导致区域公共服务差异化的根源。而现实中各个地方基于地方发展的需要而在基本公共服务政策上具有明显的差异化特征，以环境保护政策为例，东部地区由于产业发展中心的调整，高新产业、绿色产业成为了主要的产业发展政策，生态环境保护和治理成为环保政策重点；而在中西部地区，由于承接产业转移的需要，一些地方的生态环境政策往往服从于产业发展政策，这使得生态环境保护在东西部地区呈现出非均等化的态势。这引起了群众的不满，并成为了一些群体性事件和社会矛盾的重要导火索。因此，公众需要均等化的公共服务政策体系保障自身发展的机会平等。

二是区域基本公共服务投入均等化需求。如果说基本公共服务存量所代表的是区域公民在发展中机会条件的话，那么公共服务的财政投入在代表了不同区域在公共服务建设中的力度和潜力，财政投入的差异化往往加剧了基本公共服务的非均等化。如表2所示，2012年我国的东中西部[3]地区基本公共服务的财政投入仍然存在着巨大的差距，这使得存量本就具有差异性的东中西部区域，由于现量投入不均差距进一步拉大。尤其是西部地区在各项投入上都落后于东中部地区，公众迫切需要基本公共服务的全国统筹，通过均等化的公共服务财政投入推进公共服务的均等化进程，通过差异化的财政转移支付实现公共服务总量差异的缩小。

表2 2012年区域财政基本公共服务财政支出（单位：亿元）

地　　区	一般公共服务	公共安全	教　育	社会保和就业	医疗卫生	节能环保	城乡社区事务
东部平均	450.56	264.63	819.39	426.23	270.97	105.42	455.96
中部平均	399.49	171.16	681.06	426.65	254.88	93.76	217.89
西部平均	286.42	134.25	454.35	315.58	172.39	81.49	189.48

数据来源：中华人民共和国国家统计局：《中国统计年鉴（2013）》，中国统计出版社2014年版，经整理。

三是区域基本公共服务结果均等化需求。基本公共服务结果均等化是显性的均等化，是公众看得见、摸得着的关于公共服务现实感受，结果的非均等化在现实中往往直接决定着公众的所获取效益水平。区域的政策体系差异和财政投入不同造成了当前我国区域基本公共服务结果的巨大差距。以义务教育为例，经济水平和资源投入的差异导致地区间教育水平出现了差异。从教育资源的配置来看，在硬件设施方面，小学生均教学及辅助用房面积东、中、西部分别为 $5.16m^2$、$3.92m^2$ 和 $3.88m^2$，小学生均体育运动场馆面积分别为 $8.14m^2$、$7.34m^2$ 和 $5.35m^2$，东部地区远高于中西部地区，特别是西部地区；在生均费用方面，东部地区中小学生均事业费用比中西部地区平均差距在1.8—2.2倍，生均公用费用的差距在1.4—2.2倍[4]。而从特殊教育公共服务来看，如表3所示，东中西部各省份的投入资源和产出也存在巨大的差距，东中部地区在教师投入方面远高于西部地区，而从受益人来看，东部地区也大大领先于西部地区，区域的基本公共服务受益情况存在巨大差距。区域基本公共服务结果的非均衡化造成了公众"用脚投票"选择下的人口流动，而区域的户籍制度又阻碍了这一流动的正常进行，形成了当前很多地方所出现的外来人口与当地人关于基本公共服务享受的矛盾。

表3　2012年各地区特殊教育情况统计（单位：人）

地　区	教职工数	专任教师	招生数	在校学生数	毕业生数
东部地区平均	2340.3	1857.4	2295.8	14157	1866.6
中部地区平均	2056.2	1695.8	2044.2	12088.8	1258.9
西部地区平均	877.27	742.27	2027.18	10572.09	1575.91

资料来源：中华人民共和国国家统计局：《中国统计年鉴（2013）》，中国统计出版社2014年版，经整理。

（二）城乡基本公共服务均等化的需求

随着经济社会的发展，城乡发展不均衡已经成为了阻碍我国经济可持续发展、社会和谐稳定的重要障碍。而导致城乡差异的根源之一便是城乡基本公共服务的非均等化，对于公众的调查显示，73.8%的公众认为中国城市公共服务在各方面都比农村优越得多。公众对于城乡基本公共服务均等化的需求主要体现在以下方面：

一是城乡收入均等化需求。城乡收入均等化需求，并不是城乡收入的平均化，而是城乡收入比例应该不断缩小，尤其是要不断提高农村居民的收入水平。当前我国城乡居民的收入差距巨大，"以2005年为例，我国城乡名义收入差距为3.22∶1，如果将城乡基本公共服务计算在内，城乡居民实际收入差距达到5—6倍"[5]。2013年我国城市居民可支配收入和农村居民纯收入分别为26955元和8896元，收入比仍达到了3.03∶1。[6]同时，城乡居民对于基本公共服务的依赖程度也并不相同，农村居民自身的服务投入对于公共服务替代水平比城市更低，公共服务的刚性需求更强，加之城乡的公共服务投入水平差异，导致城乡居民的公共服务获取水平的形成巨大鸿沟。统计显示我国2012年城乡居民家庭恩格尔系数分别为36.2%和39.3%[7]，农村居民需要花费更多收入用于食品，用于服务购买的收入非常有限，无法对短缺的公共服务有效弥补。因此，农村居民迫切需要提高农村公共服务水平，缩小收入差距，希望政府加大对农村公共服务的财政投入,实现财政的转移支付,提高农村公共服务的整体水平。

二是城乡基本公共服务资源投入均等化需求。基本公共服务的城乡均等化是城乡一体化发展的重要内容和支撑。而现实中,城乡资源分配不均一直长久存在,并且影响到了城乡建设的不均衡以及城乡公民在发展权利上的不公平。在义务教育方面,根据2011年教育部、国家统计局、财政部所发布的《关于2012年全国教育经费执行情况统计公告》显示,2012年的教育费用支出,全国普通小学为6128.99元,而农村为6017.58;全国普通初中为8137元,而农村学生为7906元,均低于全国平均水平[8];另外关于教育资源的其他投入,包括师资水平、基础建设、教育设备差距更大,这导致了农村学生大量向城镇聚集,增加了农村学生学习成本的同时,也对城镇教育资源产生了拥挤效益,降低了城市教育服务水平。在医疗资源配置方面同样如此,2012年,全国每千人口的医疗卫生技术人员配备为4.94人,而城市达到了8.55人,农村为3.41人,两者相差2.5倍;每千人口的职业(助理)医师,全国为1.94人,城市为3.19人,农村仅为1.4人;每千人口的注册护士,全国为1.85人,其中城市为3.65人,农村仅为1.09人;每千人口的医疗卫生床位,全国为4.23张,其中城市达到了6.88张,而农村仅为3.11张。[9]农村的医疗资源配置远远落后于城市。因此,公众要求城乡的基本公共服务资源投入均等化,甚至向农村倾斜,以保障农民维护和发展基本本权利的同时,也推进农村社会的整体发展。

三是城乡基本公共服务结果均等化。投入的不同造就了城乡基本公共服务的巨大鸿沟,这一鸿沟的出现一方面导致了农村人口过度地向城市转移,造成了一系列的城市问题;另一方面,也影响了城乡资源流动的顺利进行,加剧了我国的城乡二元化。以当前的养老问题为例,北京大学国家发展研究院所发布的《中国人口老龄化挑战》报告显示:"新型农村养老保险所提供的养老金占家庭人均支出的比例为21%,而政府、事业机构和企业所提供的养老金分别占了人均支出的242.2%和192.9%。也即新型农村社会养老保险发放的养老金平均只能够支付一个人生活费用的21%,而企业、政府或事业单位的养老金金额,平均大约可以支付两个人的生活费用。"[10]因此,推进城乡一体化,不仅需要基本公共服务项目的均等化,还需要基本公共服务的实践结果均等化。

(三) 群体基本公共服务均等化的需求

群体差距目前也是我国社会矛盾的重要根源,群体之间的差距在当前主要体现为基于职业和收入而产生的社会地位差距,即所谓的贫富差距。当前我国面临着严重的贫富差距问题,一方面体现为职业,数据显示为我国城镇居民2012年不同行业的收入，收入最高的前三行业为金融行业、信息传输与计算机服务、科学研究与技术服务，年人均收入为89743元、80510元和69254元，而收入最低的农林牧渔业仅为22687元、住宿和餐饮业31267元、水利环境等公共设施管理行业32343元，最高的收入差距比达到了3.95∶1。同时，反映财富收入分配的基尼系数，我国2013年的基尼系数为0.473，仍然超过国际红色警戒线的0.4标准。另一方面，我国的群体收入差距还体现在制度上，2011年"退休人员的月基本养老金在1500元以上，而非公部门就业人员月平均工资不到2000元，其中30%的职工工资在1200元以下"[11]，甚至低于公共和国有部门的退休工资。群体收入差距决定了群体的社会地位，而社会地位又影响到公共政策和基本公共服务供给，从而导致了群体间的公共服务不均等，在当前情况下集中为流动人口的公共服务非均等化。以农民工群体为例，由于受到户籍制度的限制，农民工这一群体一直被排斥在城市公共服务体系之外，一是农民工子女的教育不均等，目前农民工子女的教育虽然目前取得了权利保障，但教育水平与城市基本教育相差甚远；二是农民工的社会保险在大部分地方仍未与城市社会保险完全对接，农民工的参保率仍旧处于较低水平；三是农民工的住房保障仍然处于城市住房保障体系之外，大大增加了农民工群体的生活成本，使得收入差距进一步被拉大。

三、基本公共服务供给制度的需求

公共服务的需求实现依赖于公共服务供给制度的作用发挥，缺乏供给制度的支撑，公共服务需求只能是空中楼阁、海市蜃楼。因此，公众在要求保障公共服务公共性、全面性、均等化的基础上，也要求通过完善的公共服务供给制度，保障公共服务供给的低成本和高效率。主要表现在以下方面：

（一）建立健全多元公共服务供给体系的需求

多元公共服务供给体系是当前破解公共服务短缺和提高公共服务质量的重要措施，而我国的公共服务供给仍然存在着"政府垄断"的现象。政府垄断公共服务供给有其历史合理性，但也制约了公共服务供给水平的提高，特别是公共服务的供给不足和供给成本过高。如表4所示，公众对政府公共服务供给的满意度并不高，各个公共服务项目满意度均未达到50%，而生态环境和保障性住房的不满意度甚至达到了51.01%和40.77%，可见政府的公共服务供给并未满足公众的要求。同时，政府单一的公共服务供给模式还带来了公共服务供给的高成本问题，对公众的调查显示，只有28.04%的公众认为政府的公共服务供给成本低于市场和社会，现实中，部分公共服务产品的政府采购价格远高于市场，造成了政府形象受损。

表 4　公众对政府公共服务满意度调查（单位:%）

公共服务情况评价	非常好	比较好	一般	比较差	非常差
义务教育情况	9.6	35.8	38.2	11.2	5.2
就业服务情况	3.3	22.0	54.8	15.5	4.3
医疗卫生情况	2.6	18.8	48.2	23.3	7.0
社会保障情况	4.2	24.4	48.4	17.8	5.2
保障性住房情况	2.4	14.7	42.1	28.6	12.2
生态环境保护情况	2.9	13.9	32.1	31.2	19.9
社会治安情况	5.4	40.7	39.9	10.9	3.1
公共文化情况	3.9	24.7	49.5	17.2	4.7
基础生活设施建设情况	4.0	29.2	48.1	14.5	4.2

破解公共服务供给不足的重要方式便在于完善公共服务的多元供给体系建设，其中社会组织参与和公共服务市场化改革是当前完善公共服务供给体系的重要内容。对于公务员的调查显示，有60.83%的被调查者认为应该扩大公共服务供给中的社会参与，充分发挥社会力量来提高公共服务供给水平，特别是政府可以通过公共服务购买来实践政府与社会的合作模式，发挥社会组织的专业技术，不断提高公共服务供给水平。而公共服务的市场化改革中，41.6%的公众认为市场在提供公共服务上比政府花费的成本更少，当前的公共服务需要推进市场化改革。对于市场化改革的方式选择，张立荣教授的调查显示，政府公务人员所认可的方式排序如下：公开招投标（77.7%[①]）、民营化（40.1%）、委托代理经营（33.5%）、使用者付费（30.2%）、特许经营（24.5%）、合同外包（22.6%）、分散决策（19.9%）、内部市场（11.1%）。[12]

（二）完善公共服务运行机制的需求

相对于供给体制所体现的公共服务供给政治属性和民主属性，公共服务的运行机制更强调公共服务供给的科学属性，即公共服务以何种方式能够最为有效地供给社会公众。

1. 建立以需求为导向公共服务供给机制的要求

需求导向是当前服务型政府建设的重要内涵，作为以公众为服务对象的公共服务首先必须坚持以公众需求作为供给决策的出发点和归宿点。而调查显示，当前所提供的公共服务对于社会公众的满足程度仍然较低，如表5所示，除了义务教育义务，公

---

① 77.7%为选择此项措施人数占总人数的比例，下同。

众对于公共服务对自身需求满足情况都未超过50%，其中的公共文化设施更是只有34.8%。这一方面是由于政府公共服务的供给数量不足，导致公众难以享受；另一方面更多表现为政府公共服务供给与公众需求之间的脱节问题，即政府的"供"非百姓的"需"，导致了资源的浪费。对此，公众需要政府和社会建立完善的公共服务需求调查机制、公共服务需求评估机制和公共服务需求满足的持续跟踪机制，保障公共服务供给与公众需求之间的有效契合。

表5 公众对于政府公共服务满足自身需求的评价（单位：%）

公共服务能否满足需求	满足	部分满足	一般	部分满足不了	无法满足
义务教育	24.1	31.5	25.9	12.3	6.2
就业服务	11.3	26.3	44.0	12.3	6.1
医疗卫生	8.8	31.8	32.3	18.6	8.6
社会保障	11.7	30.4	37.7	15.2	5.1
公共文化设施	7.6	27.2	36.5	20.0	8.7
基础生活设施	9.7	31.8	36.8	17.0	4.8

其次，还要建立公共服务供给重点工程的来满足公众的迫切需求。对于公共服务，从长远来看都需要完整和全面的公共服务，但是在社会的不同阶段，公共服务的需求重点也有所差异。对此作为公共服务供给主导的政府，应该在保障公共服务全面供给的同时，进一步推进公共服务的重点工程，以重点工程满足最为迫切的医疗卫生（48.9%）、生态环境保护（45.4%）和公共文化设施（37.0%）等公共服务。同时以重点工程为突破，带动全面公共服务体系建设，保障公众公共服务诉求得到有效满足。

再次，长久的公共服务与需求相脱节还会导致公众对于公共服务的信心不足，《中国社会发展年度报告2012》的调查也显示，如表6，公众的公共服务预期仍存在着不确定性，其中环境保护和医疗卫生是公众最为缺乏信心的公共服务。这就要求建立长期的公共服务供给发展规划和实施方案，确保公众对公共服务未来规划的充分了解，增强公众对于公共服务体系建设的信念，以外部压力推进我国的当前公共服务体系建设。

表6 公众对各类基本公共服务的预测分布

	基层设施	公共安全	社会保障	医疗卫生	基本教育	环境保护
积极预期	76.6%	68%	67.8%	64.9%	70.9%	57.4%
消极预期	9.8%	15.8%	14.6%	21.3%	13.6%	30.6%

资料来源：李汉林主编：《中国社会发展年度报告》，中国社会科学出版社2012年版，第163页。

2. 建立整体性公共服务供给机制的需求

长久以来公共服务供给中存在着政府间的协调问题和程序问题，这种协调问题集中体现为"责任不清""办事推诿""办事拖沓"等现象，导致了公共服务在政府内部部门之间和政府与社会、企业之间的职责不清晰，流程不科学。公众在办事时大多都经历过被"踢皮球"的无奈，有的公众甚至要很多次才能搞清负责部门和程序，更不用说要获取相应的公共服务。对公众公共服务获取方便性的调查显示，如表7，除义务教育以外，公共服务的便捷程度均不高，特别是公共文化设施，只有29%的公众认为方便。究其原因，多头责任主体和复杂的程序是主要障碍，因此建立整体性公共服务供给机制已经成为了优化政府职能和减少公共服务供给成本的双重需求。这就要求作为公共服务供给主体的政府推进以政府为主导、以新型网络信息技术为载体的整体性公共服务供给机制改革，一方面要进一步强化政府职能优化，推动大部制改革，完善政府的职能配置和权责体系；另一方面要推进电子公共服务体系建设，结合当前的窗口服务与电子政务系统，建立宽口径、广覆盖的电子公共服务体系，让公众能够快捷、方便地使用到公共服务。

表7 公众对公共服务供给便捷性的评价（单位:%）

能够方便享受到的服务	非常方便	方便	一般	不方便	非常不方便
义务教育	18.2	39.8	30.9	8.0	3.1
就业服务	5.3	21.1	55.2	14.1	4.3
医疗卫生	5.3	31.1	43.2	15.4	5.1
社会保障	6.1	30.0	48.3	11.9	3.6
公共文化设施	4.9	24.1	46.5	18.8	5.7
基础生活设施	5.8	32.9	45.8	12.1	3.3

3. 完善公共服务合理布局的需求

当前我国的公共服务资源面临着严重的布局不合理，多数优质公共服务资源集中在大中城市，农村和小城镇居民为了尽可能享受优质公共服务资源也舍近求远，涌向大中城市，一方面导致城市教育、医疗卫生服务、就业服务等公共服务过度拥挤，另一方面又导致农村、小城镇等基层公共服务闲置。以医疗卫生公共服务为例，我国面临着三甲医院和基层医疗诊所医疗卫生服务的分配扭曲问题，根据《2013中国卫生统计提要》，如图2所示，2009—2012年以来，基层医疗机构[①]的入院人数趋于平缓，

---

① 基层医疗机构包括社区卫生服务中心（站）、街道卫生院、乡镇卫生院、村卫生室、门诊部、诊所（医务室）。

而公立医院①的入院人数却是大量增加。特别是三级公立医院，2010—2012 年的病床使用率分别达到了 102.9%、104.2% 和 104.5，逐年增长，很多大医院"一床难求"现象相当普遍。大医院所带来的不仅仅是拥挤问题，更是费用的激增，如表 8 所示，大医院的治理费用也在逐年递增，次均医疗费用和人均医疗费用均出现逐年上升的趋势，一些普通家庭更是因为住院而出现"因病致穷"问题。公共服务的拥挤现象所带来的不仅是公共服务质量的下降，更是公共服务成本的提高，因为拥挤而带来的额外成本已经成为了一种社会"潜规则"，大大降低了公共服务的公共属性和均等属性。因此，政府需要通过合理的地理布局和资源调配，实现公共服务设施的合理布局，破解公共服务设施的拥挤问题。

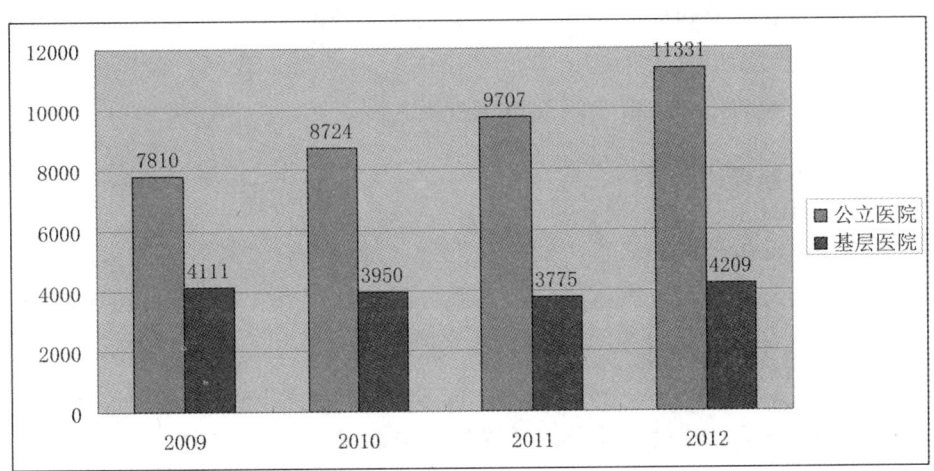

图 2　2009—2012 年各类医院入院人数统计（单位：万人）

数据来源：中华人民共和国卫生部：《2013 中国卫生统计提要》，经整理。

表 8　2009—2011 年三级公立医院医疗费用统计（单位：元）

	2009 年	2010 年	2011 年	2012 年
次均医疗费用	203.7	220.2	231.8	242.1
人均医疗费用	9753	10442.4	10935.9	11186.8

数据来源：中华人民共和国卫生部：《2013 中国卫生统计提要》，经整理。

---

① 公立医院是指经济类型为国有和集体办的意义。

四、扩大公共服务公众参与需求

公共服务的特点决定了公共服务中的公民参与不仅包括了公民通过选举制度实现专门代表履行自身利益的委托,还包括公民对于公共服务决策、供给、选择和评价的全程参与。公民参与公共服务既是宪法所规定的公民权利,也是公共服务质量提升的关键,更是当前社会民主的重要内容。推进公民参与的制度建设,一方面可以通过有序的政民对话、政民沟通、政民合作达到扩大政府群众基础的作用,促进社会的稳定;另一方面,公民参与能够切实提高公共服务的效率与质量,扩大了社会公共利益,推进社会发展,这反过来是强化了政府的公共服务能力,增强了政府自身应对并化解社会风险的能力。因此,推进公共服务中的公民参与是政府与公民的双重需求。公共服务中的公民参与需求主要表现在以下方面:

(一) 公共服务表达需求

公共服务能否满足公众的需求,前提在于公众是否具有公共服务需求的表达权与表达机会。虽然公共服务需求表达对于公共服务最终决策存在着障碍,但这并未影响公共服务需求表达对于公共服务体系建设的意义。而现实中公共服务需求已经成为了公众的重要需求,更是公众的权利,也是政府推进公共服务体系建设的重要内容。当前公众对于公共服务需求表达,主要表现在以下方面:

一是公众需要公共服务的信息知情权。在现实中的一个常见问题就是,公众知道自身所应该享有的公共服务基本权利,但并不知道这些服务的基本信息。以低保为例,很多公民需要低保,但并不知道政府所公布的申请低保的相关信息,知道以后往往已经过了申请期。对于公众的调查显示(表9),关于公共服务信息的获取,排名前三的分别为互联网(89.9%)、电视(72.4%)和报纸(59.7%)等媒体机构。而实践中很多基本公共服务供给主体实质上是基层政府,具体办理者则为社区自治机构,基层政府和社区机构的信息往往又难以登上上述媒体,这导致很多公民难以及时获取信息。对于信息获取,公众期望政府提供更为主动的信息服务,不仅包括基本宣传模式,还应包括能够确保有需求公众的专项信息推送,如手机短信、电话单线联系等方式,保障公众的信息知情权。

表9 公众信息获取路径和方式

了解公共服务信息的主要途径	所占总人数的百分比(N = 1621 人)	排序
互联网	89.9%	1
电视	72.4%	2

(续表)

报纸	59.7%	3
广播	25.9%	4
亲戚朋友	14.9%	5
宣传栏	10.7%	6
村（社区）干部	2.7%	7
其他	1.3%	8

二是公众需要制度化的需求表达渠道。一方面，公众希望政府在出台所有公共服务政策之前都将公民需求调查作为政策制定的前置条件，以确保政府出台的公共服务政策法规都是以公众需求为导向的。同时，公众需要政府开辟专门的公共服务需求表达平台，调查显示（表10），公民的需求表达意愿非常之高，但转化为具体行为较少，只有62.7%的公众进行了需求表达，而其中的表达方式最多的为网络媒介和新闻媒体，如表所示，常规的表达渠道包括听证会、人大、政协、社区干部等方式选择较少，因此政府需要推进公众的需求表达平台建设，实现公众需求的正常表达。

表10 公众认为公共服务需求表达的有效方式

表达自身的公共服务需求较为有效的方式	所占总人数的百分比（N=1621人）	排序
通过网络媒介反映	61.1%	1
新闻媒体	58.7%	2
参与政府的调查	37.3%	3
通过人大代表、政协委员反映	30.4%	4
直接向政府部门反映	29.7%	5
参加相关的听证会	21.8%	6
信访	18.0%	7
游行示威	12.3%	8
行政诉讼或行政复议	11.9%	9
直接向社区干部反映	10.4%	10
向个别政府官员反映	9.4%	11
其他	2.3%	12

三是公众需要多样化的公共服务选择权利。对于公共服务的选择也是公众需求有效表达的重要内容，而现实中公众缺乏对于公共服务的选择权利和选择机会，往往处于"被代表"的地位。这是因为当前我国公共服务供给中公众选择空间小，"用脚投票"的机会较少。对于公众调查显示（图3），有13.93%的公众选择通过地域选择来

进行公共服务选择。另有23.58%的公众选择通过自我服务替代公共服务，有24.79%的公众会选择通过付费服务进行替代。仍有37.7%的公众对于公共服务没有选择权利，只有被动的接收"政府提供什么就是什么"的公共服务供给。

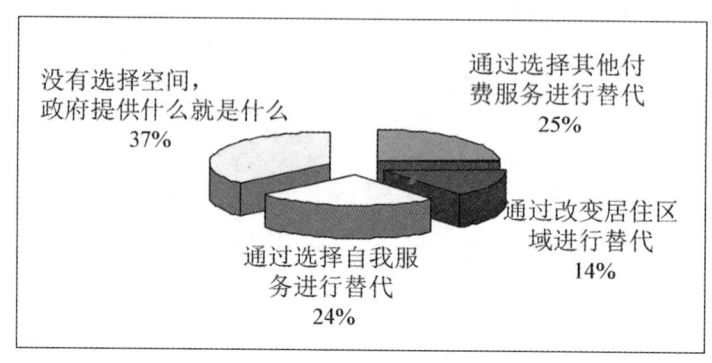

图3　公众对于公共服务的选择空间

（二）公共服务决策参与需求

公共服务的决策参与主要表现为公众对于公共服务供给的影响能力，从源头来看公众是公共服务成本的最终承担者和公共服务结果的最终使用者，那么作为委托主体的政府和社会为公众提供何种公共服务必须是一个包含了公众决定的结果，而公众决定并不一定都是直接的参与决定，也包括了其他形式的参与形式。

第一，公众需要完善公共服务决策参与渠道。调查显示当前的公众公共服务参与仍然停留在较低层次的"反映问题式"参与，即仅仅是针对实践中的问题向政府等公共部门进行反映，采用的方式主要还是舆论媒体，见表9，如网络媒体（60.63%）和新闻媒体（57.47%）。而正规的参与渠道，如社区层面上的议事会、村委会、听证会等较少，现实中部分听证会更成为了公众所谓的"涨价会"，公众缺乏公共服务的决策参与。根据国外的公共服务参与发展来看，公众的决策参与关键在于政府主动创造公民参与渠道，如西方国家流行的关键公众接触、公民发起的接触法、公民调查、新沟通技术、公民会议、咨询委员会和斡旋调解。[13]而我国的实践中缺少这些参与渠道，导致公民参与仍旧是分散的、凌乱的、无序的参与。

第二，公众需要一定的公共服务决策参与能力。如果说渠道应该是政府为公民参与所涉及的制度载体，那么能力看似更应该是公民自身的因素，但事实上建设完善的公民社会本就是政府职责的重要内容和政府优良的评价标准，正如密尔的观点，好政府的一个重要标准就是"人民本身的美德与智慧"[14]，即作为政府自身必须将公民培育作为自身的重要职责，当然也包括公民参与的培养。而实践中，我国的公民公共服务参与能力培养仍然无法应对政府和社会对于公民参与的需求，一方面公民参与的意识仍然薄弱，很多公民并未将参与作为自身神圣使命和权利的体现，而在参与存在着严重的不良倾向,访谈中,相当部分的公民将公共服务参与当作是"政府强制行为"或"村社游戏行为",对于自身的选择结果"并不太在意"。而另一个极端则是彻底的"政治冷漠",即公民对于公共事务完全漠不关心,究其原因仍在于公民对自身之于公共服务的影响力持看低态度,并认为集体决策最终会演变为部分精英的决策,与自身的关系不大。另一方面,公民的参与能力仍然不强,公民的参与更多是对于政府公共服务行为的"发牢骚",却难以形成卓有成效的对策建议,这导致政府也逐渐将公民参与定位成了"走程序和走形式",公民参与并未对公共服务决策起到实质的影响。因此,公众社会需要政府的民主和公共精神培养,更需要政府对于公民参与的宽容和耐心。

第三,公众需要参与公共服务决策的制度保障。公众参与公共服务决策的制度设计是实践公众参与公共服务决策持续进行的推进器,而当前公民参与公共服务决策的制度设计不足造成了公民参与的"运动式"特征,公众需要保障其公共服务决策参与的制度设计。一是公众需要公共服务参与的决策形成机制。当前的政府和基层组织以公民参与作为自身推进社会民主和实现决策科学化的手段,却没有将公民参与的结果真正的纳入到自身最终决策体系之中,使得公民参与成为了一种没有实质意义的华丽外衣,耗费了大量的公民参与成本,严重挫伤了公民的参与积极性。对公众的调查显示,34.54%的公众认为公众参与公共服务并未对政府和社会的公共服务决策产生影响,而产生了大量的政绩工程,与自身的需求无关。二是公众需要公共服务参与的科学决策机制。公民参与的效果在于形成公民决议,而公民参与公共服务的效果则在于公民决议对于公共服务的有效性。作为公共服务的受益者,公民参与公共服务是提高公共服务合法性和合理性的基础。而公共服务决策又是多元主体共同决定的结果,包括政府、村(社区)自治组织、社区组织和企业都是公共服务决策参与者,作为参与主体之一的公民,如何将自身的决议与上述主体进行整合正是当前困扰公民参与公共服务效果的主要因素。同时公共服务自身所涉及的专业性又对公民参与提出了重大挑战,因此公民参与所形成的公民决议与公共服务的决议存在着巨大的鸿沟,不仅包括专业因素的考量,还包括巨大的多元利益主体博弈。因此,如何将公众的民主参与和科学决策形成合力,是当前公民参与公共服务中政府和公民的双重诉求。

(三) 参与公共服务的监督评估的需求

对于公共服务中的公民参与,监督评估自始至终便是公民参与的重要内容,对于公务员的调查显示,有60.84%的受访者认为,扩大公民参与是目前政府提高公共服务体系所最应该做的事情。而对于公民参与的形式,如表11所示,有72.5%的公务员认为就是进行公共服务的监督评估参与,而68.75%的公众更是认为现实中公共服务参与最为缺乏的也是监督评估参与。因此对于公共服务而言，对于公民的监督评估参与具有很大的需求。

表 11 公务员认为公民参与最为可行的方式

现实中公共服务的公民参与比较可行的是	所占总人数的百分比（N = 240 人）	排序
参与公共服务的监督评估	72.5%	1
配合政府的公共服务政策	41.3%	2
参与公共服务的决策制定	39.2%	3
参与公共服务的直接供给	22.5%	4
参与公共服务供给的成本分担	21.7%	5

对于监督参与，公民对于公共服务的监督参与是实现公共服务有效供给的重要部分，同时也是保障公共服务效果的重要措施。而实践中公民的监督参与比较薄弱，一方面表现为公众对于公共服务的质量"关注度"不足，公众对于公共服务进行决策参与的后续参与不足；另一方面，公民的参与形式较为单一，调查显示对于公共服务的监督主要形式在于"向上反映问题"，或者向村（居）两委反映，或者直接向政府进行反映，而并未将监督参与作为公共服务质量提高的运行机制，公共服务监督并未发挥最大效用。因此，政府和公民需要通过公民的持续监督参与保障公共服务质量。

对于评估参与，当前主要表现为公众的满意度调查，而对公共服务供给的体制机制评估则较少。实质上，公共服务的结果只是公共服务体制机制运行的体现，公共服务的体制机制才是影响公共服务效用的根本，对于公共服务体制机制的评估理应成为公民评估公共服务的核心。而现实中的公共服务公众评估，仅仅是对政府公共服务结果的评价，评价结果仅仅是公众的主观意见，而并未与公共服务自身的质量标准评价相结合，导致公共服务的评估脱节。因此，公民参与公共服务评估，需要健全公共服务的主客观双重评价机制，从而实现对公共服务的全面评价。

综上所述，我国当前的社会发展阶段决定了当前的公共服务需求不仅仅是对个别结果、单一机制的需求，更是对于完善公共服务体系的需求，这一体系需要具有政治与科学的双重特征，既保障公民的民主权利和民生权利，又能够通过科学管理、质量控制推进公共服务的高绩效。公共服务体系既是公众的需求，也是政府和社会组织的需求，更是当前我国完善服务型政府建设和构建和谐社会必须要解决的问题。

四、创新我国公共服务体系建设的政策建议

我国当前的社会发展阶段决定了当前的公共服务需求不仅仅是对个别结果、单一机制的需求，更是对于完善公共服务体系的需求，这一体系需要具有政治与科学的双

重特征，既保障公民的民主权利和民生权利，又能够通过科学管理、质量控制推进公共服务的高绩效。公共服务体系既是公众的需求，也是政府和社会组织的需求，同时也是当前我国完善服务型政府建设和构建和谐社会必须要解决的问题。完善和创新我国的公共服务体系建设，我们需要从以下方面不断突破：

（一）完善多元协同的公共服务供给体制

一是强化政府的公共服务职能和责任体系建设。强化政府的公共服务职能关键在于持续推进服务型政府建设，一方面要不断提高政府的公共服务能力，通过理论培训等理念改造强化政府的公共服务意识与思维，通过流程再造等制度创新增强政府应对社会公共服务需求的供给能力，通过资源筹集与配置扩大政府公共服务资源的调配渠道，以最终实现政府供给能力与社会公共服务需求的有效对接；另一方面就是要完善政府的公共服务责任体系建设，合理划分公共服务供给中中央政府和地方政府的责任分工，明确各级政府的责任主体地位，同时在《国家基本公共服务体系"十二五"规划》的基础上进一步细化基本公共服务标准，确定各级政府的责任履行标准，保障公共服务的高效供给。

二是推进公共服务体系建设中的社会协同建设。推进社会协同机制建设关键在于扩大社会组织在公共服务体系建设中的参与渠道，这一方面要求政府要加大对于社会组织的支持，包括要加大对社会组织的准入支持，通过不断降低准入门槛鼓励社会组织的成长；要加大对社会组织的保障支持，扩大对于社会组织的资金支持力度，支持社会组织的自身制度建设和能力建设；要不断完善与扩大针对社会组织的服务购买，为社会组织的生存和发展提供项目支撑。另一方面，政府要强化对社会组织的管理，制定社会组织制度建设的统一规范，强化对社会组织评估制度和绩效管理办法，开展社会组织社会责任报告书制度，加强社会对社会组织的监督管理机制。

三是不断加强公共服务中的公民参与制度设计。完善公共服务中的公民参与制度建设，包括完善公民的公共服务需求表达和决策机制，保障公共服务的需求导向和公民导向；完善公共服务执行中的公民参与，推进公共服务供给的政民协同模式；完善公共服务监督评估中的公民参与，实现对公共服务的过程控制和效果管理。同时也应不断推进公共服务中的公民参与渠道建设，按照公共服务的性质进行分类管理，针对需求信息获取类的公共服务，可以推行关键公民接触、公民调查以及群众意见箱等公民参与方式；针对政民互动类的公共服务，可以通过公民听证、民主恳谈以及综合协调等公民参与方式；针对需要公民参与的民主类公共服务，可以推行公民会议、公民议事会和公民监事会等公民参与形式。

（二）深化推进基本公共服务均等化建设

推进基本公共服务均等化，关键就是以制度公平保障不同区域、不同群体以及城乡之间公众在基本公共服务享受方面的机会均等、结果均等和权利均衡，进而保障公民能够享受到公共、全面和均等化的服务。

一是完善基本公共服务范围扩大的保障机制。要根据对社会公共服务供给能力的评估，不断扩大基本公共服务服务范围，通过梯度式管理模式逐步推进公共服务的对于公众全面的普惠，保障公共服务的公共属性。一方面，政府要逐步打破阻碍公共服务普及性的户籍制度、城乡二元体制、双轨制下的社会保障制度等制度障碍，保障公民能够公平地享受到基本公共服务。另一方面，政府要不断构建针对农民工、失地农民等弱势群体的权利保障机制，确保这些群体能够公平享受到社会公共服务，推进社会的公平正义。

二是要完善基本公共服务标准化的保障机制。针对国家已经指定的公共服务"十二五"规划标准，应加强公共服务标准的落实保障机制建设，确保社会公众能够享受到更为全面、更为可及的基本公共服务。这就要求政府要推进基本公共服务的标准机制建设，将基本公共服务的供给范围、供给程度、所要达到的效果标准化、制度化，并确定责任归属主体，通过责任考核机制和责任追究机制确保基本公共服务的全面性与可及性，保障公民全面享受公共服务的权利。

三是要完善基本公共服务供给均等化保障机制。针对当前所存在的基本公共服务在城乡、区域和群体之间的不均等，一方面要坚持均等化的基本公共服务供给战略设计，强调公共政策在城乡、区域和群体之间的均等化特征，对所要出台的公共政策均要进行均等化的测量与估算。另一方面，按照罗尔斯的"第二个正义原则"，实现公共政策和公共服务向农村、中西部地区和社会弱势群体的倾斜，实践公共服务的补偿机制，保障社会的公平正义。

（三）完善基本公共服务均等化的质量控制与绩效评估

针对当前公众对于基本公共服务的"质""量"并重需求，要加强公共服务的质量管理，确保公共服务的高效率、高效益和高效能。

首先，要不断完善基本公共服务财政管理制度。将专业的财会管理机制引入到公共服务管理之中，对公共服务进行严格的预算管理和财务审计制度，严格控制公共服务成本，提高公共服务资金使用效率。同时，严格管理部分公共服务的收费管理机制，逐步实现基本公共服务免费推广。

其次，要不断完善基本公共服务的质量管理机制。运用全面质量管理的理论加强对公共服务的全过程质量管理,构建基本公共服务的质量监测体系,对公共服务质量进行全程监控和评估;同时,建立公共服务质量的预警机制,针对低质量的基本公共服务,及时向相关部门通报并整改,确保公众能够享受到"高质量"的公共服务。

再次,要不断完善基本公共服务的绩效评估机制。一方面完善包括政府、专业第三方组织以及公众的多元绩效评估体系,实现对基本公共服务的多元全面评估。另一方面,完善客观服务标准评价与主观满意度评价的双重评价机制,实现对公共服务从质量到效能的全面评估。另外,完善基本公共服务绩效评估的反馈机制,对相应的责任主体进行责任评估,并通过相应的奖惩机制确保对公共服务质量控制于保障的持久性。

---

[1] 詹勇:《摩擦事件刺痛人心、社会管理亟须破题》,《人民日报》,2011年6月15日。

[2] 常修泽:《中国现阶段基本公共服务均等化研究》,《中共天津市委党校学报》2007年第2期。

[3] 本文所采用的东中西部地区分类,按照国家2000年制定西部大开发中享受政策范围的省市划分,东部地区包括北京、天津、河北、辽宁、上海、江苏、浙江、福建、山东、广东和海南;中部地区包括山西、吉林、黑龙江、安徽、江西、河南、湖北、湖南;西部地区包括四川、贵州、云南、西藏、陕西、甘肃、青海、宁夏、新疆、内蒙古、广西。

[4] 国务院发展研究中心课题组:《民生为本,中国疾病公共服务改善路径》,中国发展出版社2012年版,第108—109页。

[5] 孙友祥、柯文昌:《城乡公共服务均等化:价值、困境与路径》,《中国行政管理》2009年第7期。

[6] 中华人民共和国国家统计局:《中国统计年鉴2013》,中国统计出版社2014年版。

[7] 中华人民共和国国家统计局:《中国统计年鉴2013》,中国统计出版社2014年版。

[8] http://cn.chinagate.cn/reports/2014-03/10/content_31739829.htm。

[9] 中华人民共和国国家统计局:《中国统计年鉴2013》,中国统计出版社2014年版。

[10] 南方财富网:《中国城乡养老保险待遇有差距》,网址:http://www.southmoney.com/touzilicai/baoxian/554864.html,访问日期:2013年6月5日。

[11] 国务院发展研究中心、世界银行:《2030的中国》。

[12] 张立荣:《当代中国服务型政府及公共服务体系建设状况问卷调查数据统计与展示》,中国社会科学出版社2010年版,第43页。

[13] [美]约翰·克莱顿·托马斯:《公共决策中的公民参与》,孙柏瑛等译,中国人民大学出版社2010年版,第23页。

[14] [英]约翰·密尔:《代议制政府》,汪瑄译,商务印书馆2008年版,第26页。

中西政府治理价值研究的历史嬗变

丁 煌[*]

一、问题的提出

人类的一切活动都蕴涵着价值，无论是个体行为，还是集体行动，而且，越是集体行动，就越会突出价值的问题；人的一切行为都包含着价值因素，进一步说，人的一切自觉的行为都有明确的价值目标；职业行为的价值目标是职业群体开展职业活动的基本理念，是贯穿于这个职业从业者的一切活动和行为中的基本精神和原则。政府治理的价值是政府治理所追求的一种应然状态，它反映了人们关于政府治理的希望和理想、信仰和依托，可以说，政府治理的价值就是政府治理的灵魂和基石。

关于政府治理的价值，国内外均经历了在效率与公平之间的摇摆。纵观新中国走过的六十多年光辉历程，特别是经过三十多年改革开放所取得的伟大成就，我们不仅可以自豪地感受到，无论是从综合国力的增强和国际地位的提升来看，还是从经济社会的快速发展和人民群众生活质量的不断改进观之，我们的国家都发生了举世瞩目的根本变化；与此同时，我们也不难发现，我国政府治理的价值理念也处在不断地调整、完善和转变过程之中，新中国成立六十多年来，我们既有过因政府治理的价值理念出现严重错误而造成治理失败的惨痛教训，也不乏在政府正确的治理价值取向指导下经济社会发展所取得的骄人成就，尤其是改革开放三十多年来，在曾经的"效率优先、兼顾公平"的治理价值取向下，我们的经济发展创造了非凡的奇迹，综合国力突飞猛进。但与此同时，我们也必须承认，在致力于推动经济发展的同时，对于公平正义的关注却稍显弱化，积累了一系列矛盾，更出现了诸如基本教育资源和医疗资源分布不均、居民收入差距不断拉大、低收入群体的被剥夺感日益增强、城乡壁垒

---

[*] 丁煌，法学（政治学）博士，武汉大学"珞珈学者"特聘教授、博士生导师，政治与公共管理学院院长，主要从事比较公共行政与公共政策研究。

依旧存在、农民工在为之抛洒汗水的城市中难寻归宿、弱势群体权益得不到正当有效的保护等各种社会不公正的问题，特别是少数政府公职人员，本应是社会公正的维护者，却变成了社会公正的破坏者，他们的恶劣行为打击的是社会公众对政府的信心，削弱的是公众对公权的尊敬，破坏的是社会对秩序的维护，因频繁出现政府公职人员在资源分配方面的不良行径而滋生的许多不公正现象最为社会所垢病，进而严重地威胁到政府的合法性。然而，我们必须明白：发展是为了人民，发展要依靠人民，发展成果应由人民共享，只有切实保障人民群众的经济、政治、文化、社会权益，使全体人民共享改革发展成果，朝着共同富裕的目标稳步前进，只有统筹好各种关系、兼顾好各方利益，不断促进社会公平正义，才能真正实现科学发展。所以，伴随着践行科学发展观和构建社会主义和谐社会治国新方略的提出，我国政府治理的价值取向也发生了根本性的转变，"促进社会公平正义"已经成为当下政府施政的主导价值追求，"如果说真理是思想体系的首要价值，那么公平正义就是社会主义国家制度的首要价值"；"如果说发展经济、改善民生是政府的天职，那么推动社会公平正义就是政府的良心"（温家宝语）。"公平正义比太阳还要有光辉"这句饱含诗意的话语，不仅道出了党和政府现阶段治理价值理念的重大转变，更昭示了政府治理价值研究的重要性和紧迫性。

然而，基于政治与行政二分法产生的西方传统行政管理学从一开始就认为行政管理与价值无关，价值研究被排除在行政研究之外；或许是受到西方传统行政管理学的影响，中国大陆早期的行政学者也从本质上把行政管理视为一种技术性执行性活动，认为它不应该或事实上不存在价值偏好，行政管理学研究也相应地被看成是一个应该坚持价值中立的研究领域。尽管自20世纪60年代末70年代初开始价值问题在西方公共行政学领域因新公共行政运动的勃兴而受到了广泛的关注，但是，迄今为止，无论是在西方，还是在中国，相对于公共行政与公共管理学科的其他研究领域，对政府治理价值的研究长期以来一直都是公共行政与公共管理学研究的一个较为薄弱的环节，这不仅影响到政府治理实践方向的正确选择，更削弱了公共行政与公共管理的学科基础，因为只有对政府治理价值的正确把握才能有效地统摄和提升公共行政与公共管理学的理论研究，从而跳出纯粹的形式化的技术理性，实现公共行政与公共管理学理论体系的内在和谐与统一。

作为一门源自西方世界的学科，公共行政学的历史发展之所以出现多次范式转换，其根本原因在于政府治理的价值变迁以及这种实践在学术上的反映。同时，由于对价值这一核心理念存在认识论或者方法论上的根本差异，中西方关于政府治理价值及其变迁的研究均存在明显的历史特征。

二、西方政府治理价值研究的发展

西方发达国家关于政府治理价值及其变迁的研究状况大致经历了四个发展阶段：

（一）以效率和经济为基本价值取向的传统公共行政阶段

19世纪末，西方社会进入资本主义经济的快速发展时期，但政府的低效、浪费与腐败引发了公民的普遍不满，在此背景下诞生的行政学一开始就视效率与经济为公共行政的根本价值。威尔逊在《行政学研究》中明确指出，行政学研究的目标在于首先要弄清楚政府能够适当且成功地承担什么任务，其次要弄清楚政府怎样才能够以尽可能高的效率和尽可能少的金钱或人力消耗来完成这些任务。"效率是行政管理价值尺度方面最高的原则。"[1] 传统行政学时期，学者们从不同角度指出了效率价值的实现路径：一是强调政治与行政的分离，古德诺被视为政治—行政二分法的系统化提出者；二是对行政原则的探索，代表人物有泰勒、法约尔、古利克等；三是理性官僚制的设计，德国思想家韦伯秉持效率至上的价值理念创立了"理性官僚制"，把威尔逊对效率的追求变成了可以实施的制度性方案。自从20世纪40年代起，尽管政治—行政二分法这一传统行政学的理论前提遭到了有限理性决策理论和公共选择学派的批判与否定，但后两者在价值取向上仍然指向的是经济与效率，没有突破传统行政学研究范式。

（二）以社会公平为基本价值取向的新公共行政阶段

20世纪60年代末70年代初，以美国为代表的西方国家连续出现了一系列社会、经济与政治危机，政府改革的呼声此起彼伏，传统行政学面临严峻挑战。对此，西方行政学界做出了积极且有力的回应。他们反观传统公共行政的固有缺陷，高举"社会公平"的旗帜，积极倡导关注意义和价值，着重建立规范理论，以期促使未来人类社会绽放出一线曙光，从而引发了新公共行政运动，并形成了新公共行政学派，其主要代表人物是美国行政学家弗雷德里克森。在弗雷德里克森看来，传统公共行政所追求的是一个有效、经济和协调的行政系统，它往往把研究重点放在高层管理机构和政府重要职能部门，而新公共行政则不仅认为公共行政应当以经济、有效的方式为社会提供高质量服务，更强调公共行政应该将社会公平作为其价值目标，应该改变那些在制度上妨碍社会公平实现的政策和结构。

---

[1] 达尔：《行政科学：三个问题》，见彭和平等编译：《国外公共行政理论精选》（中译本），中央党校出版社1997年版，第152页。

(三) 以多重利益诉求的最大化为基本价值取向的新公共管理阶段

20世纪70年代后期以来形成了以现代经济学和私营部门管理为理论基础，以追求经济、效率和效益为目标的新公共管理运动，并在此基础上形成了新公共管理学。新公共管理学对政府效能的价值判断从现实的人性分析出发，区分了政府管理主体与对象各自不同的利益诉求，能够实现各自利益诉求最大化的政府就可判定为高效能的政府。新公共管理的核心即管理的自由化和市场化。就管理自由化而言，该理论认为传统官僚制政府的不良绩效源于僵化的规则制度，为改进绩效，公共管理者必须从繁文缛节的枷锁中解放出来，解除规制并进行分权。就管理市场化而言，该理论主张在政府管理中引入市场竞争机制，引进私营部门的管理方法和手段。这些理念在美国学者奥斯本和盖布勒合著的《改革政府》一书中得到了提炼和普及，成为新公共管理的理论精髓。可见，尽管新公共管理强调对多重利益诉求的最大化，但其实质仍然指向经济与效率，只不过展示了不同于传统公共行政的效率实现路径而已。

(四) 以人本主义和公共利益为基本价值取向的新公共服务阶段

针对新公共管理的理论缺陷，进入本世纪以后，以美国著名行政学家罗伯特·登哈特为代表的公共行政学者提出了新公共服务理论，它以民主和公民权理论、社区和公民社会模型、组织人本主义和后现代公共行政为思想基础，强调价值定位问题是公共行政必须关注的对象，他们认为构成其理论核心和实质的有两个主题：一是促进公共服务的尊严和价值；二是将民主、公民权和公共利益的价值观重新肯定为公共行政的卓越价值观，认为公共利益源于对共同价值准则的对话协商，强调通过公民参与和对话协商促进公共利益和社会公平。基于此，它强调政府治理的公共性、回应性、可选择性、责任性、参与性、合作性、透明性，关注民主价值、公民权以及公共利益，以人本主义和公共利益为基本的价值导向。另外，在这一时期，秉承新公共行政的价值传统，以威斯利为代表的"黑堡学派"在所谓"黑堡宣言"和《重建民主行政》中也强调政府在民主治理过程中应起的重要作用，并对"公共利益"的价值取向做出了新的阐释；而且，弗雷德里克森在新公共行政运动过去三十多年后又针对美国的政府治理实践撰文指出，尽管在过去三十多年中，社会公平在美国公共行政学术研究中已日益引起广泛关注，但其在政府治理实践中却没有得到充分实现，美国的社会、经济和政治生活中社会公平日益匮乏，一个重要原因在于新公共管理所倡导的"管理主义"盛行，效率往往更容易引起政府公共部门的兴趣，因此，必须通过政府治理创新，将社会公平纳入政府治理实践，使其成为政府治理实践的首要目标。

三、中国政府治理价值研究的演进

虽然建国初期我国的学术机构对公共行政进行过初步的理论探索，但严格意义上讲，公共行政学的系统性研究始于改革开放之初。归纳改革开放以来学界对政府治理价值的探索，有两个显著特点：一是学习、借鉴国外理论成果的努力持续不断；二是研究具有强烈的中国关怀。研究者紧密结合我国社会历史背景和公共行政实践，把对现实的理论总结用于解释和指导实践，使理论研究具有鲜明中国色彩，并呈现出明显的阶段性特征。

（一）"着重突出效率价值"的20世纪80年代

1949—1978这30年间，受特殊环境影响，我国在处理公平与效率的关系上采取的是所谓"公平"的"平均主义"价值原则，这实际上是一种不健全的公平观，政府治理价值整体上处于认识的萌芽阶段。改革开放之初，邓小平充分认识到"一大二公"的平均主义分配方式对效率造成的巨大损害，提出了"让一部分人先富起来"的著名论断。我国政府对效率与公平关系的正式关注始于1987年10月党的十三大提出"在促进效率提高的前提下体现社会公平"，先后在农村和城市掀起了以"效率优先""发展才是硬道理"为价值导向的改革浪潮，"先增长、后分配"的发展模式使国民经济发展效率得到大幅度提高，以经济两位数增长创造了"中国奇迹"，既有利于经济增长、效率提高，也有利于改善收入分配、提高人民生活水平，符合当时社会发展背景以及人民实际利益的需要。在这一时期，经济发展成为第一要务，行政工作围绕改革开放而展开，行政效率价值具有至上地位，精简机构、提高效率成为政府首要的改革目标。此时的学术努力主要体现在：一是译介西方公共行政学著述；二是对行政学基本理论、分支学科和我国行政管理中的实际问题进行初步探讨，出版的行政学著作也把效率价值放置于突出地位，这些研究的共同导向明显与改革开放之初中国亟须以高效率行政推进经济发展、进而推进现代化的迫切需求紧密相连。

（二）"开始关注公平价值"的20世纪90年代

20世纪90年代以后，人们之间的收入差距迅速拉大，分配不公、不平等竞争、寻租行为等社会问题增多，在一些企业中又重现"吃大锅饭"的现象，人们劳动积极性有所减退，要效率也要公平的呼声日益高涨。在这种情况下，中央及时调整了公平与效率的关系，党的十四大把建设社会主义市场经济体制确定为我国经济体制改革的目标，在收入分配制度上提出了"以按劳分配为主体，多种分配方式为补充，兼顾效率与公平"；党的十四届三中全会阐明了公平与效率的关系："建立以按劳分配为主体、效率优先、兼顾公平的收入分配制度，鼓励一部分地区一部分人先富起来，走共同富裕的道路"；党的十五大报告还明确指出："坚持按劳分配为主体、多种分配方式并存的制度，把按劳分配和按生产要素分配结合起来，坚持效率优先、兼顾公平，有利于优化资源配置，促进经济发展，保持社会稳定"，从而冲破了计划经济体制的束缚，强调了经济及经济利益在整个社会中的中心地位，有助于形成与市场经济相适应的政府治理理念。这一阶段，打破垄断、实行机会均等，追求高效率同时兼顾分配公平，给市场竞争中的失败者和弱者以基本生存关怀，倡导建立社会保障体制，成为政府治理的主导价值。在这一时期，党和政府对现代化发展进程的规律有了进一步认识，改革逐渐突破旧体制，到1992年，建立社会主义市场经济体制的改革目标得以确立，明确以市场作为配置资源的基本方式，政府在专注于效率与秩序价值的基础上开始倡导公平、正义的扩展性行政价值。这种转变说明了理论研究造就的氛围对行政实践的发展具有重要推进作用；反过来，行政发展中遇到的难题又为政府治理价值的研究提出了新课题，成为促进学术研究的持续动力。此时，我国行政学界对于现实问题的研究主要集中在：一是从机构精简转变到关注职能转变和行政体制改革；二是对国外新理念、新制度的介绍，主要涉及西方新公共管理改革的理念与措施；三是对政府治理价值进行初步探讨，虽然对公平正义等价值有所涉及，但还主要是基于效率与经济框架之内。

（三）"凸显公平、正义、民主等多元价值"的21世纪

进入21世纪以来，社会基尼系数不断扩大的趋势表明，虽然我国居民整体收入增加，"蛋糕做大了"，但社会成员中"蛋糕分配"的非均等程度也在扩大，如果不能正视并着力解决这一问题，过大的收入分配差距必将影响到经济增长的长远效率并引发更多社会不安定因素。拉美化的教训告诉我们，总体财富增长过程中，如果忽视底层民众的利益，就有可能导致一个人口众多的社会群体享受不到经济发展所带来的好处，一旦这个庞大群体被排除在发展之外，那么这个社会很可能会孕育危机，经济无法持续、稳定增长。为此，党的十六大明确提出："坚持效率优先，兼顾公平，既要提倡奉献精神，又要防止收入悬殊"，"初次分配注重效率，发挥市场的作用，鼓励一部分人通过诚实劳动、合法经营先富起来，再次分配注重公平，加强政府对收入分

配的调节职能，调节差距过大的收入。"随后，党和政府相继提出了践行科学发展观、构建社会主义和谐社会、建设服务型政府以及实现基本公共服务均等化等一系列促进社会公平正义的价值理念和施政目标。在这一时期，中国公共行政的理论和实践话语发生了重大变化，即公共治理、协商、参与、回应、责任等价值与实现方式有了更大存在空间，"以人为本"的行政价值为政府运行机制和管理方式的创新提出了更高要求，长期以来对公共行政效率价值的追求逐渐转变为当下对公共行政的回应性、代表性、公平性和参与性等多元价值的关注。这一时期学者们所探讨的政府治理价值转变主要体现在：（1）资源配置理念上提出市场调节企业、政府调节市场，市场对资源配置起基础性乃至决定性作用，政府以宏观调控弥补和纠正市场失败、促进社会公正、安全和福利；（2）政府成本意识上倡导廉洁、廉价行政，进行高效治理；（3）法治意识上强化行政监督、监察，规范行政、依法行政，建设法治政府；（4）权责意识上建立"有限政府"，实行行政问责制度；（5）民主行政观念上建设公民本位、政府主导而非本位的政府；（6）公共服务理念上减少政府的动员控制性，建设服务型、回应性、可治理型政府；（7）专业化观念上建立专业化、知识化政府，录用公平，履政公正，政务公开、透明、开放。这些理念客观反映了执政党和政府提出的建设政治文明、构建和谐社会、实现科学发展的内在政治逻辑。

四、简短的结语

效率和公平是政府追求的两大价值目标。效率高低关系着经济增长，公平与否影响到社会稳定。从理论上说，二者不可偏废。而在现实中，政府在不同时期必须在二者间有所侧重，因此，如何正确认识和处理两者关系，不仅是各国政府面临的现实问题，而且更是政府治理价值研究不可回避且须从理论上予以澄清的问题。鉴于不同时期的社会背景，西方公共行政学中关于公平与效率这对政府价值取向出现了轮回与侧重的现象，但从公共行政学理论发展的角度来看，效率与公平的融合是一种趋势，诚如美国行政学者梅戈特所言："在不同时期，一种价值可能超过另一种价值，但就每一种价值观的合法性而言。它们之间没有拔河赛。"[①] 然而，在政府治理实践中，效率与公平如何得以统一，工具理性与价值理性怎样相互兼容，这是公共行政学需要深入探究的问题。就我国的情况而言，伴随着改革开放和社会主义现代化建设事业不断发

---

① 转引自张梦中：《美国公共行政历史渊源与重要价值取向》，《中国行政管理》2000 年第 11 期。

展,在价值取向上,我国政府治理研究相继经历了 20 世纪 80 年代"着重突出效率价值"、20 世纪 90 年代"开始关注公平价值"、21 世纪初至今"凸显公平、正义、民主等多元价值"的三个发展阶段;从实践上看,我国改革开放以来国家在每个时期的政策导向不仅是该阶段社会政治经济状况的反映,更是各个时期政府治理价值变迁的体现。改革开放前 20 年,我国面对底子薄、人口多、积累少、社会财富匮乏、收入差别不大等客观历史状况,"效率"自然成为那个时期政府治理的主导价值。然而,伴随经济的高速发展和国家整体财富的快速增长,因区域差别、城乡差别和贫富差别的日益扩大而导致的不和谐情形却越来越严重,甚至会影响到社会的安定和政府的合法性,当下社会各界普遍形成的共识是:中国政府应该强化社会公平正义的价值取向并且应该勇敢地成为促进社会公平正义的主导力量。所以,从 20 世纪 90 年代到进入 21 世纪以来,我国的政府治理价值由"效率和公平兼顾"向"更加注重公平正义"的转变无疑成为中国政府的明智选择,因为这既是科学发展的内在要求,也是构建社会主义和谐社会的基本前提,更是建设服务型政府和实现国家治理现代化的应有之义。

---

[1] Dwight Waldo, *The Study of Public Administration*, New York: Random House, INC., 1967, p.60.

[2] George Frederickson, "The State of Social Equity in American Public Administration", *National Civic Review*, Vol.94, Issue.4, 2005.

[3] 丁煌:《西方行政学说史》(第 2 版),武汉大学出版社 2005 年版。

[4] [美] 布坎南:《自由、市场和国家》,桑伍等译,北京经济学院出版社 1988 年版。

[5] [美] 奥斯本等:《改革政府》,周敦仁译,上海译文出版社 1996 年版。

[6] [美] 登哈特:《新公共服务:服务而不是掌舵》,方兴、丁煌译,中国人民大学出版社 2006 年版。

[7] 夏书章:《行政管理学》,山西人民出版社 1985 年版。

[8] 赵立波:《政府行政改革:走向 21 世纪的中国视点》,山东人民出版社 1998 年版。

[9] 张康之:《寻求公共行政的伦理视角》,中国人民大学出版社 2004 年版。

[10] 刘祖云:《当代中国公共行政的伦理审视》,人民出版社 2006 年版。

[11] 张富:《论公共行政价值的价值向度》,中央编译出版社 2007 年版。

[12] 丁煌:《寻求公平与效率的协调与统一》,《中国行政管理》1998 年第 12 期。

[13] 任晓:《中国行政改革的动力与进程(1982—1988)》,《政治学研究》1989 年第 6 期。

[14] 周志忍：《当代西方行政改革与管理模式转换》，《北京大学学报》1995年第4期。

[15] 张国庆：《试论我国政府行政改革的基本价值选择》，《中国人民大学学报》1999年第4期。

[16] 孙学玉：《当代公共行政改革的目标趋向与价值选择》，《学术季刊》1999年第4期。

[17] 王乐夫等：《公共行政的价值范畴研究》，安徽大学学报2004第2期。

[18] 周光辉：《从管制转向服务：中国政府的管理革命》，《吉林大学社会科学学报》2008年第3期。

[19] 周光辉：《政府：一个公正社会不可或缺的角色》，《吉林大学社会科学学报》2006年第4期。

[20] 达尔：《行政科学：三个问题》，见彭和平等编译：《国外公共行政理论精选》（中译本），中央党校出版社1997年版。

[21] 张梦中：《美国公共行政历史渊源与重要价值取向》，《中国行政管理》2000年第11期。

Interlocal Agreements and Regional Collaborative Governance Networks in China[*]

Liming Suo Jie Ma Bin Chen[**]

Introduction

China's phenomenal economic performance has largely been attributed to a competitive environment in which local governments compete with each other to attract business investment, resources and talents. Recently attention has turned to the efforts that involve collaboration among multiple jurisdictions at the regional level. Local governments increasingly confront policy problems that span the boundaries of individual geographic jurisdictions. The need to work together has clustered them into several large regional collaborative zones to address positive and negative inter-jurisdictional externalities caused by rapid social and economic growth. China's major regional collaborative zones formed include the Beijing-Tianjin-Hebei Metropolitan Region, the Yangtze River Delta, the Pan Pearl River Delta and the Mid-China region (Ye, 2009). Despite the fanfare of media coverage, how these regional collaborative zones work is still understudied. The purpose of this paper is to examine one type of regional collaborative mechanism—interlocal agreements (ILAs) from a network perspective. ILAs are formal and informal arrangements (joint planning, joint policy initiatives, joint programs, contracts, etc.) where one local government collaborates with another or in which multiple jurisdictions pool their resources for joint problem solving, better coordination and more innovation. Scholars and researchers also recognize that multiple local governments that

---

[*] This research is supported by the National Natural Science Foundation of China (Project Number: 71003013 & 71303032).

[**] Liming Suo, Ph. D., University of Electronic Science and Technology of China; Jie Ma, Ph. D., University of Electronic Science and Technology of China; Bin Chen, Ph. D., Tongji University and Baruch College/CUNY.

participated in multiple interlocal agreements became regional-level networked governance structures (Hu and Ma, 2011; Thurmaier and Wood, 2002). A regional network of jurisdictions connected through interlocal agreements are manifestations of regional collaborative governance.

This paper proceeds in four sections. The first section is a survey of literature on regional governance. We aim to illustrate how the scholarly and practical interests on regional governance have shifted from a vertical and hierarchical dimension to a horizontal and networked one. In the second section, we present the Pan Pearl River Delta (PPRD) as a case study of regional cooperation through interlocal agreements. Also known as "9 + 2", the PPRD is made up of nine mainland provinces of Fujian, Jiangxi, Hunan, Guangdong, Guangxi, Hainan, Sichuan, Guizhou, and Yunnan, and two special administrative regions of Hong Kong and Macau. We will analyze a data set of 191 ILAs co-participated by these eleven jurisdictions to examine what policy issues these ILAs intend to address. After categorizing them into seven policy fields, we track their trends of growth over the years and compare their scale and scope across different policy areas. We will answer the questions: What is the scope of interlocal agreements in PPRD? Are they used more in one type of policy domain than another?

Since "9 + 2" members are connected by their joint participation in 191 interlocal agreements, they constitute a number of two-mode networks for our analysis. In the third section, we construct seven two-mode networks, one for each policy area. Each two-mode network data will be transferred to two one-mode network projection data: jurisdiction-to-jurisdiction and agreement-to-agreement. By employing various network analytical techniques, we will provide answers to the questions: how interconnected are these PPRD members through ILAs? Do the degrees of joint participation and co-membership vary across different policy domains? Are some "9 + 2" members more connected than others? Which jurisdiction occupies a central position and which one are least central in each network? We conclude the paper in the fourth section with some implications of our findings for China's regional collaborative governance.

This is a three-fold study to advance our understanding of regional governance. First, most existing studies on China's regional governance tend to be theoretical. The construct of network is receiving greater attention in the literature and network analysis has been lauded as an exceptionally powerful analytic tool. Yet although "network" has become a catchy word among Chinese scholars of regional governance, none has ever applied network analysis to examining empirical cases. We empirically map the network interconnectedness of PPRD members through interlocal agreements. Second, while most network studies of regional governance were conducted in a western context (for example, Lee, Feiock and Lee, 2012,

2013; Le Roux, Brandenburger and Pandey, 2010), ours is perhaps among the first of non-western cases. Third, while the existing studies on regional networks are all about one-mode networks, we utilize two-mode network analysis in our study. The study of two-mode networks has been common in the social sciences. However, in public management and policy studies, particularly in regional governance, the analysis of two-mode networks has not yet received enough attention, despite the fact that many of the networks that scholars study are bimodal in nature.

The Road to Regional Networked Governance

We are entering an era of "Hybrid" governance, where vertical, hierarchical authorities that trickle down from higher level governments to lower level jurisdictions operate in conjunction with horizontal collaboration across sectors and jurisdictions (Kettl, 2002). The development of research on regional governance echoes Kettl's observation. There are two prominent streams of literature on regional governance — vertical versus horizontal. Vertically, there has been a long tradition of studying intergovernmental management, particularly the functioning of administrative and fiscal federalism — the relationships between federal, state and local governments as well as their implications for maintaining macroeconomic stability, creating an equitable distribution of income and efficiently allocating resources (Oates, 1999; Colan and Posner, 2008).

The literature on the horizontal stream primarily concerns about which metropolitan governance structure may help or hinder economic development (Nelson and Foster, 1999). Three schools of thoughts — centralist, polycentrist and regionalist — compete for dominance in the debate (Wallis, 1996). Centralists favor consolidation of small, multiple and fragmented local governments, by contending that large, monocentric and multiple-purpose governments are most efficient in administration and production because of economies of scale, professional accountability, internalization of externalities, and elimination of duplications in service units (Leland and Thurmaier, 2000). Yet polycentrists counter that a system of decentralized and overlapping governments is a virtue, rather than a signal of chaos or inefficiency. With the driving force of inter-jurisdictional competition, local government structures will be streamlined to produce a mixed bundle of services/taxes that matches the heterogeneous preferences of firms and residents (Ostrom, Tiebout and Warren, 1961; Tiebout, 1956).

The third school of thought, represented by regionalists, rises above the centralist versus polycentrist debate. Of their primary concern is the role of regional governance mechanism in dealing with issues of regional significance. Policy issues of economic development, air pollution control, transportation infrastructure, etc., are cross-boundary in nature and therefore require regional solutions for collaborative decision-making (Feiock and Scholz, 2010). Instead of debating about actual arrangements of consolidated or multi-tiered local government structure, regionalists focus on identifying more flexible, voluntary, and horizontally linked arrangements of delivering services and joint decision-making (Savitch and Vogel, 2000). These alternative arrangements between local governments across jurisdictions can take many forms, ranging from voluntary memorandums of understanding, mutual aid agreements, and joint planning agreements to more legally binding mutual contracts; from relatively simple joint service agreements to more complex, ongoing interactions involving multiple governments.

These collaborative mechanisms can be all categorized into interlocal agreements, ranging from simple dyadic relationships to complex networks of multiple local governments even with private and nonprofit actors. The simple dyadic case involves management of a contractual relationship (formal or informal) while the latter requires local officials to manage their duties in a network fashion. This "complex networks" approach suggests a large number of independent governments voluntarily cooperating through multiple, overlapping webs of interlocal agreements (Thurmaier and Wood, 2002). Such range in the scope and depth of interlocal agreements enables researchers to apply a network approach to studying regional governance. For example, competitive motivations were found to underlie cooperative behaviors in regional economic development policy network (Lee, Feiock and Lee, 2012). Some network structural configurations — reciprocity and clustering — were preferred in a dense network of local governments and nonprofits (Lee, Feiock and Lee, 2013). Researchers also indicate that interlocal service cooperation increases when jurisdictional actors network frequently through a regional association or council of government (LeRoux, Brandenburger and Pandey, 2010).

Research on China's regional governance also started with a vertical dimension. The earlier studies have focused on the utility of administrative and fiscal decentralization in sustaining the economic reforms in terms of central-local relationships (Shirk, 1993). The development of China's central-local interaction was touted by political economists as a model of "Market-Preserving Federalism" (Qian and Weingast, 1996) in which the central government incentivized local governments to undertake reforms, generate more revenues and allocate resources to meet their own needs. At the horizontal level, the reform unleashed the entrepreneurial spirit of local governments, fuelling the rapid growth of local economies, a market-oriented scenario that would be favored by polycentrists. Yet, just like centralists in the US, opponents pointed out that that fiscal decentralization elevated efficiency over equity, produced "race-to-the-bottom" competition between local governments and encouraged local officials to protect their own markets by erecting administrative blockades (Chen, 2004). While central authorities kept talking about coordinating the national economy as a common market, local authorities in pursuit of revenue were dividing it up. Even when the central government enjoyed authority over units of the lower level governments, it faced the problem of monitoring the compliance of multiple jurisdictions that had different local conditions.

Over time, when neither centralized authority nor market solution works, China's local governments began to recognize that a decision or action of one government affects the actions of others. According to a survey of local officials, such a recognition of interdependency led to more horizontal and collaborative approaches when two or more local governments seek to create a desirable outcome through coordination or cooperation, rather than competition (Shi, 2008). Accordingly, Chinese scholars call for a shift of scholarly interests toward regional governance (Yang and Chen, 2004). Collaboration between local governments is believed to be one of the policy instruments to address policy problems of regional significance, particularly for the purposes of economic integration, industrial restructuring and joint planning, and trans-jurisdictional problems and regional public goods (Yang and Peng, 2009). Examples of specific policy issues that require regional collaboration include environmental protection, infrastructure, economic development and public crisis and emergency (Ma, 2010; Yan and Wang, 2013). Chinese researchers also explore the motivations of forming collaborative relationships among local governments and suggest that they are heavily influenced by the factors of geographic proximity and regional economic development level, as well as political, institutional, cultural and historical factors. Yet once local governments participate in regional collaboration, it usually has a bandwagon effect — other local governments are also eager to participate for the fear of being left out (Sun, 2013).

Interlocal or intergovernmental agreements have been treated as institutional innovation in regional governance and therefore have received a lot of attention. According to Yang's study (2011), on the basis of different participating actors, these agreements can be classified along the three dimensions: vertical, horizontal and cross-jurisdictional. The vertical agreements refer to the ones signed either between central and local governments or between provincial and municipal governments in a hierarchical fashion. The horizontal agreements are those between governments in the same administrative levels, for example, inter-provincial, inter-municipality, inter-county as well as interagency agreements. Other agreements could be made between governments at the different administrative levels and therefore are cross-jurisdictional. According to their policy nature, some agreements are designed to address boundary and jurisdictional issues, some are distributive and developmental, some are regulative and others are more redistributive (Yang, 2011).

In addition to centralized authority and market competition, networked governance has been proposed to be a better regional coordinative mechanism (Lu, 2008). For example, a government-led network was proposed for the Jing-Jin-Ji metropolitan region (Ma, 2010). An interlocal agreement between two local government units constitutes a dyadic relationship. If each unit also participates in other agreements with other local governments, together, these relations form macro-level regional governance that comprises a set of actors in a network structure (Thurmaier and Wood, 2002). Over time, embedded relationships with other local governments accumulate into a regional cooperative network (Hu and Ma, 2011). However, the current studies have not yet gone beyond theoretical discussion and there is a lack of empirical studies. Even few studies apply a network approach to empirically investigating China's interlocal agreements as a regional network. This is the gap we intend to close in this study.

Interlocal Agreements in Pan Pearl River Delta

The Pan Pearl River Delta (PPRD), also known as "9 + 2", was initially suggested in July 2003 by Zhang Dejiang, the Party Secretary of Guangdong and a member of Politburo, as a development strategy of fostering an integral regional economy (Yeh and Xu, 2011). The case of PPRD regional cooperation provides us with a unique laboratory for the study of ILAs from a network perspective on the three grounds. First, as shown in figure 1, as one of China's four major regional cooperative zones, the "9 + 2" area spans across China's four geographic areas — eastern, southern, central and southwestern parts, covering nine coastal and inland provinces of Fujian, Jiangxi, Hunan, Guangdong, Guangxi, Hainan, Sichuan, Yunnan and Guizhou and the two special administrative regions (SARs) of Hong Kong and Macau. Although member provinces are mostly contiguous and located in the Pearl River Basin, it embraces one fifth of China's total territory and 55% of the mainland coastline.

Figure 1　Location and Boundary of Pan Pearl River Delta

Source: http://www.slcss.edu.hk/subjects/geog/PanPRD_e.gif.

Second, as shown in table 1, the PPRD carries a third of China's population (480 million) and contributes 36% to China's GDP. It is a very vibrant regional economy with an average growth rate of 10.8%, 0.7% higher than the national average of 10.1%. Except for Hainan, Hong Kong and Macau, the GDP growth rates of other "9 + 2" members are all above the national average. Third, statistics in table 1 also suggest that the PPRD is also marked by huge variations in economic performance. The nine provinces and two regions are categorized into four different development levels (Lei et al., 2006). While Hong Kong and Macau are considered as the two wealthiest members with per capita GDP over 5 - 10 times that of national average, Guangxi, Yunnan and Guizhou are treated as three "underdeveloped" provinces with their per capita GDPs well below the national level. In between, Guangdong and Fujian are two "developed" provinces with their per capita GDPs higher than national average by 30% - 40%. Hainan, Hunan, Jiangxi and Sichuan are four "developing" members with per capita GDPs ranging from 75 to 87% of China's national per capita GDP. The per capita GDP of Guangdong, the wealthiest province in the mainland, is almost three times that of Guizhou, the poorest. The per capita GDP in Macau is 22 times that in Guizhou.

Table 1 Socioeconomic Statistics for Pan Pearl River Delta, 2012

Province/SAR	Population (millions)	Land Area (10000 square kilometers)	GDP (billions of USD)	GDP Per Capita (USD)	GDP Growth Rate (Percentage)
Fujian	37.5 (2.8%)	12.4 (1.3%)	313.5 (3.8%)	8394 (137%)	11.4 (113%)
Jiangxi	45.0 (3.3%)	16.7 (1.7%)	206.0 (2.5%)	4582 (75%)	12.3 (122%)
Hunan	66.4 (3.9%)	21.2 (2.2%)	352.5 (4.3%)	5327 (87%)	10.1 (100%)
Guangdong	105.9 (7.8%)	18.0 (1.9%)	907.9 (11%)	8606 (141%)	11.5 (113%)
Guangxi	46.8 (3.5%)	23.7 (2.5%)	207.3 (2.5%)	4447 (73%)	11.8 (117%)
Hainan	8.9 (0.7%)	3.5 (0.4%)	45.4 (0.6%)	5151 (84%)	9.9 (98%)
Sichuan	80.8 (6.0%)	48.5 (5.1%)	379.8 (4.6%)	4711 (77%)	13.6 (135%)
Guizhou	34.8 (2.6%)	17.6 (1.8%)	109.0 (1.3%)	3136 (51%)	12.0 (119%)
Yunnan	46.6 (3.4%)	39.4 (4.1%)	164.0 (2.0%)	3531 (58%)	14.9 (148%)
Hong Kong	71.6 (0.5%)	0.1 (0.01%)	249.3 (3.0%)	35433 (580%)	1.5 (15%)
Macau	0.6 (0.04%)	0.003 (0.0003%)	39.63 (0.5%)	69628 (1139%)	9.9 (98%)
PPRD Total	479.9 (35.4%)	201.1 (21.0%)	2974.3 (36.0%)	13904 (227%)*	10.8 (107%)*
All China	1354 (100%)	960 (100%)	8256.2 (100%)	6113 (100%)	10.1 (100%)

Source: *China Statistic Year Book 2013*, http://www.stats.gov.cn/tjsj/ndsj/.
Note: 1) Numbers in the parentheses are the percentages of the national total;
  2) GDP and GDP Per Capita values were converted to US dollars at the rate of 6.2855 : 1.
* Numbers are average values of 11 provinces and special administrative regions.

To examine the scope of PPRD's regional cooperation, we compiled a dataset of 191 interlocal agreements participated by nine mainland provinces and two SARs over the time period of eleven years. These are publicly available data published by www.pprd.org.cn. We grouped them into seven areas of policy issues: environmental protection, tourism development, transportation infrastructure, science/technological/cultural collaboration (STC), migrant labor, public health, and trade development. These policy issues that involve positive and negative externalities are clearly trans-jurisdictional in nature.

The tourism promotion and trade development are typical examples of maximizing positive externality from regional cooperation. From tropical beaches to snow-capped mountain peaks, ancient history to ethnic minority cultures, the provinces within the PPRD region offer many different attractions for visitors to explore. Hong Kong and Macau also became the two primary destinations for mainland Chinese to travel overseas. A number of bilateral and multilateral agreements were signed to promote and coordinate tourism industry development. For example, in 2008, Guangdong signed agreements with its neighboring provinces of Fujian and Jiangxi to jointly market Hakka cultural heritages. In the same year, Guangdong hosted the Pearl River Delta International Tourism Festival. As developed regions, Guangdong, Hong Kong and Macau need to expand their economic forces further to neighboring areas. At the same time, neighboring regions need to realize the benefits of cross-regional development. In 2003, Closer Economic Partnership Arrangements (CEPAs) were signed with Hong Kong and Macau on June 29 and October 18 respectively. The "9 + 2" members also strive to remove intra-regional trade barriers. One of the objectives stated in CEPAs is to progressively reduce or eliminate tariffs and non-tariff barrierssubstantially on all the trade in goods.

Facing stiff global and regional competition, collaborations on scientific and technological innovations are the keys to economic success. In 2006, research institutions in Guangdong, Guangxi, Fujian and Hainan decided to share some of their advanced scientific equipment. In 2012, all the PPRD members jointly worked out a plan for scientific and technological cooperation. As such, well-developed transportation infrastructure is instrumental to the free flow of goods, material and personnel, and requires region-wide planning and coordination. In 2005, Guangdong signed collaborative agreements with Jiangxi, Hunan, Fujian and Guangxi to conduct inter-provincial highway planning. Collaboration related to regional development and infrastructure planning also extended to railway, sea and river transportation in 2011 to 2013.

As a byproduct of industrialization and rapid economic progress, China has seen its environment deteriorate. Clean air and water are clearly public goods and need the collective efforts of all parties affected. Many mainland PPRD members are loosely tied together through the tributaries of the Pearl River. Protecting water resources across the administrative boundary therefore became their common concern. In 2012, all the mainland "9 + 2" member provinces formulated a guideline on dealing with disputes on cross-boundary water pollution. In 2009, all the PPRD members worked together to create a region-wide system of monitoring air quality.

The PPRD has always witnessed huge waves of migrant workers. Millions of workers from moderately and underdeveloped provinces, say, Sichuan and Guizhou, migrated to the developed provinces of Guangdong and Fujian for job opportunities. The policies pertaining to social security and workers' rights need permanence across the region. In 2006, an agreement on protecting migrant workers' rights was signed among labor unions in different provinces. A frequent movement of people makes it increasingly difficult to manage a public health crisis. Infectious diseases, such as outbreak of severe acute respiratory syndrome (SARS) in 2002, do not recognize the administrative and geographic boundaries. As a reflection of their common concerns, many interlocal agreements on public health were signed by Guangdong, Hong Kong and Macau from 2004 to 2013.

In figure 2, we plotted 191 agreements in seven policy areas from 2003 – 2013. In the earlier years, the ILAs heavily concentrated on economic and trade development. In 2003, four agreements were signed, with one for tourism development, one for SCT and two for trade. Over the years, the number of other non-trade-related agreements began to pick up. Now, the "9 + 2" cross-regional cooperation has extended from trade and economy to many other areas of environment protection, migrant labor, and public health.

Table 2 Interlocal Agreements for Pan Pearl River Delta (2003 – 2013)

	2003	2004	2005	2006	2007	2008	2009	2010	2011	2012	2013
Environment	0	6	5	7	1	4	2	3	0	2	12
Tourism	1	1	6	2	0	7	7	8	4	3	3
Transportation	0	0	5	2	0	3	2	2	4	5	4
S&T and Culture	1	1	9	1	2	3	0	0	2	9	5
Labor	0	2	3	4	1	2	2	5	1	0	0
Public Health	0	1	0	3	1	2	0	0	1	2	0
Trade	1	1	3	0	0	3	6	3	0	0	0

We also present the distribution of ILAs along seven policy arenas in figure 3. As seen in figure 3, environmental protection and tourism development are the two largest groups of ILAs between 2003 and 2013 (42 agreements each). The second and third largest groups of agreements fall in the areas of STC (33 agreements) and transportation infrastructure (27 agreements) Together, these four groups account for nearly three quarters (75%) of the total agreements. The fourth largest group of agreements is in the area of migrant labor, including 20 agreements. The group of trade agreements ranks fifth (17 agreements). There are only 10 agreements in the area of public health, ranking sixth.

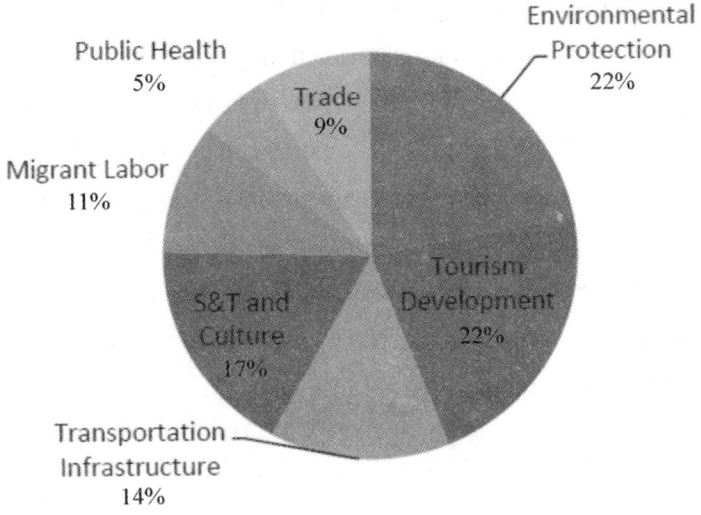

Figure 2 Distribution of 191 Interlocal Agreements

Pan Pearl River Delta as Regional Networks

Although giving us some idea on distribution and trend of the "9 +2" interlocal agreements in seven policy domains, the analyses above only reveal part of the whole picture. They do not tell us much about how the PPRD as a regional cooperative network looks. To explore the PPRD regional governance from a network perspective, we turned to the two-mode network analysis of the "9 +2" interprovincial networks, defined as the set of relationships among provinces and SARs created by their common participation on agreements. Most social network analyses involve one-mode networks that consist of a single set of actors. The "9 +2" regional networks we studied are two-mode, consisting of one set of actors and one set of events. Such networks of actors tied to each other through their participation in common events, and common events linked through multiple memberships of actors, are also referred to as affiliation networks (Wasserman and Faust, 1994).

We employed UCINET, analytical software for network analysis (Bargotti et al., 2002) to create seven two-mode affiliation networks, one for each policy area, that linked individual "9 +2" members based on their joint participation on agreements. In a two-mode network matrix, when province i participates in with agreement j and otherwise. A two-mode matrix can be transferred to two one-mode projection matrices: jurisdiction-to-jurisdiction) and agreement-to-agreement. The former is a network of ties between the PPRD members that develop on the basis of joint involvement in common agreements. A one-mode network projection of jurisdiction-to-jurisdiction reveals how many agreements any pair of jurisdictions jointly signed. For example, if eight agreements were participated by two jurisdictions and together, the value in the matrix cell would be . The latter is a one-mode network projection of connections between agreements, derived from the co-memberships of jurisdictions. This reveals the number of jurisdictions where any pair of agreements are jointly involved. In the similar vein, if four jurisdictions were all found to participate in agreement and agreement, the matrix cell. The network data in these two one-mode projections are all valued rather than binary.

Network Cohesiveness

To what extent the collaboration developed among the "9 + 2" members is cohesive? Do their connections vary across different policy issue networks? To answer these two questions, we look at one network metric — density, measuring the degree to which a network is connected. In binary one-mode networks, network density is the number of ties in a network, expressed as a proportion of the maximum possible number of ties. In valued one-mode projection of two-model networks, the network density is calculated as the average value of tie strength across all ties. By using measure of density, we could determine the degree of shared participation of interlocal agreements that existed among the PPRD members. The larger the density score, the more cohesive the network is. In table 2, we present the network density values of jurisdiction-to-jurisdiction and agreement-to-agreement networks in seven policy issues.

Table 3 Densities of Jurisdiction-to-Jurisdiction and Agreement-to-Agreement Networks in Seven Policy Areas

Inter-jurisdictional Networks (Co-Participation)	Inter-agreement Networks (Co-Membership)
Environment (14.84)	Migrant Labor (4.92)
S&T and Culture (13.52)	Transportation (3.51)
Migrant Labor (12.15)	S&T and Culture (3.47)
Transportation (11.60)	Environment (2.96)
Tourism (11.31)	Public Health (2.6)
Trade (2.98)	Tourism (2.12)
Public Health (2.73)	Trade (1.21)

The comparison of results in figure 3 and table 2 reveal some interesting findings. For the inter-jurisdictional networks, the largest group (environment) in figure 3 still topped the list in table 2 with a density score of 14.84, indicating that the policy issue of environmental protection sees the most connected and cohesive networking ties among 11 jurisdictions. The group of tourism development agreements also accounts for the largest share of total agreements in figure 3. Yet the jurisdiction-to-jurisdiction network on policy issue of tourism only ranks fifth with a density score of 11.31. In other words, the average number of tourism agreements that the PPRD jurisdictions co-participated is around 11. The third largest group of S&T and culture agreements upgraded to the second place in terms of density. It is the network of migrant labor policy issue that has the largest gains, moving from the fifth in figure 3 up to the third in network density ranking. The rankings for trade and public health policy networks remain unchanged.

The results of inter-agreement networks are different. The largest number of co-membership is seen in the area of migrant labor. For any pair of agreements, on average there are five overlapping PPRD members. S&T and Culture moved down to the third place with a density score of 3.47. The environmental group further moved from the first place to the fourth one. The rankings of two groups upgraded with the transportation group from the fourth to the second and public health group from the bottom to the fifth. Another two groups downgraded their rankings with tourism from the fifth to the sixth and trade from the sixth to the bottom.

Network Visualization

To ascertain the extent to which there were overlapping participations of multiple agreements among the PPRD members, we used Net–Draw, a network visualization function embedded in UCINET to visually display the structural configuration of inter-jurisdictional network in seven policy areas. Net–Draw allows for a number of analytical procedures to be undertaken to determine the kinds of shared relationships among the "9 + 2" members entered into the software program. The findings are presented as seven sociograms from figure 4a to figure 4g. In each figure, the symbols of a square represent jurisdictions. To better visually represent the network structure, we deliberately placed provinces and SARs into the diagram layout that is consistent with their administrative boundaries and geographic locations. The lines connecting squares refer to their joint participation of agreements. Since one-mode network projections derived from two-mode networks are necessarily symmetric, we dropped off the arrows of the lines. Also note that some lines are thicker and some are thinner. The sizes of lines indicate the strength of connections and are in proportion to the number of agreements they have in common. The thicker lines represent more agreements and the thinners lines less agreements. As we illustrate each of the figures below, one of the strengths of network visualization is that it can reveal both loose and tight structures (Fataar, 2006).

The inter-jurisdictional network connected through collaborative agreements in environmental protection is shown in figure 3a. The six provinces of Yunan, Guizhou, Hunan, Jiangxi, Guangdong and Guangxi are found to form a tight substructure in the center of the PPRD, primarily because of their geographic proximity. The structural configuration looks like one where a square, consisting of four immediately neighboring provinces (Guizhou, Hunan, Guangdong and Guangxi) is embedded in a large trapezoid (Yunan, Guizhou, Hunan, Jiangxi, Guangdong and Guangxi). The network structural configurations of transportation infrastructure and trade in figure 3b and figure 3c look very similar to that of environmental protection. This is perhaps because geographic proximity is a key determinant in fostering inter-jurisdictional collaboration for addressing the issues of environmental protection, transportation infrastructure and trade development.

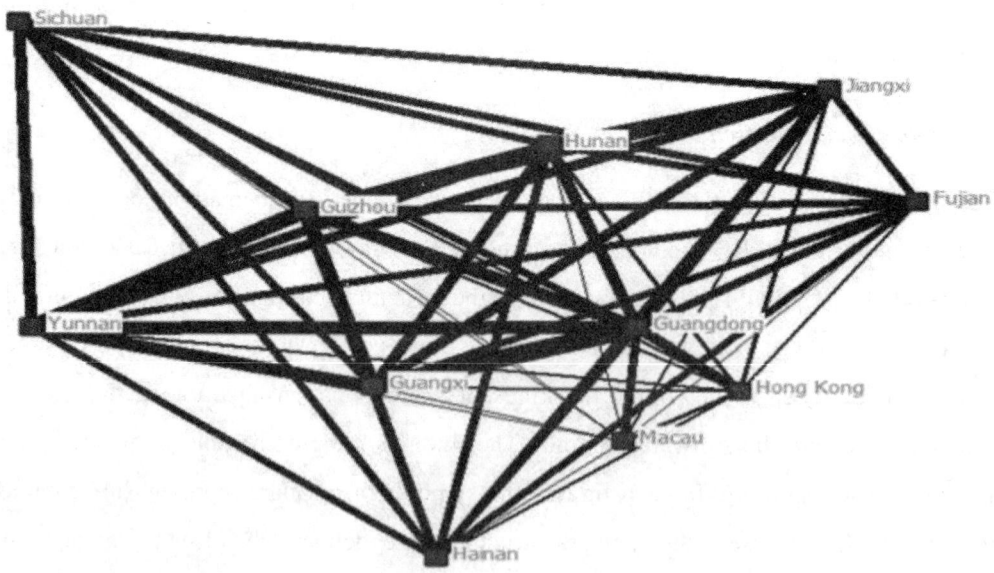

Figure 3a Environmental Protection

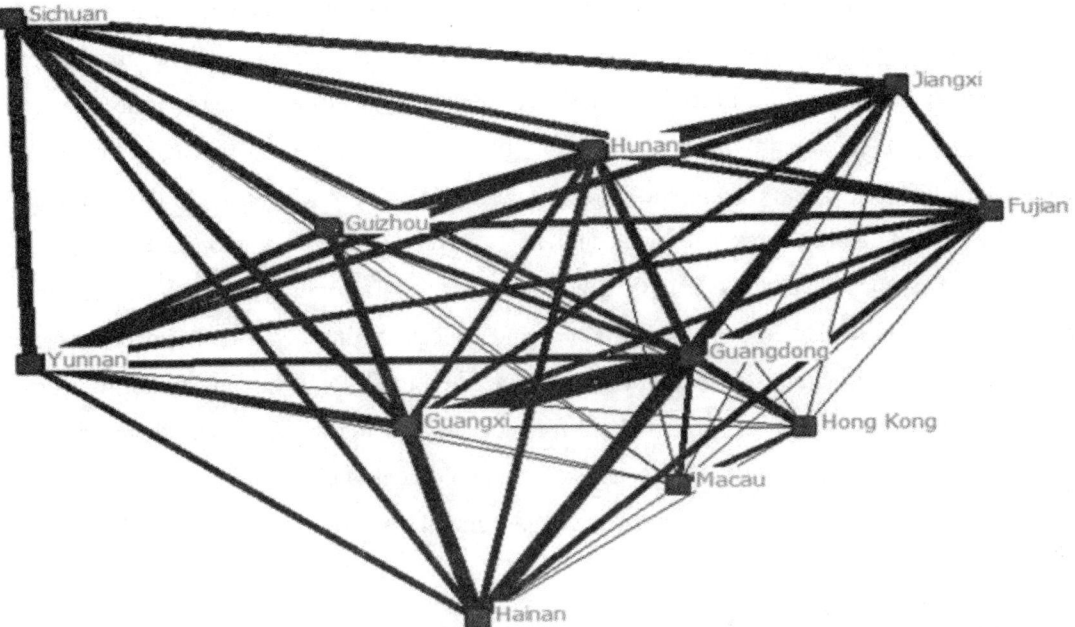

Figure 3b   Transportation Infrastructure

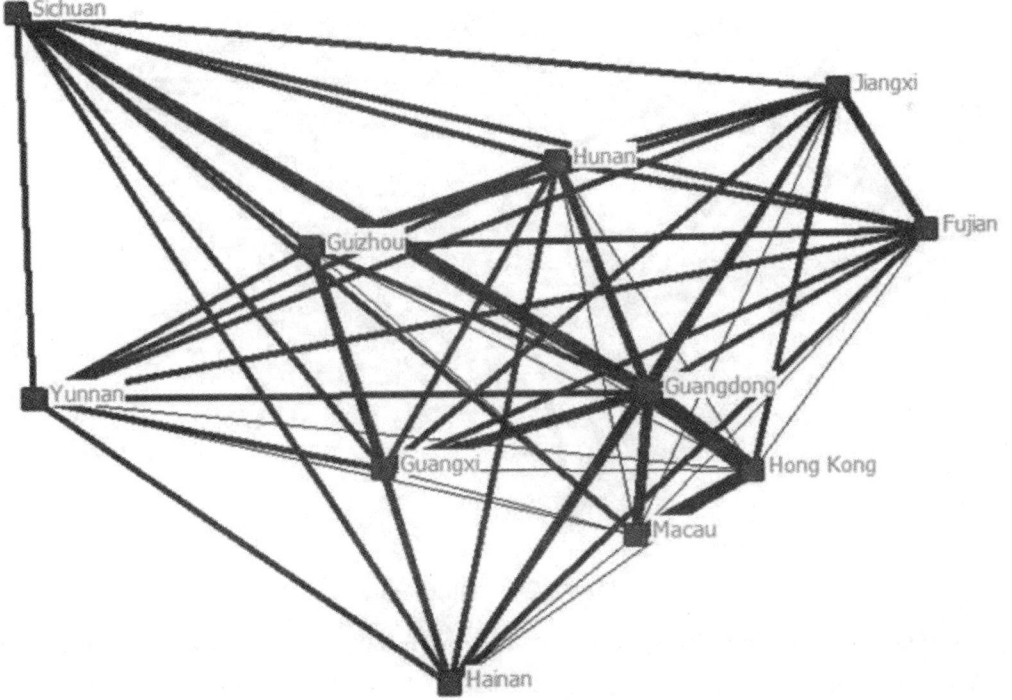

Figure 3c   Trade

Figure 3d depicts inter-jurisdictional network formed through collaborative agreements in scientific, technological and cultural collaboration. There are fairly extensive amounts of agreement shared among the PPRD members. Yet the strength of ties varies. As the sizes of lines indicate, mainland provinces have much stronger relationships with each other than their interactions with Hong Kong and Macau. There are two sub-networks: all the mainland members tightly connected as one block and Pearl River Delta (Guangdong, Hong Kong and Macau) as the other block. It is Guangdong as a coastal province that plays a bridging role between mainland members, Hong Kong and Macau through S&T cultural collaboration. This structural pattern is consistent with the fact that the "9 + 2" members are in different economic development stages. It is hard for most developing and underdeveloped inland provinces to engage in substantial scientific, technological and cultural exchanges with Hong Kong and Macau as the two most developed members.

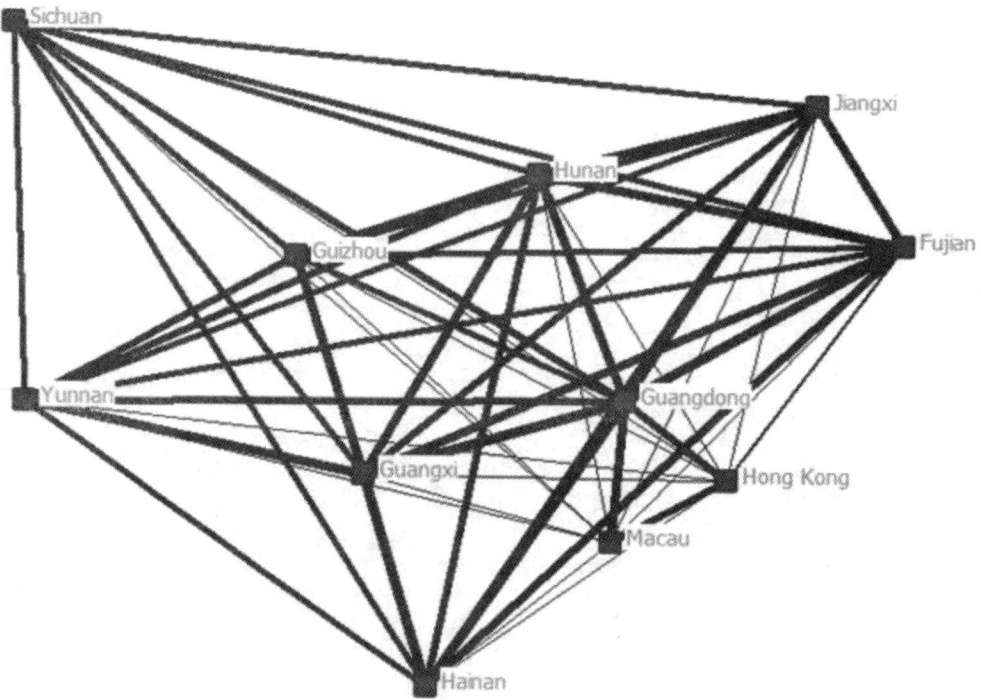

Figure 3d S & T and Culture

The sociogram in figure 3e clearly demonstrates a pattern of workers migrating from underdeveloped and developing inland provinces to developed coastal areas. Cities in Guangdong Province have been destinations for workers migrating from poor inland provinces. What emerged is a star-like structure where strong ties radiated from Guangdong, situated as the hub, to the provinces of Sichuan, Yunnan, Hainan, Fujian, Jiangxi and Hunan at the rim. Although also being part of inland provinces, Guizhou and Guangxi had less extensive ties with Guangdong. It might be because these two provinces are overshadowed by Sichuan as the largest labor-exporting province. For pairs of Sichuan and Guizhou, and Hong Kong and Macau, they are geographically neighboring with each other and therefore each has witnessed extensive co-participation of agreements on labor and manpower. However, an examining of agreements suggests a difference. While the focus of collaboration between Sichuan and Guizhou is on low-skilled workers, Hong Kong and Macau are primarily involved in exchange of highly-educated talents.

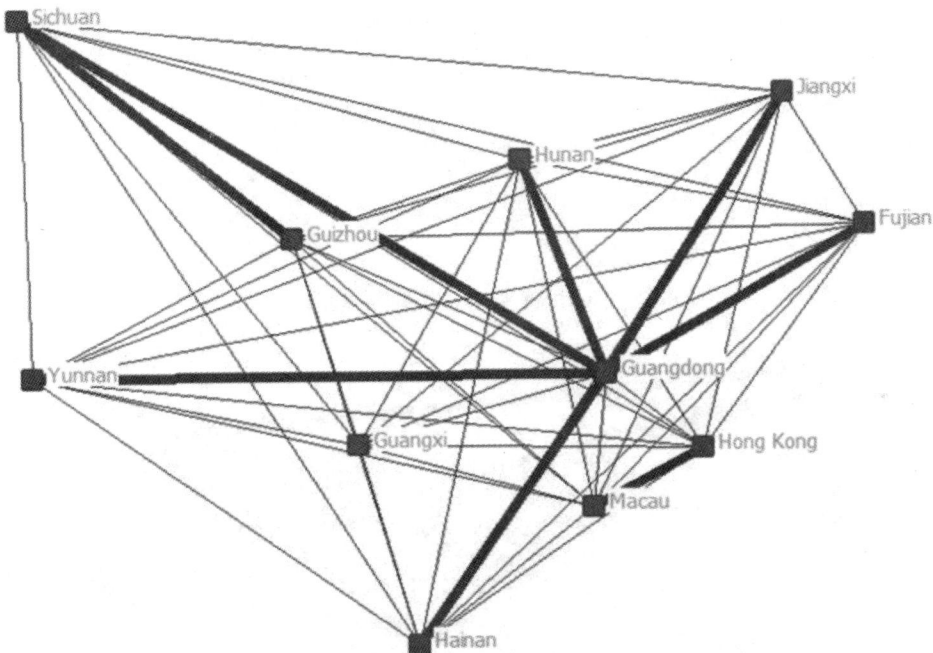

Figure 3e　Migrant Labor

Figure 3f displays the sociogram of inter-jurisdictional network in the policy issue of tourism development. The three provinces of Guangdong, Jiangxi and Fujian developed a strong triangle among themselves and Guangdong also built a strong tie with Guangxi. The sociogram in the public health area (Figure 3g) demonstrates a fairly strong and equally distributed degree of interconnectedness among geographically close mainland provinces. What is worth noting is that Guangdong, Hong Kong and Macau are so connected to each other that they developed an "iron triangle" with very thick lines connecting them. The closure of the triangle is usually an indicator of a strong and bonding network structural configuration. Across all the seven networks, Hong Kong and Macau as two special administrative regions, under the institutional arrangement of "one country and two systems", were usually loosely connected to most mainland provinces. Their connections with mainland were primarily through Guangdong.

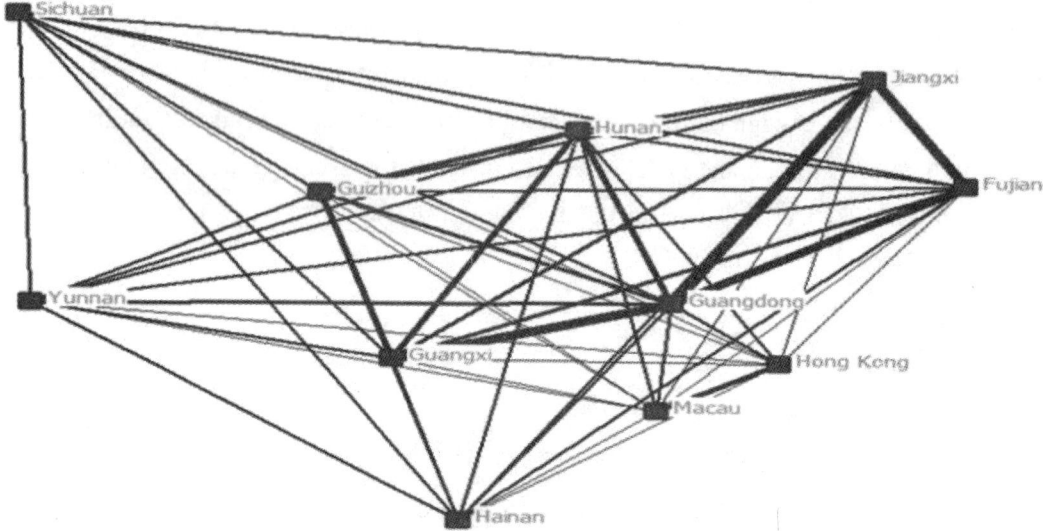

Figure 3f   Tourism Development

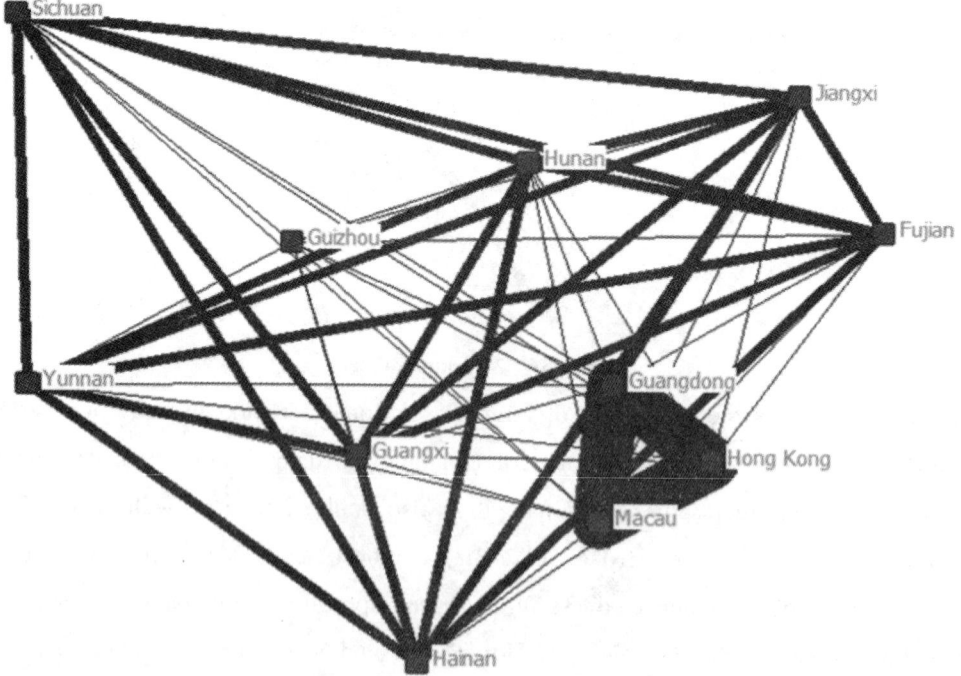

Figure 3g   Public Health

Degree Centrality

Social network analysis can also help identify most central and least central actors in a network. We used the network metric of degree centrality to measure the degree to which a jurisdiction is centrally located in the "9 + 2" networks. Degree centrality is an important structural attribute of social network studies because it identifies how important an actor is within a social network. It is usually an indicator of an actor's prominence and power within a network. By comparing the positions of specific jurisdictions — in terms of their relative centrality — across the networks, we provide information about the role of each jurisdiction — in the PPRD regional cooperation. In one-model networks, degree centrality is simply the count of the number of an actor's ties, which is then normalized by network size. In two-mode networks, there are one set of actors and one set of events. The affiliation relation relates each actor to a subset of events and relates each event to a subset of actors. Consequently, the centrality of an actor is proportional to the sum of the centralities of the events to which it belongs and the centrality of an event is proportional to the sum of the centralities of the actors that are members of the event (Faust, 1997). To take into account such duality, we applied a 2-mode centrality analysis in UCINET to our data. The UCINET generated two sets of degree centrality scores: one for jurisdictions and the other for agreements. We present the results of jurisdictions in table 3 where the PPRD members are ranked on the basis of their degree centrality scores.

The most obvious finding is that Guangdong is the most central member as its degree centrality scores topped across all the seven policy areas. The result comes as no surprise. The pivotal network position Guangdong occupied is mainly due to its economic power, geographic advantage, and political status. As the wealthiest among the mainland members, Guangdong is among the first Chinese provinces to benefit from the economic reforms following 1978 and is always considered to be one step ahead of the rest of China. The province is located at the end of Pear River Basin and connects the mainland to Hong Kong and Macau. The Party Secretary of Guangdong is usually a member of the Politburo (the Political Bureau of the Central Committee of the Communist Party of China), which is the highest decision-making body in China. This gives Guangdong a higher political status than other provinces with regard to the PPRD cooperation. Fujian, though as one of the two developed provinces, does not enjoy the same prestigious status as Guangdong. Most of its rankings are above or around middle levels with even one in the low end (trade).

Three underdeveloped provinces of Guangxi, Guizhou and Yunnan are in the low range of rankings in the areas of migrant labor, public health and trade. While Guizhou and Yunnan remains at or below the middle level, Guangxi became the second in the areas of environment, tourism, transportation, and S & T and culture. Guangxi's relative central network position in these areas is due to its geographic advantage. It is located in the place where China-ASEAN Free Trade Zone and the PPRD connects. Despite their low rankings in most policy areas, Guizhou and Yunan moved up to the third and fourth third in the policy area of environmental protection as these two provinces are rich in environmental resources.

Table 3 Two-Mode Centrality Ranking of Provinces/SARs in PPRD Networks of Interlocal Agreements (Measured as Degree Centrality)

Ranking	Provinces and SARs (Normalized Degree Centrality Score)						
	Environment	Tourism	Transportation	S & T and Culture	Migrant Labor	Public Health	Trade
1	Guangdong (0.94)	Guangdong (0.83)	Guangdong (0.93)	Guangdong (0.88)	Guangdong (0.90)	Guangdong (0.90)	Guangdong (0.65)
2	Guangxi (0.60)	Guangxi (0.55)	Guangxi (0.70)	Guangxi (0.64)	Sichuan (0.70)	Hong Kong (0.80)	Hong Kong (0.48)
3	Guizhou (0.55)	Jiangxi (0.52)	Hainan (0.56)	Fujian (0.58)	Fujian (0.65)	Macau (0.80)	Sichuan (0.35)
4	Yunnan (0.55)	Fujian (0.48)	Jiangxi (0.52)	Hainan (0.58)	Jiangxi (0.65)	Jiangxi (0.40)	Macau (0.35)
5	Jiangxi (0.50)	Hunan (0.41)	Hunan (0.52)	Hunan (0.55)	Hunan (0.65)	Fujian (0.30)	Jiangxi (0.30)
6	Hunan (0.48)	Guizhou (0.33)	Sichuan (0.52)	Macau (0.52)	Hainan (0.65)	Hunan (0.30)	Hunan (0.30)
7	Hong Kong (0.45)	Hong Kong (0.31)	Yunan (0.52)	Jiangxi (0.49)	Guizhou (0.65)	Guangxi (0.30)	Guangxi (0.30)
8	Sichuan (0.41)	Macau (0.31)	Fujian (0.48)	Guizhou (0.49)	Yunnan (0.65)	Hainan (0.30)	Guizhou (0.30)
9	Fijian (0.38)	Yunnan (0.29)	Guizhou (0.48)	Yunnan (0.49)	Hong Kong (0.65)	Sichuan (0.30)	Fujian (0.24)
10	Hainan (0.36)	Hainan (0.26)	Hong Kong (0.48)	Hong Kong (0.49)	Macau (0.65)	Yunnan (0.30)	Hainan (0.18)
11	Macau (0.36)	Sichuan (0.26)	Macau (0.41)	Sichuan (0.45)	Guangxi (0.60)	Guizhou (0.20)	Yunnan (0.18)

Among four developing provinces, Hunan is mediocre with all the ranking around the middle level. Jiangxi is seen to have some fluctuations with some rankings slightly above and others below the middle levels. Hainan's ranking is even more fluctuated than Jiangxi's. On the one hand, Hainan ranks almost to the end in three areas (environment protection, tourism and trade); on the other hand, its rankings in other areas are well above or slightly below the middle. Sichuan is perhaps the biggest outlier. As the second populated province and second largest economy in PPRD, Sichuan is neither a part of the Pearl River Basin nor contiguous to Guangdong geographically, ranking second and third in the areas of migrant labor and trade. Yet its rankings in other areas are well below the middle and even towards the bottom. Overall, Sichuan does not seem to be very active in "9 + 2" cooperation.

Hong Kong and Macau as the two special administrative regions have very different legal and administrative systems from mainland provinces. Their rankings in most areas are below the middle with some at the bottom. Yet they are the PPRD's windows to the outside world. Because of geographic proximity and economic interdependence, they have higher stakes in the areas of public health and trade relationships. Their rankings in the area of public health jumped to second and third and in the network of trade agreements they are positioned in second and third.

Concluding Discussion

Since the late 1990s, efforts to form regional collaborative networks have been proliferated in many parts of China. This has led to a shift of scholarly interest in horizontal and networked regional governance, as our literature review concludes. What we know little about is how they are actually working. As network analysis can be a powerful analytic tool in researching governance, this paper contributes to the literature about China's regional governance, empirically and conceptually, using an analysis of inter-jurisdictional networks of nine provinces and two special administrative regions, connected through interlocal agreements within the Pan Pearl River Delta. We draw three implications and one caveat of our findings for theory and practice.

First, local governments in China have been always criticized for diversion of scarce public resources to economic development and diverted attention away from environmental and social concerns (Xu and Yeh, 2011). Even in regional cooperation, the primary focus has always been on the issues related to local economic development. Yet the results of our analysis suggest a different story. The total number of agreements on economic development (tourism, transportation and trade) is 86, less than 105 agreements concerning social issues (environmental protection, public health, labor and SCT). Our network analysis further reveals that on average, the PPRD members have the highest co-participation of agreements and the interlocal agreements have the highest co-memberships of the "9 + 2" members on policy issues of environmental protection, S & T and culture, and migrant labor, suggesting that local governments have begun to assume the role they are supposed to play-providing public goods and services, as opposed to simply pursuing economic growth. However, the issue of public health does not receive a lot of attention for the "9 + 2" inter-jurisdictional collaboration. With the smallest share of total agreements, its shared participation of "9 + 2" members is also the lowest.

Second, the visualization of the PPRD network structures provides us with some clues on what may drive the PPRD members' participation of regional cooperation. The "9 + 2" is intended to serve as an informal partnership in which its members participate on a voluntary basis and are free to pursue strategies on which they agree. In the absence of a centralized decision-making authority, geographic proximity and resource complementarity seem to determine the PPRD members' commitment to work with each other. The provinces of Guizhou, Hunan, Guangdong and Guangxi, located in the PPRD's heartland, neighboring immediately with each other, are found to have a very extensive shared participation in multiple areas of agreements. Hong Kong and Macau, on the other hand, are geographically far away from many inland provinces and thus do not have much co-participation with them. The network structure of migrant labor demonstrates the role of resource complementarity in fostering collaboration between many inland provinces as homes of migrant workers, and Guangdong as their final destination.

Third, the central positions of Guangdong in all the networks, identified by our analysis, illustrate its leading roles in the PPRD regional governance. Being cognizant of its prominence, the leadership in Guangdong should not only take initiatives in addressing key regional issues, but also be careful not to compromise other PPRD members' autonomy. Understanding the network structure will also help them identify the gaps in regional cooperation. Guangdong may encourage those more peripheral provinces to increase their participation in addressing the issues of regional concerns. The network analysis of this nature can also help individual "9 + 2" members have a better understanding of their roles and positions in PPRD. They might contemplate the strategies of being more engaged with other members. For example, despite the fact that they are under different political and administrative systems in one country, Hong Kong and Macau should find ways to be more integrated into the "9 + 2".

Finally, the findings from this study should be interpreted with cautions. One important caveat is that we only examined the network connections through interlocal agreements signed by PPRD members. A wide scope of co-participation and a large number of co-memberships do not necessarily foretell effective implementation of these interlocal agreements and ultimate successes of addressing these policy issues. More research needs to be done to investigate the extent to which regional issues are addressed by these joint efforts. Future research should also be conducted to study China's other regional collaborative zones from a comparative angle.

---

[1] Borgatti, S. P., Everett, M. G. and Freeman, L. C., *Ucinet 6 for Windows: Software for Social Network Analysis*, Harvard, MA: Analytic Technologies.

[2] Chen, Bin, "Reforming Intergovernmental Fiscal Relationships in China: A Political Economy Perspective", *Chinese Public Administration Review*, 2 (3/4), 2004, pp. 1 – 8.

[3] Colan, Timothy J. and Paul L. Posner (eds.), *Intergovernmental Management for the 21st Century*, Washington, DC: The Brookings Institution Press, 2008.

[4] Fataar, A., "Policy Networks in Calibrated Political Terrain", *Journal of Education Policy*, 21(6), 2006, pp. 641 – 659.

[5] Faust, Katherine, "Centrality in Affiliation Networks", *Social Networks*, 19, 1997, pp. 157 – 191.

[6] Feiock, Richard C. and John Scholz, *Self-organizing Federalism: Collaborative Mechanisms to Mitigate Institutional Collective Action Dilemmas*, Cambridge, MA: Cambridge University Press.

[7] Feiock, Richard C., "Policy Networks among Local Elected Officials: Information, Commitment, and Risk Aversion", in Won Lee, Hyung Jun Park and Keon Hyung Lee, *Urban Affairs Review*, 46 (2), 2010, pp. 241 – 262.

[8] Hu, De and Hailong Ma, "Government Power and its Impact on Pan-Pearl River Delta Regional Cooperation: Cooperative Networks and Regional Governance", in Anthony G. O. Yeh and Jiang Xu (eds.), *China's Pan-Pearl River Delta Regional Cooperation and Development*, Hong Kong: Hong Kong University Press, 2011, pp. 181 – 190.

[9] Kettl, Donald F., *The Transformation of Governance: Public Administration for 21st Century America*, Baltimore: Johns Hopkins University Press, 2002.

[10] Lee, In-Won, Feiock, Richard C. and Youngmi Lee, "Competitors and Cooperators: A Mi-

cro-Level Analysis of Regional Economic Development Collaboration Networks", *Public Administration Review*, 62 (5), 2012, pp. 585 – 596.

[11] Lee, Youngmi, Feiock, Richard C. and In Won Lee, "Interorganizational Collaboration Networks in Economic Development Policy: An Exponential Random Graph Model Analysis", *The Policy Studies Journal*, 40 (3), 2013, pp. 547 – 573.

[12] Lei, X. L., G. Z. Li and G. H. Chen, "Assessment and Analysis of Pan-Pearl River Delta Regional Economic and Social Development", in Q. Y. Liang (ed.), *Research Reports on Cooperation and Development in Pan-Pearl River Delta Region*, Beijing: Social Science Literature Press, 2006, pp. 81 – 120.

[13] Leland, Suzanne M. and Kurt Thurmaier, "Metropolitan Consolidation Success: Returning to the Roots of Local Government Reform", *Public Administration Quarterly*, 24 (2), 2000, pp. 202 – 213.

[14] LeRoux, Kelly, Brandenburger, Paul W. and Sanjay K. Pandey, "Interlocal Service Cooperation in U. S. Cities: A Social Network Explanation", *Public Administration Review*, March/April, 2000, pp. 268 – 278.

[15] Lu, Lina, "Literature on Horizontal Relationships", *Social Sciences in Hubei*, 5, 2008, pp. 39 – 41.

[16] Ma, Hailong, "Models of the Jing – Jin – Ji Regional Governance", *Beijing Administrative College Journal*, 6, 2010, pp. 7 – 11.

[17] Nelson, Arthur C. and Kathryn A. Foster, "Metropolitan Governance Structure and Income Growth", *Journal of Urban Affairs*, 21 (3), 1999, pp. 309 – 324.

[18] Oates, Wallace E., "An Essay on Fiscal Federalism", *Journal of Economic Literature*, 27, 1999, pp. 1120 – 1149.

[19] Ostrom, V., Tiebout, C. and Warren, R., "The Organization of Government in Metropolitan Areas: A Theoretical Inquiry", *American Political Science Review*, 55, 1961, pp. 831 – 842.

[20] Qian, Yingyi and Barry Weingast, "China's Transition to Markets: Market-Preserving Federalism, Chinese Style", *Journal of Policy Reform*, 1, 1996, pp. 149 – 185.

[21] Savitch, H. V. and Ronald K. Vogel, "Paths to New Regionalism", *State and Local Government Review*, 32 (3), 2000, pp. 158 – 168.

[22] Shi, Yajun (eds.), *Statistics of Suveying China's Administrative System*, Beijing: China University of Political Science and Law Press, 2008.

[23] Shirk, Susan L., *The Political Logic of Economic Reform in China*, Berkeley, Los Angeles & Oxford: University of California Press, 1993.

[24] Sun, Bing, "On the Factors and Mechanisms of Cooperation among the Local Governments in China", *Nankai Journal*, 2, 1993, pp. 23 – 30.

[25] Thurmaier, K. and Wood, C., "Interlocal Agreements as Overlapping Social Networks: Pick-

et-fence Regionalism in Metropolitan Kansas City", *Public Administration Review*, 62 (5), 2002, pp. 585–598.

[26] Tiebut, C. M., "A Pure Theory of Local Expenditures", *Journal of Political Economy*, 64, 1956, pp. 416–424.

[27] Wallis, A. D., "Regions in Action: Crafting Regional Governance under the Challenge of Global Competitiveness", *National Civic Review*, 85, 1996, pp. 15–24.

[28] Wasserman, S. and K. Faust, *Social Network Analysis: Methods and Applications*, Cambridge: Cambridge University Press, 1994.

[29] Xu, Jiang and Anthony G. O. Yeh, "Political Economy of Regional Cooperation in the Pan-Peal River Delta", in Anthony G. O. Yeh and Jiang Xu (eds.), *China's Pan-Pearl River Delta Regional Cooperation and Development*, Hong Kong: Hong Kong University Press, 2011, pp. 103–124.

[30] Yan, Lirong and Wei Wang, "Literature Review on Intergovernmental Cooperative Governance: A Perspective of Regional Public Crisis", *Political Studies*, 2013, pp. 12–14.

[31] Yang, Aiping and Ruiliang Chen, "From Regional Administration to Regional Public Administration: A Comparative Analysis of Changing Governance", *Social Sciences in Jianxi*, 11, 2004, pp. 23–31.

[32] Yang, Aiping, "Intergovernmental Agreements in Regional Collaboration: Concepts and Classification", *Chinese Public Administration*, 6, 2011, pp. 100–104.

[33] Yang, Long and Yanqian Peng, "Understanding China's Local Government Collaboration: A Perspective of Administrative Authority Concession", *Political Studies*, 4, 2009, pp. 61–66.

[34] Ye, Lin, "Regional Government and Governance in China and the United States", *Public Administration Review*, Special Issue, 2009, pp. 116–121.

[35] Yeh, Anthony G. O. and Jiang Xu (eds.), *China's Pan-Pearl River Delta Regional Cooperation and Development*, Hong Kong: Hong Kong University Press, 2009.

从竞争走向合作：打破土地资源利用的路径依赖[*]

李永乐　刘玉山[**]

一、引言

"兄弟竞争"和"父子争议"等政府间竞争在中国经济崛起和转型过程中扮演着重要角色。[1]兄弟竞争主要包括地方政府间的财政收入竞争[2]、支出竞争[3]和晋升竞争[4]，父子争议主要指中央和地方政府间的财政收入竞争[5]。"央地不同级"和"同级不同地"政府间竞争的识别和效应主题引起了学者的广泛关注，但对于"同地不同届"政府间的策略行为关注较少，仅见于报刊报纸的描述性分析和实例阐释。[①] 习近平在2011中央党校春季开学典礼的讲话中特别指出山西省右玉县19任县委书记连续种树60年，同地不同届政府贯彻"一张蓝图绘到底"的精神，让昔日的不毛之地变成现在的满目葱茏。与之形成对比的是"一任市长一张蓝图"的做法，急功近利的短期行为不利于可持续发展。因此，"同地不同届"的政府间行为也会对地方经济发展产生重要影响，值得关注、讨论与剖析。

基于此，笔者将"央地不同级"、"同级不同地"和"同地不同届"三种竞争纳入统一的三维立体结构分析框架，拓展中国政府间竞争的研究范畴，丰富该研究的主题和新鲜事实。另外，本研究认为由于土地资源分散管理赋予了地方政府对辖区内土

---

[*] 本文受到国家自然科学基金重点项目"我国土地资源效率提升能力与系统建设研究——基于转变经济发展方式的视角"（71233004）、教育部哲学社会科学研究重大课题攻关项目"我国土地出让制度改革及收益共享机制研究"（13JZD014）和江苏省自然科学基金青年基金"土地城镇化与人口城镇化协调研究：财政分权视角"（BK20131008）的资助。

[**] 李永乐，南京财经大学城市发展研究院博士，副教授；刘玉山，南京财经大学公共管理学院在职博士，助理研究员。

① 如山西右玉、郑州郑东新区、山东日照等地的报道。

地的实际管辖权,地方政府具备"各自为政"的基础,土地资源成为当前中国大陆地方政府在此立体结构下行为选择的落脚点,因其已经成为地方政府获得经济收益和政治收益的载体,通过出让城市国有土地获得预算外财政收入(土地出让金),通过开发区\园区圈地建设获得投资和经济增长,通过土地规划调整获得新的政绩增长点等等。本文的第二部分构建了一个三维立体的竞争分析框架,第三部分是对三种竞争的理论阐释和现实解读,第四部分是结论与讨论。

二、三维立体的竞争分析框架

在当前中国式分权体制以及土地制度(土地出让、土地征收和土地规划)背景下,政府间竞争主要表现在三个方面(图1),分别用X、Y和Z轴表示。

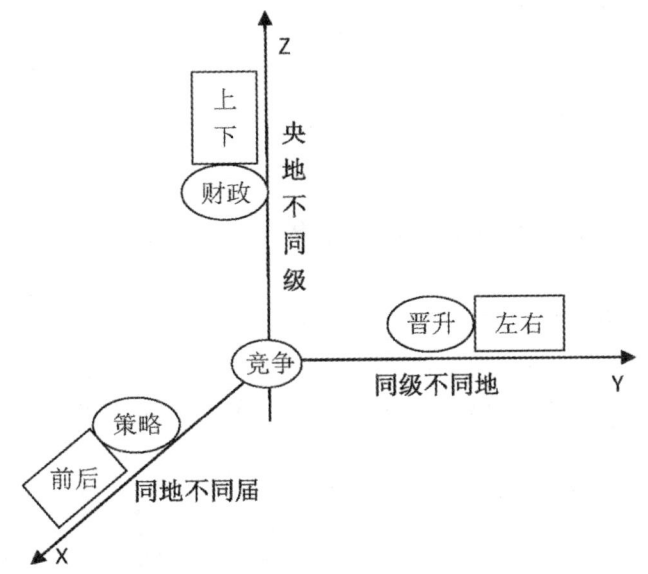

图1 政府间竞争的三维空间结构图

一是上下竞争(Z轴表示),主要为央地不同级政府间的财政竞争。分税制实施后,中央政府和各级地方政府的预算内财政收入结构出现改变,土地出让收入成为地方政府尤其是市县政府弥补预算内财政入不敷出的关键,城市土地有偿使用制度和土地出让制度成为上下财政竞争的制度基础,土地财政成为地方政府追逐的焦点。二是左右竞争(Y轴表示),主要为同级不同地政府间的晋升竞争。在官员晋升锦标赛约束下,地方政府为获取新的经济增长点,进行城市扩张,实行趋于一致的城市倾向经济政策,土地征收成为地方政府进行城市扩张的制度基础,廉价土地引资成为地方政府竞相采取的手段。三是前后竞争(X轴表示),即同地不同届政府间的策略竞争。为获得与前一届政府的不同业绩,取得新的经济增长点或者政绩点,不遵循前一届政府的发展思路，需要对土地规划（城市规划）进行调整和修编。这三种竞争都需要以现有的土地制度为基础，巧合的是土地征收、土地出让和土地规划的主体都是国务院授权下的市县政府，因此市县政府具有依赖土地进行竞争的基础。因此，土地成为政府间竞争的落脚点，地方政府依赖土地进行三维立体框架下的竞争（图2）。

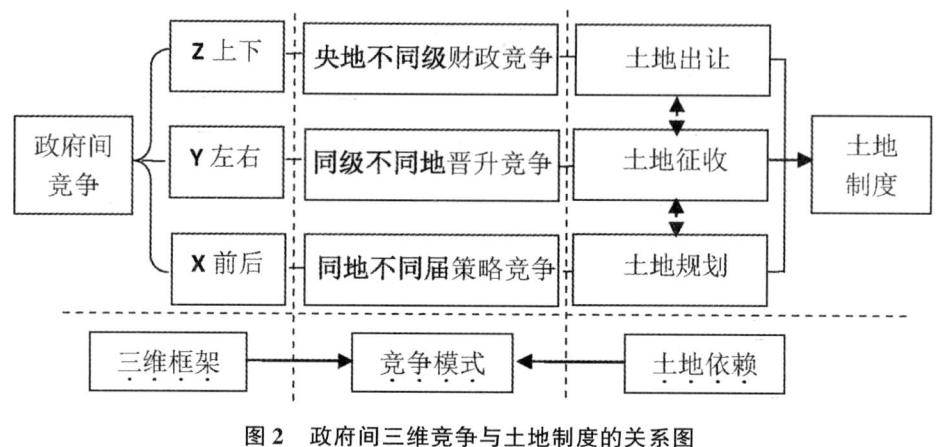

图 2　政府间三维竞争与土地制度的关系图

三、三种竞争的理论阐释与现实解读

地方政府尤其是市县政府在上下、左右、前后三维竞争框架下，有着各自的行为选择，如通过土地财政优化自身的财政状况，通过土地征收（城市扩张）而引资，实现更快的经济增长，通过土地规划修编获得与前一届政府不同的政绩点等等。

（一）上下竞争：央地不同级政府间的财政竞争

1994年分税制开启了我国分税种和分税率相结合的财政体制，中央和省级政府税收划分由中央政府确定。不仅中央和省级政府实行分税制，省级政府对市县政府也有税收分享和独享的分类，即省级以下地方政府也有税收划分。[①] 由于各级政府的理性利己行为，这种自上而下层层设置税收分成比例导致层级越低的政府所分享的预算内税收收入越低，从而形成了预算内财政"中央喜气洋洋、省级勉勉强强、市县拆东墙补西墙、乡镇哭爹叫娘"的顺口溜，这是对预算内财政收入的真实写照。除了中央政府和省市县乡等地方政府，村作为最基层的"准政府"，也承担了相当的公共服务供给和基础管理工作。村里有企业的还好，没有企业的，农地流转部分收益能够贴补

---

① 对大多数省份来说，增值税、所得税、营业税和城镇土地使用税主要采取的是共享的方式，资源税、城市建设维护税、契税、耕地占用税等主要归市县政府所有。

"家"用,但多数村受到严重的资金短缺制约,存在维持现状、消极应付、借债度日等现象。根据笔者对东部沿海某村调研,村级财务有镇政府主管,而镇级政府负有巨额债务,导致村集体资金涉嫌被挪用。该村因农地流转所获得的服务费为100元/亩,难以弥补村级公共基础设施建设资金投入。

1994年分税制前,城市土地有偿使用制度实施尤其是土地市场尚未建立以前,地方政府仅从土地税收获得的土地财政收入并不多,因此地方政府热衷于兴办自己的企业,从企业税收中做大自己的"财政蛋糕",通过"工业化"来扩大财政收入,而且大多地方政府还有"藏富于企"的行为,导致中央财政支出占总财政支出的比重始终大于收入比重,中央不但要靠地方政府的财政收入上解,而且还有中央向地方"借债"一说;分税制后,各级政府根据自身财政状况有了自己的行为选择变化。中央政府财力不断提升,改变了分税制改革前向地方政府"借债度日"的窘境,不但不会抽调地方财政收入,反而会主动通过转移支付或专项补贴财力较弱省份。市县政府开始从预算外收入尤其是土地出让金收入攫取资金[6],通过"经营城市土地"和"推进城市化"来增加自己的财政收入。同时通过土地抵押获得高额信贷,土地出让金和土地抵押融资成为地方政府获取财政收入的重要途径,土地抵押主要是用未来土地收益来作为还款担保,银行信任政府,且不少银行受地方政府管理。据刘守英等[7]对东部发达地区两市一县的调查,土地出让金收入占到预算外收入的58%—69.3%,从土地上产生的收入占到地方财政收入的一半以上,土地出让金已成为地方政府"第二财政"[8],土地收益的巨额诱惑,大大刺激了地方政府通过谋求土地收益来扩大其可支配财力动机,并通过土地征收来实现"不缺地""不断地"和"持续供地"。通过预算外资金的攫取,弥补了市县政府预算内财政入不敷出的窘境,基本不从乡镇计提其他资金,有时还会通过融资平台建设分享部分土地收益给乡镇(街道办事处)政府。

作为土地征收和国有土地使用权出让的实际控制方,市县政府有条件通过土地增加自身的财政收入总量,因为市县政府具有对土地出让金的"剩余控制权"。主要做法是:成立类似于公司的经济行为主体,如成立土地资产运营公司来储备土地。储备土地主要有两类,一类来源于存量土地,即城市内已经使用后被地方政府收回的土地;一类来源于增量土地,即通过土地征收的方式"变性"为城市土地。相对于存量土地,增量土地付出的成本较小,因此地方政府乐于采取的方式是:征收土地后进行基础设施建设—出让土地获得出让金—发展建设过程中收取各类税收—成为新的经济增长极—进行新一轮的征地。土地成为地方政府尤其是市县政府获得财政收入的重要源泉。

(二)左右竞争:同级不同地政府间的晋升竞争

上下级政府间的财政竞争体现了不同层级政府的理性行为选择导致的财政分配现

状，我国地方官员不仅是"经济参与人"，而且是"政治参与人"，他们关注政治晋升和政治收益，各地官员不仅在经济上为财政税收而竞争，同时也在"官场"上为晋升而竞争[9][10]，要真正全面理解政府行为，还应深入到"政"的方面。[11]在中国式分权体制下，晋升激励使得地方政府官员有着非常强的激励促进地方经济发展。[12]经济不仅要增长，而且要比其他地区更快地增长。实际上，不管是基于民意调查的自下而上的竞争，还是基于上级政府评价的自上而下的竞争[13]，当地民众和中央政府都处于信息劣势，很难有一个完全充分合理的指标对官员进行全面评估，更多的是采用自身感受（福利，民众）或某个指标的相对绩效（GDP增长率，中央政府）来进行比较，这就造成了地方政府不遗余力片面追求经济数量的高增长，并不注重经济发展的质量。

为获得更快的经济增长，发展非农产业比发展农业更有效果，城市倾向比农村倾向更有实效，因此城市扩张发展模式成为地方政府竞相选择的策略，设立建设并发展开发区\园区成为地方政府争相选择的方式，因而"圈地""引资"成为地方政府青睐的手段，城市土地扩张成为地方政府获取经济增长的载体。有地才能投资，投资才能生效，土地一度成为地方政府竞争的砝码，成为地方政府获取政治收益的载体。东部发达地区甚至出现"拼地价"的让利竞赛，新华社记者将之概括为"门槛一降再降，成本一减再减，空间一让再让"[14]，地区间竞争越是激烈，就越倾向于低价甚至"零地价"出让土地。① 由于各地趋于一致的策略选择，结果最优点个人边际成本小于社会边际成本，各地区纳什均衡所确定的城市扩张面积总和大于全国最优的城市扩张面积，导致城市过度扩张，土地资源遭受不同程度的浪费。

只有通过上一级政府在更高层次上调节区域内城市的利益和各地的城市扩张行为策略（即"做对协调"）才能使得城市扩张在更大范围内实现边际收益等于边际成本，减少重复建设和土地资源浪费。[15]习近平总书记在2014年2月26日就推进京津冀协同发展提出的七点要求中包括："明确三地功能定位、产业分工"、"自觉打破自家'一亩三分地'的思维定式"和"不搞同构性、同质化发展"。这些均体现了区域发展更高层次协调所解决的关键问题。地处长三角的江苏、浙江和上海的产业结构趋同现象一直是讨论的焦点和热点问题，虽然产业趋同现象较为严重，但是无论是《上海优先发展先进制造业行动方案》，或是《浙江省先进制造业基地建设纲要》，还是江苏省份"沿江开发战略"，都把汽车、石化、电子信息等产业作为未来发展的主导产业。[16]2010年5月国务院正式批准实施的《长江三角洲地区区域规划》也是"做对协调"的直接体现。

---

① 或是通过返还出让金方式赢得企业投资。

(三) 前后竞争：同地不同届政府间的策略竞争

实际上，每一届政府发展经济的初衷是好的，总想做出别人尤其是上级政府看得到的成绩，做出比前一届政府更好的成绩，因而会寻找新的经济增长点。开发区一度被认为是地方经济发展的增长极，在地方政府找不到更好地办法的时候，只能从招商引资中获取更多收益。招商引资需要落地，必然要占用土地。地方政府为吸引更多的企业落地，要为开发区建立更好的硬环境。囿于土地利用总体规划和城市规划是10—15年，但一任市长任期一般为5年，年限的不协调导致修改规划的现象并不少见。在很多地方政府领导心中，认为延续前一任的做法是"为他人做嫁衣"，因而容易出现另建新区、另赋新篇的思想，而且由于"功成必在我任期"的思想作怪，急功近利的做法不断出现，最终导致呈现出"一任市长一张蓝图"的怪象，规划没有连续性。

后一届政府没有继承前一届政府的规划，却模仿了前一任政府的做法，比如前一届政府通过土地征收设立开发区取得了较快的经济增长，后一任政府为实现更大的相对经济绩效则会很自然地选择进一步土地征收获取新一轮的经济增长，这种做法继承一定程度上会导致上一届政府所重点发展区域的减速、衰退甚至消失，也会导致土地利用效率的低效甚至闲置。因此，亟须改变一个地区内不同届政府间的不同策略竞争，要有"功成不必在我任期"的理念和境界，注意防止和纠正各种急功近利的行为，不贪一时之功，不图一时之名，多干打基础、利长远的事[17]，才能成功改变一个地区，成就一番事业。如山西省右玉县19任县委书记连续种树60年，一张蓝图绘到底，才让昔日的不毛之地变成现在的满目葱茏。又如河南郑州郑东新区开建至今，虽历经了郑州市四任市委书记和五位市长的领导变更，但李克强当年提出的"三年出形象，五年成规模，一张蓝图绘到底"思想，却是历届领导班子始终坚持的原则，一任接着一任干，保持工作连续性。《人民日报》评论员在《领导文萃》上撰文提及山东日照11任市长一个规划，打造出黄海之滨的黄金海岸。[18]这些实例均体现了换届不换方向，一任接着一任往下干的持续性和优越性，变前后任政府的策略竞争转为接力继承。

当然，如果前任的举措已不符合时代发展的要求也应及时修订，但不能做全盘否定、完全更改的事情，这不利于发展的持续性和稳定性，会产生资源浪费和产能过剩。好的发展思路和规划，要一以贯之，也要与时俱进。认准的项目要传好，接稳接力棒。不能推倒重来，也不能一味坚持，要用科学发展的眼光看待问题。蓝图要绘得对，绘得远，绘得有空间。

四、结论与讨论

"央地不同级"政府间财政竞争催生了地方政府以土地出让和土地财政为主的土地策略,"同级不同地"政府间晋升竞争导致了地方政府以土地征收和土地引资为主的土地策略,"同地不同届"政府间策略竞争引起了地方政府对土地规划和城市规划的调整,三种政府间竞争模式最终固化了地方政府尤其是市县政府以土地为落脚点的政策取向,土地资源已成为地方政府经济收益和政治收益的载体,各地政府趋于一致的土地利用策略导致了土地资源的过度利用,不利于经济社会可持续发展。因而打破中国特有的三维立体结构下的政府间竞争,构建合理的激励和约束机制是土地资源可持续利用的前提保障,笔者认为可从"做对价格"、"做对协调"和"做对激励"三条路径入手实现政府间有机合作,三条路径并没有严格的界限,相互作用,相互影响,但做对价格主要是调节上下财政竞争,做对协调主要是调节左右晋升竞争,做对激励主要是调节前后策略竞争。

(一) 做对价格:成本与收益的比较

地方政府在面对自力更生创造更多税收和储备土地创造更多出让金两个选择时,面对前者成本高、收益慢后者成本低、收益快的状况,地方政府自然选择后者。地方政府面对存量土地更新和增量土地征收两个城市发展选择时,面对存量土地的在开发利用成本远高于增量土地的征收利用,地方政府倾向于选择土地征收。因此,地方政府逐渐形成了以土地出让为主的土地财政策略。这种策略的前提是中央政府赋予地方政府拥有全部土地出让金的索取权,地方政府通过成本与收益的函数比较确立了当前的财政收入增长方式。因此,打破现有的土地财政分享模式,做对地方政府获得土地财政的价格(即成本与收益的比较),扭转地方政府的土地财政依赖症,同时赋予地方政府新的税源,满足地方政府财政收支基本平衡的目标,对土地资源可持续利用会起到正向促进作用。

(二) 做对协调:边际成本与边际收益的比较

地方政府尤其是市县政府具有本辖区的土地实际管辖权,土地征收、土地规划和土地引资政策均是以市县政府为主体设立,因此地方政府具备"各自为政"的基础。各自为政的时候都是以自身利益最大化为己任,不仅会减少具有正的外部性效应项目的建设,而且会产生"以邻为壑"的做法,目的是为了获得比同级其他地区更快的经济增长,获得比其他同类地区主要官员更多的晋升筹码,这种做法不利于经济的可持续发展和优化。

面对此种情况,通过上一级政府在"战略"层面的协调和"战术"层面的差别对待可以缓解竞争态势,由竞争走向合作。如不同类型城市需要差别化管理,资源型城市以保护资源为第一要务,区域中心城市以发展经济为第一要务,环境恶劣地区以保护改善环境为第一要务,并不需要一切均以GDP为考核指挥棒。对土地利用而言,各自为政导致的结果是最优点个人边际成本小于社会边际成本,纳什均衡所确定的各地城市扩张面积总和大于全国最优的城市扩张面积,导致城市过度扩张,土地资源遭受不同程度的浪费。因此,只有"做对协调"才能使得土地利用在更大范围内实现边际收益等于边际成本,在更大区域内实现一体化土地利用,才能更好地实现高效合理利用土地资源。

(三) 做对激励:总成本与总收益的比较

不断改变某一地区规划和发展战略会产生不必要的成本浪费和收益减少,导致地区发展的总成本增加、总收益减少。一个地区的发展,需要经历几代人的努力,更需要几代人向着一个共同的目标努力,因此"一届政府一个规划"的做法值得商榷,"纸上画画、墙上挂挂"的规划效应值得反思,如何提升土地规划和城市规划的科学性、严肃性和法律性成为亟待解决的关键问题。事业是铁打的营盘,党员干部是流水的兵。虽然党员干部换了一届又一届,但"右玉精神"得到了传承,才让昔日的不毛之地变成现在的满目葱茏。任何一届政府需要从长远考虑,不能仅仅看到自己任内的发展总成本和总收益,而要想到建设完成一个城市的总成本和总收益。上一级政府在制定考核标准时,不仅看"显绩"和发展现状,更注重"潜绩"和发展后劲,急功近利的短视做法不能加分、甚至减分,激励同地不同届做成一个事业,绘完一张蓝图。

---

[1] 王美今、林建浩、余壮雄:《中国地方政府财政竞争行为特性识别》,《管理世界》2010 第 3 期,第 22—33 页。

[2] 郭杰、李涛:《中国地方政府间税收竞争研究》,《管理世界》2009 年第 11 期,第 54—64 页。

[3] 李涛、周业安:《中国地方政府间支出竞争研究》,《管理世界》2009 年第 2 期,第 12—22 页。

[4] 周黎安:《中国地方官员的晋升锦标赛模式研究》,《经济研究》2007 年第 7 期,第 36—50 页。

[5] 周飞舟:《分税制十年:制度及其影响》,《中国社会科学》2006 年第 6 期,第 100—

115页。

[6] 吴群、李永乐：《财政分权、地方政府竞争与土地财政》，《财贸经济》2010年第7期，第51—59页。

[7] 刘守英、蒋省三：《土地融资与财政和金融风险》，《中国土地科学》2005年第6期，第3—9页。

[8] 周飞舟：《分税制十年：制度及其影响》，《中国社会科学》2006年第6期，第100—115页。

[9] Li, Hongbin and Li-An Zhou, "Political Turnover and Economic Performance: the Incentive Role of Personnel Control in China", *Journal of Public Economics*, 89, 2005, pp. 743-1762.

[10] 周黎安：《中国地方官员的晋升锦标赛模式研究》，《经济研究》2007年第7期，第36—50页。近期有学者（杨其静、郑楠，2013）指出是晋升资格赛，但也必须达到资格才行，这个资格很大程度上是通过经济增长而获得的。笔者认为这一提法实质是弱化了经济增长指标比重，增强了其他项目比重而已，但经济增长还是要达到一定水平才行。

[11] 周飞舟：《分税制十年：制度及其影响》，《中国社会科学》2006年第6期，第100—115页。

[12] 王永钦、张晏、章元、陈钊、陆铭：《中国的大国发展道路——论分权式改革的得失》，《经济研究》2007年第1期，第4—16页。

[13] 张晏、龚六堂：《分税制改革、财政分权与中国经济增长》，《经济学》（季刊）2005年第4期，第75—108页。

[14] 参见新华社记者车晓慧、陈钢的报道《级级下任务层层压指标，招商引资成"让利竞赛"》，新华社2003年11月11日。

[15] 李永乐、吴群：《中国式分权与城市扩张——基于公地悲剧的解释》，《南京农业大学学报》（社会科学版）2013年第1期，总第13期，第73—79页。

[16] 齐峰：《泛长三角区域合作机制之探讨》，《宁波经济》（《三江论坛》）2009年第1期，第17—20页。

[17] 习近平在2011中央党校春季开学典礼的讲话。

[18]《人民日报》评论员：《不要再"一任市长一张蓝图"》，《领导文萃》2014年第2（下）期，第23—24页。

不公平感与反腐败效能感——什么塑造了个体对反腐败的态度?*

李 辉 公 婷 肖汉宇**

前 言

自改革开放以来,中国政府已做了三十余年的努力,试图通过运动反腐、严厉惩办和制度建设等多种方式控制和预防腐败。学界对中国政府的反腐败成效评价不一。有些学者认为这些尝试取得初步成效。有些则认为他们只是隔靴搔痒,甚至认为这些努力只是表面文章走过场。更多学者在肯定政府反腐努力的同时,指出反腐举措存在的种种缺陷(He, 2000; Gong, 2009; Ma, 2009; Quade, 2007; Manion, 2004)。然而,很少有研究触及民众对反腐败的看法。民众是如何评价反腐败的在当今中国社会变得日趋重要。因为,民众如何看待政府反腐可以反映一个社会对腐败的容忍度,对政府反腐工作的满意度,甚至影响到政府的合法性(Seligson, 2002),从而在很大程度上决定反腐败的未来走向。

本文试图通过"反腐败效能感"的测量就民众对于反腐败的认知和态度进行分析。我们把反腐败效能感定义为:民众对反腐败的正向功能的主观期待。也即,个体对反腐败正向功能期待越高,则其反腐败效能感越高,反之则反腐败效能感越低。这里,我们需要回答的问题是:民众对于反腐败这一问题是如何认识的?是倾向于肯定反腐败的积极作用,还是认为反腐败实际效果有限,不会对社会带来多大影响?在此

---

* 本文为李辉主持的国家社会科学基金青年项目"东亚儒家文化圈预防腐败制度研究及对中国的启示研究"(批准号:11CZZ015)的阶段性成果。感谢上海社会科学院潘大渭研究员主持上海哲学社会科学基金项目"中俄社会结构与社会认同比较研究"(2007BSH004)提供的数据,感谢上海社会科学院朱妍博士,上海同济大学孙明博士在写作过程中给予的无私帮助。

** 李辉,复旦大学国际关系与公共事务学院;公婷,香港城市大学公共政策学系;肖汉宇,香港城市大学公共政策学系。

基础上，我们进一步探讨是什么因素决定了民众对反腐败的认知态度。本文通过对实证数据的分析发现，不公平感会显著影响民众对反腐败效能的评估。在基于收入分配的不公平感上，收入分配不公和收入差距过大都会提高个体的反腐败效能感；而在基于对权力不平等的容忍度上，权力距离则会降低个体的反腐败效能感；同时，二者之间对因变量反腐败效能感的影响还存在交互效应，个体对权力不平等的容忍还会稀释基于收入分配的不公平感对反腐败效能感的正向效应。

我们的研究还意味着：如果转型中国的分配不公现象继续加剧，收入差距不断拉大，则民众会对分配制度更加不满，会更加强烈地提出反腐败的诉求，党和国家要继续提高反腐败的供给，要更加行之有效地抑制腐败的蔓延，也要提供更多的渠道给普通民众来监督政府官员的权力滥用。同时，党和国家如果能够实施卓有成效的反腐败行动，不仅仅可以遏制腐败的蔓延，在民众看来，还可以降低社会不平等的程度，反腐败会产生超过自身的多重效果，对提高民众对政府的信任至关重要。

文章接下来的部分将按以下几个部分展开。

在第一部分我们回顾了在腐败研究领域中基于个体的微观态度和感知视角的研究取向，其中包括对腐败感知和腐败容忍度的研究，并且提出和定义了一个新的用以测量民众关于反腐败的感知概念——反腐败效能感。第二部分集中探讨了个体的不公平感和反腐败效能感的关系，从理论上说明基于分配的不公平感（包括宏观和微观）和权力距离与反腐败效能感的关系，并且提出本文的三个核心假设。第三部分对数据来源和核心变量进行了统计描述。第四部分使用 Ologit 模型对前面提出的三个核心假设进行了验证。最后结论部分对本文的观点进行了一定扩展，并尝试提出了其政策含义。

（一）腐败感知、腐败容忍度与反腐败效能感：腐败研究中的微观态度

对于腐败和反腐败问题的主流研究主要强调的是宏观的结构性因素，如国家的富裕程度、民主程度、对外贸易、殖民地传统、宗教信仰等等（Treisman，2000，2007；Sun，2009）。在这种研究路径下，实实在在的微观个体与腐败和反腐败的关系在这些研究中很少受到关注。[①] 但是这一趋势近年来在逐渐发生改变，学者们开始逐渐意识到公众对于腐败和反腐败的主观态度的重要性。理论上来说，实际腐败率（the real rate of corruption）是不可能被直接度量的（Svensson，2005；Wedeman，2009）。因此，目前国际上较为流行的做法是通过"腐败感知"来测量一个国家的腐败程度，最著名的数据就是"透明国际"从 1996 年开始逐年发布的"清廉指数"（Corruption

---

[①] 对于腐败问题的跨国（cross-national）研究中也面临同样的问题，Treisman 在对腐败研究的批评中，认为腐败研究中基于个体经验的研究匮乏，应当是今后腐败研究重点发展的方向（Treisman，2007）。

Perception Index，CPI）①。其实这一指数的度量方法也离不开所谓的"感知"（perception），只不过他们使用了多个来源的感知而已（包括各种国际组织的内部专家以及跨国公司的商业精英）。由于其号称是目前度量国家腐败程度最权威的数据，因此研究者们在使用这一数据时也就直接忽略其"感知"的因素，直接作为一国腐败程度的有效度量来使用（Treisman，2000，2007）。但由于其毕竟不是纯粹客观的度量，因此这一指数也不断受到各种指责和挑战，主要归咎于其中"人为"的因素，这一指数极易受到外在于腐败的各种因素的"渲染"，包括意识形态，重要政治事件的冲击（转型、革命）等，以及经济的危机或衰退（Kurtz and Shrank，2007；Maria，2008；Johnston，2010）。

1. 腐败感知

在腐败感知的研究中，有些学者致力于发现民众的腐败感知（perceptions）和实际腐败（realities）之间的关系。Olken 在印度尼西亚的一个村庄里做了一个实验性的研究，他在村庄的一项公共工程项目中，使用了两种不同的方式来测量腐败，一种是对腐败程度的客观测量，一种是村民对于腐败的主观态度，结果发现主观态度与腐败的现实之间确实存在很大的落差（Olken，2009）。同样，Seligson 比较了拉美四个国家的国民对政府腐败的态度，然后将这一数据与透明国际所发布的"腐败感知指数"（Corruption Perception Index，CPI）② 相比较，发现二者之间有巨大差距（Seligson，2006）。

另外一些学者则在探讨是什么影响了民众对政府腐败程度的认知，结果发现媒体是非常重要的因素。朱江南等人利用亚洲晴雨表第一波（Asian Barometer Survey I，ABS I）调查数据，结合张光对中国各省官方媒体报道的腐败案件数量的统计，把公众腐败感知的信息来源分为两类：一是主流官方媒体的影响；二是非正式的"小道消息"（grapevine news）的影响。结果发现，被政府控制的官方媒体降低了民众的腐败感知，但是非官方的小道消息恰恰相反，提升了民众的腐败感知（Zhu，Lu and Shi，2012）。Arnold 也发现，在拉丁美洲，民众对于政府的腐败感知取决于他们的政治知识，媒体自由程度越高的国家民众的政治知识越充分，对政府的腐败感知也越准确（Arnold，2012）。余致力等人利用台湾本土的清廉调查数据（Taiwan Integrity Survey）发现，民众的腐败感知是自下而上的，而不是自上而下被灌输的，民众与政府的接触经历、政党认同和观看电视节目偏好（蓝、绿）与腐败感知显著相关（Yu，Chen and Lin，2013）。

---

① 更多的细节参见：http://www.transparency.org/。

② 更多细节参见：http://www.transparency.org/。Kurtz &Shrank（2007）对这一指数测量方法中所存在问题，以及对其使用方式中的错误做了一个极为有力的批评。

李辉等人利用亚洲、非洲和拉美晴雨表的合并数据做了一项关于腐败感知的多层分析（multilevel analysis），结果发现民众的自我经济评价、民主价值观以及国家的民主程度都与腐败感知有显著相关性，亚非拉地区的民主化不是降低而是提高了民众对政府的腐败感知（Li，Tang and Huhe，2013）。

2. 腐败容忍度

公婷和王世茹利用对香港大学生的抽样调查数据，研究了个体对于腐败容忍度的决定因素。结果发现社会环境对个人的腐败容忍度有重要影响，在她们的统计模型中，"在香港的居住时间"与腐败容忍度显著正相关，因此她们认为受到香港"零容忍"文化影响越深的个体，其对腐败的容忍度也越低（Gong and Wang，2013）。

但无论是对个体腐败感知的研究，还是对腐败容忍度的研究，都主要衡量的是个体对于腐败的看法，个体对于反腐败的看法的研究目前从理论到实证都非常匮乏，甚至连可以直接借用的概念工具都很少。因此，本文希望能够同时在这两个方向上做一些贡献：一是提供一个可以用以分析民众对于反腐败的主观态度的概念工具，即本文所提出的"反腐败效能感"这一概念；二是从实证上利用上海地区的调查数据，发掘一些决定这一态度的重要因素。

3. 反腐败效能感

本文的核心概念"反腐败效能感"的理论资源来自政治学中的一个重要概念"政治效能感"（sense of political efficacy）。政治效能感这一概念最初来自坎贝尔（Angus Campbell）等人，在他们看来，与对政治兴趣（political interest）和政治关心（political concern）的测量不同，效能感指的是"公众对于自身参与和影响政治的能力的感知"（Campbell et al.，1954；Campbell et al.，1960：104-105）。今天，政治效能感主要被分为两类：内部（internal）效能感和外部（external）效能感。内部效能感依然指的是民众对于自身参与和影响政治的能力的评价；而外部效能感指的是民众对于政治回应性（responsiveness）的评价，即政府是否真正地聆听了民众的呼声（Craig，1979；Craig and Maggiotto，1982）。在政治学对政治态度的研究中，政治效能感已经成为衡量个体"政治疏离"（political alienation）程度的重要概念。

借用政治效能感这一概念，我们认为"反腐败效能感"也可分为内部和外部两种类型。其中内部反腐败效能感指的是民众对自身参与和影响反腐败的能力的评价；而外部反腐败效能感则指的是民众对政府反腐败的期望值。由于数据本身的限制，本文所讨论的反腐败效能感主要指的是外部的，即民众对反腐败产生的正向功能的期望程度，个体反腐败的正向功能的期望值越高，则其反腐败效能感越高，反之则反腐败效能感越低。

反腐败效能感衡量的是个体对于"抽象"的反腐败正向功能的期望，而不是对于政府具体的反腐败措施和政策的评价和评估，因此其不是一个政策评估意义上的概念，反映的是个体的反腐败认知（cognition）。其在一定程度上可以反映民众对反腐败的期望程度，以及政府的反腐败改革和打击腐败行为的潜在支持程度。当一个个体的反腐败效能感越高时，其对于反腐败的潜在支持程度也越高。

反腐败效能感与腐败感知不同。腐败感知反映的是被访者对于当前政府或者其他政治主体（政党、议会、警察、法院等等）腐败程度的认知和评价（Zhu, Lu and Shi, 2012; Yu, Chen and Lin, 2013; Arnold, 2012; Li, Tang and Huhe, 2013）。由于一个社会中的实际腐败率是不可能被客观度量的，因此腐败感知也经常被用来作为衡量一个政府腐败程度的替代指标，但是这一方法也颇受诟病。另外一些学者也认为，腐败感知可能比实际腐败程度更为重要，因为一个政府可能实际上没有那么腐败，但是在民众的观念和想象里，这个政府已经腐烂变质，糟糕透顶，这时民众的政治行为会走向极端，要么对政府采取强烈的怀疑态度，质疑政府的各种作为，要么则完全从政治参与中退出，不再与政府合作（Warren, 2004）。

反腐败效能感与腐败容忍度也不同。腐败容忍度反映的是个体对社会中的腐败现象的宽容程度（tolerance）。但是到目前为止，在对腐败的个体态度的研究中，这两个概念只能用来探讨个体对于"腐败"的看法，而无法反映民众对于"反腐败"的认知。实际上到目前为止，由于各种条件的限制，我们还没有一个行之有效且带有一定理论程度的概念来反映民众对于"反腐败"的态度，这也是本文尝试提出"反腐败效能感"这一概念的原因。

（二）不公平感与反腐败效能感：理论建构与核心假设

腐败，尤其公共部门的权力寻租、裙带关系以及滥用自由裁量权所产生的形形色色的掠夺性行为，会减少社会公平和加剧社会不平等的程度（Alesina and Angeletos, 2005; Mauro, 1995, 1998; Gupta, Davoodi and Alonso-Terme, 2002; Fisman and Svensson, 2000; Gyimah-Brempong, 2002; Gyimah-Brempong and de Camancho, 2006; Uslander, 2008）。同时，由于较高程度不平等的存在（包括经济不平等和政治不平等），以及整个社会公平正义的丧失，又会反过来恶化一个社会的腐败程度（You and Khagram, 2005）。因此，腐败与不平等之间会形成一个恶性循环的陷阱（corruption-inequality trap）（Chong and Calderon, 2000; Chong and Gradstein, 2007）。越是腐败的政府体系，越容易加剧不平等（政治的和经济的）的现状，同时，越是不平等，包括权力垄断和经济收入的两极化，则越容易巩固富人的权力和利益，会产生更多的腐败现象。奥尔森（Mancur Olson）就认为只有当有权者和无权者有较多的共容性利益时，政体的腐败程度才会降低，而且会反过来促进整个社会的经济发展（Olson, 2000）。

研究表明，许多政府之所以会失败，原因在于其选择的"榨取型制度"（extractive institutions）（包括政治的和经济的）（Acemoglu and Robinson，2012：398－403）以及由此引发的民众的强烈的不公平感。不公平感（perceived unfairness）是一个非常重要的社会议题（Cohen，1986）。目前对于公平感的研究主要集中在"分配公平"这个问题上（Alves and Rossi，1978；Robison and Bell，1978；Bos，Vermunt and Wilke，1997），即个体对于收入分配也即经济不平等的感知和评价，一般分为宏观不公平感和微观不公平感两类。宏观不公平感指的是个体认为整个社会的收入分配是不合理的，以及认为自身所处的社会收入差距过大等；而微观公平感指的是个体对自身收入分配情况的感知和判断（Adams，1965；Walster，Walster and Bersheid，1978）。除此之外，"相对剥夺感"也反映了个体的不公平感，即当个体的实际所得少于其期望所得时，所产生的不公平感（Runiciman，1966；Crosby，1976；Panning，1983；Tropp and Wright，1999；Kus，Liu and Ward，2013）。

从理论上来说，腐败与不公平之间是一个主要包括两个相互关联过程的因果机制。首先，腐化的官僚系统（即提供了足够多的收买渠道和机会）有强烈的冲动与富人群体形成共谋关系，在制定再分配制度与执行再分配政策的过程中，帮助富人群体巩固自己的财富和社会地位，这会固化或者拉大已有的不平等程度。市民成为了"受挫折的成功者"（frustrated achievers）（Hilke，Delhey，et al.，2009）。其次，随着不平等程度的扩大，富人群体会积累更多的资源来收买或者影响（合法或者不合法的）法律和政策的内容，这里的富人群体可以是利益集团、大的公司组织，也可以是个人，当他们通过私人关系网络、行贿受贿、游说等方式"俘获"了政府之后，再分配系统会更加有利于富人群体（You and Khagram，2005：138）。在这种情况下，整个国家被利益集团所控制，成为一个"赢者通吃"（winners-take-all）的社会（Stiglitz，2012；Hacker and Pierson，2010）。Hellman（1998）的研究指出，与那些实施较全面改革甚至没有改革的国家相比，那些只实施了部分改革（partial reform）的国家的收入分配更集中于少数的精英群体。因为从长期来看，部分改革会形成获利群体，这些群体有很大的冲动来阻碍未来的改革。有学者指出，中国实施的三十多年经济改革也出现了类似的精英群体与利益集团。[①] 在这种情况下，民众（无权群体）会寄希望于政府加大打击腐败的力度和出台更多真正的反腐败措施来降低不平等的程度。

对于反腐败效能感来说，个体自身强烈的不公平感以及由此产生的对于公平价值的追求可能会驱动个体支持政府的反腐败行动。原因至少有两个：第一，个体很容易将基于收入分配的不公平归因于富人和政府在政策和制度设计上的共谋，而当个体将

---

① 孙立平：《走出转型陷阱》，《经济观察报》2012 年 2 月 24 日，网址：http://www.chinainnovations.org/Item/35264.aspx（访问日期：2013 年 9 月 6 日）。

不公平归因于腐败行为时，则相应地会希望通过降低腐败来使得收入分配重新回归公平，而且当收入分配不公平程度越高时，通过反腐败来改善公平状况给普通民众带来的好处就越大（Alesina and Angeletos，2005）。由于公民的政治态度在很大程度上受工具理性的影响（Bratton and Mattes，2001；Norris，1999；Rose，Mishler and Munro，2011），李辉等人研究发现，个体的腐败感知与其对自身的经济状况的评价高度相关，当个体认为自己的经济状况较好时，会认为政府比价清廉，而当个体认为自己的经济状况很差时，会倾向于认为政府比较腐败（Li，Tang and Huhe，2013）。因此，个体很容易将自身基于收入分配的不公平遭遇归因于政府的腐败，或者富人群体对政府的俘获和政策合谋。第二，很多社会不公平本身会以腐败的方式表现出来，比如"特权"（privilege）行为，其本身是严重的不公平行为，但是在很大程度上也是官员利用公共权力满足个人需求的腐败行为，这一点在中国表现得尤为明显（Sun，2004；Lu，2000；Yao，2002）。在一个特权和腐败并重的国家里，公民更容易将不公平归因于腐败，更希望通过打击腐败来恢复和提高社会公平。因此，我们认为，收入分配不公平感越高的个体，其反腐败效能感也越高。据此我们提出以下假设：

假设1（H1）：越倾向于认为收入分配不公平的个体，其反腐败效能感也越高。

然而，无论是宏观还是微观的不公平感，都是基于个体对收入分配的评价，这种基于分配公平的不公平感忽略了另外一个重要问题，即个体对权力（政治不平等）的认知，这里我们借用了"权力距离"（power distance）这一概念来表达个体对于权力不平等的认知。"权力距离"这一概念是由吉尔特·霍夫斯塔德（Geert Hofstede）提出来的，用以衡量一个社会中的无权者（less powerful person）对权力不平等的接受程度，也即是对于权力不平等的容忍度（Hofstede，1983，1984）。他发展出了一套全球权力距离指数（Power Distance Index，PDI）[①]，用以区分不同国家对权力不平等的容忍度。

从理论上来说，在一个权力距离较高的文化下，由于个体对权力不平等的接受程度比较高，则国家和政府也更容易垄断更多的政治权力（公权力）。而腐败的较为公认的定义就是"公职人员利用公共权力牟取私利"（Treisman，2000：399；Svensson，2005：20），而在一个制度体系中，对于公权力的垄断程度越高，产生腐败的几率就越大，因此也有研究表明，权力距离越高的社会，越容易产生腐败（Davis and Ruhe，

[①] 更多细节参见：http://www.clearlycultural.com/geert-hofstede-cultural-dimensions/power-distance-index/（访问日期：2013年8月16日）。

2003)。

从理论上来推断,如果个体的权力距离感越高,则其越可能接受权力的重要作用(包括决定收入分配上),无论是违心地接受现实还是承认权力的正当性。因此,较高的权力距离感会降低民众对自身参与和影响反腐败能力的评价(内部效能感),同时也会减弱对政治回应性的期盼(外部效能感),而这两者都会直接提高民众对反腐败的期望值。因此,权力距离感越高的个体,他们通常不会对反腐败的正向功能有很高的期望值,其反腐败效能感也相对较低。据此我们提出第二个假设:

假设2(H2):权力距离感与反腐败效能感呈负相关,权力距离感越高的个体,其反腐败效能感越低。

除了分配公平感和权力距离感这两个变量对反腐败效能感的影响外,我们认为这两个维度之间本身还有着一定的交互作用。由于权力距离感强化了个体对权力不平等的容忍度,因此会降低个体基于收入分配的不公平感,因此权力距离会对基于收入分配的不公平感的影响产生调节(moderating)作用。下面我们就来具体看一下这两种不公平感之间及它们与反腐败效能感的相关性。

从理论上来说,权力距离感越高,个体的参与和影响决策的机会和可能性就越小,而只能接受权力对收入分配的决定作用。进而,如果个体认为权力对于收入分配的影响持容忍和接受态度,则通常不会把收入分配的不公平归因于权力的不平等和腐败。因此,权力距离感会降低分配不公平感对反腐败效能感的正向效应。据此我们提出第三个假设:

假设3(H3):权力距离会稀释分配不公平感对反腐败效能感的正向影响。

为了更直观地表达权力距离、分配不公平感和反腐败效能感三者之间的关系,我们使用图1构建了三者的关系:

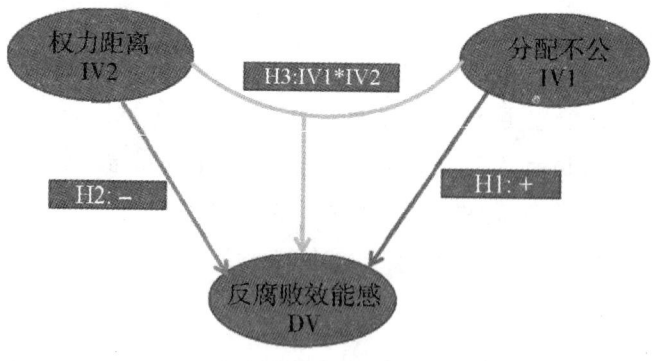

图1 权力距离、分配不公平与反腐

(三) 数据、变量与测量

本文实证分析部分的数据来源为《上海市民社会生活调查数据（2008）》，数据调查工作受到上海社会科学院"中俄社会结构与社会认同比较研究"项目的资金支持。采用的是多阶段概率比例抽样方法，样本覆盖了上海市的11个行政区。具体抽样方法为：对于9个老中心城区，首先按照上海市行政区划的人口比例在各区抽取1—3个街道，并按照人口比例在各个街道分配样本数，在各个街道等距抽取54个居委会，然后根据居委会提供的家庭住户名单抽取家庭，入户之后根据Kish表确定访问对象。对于浦东和闵行两个新城区，首先按照人口比例确定了500个样本数，然后按照行政区划的居委会名单抽取20个居委会，每个居委会分配25户家庭，其余抽样方法同前。总共覆盖了上海市下辖的74个居委会，完成有效样本1604份：在老城区9个区的调查中，共接触1731户，完成问卷1140份，其中有效问卷1114份；在浦东和闵行两区，共接触1178户，完成有效问卷490份。在最后的数据中提供了居委会编号和权重信息。之所以选择这一数据主要原因在于，中国目前对于腐败和反腐败的研究还存在着诸多禁区，很少有严格的抽样调查数据中能够提供关于腐败的测量问题，这也是为什么中国目前的腐败研究中，使用定量方法的实证研究简直凤毛麟角的重要原因。这一数据虽然只能反映上海一个城市的情况，并不能代表整个中国，但对于中国的腐败研究者来说也是弥足珍贵的。下面就介绍一下相关变量的编码和处理方式。

1. 因变量：反腐败效能感

用以测量民众反腐败效能感的问题为："您是否同意下列说法：如果加大反腐败力度，社会不平等就会减少。"选项包括"非常不同意""不太同意""比较同意""非常同意"，编码为取值在1—4之间的定序变量，数值越大表示越同意题干描述的信息，也即个体的反腐败效能感越高。图2中报告了在本数据中被访者的反腐败效能感分布情况。可以发现中国民众有着很高的反腐败效能感，接近50%的被访者选择了"非常同意"，只有13.37%的人选择了"非常不同意"和"不太同意"。

2. 核心自变量：收入分配公平感与权力距离感

首先来看基于收入分配的不公平感。如前所述，基于收入分配的不公平感可以体现在宏观与微观两个层面。在问卷中，有一道题测量了宏观的收入分配不公平感："总的来看，您认为目前我们这个社会的收入分配是否公平？"答案选项1—5之间取值，1代表很不公平，5代表很公平。为了能够更方便地反映不公平感与因变量之间的关系，我们对原结果进行了重新编码，取值为0—4之间的定序变量，数值越大代表个体认为目前社会的收入分配越不公平，也即个体的不公平感程度越高，具体见图3。

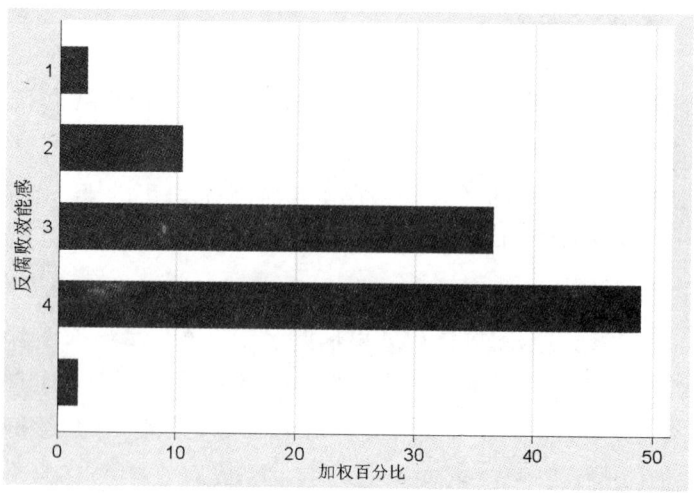

图 2　反腐败效能感分布

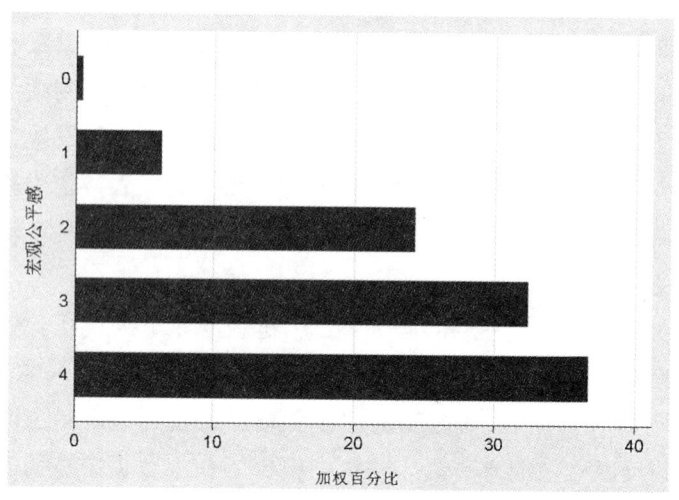

图 3　分配不公平感分布

另外还有一道题测量被访者对目前收入差距的判断："现在收入差距已经过大了。"选项包括"非常同意""比较同意""不太同意""非常不同意",编码为取值在 0—3 之间的定序变量,数值越大代表越同意题干描述的信息,也即不公平感越高。我们认为个体对于总体收入分配状况的判断和收入差距的整体认知共同构成了基于收入分配的宏观不公平感,具体见图 4。

除了宏观的不公平感之外,我们还使用另外一道题度量了个体的微观公平感:"考虑到您的教育背景、工作能力、资历等各方面的因素,您认为自己目前的收入是否合理?"选项取值区间为 1—5,数值越大代表越合理。这道题反映了人们对自己收入所得是否公平的主观评价,是对收入分配的微观层面的感知。为了与前面两个变量的编码方向一致,我们重新编码为取值在 0—4 之间的定序变量,数值越大代表越不合理。

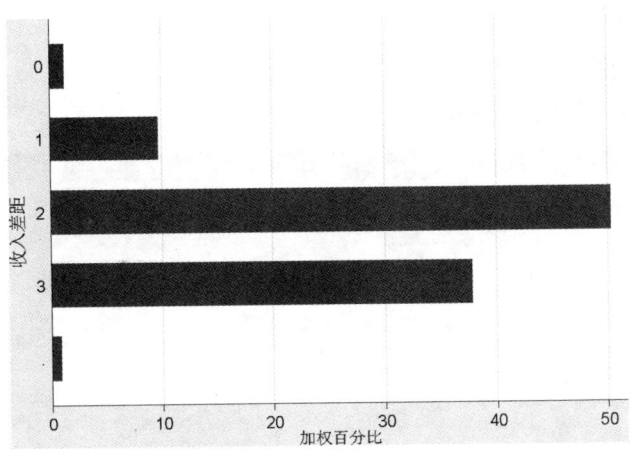

图 4　收入差距分布

其次为权力距离。如前文所示,权力距离是一个个体权力认知的概念,它反映了个体对权力"应该"在社会中起多大作用这个问题的认识,如果一个无权者对权力不平等的接受度越高,则相应地会越认可权力应该发挥的作用,反之亦然。

我们使用下列问题来测量一个个体的权力距离:"下列因素都可能影响一个人的收入水平,您觉得这些因素应该起多大作用?实际上起了多大作用?——有没有权力。"选项包括"不起作用""作用不大""一些作用""很大作用""极大作用"。被访者需要同时回答权力"应该"和"实际上"起的作用有多大,当被访者越是肯定权力"应该"起的作用时,代表其越认可权力在社会中的作用。但是仅仅依靠这一题还不足以测量权力距离,为了更准确地反映个体对权力在社会作用中的认知,我们用权力"应该"起的作用减去权力"实际"起的作用,得到二者的差。由于两道问题都是取值在 0—4 之间的定序变量,因此其差值的取值范围在 -4 和 -3 之间,即为个体的"权力距离"。这个差值越高,代表个体的权力距离越高,其越认可权力在收入分配中应有的作用,而数值越小,则代表越不能容忍权力在收入分配中的作用,其应该与反腐败效能感之间成负相关关系,其在样本中的分布情况如图 5 所示。

3. 控制变量

除了核心自变量之外,我们还纳入了性别、年龄、党员身份、收入和教育程度等人口学变量作为控制变量。其中性别为 0 和 1 的二分变量,男性编码为 1;年龄为 18—65 周岁之间的连续变量;在原数据中,党员身份包括三个类别:中共党员、民主党派和群众,我们把中共党员和民主党派编码为 1,代表有党员身份的,群众

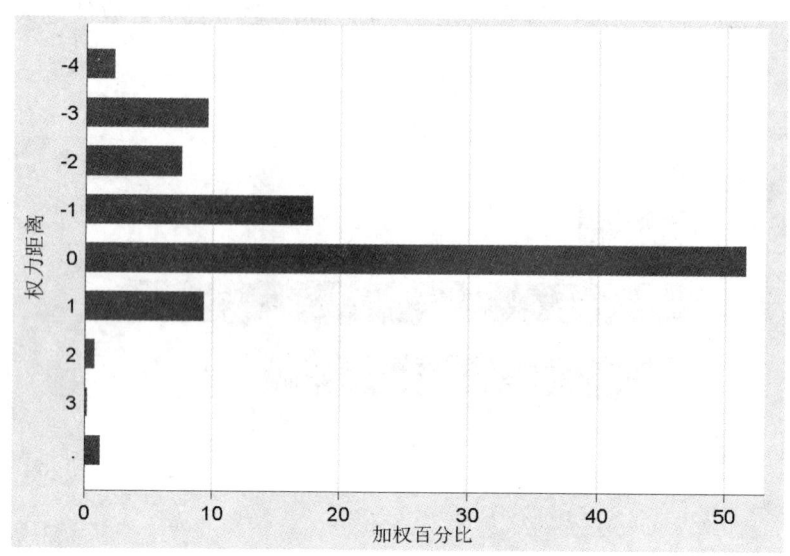

图 5　权力距离分布

编码为 0，代表无党员身份的。在《上海市民社会生活调查数据》中，对于收入的测量包括三种方式：上个月的个人总收入，上个月的家庭总收入，以及上一年（2007）的个人总收入。我们使用"上个月个人总收入"来作为测量被访者收入情况的变量，由于数值较大，为 0—21000 之间的长尾变量，因此我们对个人月收入做了取对数的处理。这一数据对教育程度的分类比较细致，包括从没有受过任何教育到全日制研究生以上 14 个类别，经过重新编码最后合并为三个类别：没有受过教育到小学编码为 0，初中到中专编码为 1，大学专科以上编码为 2。在表 1 中报告了所有相关变量的描述统计情况。

表 1　相关变量的描述统计

变量	样本数	均值	标准差	最小值	最大值
反腐败效能感	1588	3.35	0.76	1	4
权力距离	1588	−0.65	1.21	−4	3
宏观收入分配	1604	2.99	0.95	0	4
收入差距认知	1588	2.26	0.68	0	3
微观不公平感	1577	2.46	1.11	0	4
性别	1604	0.51	0.50	0	1
年龄	1604	39.09	13.10	18	65
教育程度	1604	1.24	0.50	0	2
个人月收入（log）	1470	7.52	0.72	3.69	9.95
党员身份	1604	0.10	0.31	0	1

(四) 模型与回归结果

由于因变量"反腐败效能感"为一个取值在 1—4 之间的定序变量,因此我们选取用以处理定序变量的序次逻辑斯蒂回归(ordered logistic regression)。但是在回归过程中还有一个问题需要处理,那就是由于复杂抽样方法带来的集群效应问题(cluster effect)。前面已经介绍过,在《上海市民生活调查数据(2008)》的抽样方法说明中,是先划分为 80 个居委会,然后再在居委会之下抽取居民样本,很显然,来自同一个居委会或者社区的被访者,他们之间的相同点肯定要多于来自不同居委会或社区的居民。因此在拟合模型时不能把样本看作是一个简单随机抽样的结果,否则会降低变量的标准误,使得变量更加容易通过显著性简单,因此我们拟合模型时我们使用了"居委会编号"来控制集群效应。在表 2 中报告了使用这一方法回归的结果。

表 2 反腐败效能感的序次逻辑斯蒂(Ologit)回归结果

	模型 1	模型 2	模型 3	模型 4	模型 5	模型 6	模型 7
性别 (男性 =1)	-0.049 (0.16)	-0.096 (0.16)	-0.074 (0.18)	-0.085 (0.16)	0.030 (0.16)	-0.033 (0.16)	-0.0048 (0.16)
年龄	-0.0042 (0.0071)	-0.0026 (0.0069)	-0.0011 (0.0080)	-0.0041 (0.0074)	-0.005 (0.007)	-0.001 (0.0076)	-0.0025 (0.0077)
教育程度	0.22 (0.21)	0.32 (0.20)	0.25 (0.22)	0.25 (0.22)	0.26 (0.22)	0.37* (0.21)	0.33 (0.21)
个人收入 (取对数)	0.093 (0.13)	0.24 (0.15)	0.14 (0.15)	0.23 (0.17)	0.071 (0.12)	0.26 (0.16)	0.22 (0.17)
党员身份 (党员 =1)	0.30 (0.25)	0.27 (0.24)	0.22 (0.24)	0.31 (0.26)	0.24 (0.25)	0.15 (0.23)	0.24 (0.23)
宏观不公平感							
宏观收入分配		0.37*** (0.10)				0.27** (0.11)	0.13 (0.10)
收入差距认知			0.55*** (0.16)			0.52*** (0.16)	0.53*** (0.16)
微观不公平感				0.20** (0.095)		0.062 (0.098)	0.066 (0.10)

(续表)

	模型1	模型2	模型3	模型4	模型5	模型6	模型7
权力距离					-0.38***	-0.39***	0.49**
					(0.105)	(0.105)	(0.24)
权力距离*宏观收入分配							-0.29***
							(0.077)
Pseudo R²	0.0061	0.021	0.025	0.011	0.029	0.059	0.069
N	1457	1457	1445	1453	1446	1431	1431
Wald chi²	7.63	22.8	23.6	12.2	24.6	62.0	83.7

注：1. 所有模型的因变量为反腐败效能感；
2. 所有模型为 Ologit 模型；
3. 所用模型在回归时都使用了加权信息，并控制了集群效应；
4. 括号中为稳健标准误；
5. *p<0.1，**p<0.05，***p<0.01（双尾检验）。

在模型1中我们只加入了控制变量性别、年龄、教育程度、收入的对数和党员身份作为模型比较的基准模型，结果发现所有的人口学特征都不显著，即反腐败效能感不随着人口特征的变化而有明显区别。在接下来的模型2到模型4中，我们分别检验了核心自变量宏观不公平感、收入差距、微观不公平感对反腐败效能感的影响，结果显示无论是宏观不公平感、收入差距还是微观不公平感，在控制人口学特征的基础上都可以对反腐败效能感呈现显著的正相关关系，这在实证上验证了我们的假设1，即基于收入分配的不公平感越高的个体，其反腐败效能感也越高。而权力距离刚好相反，在模型5中，权力距离与反腐败效能感之间为稳健的负相关关系这验证了我们的假设2，即权力距离会降低个体的反腐败效能感。在模型7中我们纳入了全部的用来度量不公平感的四个变量，结果发现除了微观不公平感感之外其余三个变量依然在最高水平上显著，且方向一致。大致可以推断，反腐败效能感更容易受到个体对宏观不公平感和权力距离的影响，微观不公平感的解释力与其他三个变量相比较弱一些。

由于宏观不公平感对于反腐败效能感的影响更为显著和稳定，因此，为了进一步检验权力距离对收入分配的不公平感的调节效应（moderating effect），我们在模型8中纳入了交互项"权力距离*宏观不公平感"。结果显示，在控制所有相关变量的情况下，交互项与因变量之间呈现出负相关关系，且在1%水平上通过了显著性检验。由于交互项在数学上体现为两个变量的乘积，很难从系数上加以解释，因此一般来说要通过作图来说明。根据模型7的回归结果，我们制作了图6，以更直观地反映权力距离的条件效应。其中横坐标为权力距离，纵坐标为分配不公平对反腐败效能感影响的边际效应，可以看到随着权力距离的提高，分配不公平对反腐败效能感影响的正效应的速度逐渐下降，因此权力距离会稀释分配不公平对反腐败效能感的正向影响。而且 Y 轴的 0 线处于置信区间之中，这说明交互项对反腐败效能感有显著影响。从图 6 中可以看出，当权力距离为负时，分配不公平感对反腐败效能感的影响为正。当权力距离为正时，分配不公平感对反腐败效能感影响变为负，我们的假设 3 在这里得到了证实。

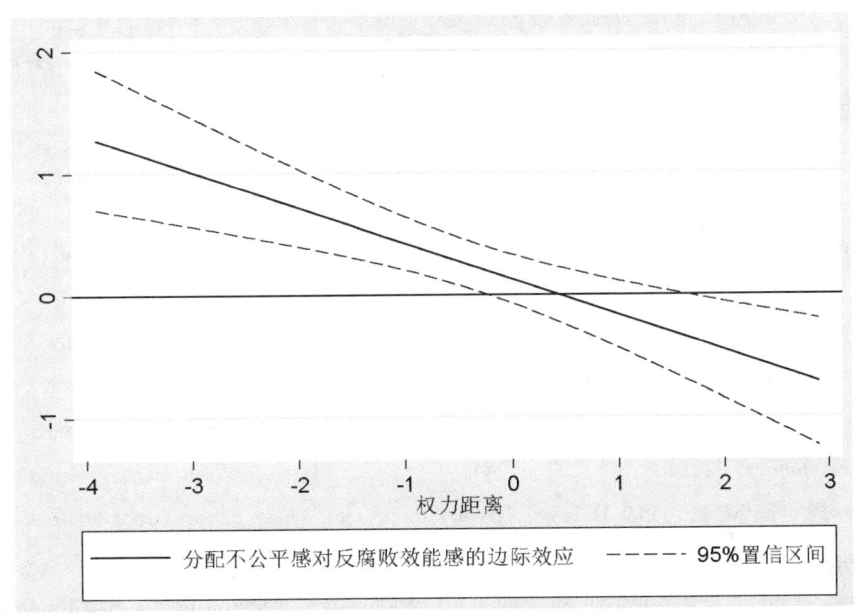

图 6　宏观分配公平对反腐败效能感的边际效应

（五）结论

几十年的经济增长奇迹给中国带来了财富，但是由于没有能有效解决腐败问题，也没有建立起公平的收入分配体系，低质量的经济增长给中国留下了严重的贫富差距和收入分配不公平问题（Carl，Zhao and Li，2001；Li，Sato and Sicular，2013；Davis and Wang，2009），有人认为这是中国为经济增长付出的代价（Shue and Wong，2007）。这一点在我们的数据中也有所体现，在 1604 份样本中，有 35.41% 的被访者认为整个社会的收入分配"很不公平"，认为"很公平"的只有 0.5%。此外，有 34.91% 的被访者认为我们现在的收入差距已经过大了，而不同意这个说法的只占 1.37%。除此之外，我们的研究还发现，虽然大多数东亚国家和社会被归类为权力距离比较高的政治文化系统内（包括中国），但是从图 5 中可以观察到，负值的比例要高于正值，这实际上说明了大多数民众不能容忍权力在收入分配中的作用。因此，虽然权力距离对反腐败效能感有显著的负面作用,但是由于大部分的中国民众越来越不能容忍权力在收入分配中的作用,再加上不断拉大的收入差距和严重的分配不公,使得中国民众的反腐败效能感处于很高的水平。在图2中,有49.13%的民众认为"加大反腐败力度就能降低社会不平等"。

这两点对于反腐败的意义在于,其提高了民众对于反腐败的诉求,民众越来越认识到政府的反腐败举措不仅仅是打击腐败分子那么简单,而是有着在腐败之外的积极意义,包括使得收入分配更加公平化。因此,对于中国政府来说,打击腐败有着多重的积极后果,不仅可以帮助遏制腐败的蔓延,在民众看来,对于腐败问题的治理还会使得整个社会的收入分配更加公平,反腐败是政府赢得民众信任和提高合法性的重要措施(Seligson,2002)。

---

[1] Acemoglu, Daron and James A. Robinson, *Why Nations Fail: The Origins of Power, Prosperity, and Poverty*, New York: Crown Publishers, 2012.

[2] Adams, J. Stacy, "Inequality in Social Exchange", in L. Berkowitz (ed.), *Advances in Experimental Social Psychology* (2), New York: Academic Press, 1965.

[3] Alesina, Alberto and George-Marios Angeletos, "Corruption, Inequality, and Fairness", *Journal of Monetary Economics*, 52, 2005, pp. 1227 – 1244.

[4] Alves, Wayne M. and Peter H. Rossi, "Who Should Get What? Fairness Judgments of Distribution of Earnings", *American Journal of Sociology*, 84 (3), 1978, pp. 541 – 564.

[5] Andres, Antonio R. and Carlyn Ramlogan – Dobson, "Is Corruption Really Bad for Inequality? Evidence from Latin America", *Journal of Development Studies*, 47 (7), 2011, pp. 959 – 976.

[6] Arnold, Jason Ross, "Political Awareness, Corruption Perceptions and Democratic Cccountability in Latin America", *Acta Politica*, 47 (1), 2012, pp. 67 – 90.

[7] Bratton, Michael and Robert Mattes, "Support for Democracy in Africa: Intrinsic or Instrumental?", *British Journal of Political Science*, 31 (3), pp. 447 – 474.

[8] Bos, Kees van den, Riel Vermunt and Henk A. M. Wilke, "Procedural and Distributive Justice: What Is Fair Depends More on What Comes First Than on What Comes Next", *Journal of Personality and Social Psychology*, 72 (1), 1997, pp. 95 – 104.

[9] Campbell, A., Converse, P. E., Miller, W. E. and Stokes, D. E., *The American Voter*. Ann Arbor: University of Michigan Press, 1960.

[10] Campbell, A., Gurin, G. and Miller, W. E., *The Voter Decides*, Evanston, IL: Row, Preston, 1954.

[11] Carl, Riskin, Renwei Zhao and Shi Li (eds.), *China's Retreat from Equality: Income Distribution and Economic Transition*, Armonk, N. Y., Mesharpe, 2001.

[12] Chong, A. and Caldero N., C. A., "Institutional Quality and Income Distribution", *Economic Development and Cultural Change*, 48 (4), 2000, pp. 761-786.

[13] Chong, A. and Gradstein, M., "Inequality and Institutions", *Review of Economics and Statistics*, 89 (3), 2007, pp. 454-65.

[14] Cohen, R. L. (ed.), *Justice: Views from the Social Sciences*, New York: Plenum, 1986.

[15] Craig, S. C. and Maggiotto, M. A., "Measuring Political Efficacy", *Political Methodology*, 9, 1982, pp. 341-354.

[16] Craig, S. C., "Efficacy, Trust, and Political Behavior: An Attempt to Resolve a Lingering Conceptual Dilemma", *American Politics Quarterly*, 7, 1979, pp. 25-29.

[17] Crosby, Faye, "A Model of Egoistical Relative Deprivation", *Psychology Review*, 83 (2), 1976, pp. 85-113.

[18] Davis, James H. and John A. Ruhe., "Perceptions of Country Corruption: Antecedents and Outcomes", *Journal of Business Ethics*, 43 (4), 2003, pp. 275-288.

[19] Davis, Deborah S. and Wang Feng, *Creating Wealth and Poverty in Postsocialist China*, Stanford, Calif.: Stanford University Press, 2003.

[20] Dobson, S. and Ramlogan-Dobson, C., "Is There a Trade-off Between Inequality and Corruption? Evidence from Latin America", *Economics Letters*, 107 (2), 2010, pp. 102-104.

[21] Fisman, R. and Svensson, J., "Are Corruption and Taxation Really Harmful to Growth? Firm Level Evidence", World Bank Policy Research Working Paper WP2485, 2000.

[22] Gyimah-Brempong, K., "Corruption, Economic Growth and Income Inequality in Africa", *Economics of Governance*, 3 (3), 2002, pp. 183-209.

[23] Gyimah-Brempong, K. and Mun oz de Camacho, S., "Corruption, Growth, and Income Distribution: Are There Regional Differences?", *Economics of Governance*, 7 (3), 2006, pp. 245-269.

[24] Gong, Ting, and Wang Shiru, "Indicators and Implications of Zero Tolerance of Corruption: The Case of Hong Kong", *Social Indicators Research*, No. 112, 293, pp. 569-586.

[25] Gupta, S., Davoodi, H. and Alonso-Terme, R., "Does Corruption Affect Income Inequality and Poverty?", *Economics of Governance*, 3 (1). 2002, pp. 23-45.

[26] Guo, Y., "Political Power and Social Inequality: The Impact of the State", in Sun W. and Y. Guo (eds.), *Unequal China: The Political Economy and Cultural Politics of Inequality*, 2013, pp. 12-26.

[27] Hacker, Jacob S. and Paul Pierson, "Winner-take-all Politics: Public Policy, Political Organization, and the Precipitous Rise of Top Incomes in the United States", *Politics & Society*, 38 (2), 2010, pp. 152-204.

[28] He, Zengke, "Corruption and Anti-corruption in Reform China", *Communist and Post-Communist Studies*, 33, 2000, pp. 243-270.

[29] Hellman Joel, "Winners Take All: The Politics of Partial Reform in Post-Communist Transi-

tions", *World Politics*, 1998.

［30］Hilke, B., Delhey, et al., "The China Puzzle: Falling Happiness in a Rising Economy", *Journal of Happiness*, 2009.

［31］Hofstede, Geert, "The Cultural Relativity of Organizational Practices and Theories", *Journal of International Business Studies*, Vol. 14, No. 2, 1983, pp. 75 – 89.

［32］Hofstede, Geert, "The Cultural Relativity of the Quality of Life Concept", *The Academy of Management Review*, Vol. 9, No. 3, 1984, pp. 389 – 398.

［33］Johnston, Michael, "Assessing Vulnerabilities of Corruption: Indicators and Benchmarks of Government Performance", *Public Integrity*, Vol. 12, No. 2., 2010, pp. 125 – 142.

［34］Kurtz, Marcus J. and Andrew Schrank, "Growth and Governance: Models, Measures, and Mechanisms", *The Journal of Politics*, Vol. 69, No. 2, May 2007, pp. 538 – 554.

［35］Kus, Larissa, Jamse Liu and Colleen Ward, "Relative Deprivation versus System Justification: Polemical Social Representations and Identity Positioning in a Post – Soviet Society", *European Journal of Social Psychology*, 43, 2007, pp. 423 – 437.

［36］Li, Hui, Min Tang and Huhe Narisong, "Does Democratization Color Citizen's Ideas: The Role of Democracy as the Contextual Condition of Corruption Perceptions", Working Paper, 2013.

［37］Lü, Xiaobo, "Booty Socialism, Bureau-Preneurs, and the State in Transition: Organizational Corruption in China", *Comparative Politics*, 32 (3), 2000, pp. 274 – 275.

［38］Manion, M., *Corruption by Design: Building Clean Government in Mainland China and Hong Kong*, Cambridge, MA: Harvard University Press, 2004.

［39］Maria, William de, "Measurements and Markets: Deconstructing the Corruption Perception Index", *International Journal of Public Sector Management*, Vol. 21. No. 7, 2008, pp. 777 – 797.

［40］Mauro, P., "Corruption and Growth", *Quarterly Journal of Economics*, 110 (3), 1995, pp. 681 – 712.

［41］Mauro, P., "Corruption and the Composition of Government Expenditure", *Journal of Public Economics*, 69 (2), 1998, pp. 263 – 279.

［42］Norris, Pippa, "Introduction: The Growth of Critical Citizens?", in Pippa Norris (ed.), *Critical Citizens: Global Support for Democratic Government*, Oxford and New York: Oxford University Press, 1999, Chapter 1, pp. 1 – 27.

［43］Olson, Mancur, *Power and Prosperity: Outgrowing Communist and Capitalist Dictatorships*, New York: Basic Books, 2000.

［44］Panning, William H., "Inequality, Social Comparison, and Relative Deprivation", *American Political Science Review*, 77 (2), 1983, pp. 323 – 329.

［45］Quade, E. A., "The Logic of Anticorruption Enforcement Campaigns in Contemporary China", *Journal of Contemporary China*, 16 (50), 2007, pp. 65 – 77.

［46］Ray, James Lee, "Explaining Interstate Conflict and War: What Should be Controlled for?",

Conflict Management and Peace Science, 20 (1), 2002, pp. 1 – 30.

[47] Li, Shi, Hiroshi Sato and Terry Sicular (eds.), *Rising Inequality in China: Challenges to a Harmonious Society*, Cambridge University Press, 2013.

[48] Robinson, Robert V. and Wendell Bell, "Equality, Success, and Social Justice in England and the United States", *American Sociological Review*, 43 (2), 1978, pp. 125 – 143.

[49] Rose, Richard, William Mishler and Neil Munro, *Popular Support for an Undemocratic Regime: The Changing Views of Russians*, Cambridge and New York: Cambridge University Press, 2011.

[50] Runciman, W. G., *Relative Deprivation and Social Justice*, London: Routlege and Kegan Paul, 1966.

[51] Seligson, A. M., "The Impact of Corruption on Regime Legitimacy: A Comparative Study of Four Latin American Countries", *The Journal of Politics*, 64 (2), 2002, pp. 408 – 433.

[52] Shue, Vivienne and Christine Wong, *Paying for Progress in China: Public Finance, Human Welfare and Changing Patterns of Inequality*, New York: Routledge, 2007.

[53] Stiglitz E. Joseph, "The Price of Inequality", *New Perspectives Quarterly*, 30 (1), 2013, pp. 52 – 53.

[54] Sun, Yan, *Corruption and Markets in Contemporary China*, Cornell University Press, 2004.

[55] Sun, Yan, "Does Democracy Check Corruption? Insights from China and India", *Comparative Politics*, 42 (1), 2009, pp. 1 – 19.

[56] Svensson, Jakob, "Eight Questions about Corruption", *The Journal of Economic Perspectives*, Vol. 19, No. 3, 2005, pp. 19 – 42.

[57] Treisman, Daniel, "The Causes of Corruption: ACross-national Study", *Journal of Public Economics*, 76 (3), 2000, pp. 399 – 457.

[58] Treisman, Daniel, "What Have We Learned About the Causes of Corruption From Ten Years of Cross-national Empirical Research?", *Annual Review of Political Science*, 10, 2007, pp. 211 – 244.

[59] Tropp, L. R. and S. C. Wright, "Ingroup Identification and Relative Deprivation: An Examination across Multiple Social Comparisons", *European Journal of Social Psychology*, 29 (5/6), 1999, pp. 707 – 724.

[60] Uslander, E. M., "Corruption and Inequality", World Institute for Development Economic Research (WIDER), Research Paper No. 2006/34.

[61] Uslaner, Eric M., *Corruption, Inequality, and the Rule of Law: The Bulging Pocket Makes the Easy Life*, Cambridge University Press.

[62] Varshney, Ashutosh, "Nationalism, Ethnic Conflict, and Rationality", *Perspectives on Politics*, Vol. 1, No. 1, 2003, pp. 85 – 99.

[63] Walster, E., Walster, G. W. and Berscheid, E., *Equity: Theory and Research*, Boston: Allyn & Bacon, 1978.

[64] Warren, Mark E., "What does Corruption Mean in a Democracy?", *American Journal of Polit-

ical Science, Vol. 48, No. 2, 2004, pp. 328 – 343.

[65] Wedeman, A., "China's War on Corruption", in Gong T. and Ma S. K. (eds.), *Preventing Corruption in Asia*, 2009.

[66] Yao, Shuntian, "Privilege and Corruption: The Problems of China's Socialist Market Economy", *American Journal of Economics and Sociology*, 61 (1), 2002, pp. 279 – 299.

[67] You, Jong-Sung and Sanjeev Khagram, "A Comparative Study of Inequality and Corruption", *American Sociological Review*, Vol. 70, No. 1, 2005, pp. 136 – 157.

[68] You, Jong-Sung and Sanjeev Khagram, "A Comparative Study of Inequality and Corruption", *American Sociological Review*, 70 (1), 2005, pp. 136 – 157.

[69] Yu, Chilik, Chun-Ming Chen and Min – Wei Lin, "Corruption Perception in Taiwan: Reflections upon a Bottom-up Citizen Perspective", *Journal of Contemporary China*, 22, 2005, pp. 79, 56 – 76.

[70] Zhu, Jiangnan, Jie Lu and Tianjian Shi, "When Grapevine News Meets Mass Media: Different Information Sources and Popular Perceptions of Government Corruption in Mainland China", *Comparative Political Studies*, XX (X), 2012, pp. 1 – 27.

从女权主义视角探讨澳门女性领导及主管公务员之玻璃天花板

谢启耀*

一、研究动机与目的

近年来随着全球经济的发展及教育的普及，以及女性地位的提升和经济独立的需要，女性的劳动参与率大量增加，成为现今世界各地最值得关注的社会变化及现象（International Labor Office，ILO，2010）。根据全球劳动力的统计公布，女性占全球劳动人口的比例不断上升，从1970年的38%提升到近年47.3%的水平（ILO，2010）。然而，随着全球的趋势，两性工作平等和工作权益的保障已广泛地被许多国家优先纳入为政策目标范围（Connell，2006）。尽管"玻璃天花板"一词源于20世纪70年代，其后各国积极改革以让更多女性成功发展进入团队之领导阶层，但结果显示她们所占的比例仍是相当有限（Connell，2006）。

统计暨普查局公布的澳门特别行政区最新人口数据，显示了澳门女性劳动人口由2003年的10.34万人，提升至去年的18.19万人。在公共行政人力资源方面，按现职公务人员的男女性比例进行分析，女性比例从2003年占35.06%一直持续上升至2012年占42.01%，这种趋势由2005年起较为明显。而自2003年至2012年之间，女性公务人员所占比例每年平均上升约1.83%。虽然女性担任公职人员的数目快速增加，但统计数据清晰地表明男性还是占领导及主管公职人员绝大多数，而自2003年起，女性在这一类高层次职位所占比例则平均每年下降约0.3%。初步说明了女性的向上流动性仍受到一定的限制，因为她们多集中分布于澳门特区政府的中、低阶层职位。在美国，Riccucci（2009）对联邦政府内任职的女性公务人员进行了深入的研究，还概括了二十多年（1984—2004）的数据来了解女性与男性公务人员在行政机关的情况，

---

* 谢启耀，浙江大学公共管理学院行政管理博士研究生。

并表明尽管在推动两性平等工作上近来取得了进展，但涉足联邦政府较高层的公职仍是以男性为主。此外，在 2007 年的统计数据显示，在联邦政府担任高级行政人员的女性比例也只有 30%（U. S. Office of Personnel Management：OPM，2007）。上述的比较可显示出，男性占组织高层大多数的比例是两地政府部门普遍的现象，故有学者称此为"男性治理铁律"（赖维尧，1996）。

澳门特别行政区的女性公务人员，在相关的法规制度上已受到较好的保障，并未发现有对女性明显的歧视或不公的情况。根据澳门第 52/95/M 号法令规定，保障男性和女性在就业上获得平等的机会及待遇，澳门公职人员章程相关法例第 87/89/M 号法令核准《澳门公共行政工作人员通则》中第九十二条，也清楚列明了女性公务人员因成为母亲而享有的优待条款。因此，从澳门特区政府现行的法规制度来看，对于女性公务人员，并没有异于男性公务人员的待遇，而且还给予了较好的优待。然而，法律的保障并不代表能保证女性在公共行政当局已获致平等的地位，进而提升她们在领导及主管职务之整体比例；因为，现时她们所遭遇的并非是公然的歧视，而是隐形的障碍。所以，本研究透过文献回顾、组织结构和组织实际运作的特质去探讨澳门女性领导及主管公务员现时在事业发展上所面临的困境，借此解释她们是否受限于玻璃天花板之隐形障碍，同时按实际情况加以分析讨论。最后，提出结论与建议。

二、相关理论与文献探讨

（一）组织结构理论

从结构论的观点来看，女性在事业发展上所面临的困境，主要是由于组织偏差的因素而导致的。对于任何形式的政治组织都隐含着特定的偏差，这种偏差仅利于某种冲突的显现而压制其他冲突的表面化。因为组织本身就是某种偏差的动员，所以某些议题被安排进入政治领域，而其他则被排除出去（Schattschneider，1960）。

由于特定的偏差隐含着特定的利害关系，而组织的参与者必定会权衡各种利害关系，以选择最有利的情况。因此，这种偏差便会渐渐地渗透于整个组织结构和组织文化之中，使得女性在组织中所遭受到的不平等长期不受到重视。而且这种组织偏差与父权体制息息相关，女性在组织中处于较不利的地位，主要是因为在政策或实际运作上，组织权力和控制结构都有利于男性支配的地位。而男性之所以能够取得此支配地位，是父权体制下长期社会化过程所造成的结果（黄焕荣，2011）。

此外有学者研究表示，女性可能因过于"女性化"（Branson，2006），较缺乏"阳性气质"（Belt，2002）而导致丧失晋升机会。而有些经验性的研究更指出具有阳性气质倾向的女性较具有被提拔晋升的机会（Foster，1995；Hull and Umansky，1997）。对于这一观点，管理学者 Fagenson（1986，1990）又做了进一步的解说。他认为男性和女性在态度、行为及认知等方面的差异，主要是由于男性和女性在组织中的人员数目和权力等因素的差距所形成，并不是由于性别因素而导致。从上述的理论可以得知，如果当女性拥有像男性一样的高职阶时，她们所表现的行为和态度也会像男性一样。而这种情况，有学者称此为"女王蜂症候群"现象，指的是女性主管人员会将其他女性人员当作竞争者，担心自己本身的利益或原有的地位因其他女性的加入而受到威胁，这种对其他女性的敌意态度，其行为结果是较不喜欢提拔女性，也不喜欢与女性共事，而且其行事风格与男性主管渐趋一致（邓慧文，1996）。

（二）玻璃天花板效应

近年来女性进入就业市场的人数逐渐增加，但不论是私人企业，还是公共行政当局，仅有少数的女性能够晋升至组织高层的职位，此种现象称为"玻璃天花板效应"。而玻璃天花板界定为"基于一些态度偏差或组织偏差所造成的人为障碍，使得具备资格的人无法在其组织中升迁至管理阶层的职位"（U. S. Department of Labor, 1997）。玻璃天花板的隐喻是认为女性无法晋升至高层的管理职位，这并非由于其资历不足或不想获得这些职位，也不是公然的歧视所造成；而是一些针对女性事业生涯发展所设下的巧妙障碍，人们甚至几乎看不到它的存在。然而，若组织中女性顺着组织生涯的阶梯不断地往上爬，当接近顶端时，就会碰撞到这面隐形的玻璃天花板障碍（Naff，1997）。

对于玻璃天花板的成因，虽然可以从人力资本、社会心理或歧视偏差等各方面的不同理论观点去加以解释。但是，组织这一项还是最重要的因素（黄焕荣，2000），而组织的因素有两项较为重要的层面。

1. 人力的输送带：对于玻璃天花板的现象，美国官方通常是从所谓"输送带定理"的观点来加以解释，此种观点认为一个高层主管的培养需要经历一段相当长的时间，大约需要 15 至 20 年的经验累积，所以当人们意识到女性面临玻璃天花板的障碍时，并无法运用政策去改变此现况，而是需要等待时间去慢慢突破（U. S. Glass Ceiling Commission, 1995a）。换言之，由于过去 20 年澳门特区政府的女性公务人员的数目偏低，男性公务人员数目一直较女性为多，尤其在 1994 年期间大约有 65% 的公职人员为男性。所以，造成这种"男高女低"的不平衡现象，并非目前才发生，而是过去历史所累积下来的。因此"输送带定理"可以解释现时女性担任高层公职人员的数目仍偏低的一部分原因，还有其他的因素需要考虑。

2. 组织权力与网络关系：组织权力可以分为正式权力和非正式权力，组织权力源于组织成员所占的职位，而非正式权力则来自于组织内外人员之间的关系和互动行为。所以，作为一位管理者除了因职位而产生的正式权力外，还要发展出能够提供非正式权力的网络关系，这样才能够使他们顺利地进行工作和事业生涯的发展（Kottis, 1993）。而且多数组织非正式的关系系统，不论是其根源或目前的功能，都是从男性文化与男性经验中发展出来的。从其形态、行为准则、沟通模式，以及关系的表现方式，都是由男性文化所主导；尤其在较高的组织阶层中，非正式的系统更是男性生活形态的一个堡垒（陈怡芬译，1983）。

除了以上的因素外，还有其他关键因素影响女性事业生涯的发展，特别是在高层的管理职位。本研究透过文献分析，对于女性担任领导及主管比例之发展缓慢归纳出以下三种原因：（1）女性担任助手角色；（2）性别刻板印象；（3）男性主导的权威（Connell, 2006；Guy, 1993；Newman, 1993）。

（1）女性担任助手角色：意指在组织中女性多被分派到支援性的职位，而非指挥性的职位，使她们在争取较好的职位晋升机会时，缺乏了有利的竞争条件。

（2）性别刻板印象：意指是对女性作为领导的角色存在着偏见，Eagly and Karau (2002) 发现女性要进入领导阶层且成为一个成功的领导者是很困难的，而且认同度也不高。这几年，有许多学者指出这些刻板印象，使女性比男性较难进入公共行政机关之较高职位，是导致女性占有较少领导阶层职位的原因之一。另外，一些女性领导者的刻板印象及传统要求，也形成女性在领导路上的一些阻碍。例如：一般而言，大部分的人都觉得女性领导及主管者比较挑剔，要求比较高，易执着于小细节和常犹豫不决迟迟无法下决定等。因此，她们必须花更多时间与别人好好相处，才能打破别人心中的刻板印象。

（3）男性主导的权威：以男性为主导的世界观被当作普遍的准则，并用来评量所有人的经验。Cubillo and Brown (2003) 的研究发现女性共同的障碍是"女性生活在传统男性的主宰文化中，一般人的知觉是认为领导与管理是属于男性所宰制的"。

三、澳门女性领导及主管公务人员的现况分析

近年随着澳门经济的急速发展和教育的普及，女性接受教育的机会大大增加。图1显示了在2012/2013学年获澳门特区政府"大专学生学习用品津贴"资助的高等教育课程的女性比男性多，占了53.21%，而就读研究生课程的学生中，则有53.67%是女性。与此同时，女性担任公务人员的数目也快速增加，从图2可以发现，澳门特别行政区的女性公务人员比例从2003年占35.06%持续上升至2012年占42.01%，这种趋势由2005年起较为明显。而自2003年至2012年之间，女性公务人员所占比例每

年平均上升约 1.83%，并依这过去 10 年的成长趋势，估计还需要大概 10 年的时间男性及女性公务人员的比例才会相当。相对而言，女性在"领导及主管官员"一类的高层次公职所占比例则由 2003 年的 42.26%，到 2012 年已下降到 41.02%，每年平均下降约 0.3%。但是，女性人数的增加在部分领导及主管阶层均显现上升的趋势。与 2003 年比较，2012 年担任处级官职中的女性由 110 人提高至 139 人，增长了 26.36%；厅级由 59 人提高至 69 人，增长了 16.95%；副局级由 27 人提高至 31 人，增长了 14.81%；而局级则由 14 人提高至 17 人，增长了 21.43%。然而，从性别比例成长的角度来看，这 10 年来女性比例没有较为明显的成长幅度，而统计数据清晰的表明男性还是占了绝大多数。这种情况尤其突显在澳门特区政府辖下局级官职中（如图 3 所示），从 2003 年至 2012 年之间，显示了女性比例在 2006 年占了最高的 27.27%，但也达不到三成；故实际情况是女性占澳门特区政府的高层公职人员比例仍然偏低。

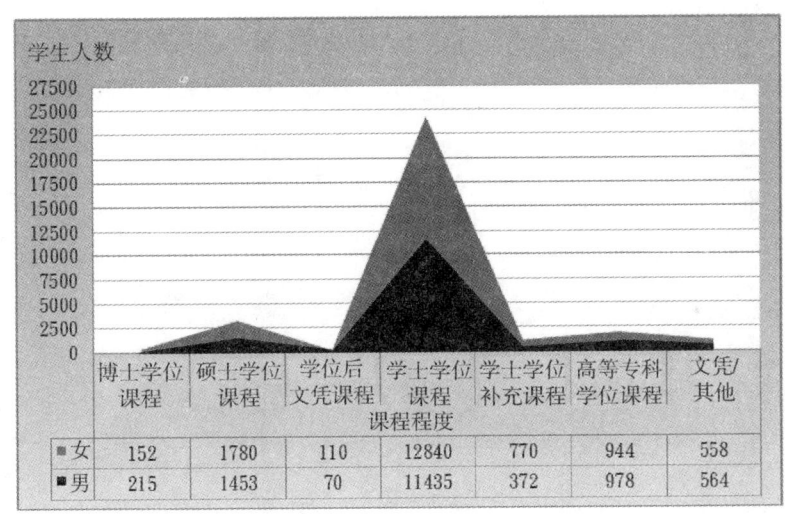

图 1 2012/2013 学年获"大专学生学习用品津贴"资助学生的升学类别及性别分布

资料来源： 高等教育人才数据库，此部分为本研究绘制及整理。

除了上述"男高女低"的现象相当明显外，在观察领导及主管公务人员的结构，还可以发现以下几点特别值得关注的现象：

（1）领导及主管公务人员的结构中，没有 29 岁或以下者，约 75% 的现职人员有 15 年以上的年资，约 1.9% 的人员年资则在 5 年或以下。而在局级官职中，局级领导人员当中以 40—49 岁的人数占最多（如图 4 所示），这一年龄组别的男性及女性在人员总数中分别占了 36.51% 及 14.29%。而更重要的是，绝大多数的局级领导人员，其育成需要经历一段长的时间。

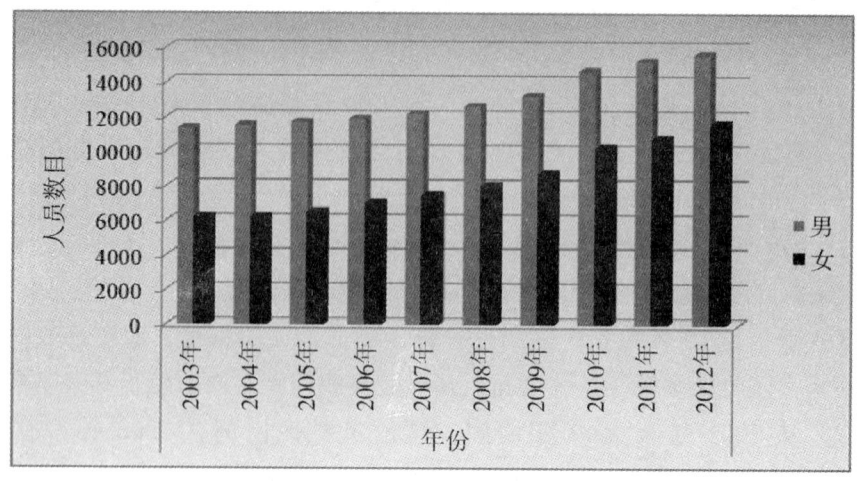

图 2　2003 年至 2012 年公共行政现职人员性别结构的演变

资料来源：澳门行政公职局（2012），此部分为本研究绘制及整理。

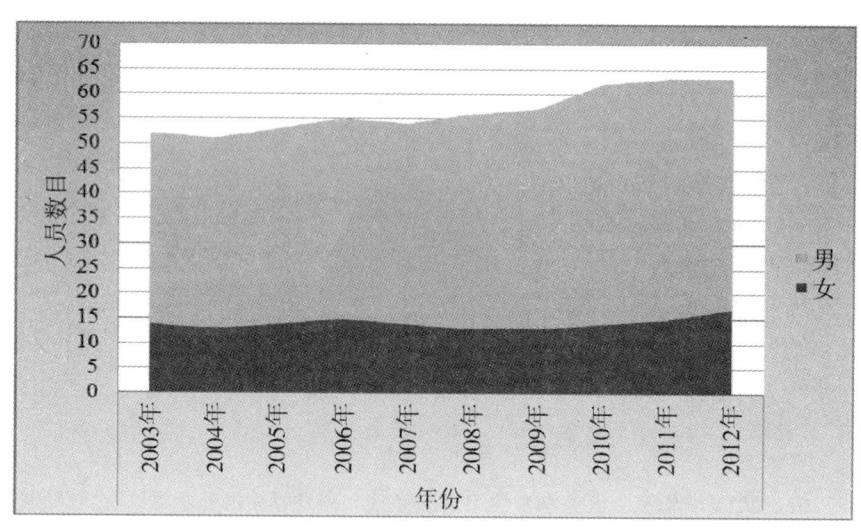

图 3　2003 年至 2012 年局级领导人员性别分布及人数的演变

资料来源：澳门行政公职局（2003—2012），此部分为本研究绘制及整理。

（2）在领导及主管公务人员的结构中，女性公务人员具有硕士学位的比例较男性公务人员为高（如图 5 所示），而且平均学历程度也与男性公务人员为相当。虽然这样，但统计数据清晰的表明男性还是占领导及主管人员绝大多数，显示了女性的晋升及所占比例并未有因具有高学历程度而做出明显的改变。

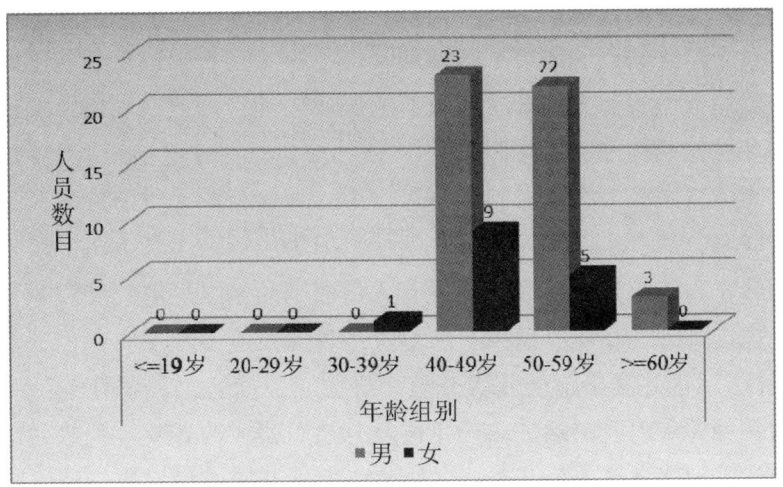

图4　2011年局级领导人员的年龄组别及性别分布

资料来源：澳门行政公职局（2011），此部分为本研究绘制及整理。

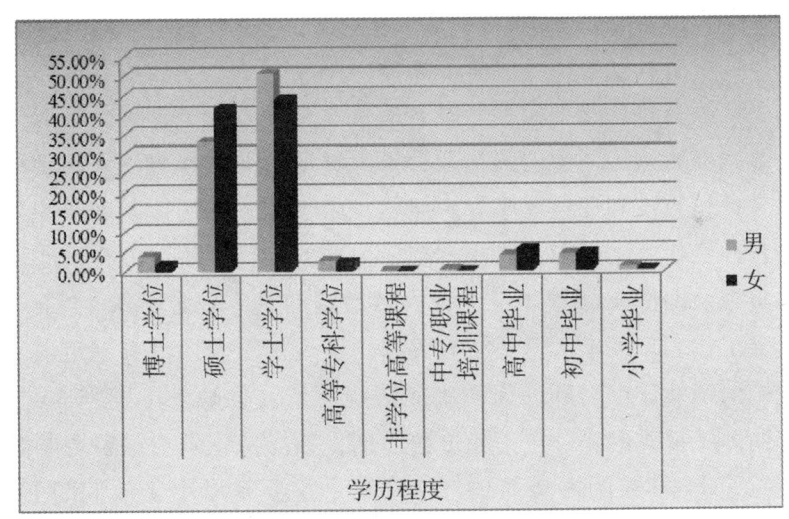

图5　2011年领导及主管人员的学历程度及性别分布

资料来源：澳门行政公职局（2011），此部分为本研究绘制及整理。

四、结论与建议

上述相关分析之论述，说明了澳门特区政府公共行政机关中的女性局级领导人员比例偏低的情况，及其面临的困境所在。对于上述她们所面对的多项因素而导致的困境，不能只透过时间去解决，而需要特区政府有更积极的行动去构建公平的竞争环境与制度来达成性别平衡的目标。

对此，面对全球化的竞争环境下，性别管理不再只是平等或伦理的问题，而是如何有效地充分运用人力资源去提升特区政府的施政效能。因此，政府需要在公务员入职、升迁及领导层流动性等三个层面着手。

事实上，澳门特区政府在现有制度的运行中，一般公务人员与领导及主管人员之间并没有晋级联系，两者也以不同的方式聘任。因为领导及主管人员的聘任、任用及选拔、中止及终止委任都是以《领导及主管人员通则的基本规定》和《领导及主管人员通则的补充规定》作为依据。所以，一般资历再深及能力水平再高的公务人员（不论是女性或男性），都并非必定会获晋升至领导主官。简言之，要杜绝一些在人事行政管理方面的各种弊病以及消除玻璃天花板之升迁障碍，改善女性局级领导人员比例偏低的情况，就必须要从统一公开考试录取公务人员开始。目前澳门特区政府的"中央招聘"并不适用于领导及主官人员的聘任，而只局限于"高级技术员职程"和"技术辅导员职程"。因此，领导及主官人员的甄选应该要有明确的客观标准与条件，引入"公平竞争"机制，让所有合资格者（不论是女性或男性）都能在公平的环境下公开竞争，加强职位的认受性。

其次，在公职人员升迁方面，应从改善评核制度着手，能选拔有能力、才干、责任感及热诚的公务人员担任重要官职。从现有的法律来看，《公共行政工作人员的工作表现评核一般制度》规定了主管人员及公务人员适用的工作表现评核制度，包括了相关评核项目、评核方式和评核程序等。但是，由于相关的法律制度较为分散，而且在其所分布的各种法律、法规中，并非占有最主要的地位，所以一直没能得到部分领导人员的足够重视。即使在《领导及主管人员通则的基本规定》第14条规定了领导人员每年须接受工作表现评审，但是，有关细则性规定至今还没有制定出来。在此情况下，有关他们的绩效评审实际尚无明确的法规可依，也缺乏了细则性的指标体系。再加上在现有的评核模式中，公众不能参与评估，领导及主管人员普遍眼睛向上，即只"对上负责"，而且评核的方法简单，评核结果主要是取决于他们的上级。因此，其评核结果与外界公众的感受往往有一定差别，亦不可能科学地反映实情。最后，在领导层流动性方面，主要领导层长期据位，多个部门的领导及主官人员，十多年来均集体连任，因而有机会导致公共利益个人化。所以，建议加大领导及主官人员的流动性，鼓励精英公仆向上流动，建设培养与输送机制，使有能力、才干、责任感及热诚的公务人员能"晋升"至领导及主官人员。这样，才能有效地排除妨碍女性职业生涯发展之障碍，以打造公平正义的组织文化。

[1] 澳门统计暨普查局：《就业调查》第4季。

[2] 澳门行政公职局：《澳门特别行政区公共行政人力资源报告，2003—2012》。

[3] 吴定、张润书、陈德禹、赖维尧：《行政学》（一），"国立"空中大学，台北县。

[4] 《澳门公职人员章程》（1989），《澳门公共行政工作人员通则》，见《澳门政府公报》，第51期。

[5] 黄焕荣、方凯弘、蔡志恒：《公务人力资源管理之性别议题与对策：组织建筑模式之分析》，《文官制度季刊》第3卷，2011年第2期，第49—80页。

[6] 邓慧文：《主管性别、应征者性别与晋升潜能对甄选决定的影响》，国立政治大学硕士论文，台北市，2011年。

[7] 黄焕荣：《组织中玻璃天花板效应之研究：行政院部会机关女性升迁之实证分析》，国立政治大学博士论文，台北市，2000年。

[8] 玛格丽特·亨宁、安妮·J.（Margaret Henning and Anne Jarbim）：《女性管理者》，陈怡芬译，台北：允晨出版社1983年版。

[9] International Labor Office, *Global Employment Trends*, Geneva, Switzerland: International Labor Organization, 2010.

[10] Connell, R., "Glass Ceiling or Gendered Institutions? Mapping the Gender Regimes of Public Sector Worksites", *Public Administration Review*, 66, 2006, pp. 837 – 849.

[11] Riccucci, N. M., "The Pursuit of Social Equity in the Federal Government: A Road Less Traveled?", *Public Administration Review*, 69, 2009, pp. 373 – 382.

[12] U. S. Office of Personnel Management, *Fed Scope: Federal Human Resources Data*, Available from http://www.fedscope.opm.gov/, 2007.

[13] Schattschneider, E. E., *The Semi-Sovereign People: A Realist's View of Democracy in American*, Hinsdale, Illinois: The Dryden Press, 1960.

[14] Branson, D. M., *No Seat at the Table: How Corporate Governance Keeps Women out of America's Boardrooms*, New York: New York University Press, 2006.

[15] Belt, V., "A Female Ghetto?: Women's Careers in Call Centres", *Human Resources Management Journal*, 12 (4), 2002, pp. 51 – 66.

[16] Foster, S. Elizabeth, "The Glass Ceiling in the Legal Profession: Why Do Law Firms Still Have So Few Female Partners?", *UCLA Law Review*, 42 (6), 2002, pp. 1631 – 1689.

[17] Hull, Rita P., Philip H. Umansky, "An Examination of Gender Stereotyping as an Explanation for Vertical Job Segregation in Public Accounting", *Accounting Organizations and Society*, 22 (6), 1996, pp. 507 – 528.

[18] Fagenson, Ellen A., "Women's Work Orientations: Something Old, Something New", *Group & organization Studies*, 11 (1 – 2), 1986, pp. 75 – 100.

[19] Fagenson, Ellen A., "At the Heart of Women in Management Research: Theoretical and Meth-

odological Approaches and Their Biases", *Journal of Business Ethics*, 9 (4-5), 1990, pp. 267-274.

[20] U. S. Department of Labor, *The Glass Ceiling Initiative: Are There Cracks in the Ceiling?*, Washington, DC: U. S. Department of Labor Employment Standards Administration Office of Federal Contract Compliance Programs, 1997.

[21] Naff, K. C., "Colliding with a Glass Ceiling: Barriers to the Advancement of Women and Minorities", in Carolyn Ban and Norma M. Riccucci (eds.), *Public Personnel Management: Current Concerns Future Challenges* (2nd Ed.), New York: Longman, 1997, pp. 91-108.

[22] US Glass Ceiling Commission, *Good for Business: Making Full Use of the Nation's Human Capital*, Washington, DC: Recommendation of Federal Glass Ceiling Commission, 1995.

[23] Kottis, Athena Petraki, "Women in Management: The 'Glass Ceiling' and How to Break It", *Women in Management Review*, 8 (4), 1993, pp. 9-15.

[24] Guy, M. E., "Three Steps forward, Two Steps Backward: The Status of Women's Integration into Public Management", *Public Administration Review*, 53, 1993, pp. 285-292.

[25] Newman, M. A., "Career Advancement: Does Gender Make a Difference?", *American Review of Public Administration*, 23, 1993, pp. 361-383.

[26] Eagly, A. H. and Karau, S. J., "Role Congruity Theory of Prejudice toward Female Leaders", *Psychological Review*, 109 (3), 2002, pp. 573-589.

[27] Cubillo, L. and Brown, M., "Women into Educational Leadership and Management: International Differences?", *Journal of Educational Administration*, 41 (3), 2003, pp. 278-291.

[28] 高等教育人才数据库, http://www.gaes.gov.mo/hetdb/hr_curr_main.html。

澳门公务法人制度改革探析——兼比较法的借鉴

张异和[*]

公务法人的研究，涉及多个学科领域的知识，包括法学、行政学、企业管理学、财务会计学等等。本文仅从法学角度出发，探讨公务法人所涉及的法律建制问题。[1] 本文将首先分析公务法人在行政组织法上的概念，然后梳理在澳门特别行政区法律体系中有关公务法人的规定以及各公务法人的组织法规，分析存在的问题，继而说明在公共行政改革的大背景下，应考虑制定关于构建公务法人一般制度的法律，之后简介葡、日，以及中国台湾的相关法律，认为澳门可适当借鉴葡、日，以及中国台湾地区的立法经验，开始改革公务法人。

一、公务法人概念分析

在行政法理论中，将行政分为直接行政与间接行政两种，直接行政是指通过国家行政机关进行的行政活动，间接行政是指由拥有法律人格、行政及财政自治权的公共实体开展的行政活动。[2] 直接行政机关的架构是金字塔式的，上下之间存在等级关系；间接行政是通过设立新的行政主体，赋予其一定职能，以实现母体的利益，母体为其订定目标与方向。[3] 存在间接行政的理由主要是基于分权理论，将国家任务分解到其他独立的行政主体，从而减轻国家的负担，因此也称为国家的工具性实体。

实施间接行政的机构主要分为地方自治团体、公务法人、公营企业和公共社团。① 这些都是独立的行政主体。行政主体是指在行政法/公法上具有权利能力承担权利、

---

* 张异和，澳门大学法学硕士，立法会顾问团高级技术员。本文仅代表作者个人观点，与所属机构无关。

① 但是，也有学者认为这只是广义上的间接行政，除国家以外的所有行政实体实施的行政，狭义的间接行政将地方自治团体、公共社团排除在外，它们构成自治行政。参见 Diogo Freitas do Amaral, *Curso de Direito Administrativo*, 3rd Ed., Almedin, Vital Moreira, pp. 106, 107。

义务的主体。① 享有权利能力的有人或法人，根据权利能力来自于公法还是私法，法人有公法人和私法人之分。

（一）公法人

公法人是在将法人的概念从私法领域中移植到公法领域之后出现的[4]，公法人主要回应了公共行政分权和自治的要求。有学者这样总结公法人的出现与演变，"法人理论在公法上的使用，被证明具有强大的解释力，它使权力的归属抽象化成为可能。过往无法解决的问题（例如如何约束拥有绝对权力的君主；如何区分国家财产与君主私人财产等等）现在都得以迎刃而解。公法人作为机构的法律组织方式，是在19世纪中期国家被构建为法人以后才开始的。开始的时候，这个概念只用于国家以及地区实体，后来逐渐扩散。首先是一些社团也被赋予公法人的资格，然后一些公共部门也被法人化。[5]

也就是随着国家加强在经济和社会领域的干预，公法人数目逐渐增多，成为国家对经济和社会控制的工具。

公法人具有以下三个特征：必然是处理公共利益；因公权力的行为而设立；具公法上的权利能力，以自身名义行使权力。[6]

（二）公务法人[7]

公务法人是指为履行属于国家或另一公法人的一定行政职能而设立的机构性质的公法人。[8]

公务法人具有以下几个特征。[9]首先，公务法人一定是法人，具法人资格，这个特征将其隶属于直接行政中的有一定自治权的机构区分开来，因为后者不具法人资格。而且公务法人是具公法人资格，而非私法人资格，这一点将其与公用事业机构区分开来，后者是私法人。

其次，公务法人也一定是机构性质法人，不是社团，并非是社员的结合，这一点将其与公共社团区分开来。

再次，公务法人是为履行特定行政职能而设立。行使的是公共职能而非私人职能，是行政而非立法或司法职能。而且履行的仅是特定职能，而非一般性的行政职能，后者只能由国家或地方实体来履行。

---

① 行政主体指公法上权利义务的最终归属者。如果某一行政部门的行为在法律上不能再归属于其他行政部门时，则该行政部门即属"行政主体"；反之，该行政部门的行为，若尚有可归属的部门时，则其仅属行政主体的一个部分，而非行政主体，故行政主体乃是行政行为"层层归属的终点"。转引自李建良：《论公法人在行政组织建制上的地位与功能——以德国公法人概念与法制为借镜》，《月旦法学》第84期，2002年5月，第45页。

最后，其实施行政是间接性的，行使的职责归根结底属于国家或作为其设立者的其他公法人。

公务法人的设立理念在于实现行政的分权，以独立法人的组织形式来完成一些公共任务，以达到行政更灵活更有效率的目的。[10]

公务法人的种类包括：具法律人格的机关（serviços personalizados）、公共基金（fundações públicas）以及公共机构（estabelecimentos publicos[11]）三种。[12]

具法律人格的机关是由法律赋予法律人格以及行政自治或行政与财政自治权的行政机构。在澳门有澳门贸易投资促进局、消费者委员会、环境委员会、民政总署、房屋局、民航局、金融管理局。它们与隶属于直接行政不具法人资格但具一定自治权的部门不同，后者不属于公务法人。[13]

公共基金，是指有为完成特定公共目的、实现公共利益而设立的具公法人资格的基金，它们由行政法规范，而不同于受民法规范的具私法人资格的基金。在澳门设立的公共基金有澳门社会保障基金、澳门基金会、科学技术发展基金、渔业发展及援助基金等等。

第三类公务法人即公共机构，指的是具有社会或文化性质、向公众开放的旨在为大众提供服务的实体[14]。在澳门这类公务法人包括澳门大学、澳门理工学院、旅游学院。

公务法人有独立的公法人资格，具行政、财政自治权，但它们与独立机构不同。公务法人是工具性机构。公务法人虽然具有法律人格，但是并非真正地独立于国家机关，它们是由一个母体机构设立或取消的，母体机构对于它们行使极大的权力，财政、人事监督权、领导机关任命或罢免权等等。而独立机构不受其他机构控制或指导。独立机构首先现于北美，20世纪最后20年逐渐出现于欧洲，多是关于电视媒体规管、基本权利保护、经济领域例如市场监管、反垄断等监管机构，等等。[15]

二、澳门行政架构中的公务法人

虽然公务法人在澳门早已出现，但公务法人在澳门的法律体系中并没有一个统一的规定公务法人制度的通则性法律，有关公务法人的一般性规定分散载于几个法律里。

首先，8月11日第85/84/M号法令制定了澳门公共行政当局组织结构一般基础，该法令所订立之原则同样适用于自治机关（serviços autónomos）。而"公务法人"具行政与/或财政自治权，属于自治机关的范畴。该法规定了公共机关须从属于总督、遵守法院命令、依法为居民谋取正当利益而开展活动的原则以及公共机关组织灵活性原则，规定了公共部门的组织结构，人员编制原则，以及机关组织法规的内容，更特别指出自治机构得于组织法规内订定有关行政及财政制度，以及机关裁撤之前提，在架构之合理化过程完结之后或者以实现某一机关之设立目标时，应裁撤该机关或将之与其他现存机关合并，等等。

回归后制定的第 2/1999 号法律《政府组织纲要法》第 6/1999 号行政法规《政府部门及实体的组织、职权与运作》都适用于公务法人，但并未因应其性质订定特别的规定。

其次，财政制度方面，澳门曾专门在法律上就自治实体订定财政制度，见于 5 月 30 日第四二/八八/M 号法令以及 9 月 27 日第五三/九三/M 号法令，后者废止了前者。由 9 月 27 第五三/九三/M 号法令制定的自治实体财政制度的具体内容有，具有财政自治权的条件（其本身收入、指定之收入及共享收入的总额不少于其开支之首次预算的 30%），自治实体通过其本身预算反映其财政状况，预算由总督核准，编制其预算须根据现行之公告会计之规定、自治实体财政制度之原则及监督实体之指引为之，由自治实体编制之本身预算草案须成交监督实体作审议，行政管理委员会由总督应监督实体之建议以批示委任其成员，须由最少三名最多五名成员组成，当中须有一名财政局代表，行政管理委员会权限包括批准自治实体开支，明确订定行政管理委员会批准开支之金额限制（不得超过自治实体首次预算总额百分之一，或任何情况下不得超过澳门币 500000 元）。财政局有监察自治实体财政活动之一般权利，且总督得透过批示命令审计自治实体的管理，得透过专家为之。

回归后于 2006 年废止了上述 9 月 27 日第五三/九三/M 号法令，将自治实体的财政制度纳入由第 6/2006 号行政法规通过的统一的《公共财政管理制度》。该行政法规的第一编中的第四章规定享有财政自治权的部门及机构的财政制度，完善了已废止的法令中的制度，继承法令中的大部分内容，增加了一些技术性规则。

除了这些散见于其他法律的适用于作为自治机构的公务法人的一般性规定以外，各公务法人尚由其各自设立法律或组织法规管。目前在法律中明确指出具公务法人地位的实体包括：澳门贸易投资促进局[16]、房屋局[17]、民政总署[18]、社会工作局[19]、民航局[20]、社会保障基金[21]、消费者委员会[22]、司法警察局福利会[23]、海关福利会[24]、港务局福利会[25]、治安警察厅福利会[26]以及消防局福利会[27]。

具有公法人地位并且有行政及财政自治权的类公务法人包括：金融管理局[28]、卫生局、邮政局[29]、印务局、澳门基金会、科学技术发展基金、渔业发展及援助基金、楼宇维修基金、工商业发展基金、汽车及航海保障基金、退休基金会、教育发展基金、学生福利基金、澳门公共行政福利基金、环保与节能基金、澳门大学、澳门理工学院、旅游学院。之所以称它们为类公务法人，是因为他们既有行政及财政自治权，又是公法人，而且也依其所负责的事务落入学理上公务法人的类别，有学者直接称其中一些为具公务法人性质的公法人。[30]

在梳理了澳门法律体系中关于公务法人的规定之后，可以发现如下几个问题。

首先，在澳门的各个法律中，有关"公务法人"的提述比较混乱，其与自治机构、自治基金的关系并未理顺。

一些一般性法律当提及公务法人时，是将其与行政机关、地方自治团体、公共团体并列的，例如《行政程序法典》第十五条规定："为着本法典之效力，公共行政当局之机关系指：a) 行使行政职能之机关；b) 公务法人之机关及公共团体之机关。"类似的还有七月十二日第34/93/M号法令[31]，以及第9/1999号法律《司法组织纲要法》[32]。这与学理上有关公共行政的种类以及公务法人性质的通说是一致的。

规定自治机构财政制度的5月30日第四二/八八/M号法令第一条规定"该法适用于以法人机关及自治基金形式设立的公务法人，在本法中以自治实体称之。"这里是将自治实体等同于公务法人的概念。而9月27日第五三/九三/M号法令第一条第二款规定："自治实体（entidades autónomas）系指以法人机关（serviços personalizados）及自治基金（fundos autónomos）组织形式而设立之公务法人（institutos públicos），以及其他具有财政自治权之机构。"这里明确地将公务法人置于自治实体的大概念下，公务法人包括法人机关及自治基金，而自治实体也包括其他具有财政自治权但不为公务法人的机构或不具公法人资格的机构。

第6/2006号行政法规《公共财政管理制度》第五十四条规定"所有自治机构均具备法律人格以及行政、财政及财产自治权"，这里与9月27日第五三/九三/M号法令的取向不同，将自治机构的范围缩窄，指具有法律人格且行政、财政及财产自治权的实体。在该法律中并未提及公务法人，当然，很明显依该法律的定义，自治机构包括但不限于公务法人①，自治机构还包括公共团体。

可能有人会提出疑问，自治机构的法律建制是否已足够，是否可以弃用公务法人的概念，毕竟公务法人在法律中并未有定义，是否还有必要再固守公务法人，遑论建立公务法人的一般法律制度。笔者认为，在法律意义上，自治机构是一个大的概念，甚至是讨论财政制度时将几个不同属性的机构结合起来取之共性（财政自治权）而成立的一个集合概念。而公务法人是有独特性的，其存在在行政组织学上有其原因，而且可以通过制度改革更加发挥其对于推动行政组织现代化的作用，因此不可言废。

在一些法律中对自治基金与公务法人的提述也不协调。有法律将自治基金与公务法人的概念并列置于公共部门的大概念下，例如第8/2006号法律《公务人员公积金

---

① 例如，澳门监狱基金，"为一在澳门监狱职责范围内运作并享有行政及财政自治权的实体"，属于一自治机构，但并非公务法人。

制度》[33]、第 13/2009 号法律《关于订定内部规范的法律制度》[34]、第 13/2010 号法律《因执行公共职务的司法援助》[35]、第 2/2011 号法律《年资奖金、房屋津贴及家庭津贴制度》[36]。采取相同做法的还包括尚在立法会进行细则性讨论的《公共部门劳动合同制度》法案[37]。然而，令人疑惑的是，一些法律却将自治机关及自治基金组织纳入在公务法人的范围内，例如第 3/2001 号法律《澳门特别行政区立法会选举制度》[38]、第 11/2003 号法律《财产及利益申报法律制度》[39]。到底公务法人是包括所有的自治基金、部分的自治基金，还是自治基金并不是公务法人？

由此可见，公务法人的概念在一些法律中的使用存在一定的混淆，容易引起对公务法人的地位、性质的误解。

第二个问题是，规定公共部门组织制度的法律是一般性适用于政府直接行政部门和公务法人的，因此并未有很多针对公务法人的特性而制定的规定。而上文提及的个公务法人或类公务法人的设立法规或组织法数目众多，于不同时期制定，各自的制度差别很大。

例如，在机关组成方面，一般都设有行政管理委员会、执行委员会等决策机关，少数设有咨询委员会①，但并非都设有内部监督机关。有内部监督机关的只有九个，分别是民政总署、贸易投资促进局、金融管理局、澳门基金会、社会保障基金、退休基金会、科学技术发展基金、汽车及航海保障基金，以及澳门大学，其他的都没有内部监督机关，就只受外部监督实体监督。

人员制度方面，对其所属人员适用个人劳动合同制度且制定专有通则约束人员之招聘、甄选、聘请等事宜的公务法人有民政总署、民航局、金融管理局、贸易投资促进局、澳门基金会、科学技术发展基金、澳门大学、旅游学院以及理工学院。有一些公务法人实行双轨制，既可以合约制招聘人员且适用规范私人劳动关系之制度，也可以聘请公共行政机关工作人员担任职务，且对其适用公共行政工作人员一般制度，例如消费者委员会、房屋局。第三种情况就是对其工作人员统一适用澳门公共行政工作人员一般制度，例如社工局。

在缺乏一个统一规定公务法人制度的法律的情况下，可看出衍生了一些问题，例如没有一个公务法人的定义以及裁撤公务法人的条件，客观上导致在设立或裁撤公务法人时无统一的标准；有的公务法人的人事制度并未真正地松绑，与一般的直接行政范围内的公共行政机关无异，例如房屋局委任编制内人员以及聘请其他人员都要受监督实体（运输工务司司长）许可[40]；缺乏内部监督和控制制度；关于外部监督实体的权力的规定也极不统一，有的过松，有的过紧；缺乏绩效评鉴制度；缺乏

---

① 民政总署、金融管理局、汽车及航海保障基金、退休基金会以及理工学院设有咨询委员会。

信息公开的规定。

三、澳门公共行政部门架构改革与公共行政改革

澳门公共行政部门架构模式改革其实早在20世纪80年代末就开始了，这是由澳门的宪制地位改变所引起的，澳门由葡萄牙的海外省成为受葡萄牙行政管理并以适合其当地特殊情况章程约束的一个地区，澳门于1976年颁布《澳门组织章程》，开始建立自主、健全的公共行政组织，后来又历经多次变革，第10/79/M号法律、第85/84/M号法令、第67/85/M号法令都是具体调整政府架构体制的法律法规。[41]于过渡期以及特区政府成立初期①亦有依照基本法的要求进行了一系列的重组和调整，包括司级机构由七个减至五个，撤销一些临时机构，对一些职能重叠的机构进行重组等，减少了政府部门总数。[42]法律方面，制定了第2/1999号法律《政府组织纲要法》、第6/1999号行政法规《政府部门及实体的组织、职权与运作》以及第6/2006号行政法规《公共财政管理制度》。

澳门特区政府在2007年提出的《澳门特别行政区2007—2009年度公共行政改革路线图》中，包括了改革政府组织架构的内容，具体政策是"启动对澳门特区政治架构、政府宏观及微观组织的研究，更科学及合理地配置职权职能，理顺分工，增强跨部门的协调机能，解决'政出多门、各自为政'，提升执政团队的施政绩效"。之后在《公共行政改革路线图》的总结及执行情况报告中指出于2009年6月完成特区政治架构、政府宏观及微观组织的研究及评估工作，于2007年至2009年期间，重组或调整了13个公共部门的架构，这中间包括了五个公务法人②，而且撤销了环境委员会这个公务法人，改设环境保护局，成为政府的公共部门。

上述的公务法人调整很大程度上是针对具体的公务法人而言的，而不是从整个制度出发。笔者认为，对公务法人在制度上进行研究与改革以及进一步对各个公务法人进行必要的评估、重组、改制或裁撤是与特区政府改革政府组织架构的方向是一致的[43]，应该成为改革的一个重要组成部分，毕竟公务法人在特区公共部门中所占的比例不低。而且正好可以借鉴国际上关于公务法人制度的一些新的趋势，更新制度，让公务法人适应现今行政的需要。

事实上，对公务法人的制度创新和改革在其他国家或地区已经开展，澳门继受葡

---

① 在澳门特别行政区政府2000年施政报告中提及有关公共行政改革的内容中，与政府架构改革有关的几点是：精简政府架构，节省政府开支，重新检讨公共行政部门的结构及人员编制，积极改善公共部门的臃肿性，减少职能重叠的情况。

② 分别是贸易投资促进局、司法警察局福利会、澳门大学、澳门理工学院以及旅游学院。

国的法律传统，葡国长期也未有关于公务法人一般制度的法律，但是在 21 世纪初开始研究改革①，并于 2004 年通过 1 月 15 日第 3/2004 号法律《公务法人框架法》。日本与中国台湾也分别通过了类似法律。下文将介绍对这三部法律的主要内容，以期能够总结出一些一般规律，为澳门的公务法人制度构建提供一些参考。

四、葡、日以及中国台湾地区公务法人法

（一）葡萄牙 1 月 15 日第 3/2004 号法律《公务法人框架法》

该法的提案人曾于法案序言指出：该法是为了规范公务法人的设立、在其运作模式方面建立系统性的统一的模式、避免不合理的差异；制定有关公务法人的必要监管、自治管理以及责任的规则。[44]

该法共分为五编五十五条，第一条指出该法制定适用于公务法人的原则和规定。如若现已生效的各公务法人的组织法规定与框架法的规定抵触，框架法的规定优先适用。

第四条明确规定了公务法人的概念：公务法人是具有自身机关和财产的公法人。原则上公务法人需满足拥有行政及财产自治权的条件。在已适当说明理由的例外情况下，可以设立仅具行政自治权的行政法人。

第二条及第三条规定了该法的适用范围，该法适用于国家或者自治区设立的公务法人，不适用于公共企业、国家或自治区设立的私法团体或基金会。

须依法定目的设立公务法人，在需要处理技术性的事务、且有必要不由政府部门处理的情况下，设立公务法人。公务法人不应履行宪法规定应有国家直接行政机关履行的职务，以及研究服务或协调、支援和控制其他行政部门的职能。② 而且禁止公务法人履行其他非为实现设立其所欲达到的特定目的的职能。③

公务法人须通过立法行为④设立。该法律规范或公务法人的组织法应该订定公务法人的名称、管辖地域、目的或职能、有监督权的政府成员、机关、财产以及其他必要的特别规定，尤其是通则法未有规定的内容。⑤

---

① 2000 年 7 月 11 日葡萄牙国家及公共行政改革部设立分析公务法人制度的研究小组，该小组于 2001 年 9 月提出了报告以及公务法人框架法的草案。
② 第八条。
③ 第十四条。
④ 葡萄牙宪法规定，议会、政府和地方自治团体各自就特定范围事宜享有立法权。
⑤ 第九条。

适用于公务法人的法律包括该通则法、各公务法人的组织法、行政程序法典、公共行政人员通则、公共财政制度、公共采购制度、公共支出与公共合同制度、兼职禁止、国家民事责任制度、行政诉讼法、税务法院有关制度。[①]

设立一公务法人须满足下列条件：（1）有必要设立一新机构去实现拟实现的目的；（2）有必要赋予法人资格，以及政府无须干涉；（3）满足自治机关或基金的财政条件；（4）为成为各类型公务法人需满足的其他特定条件。而且在设立前要开展有关设立行政法人的必要性、财政影响以及其设立对所属领域的效果的评估。[②]

财政部及行政法人的监督实体得命令对各公务法人进行评鉴，由外部审计或官方监督机构评价公务法人完成任务和目标的程度。但并未规定是定期还是不定期评鉴。[③]

在下列情况下，应裁撤公务法人：当存续期限届满；当设立目的已实现或不可能实现时；当设定其为公务法人的理由不存在时；当公务法人的财产/设施不足够而必须由国家来履行有关义务时。[④]

组织制度方面，公务法人所必须设立的机关是管理委员会和独任监事。公务法人也可以视情况设立其他的机关，例如咨询机关。[⑤]

执行委员会由一位主席和一至两位委员组成，都由有监督权的政府官员以批示任命，任期五年，可以相同任期续期一次。独任监事负责监管公务法人运作的合法性、合规性以及对财产的妥善管理。由有监督权的政府官员与负责财政的政府官员联合任命，任期五年，可以相同任期续期一次。

人事制度方面，该法最初有三条原则性条文，第34条规定公务法人对全体人员或对部分人员适用个人劳动合同制度，在由合理理由的情况下可以适用公职人员制度，第35条规定公务法人人员制度变更的处理措施，但后来这两条于2008年被废止，只剩下一条，即第33条一条原则性规定，公务法人配备为履行职能所必需的人员，内部组织应有灵活性，较少等级制，在需要的情况下可以购买外部服务。可以理解为改为因应不同情况在各公务法人组织法内规定有关制度。

透明度与信息公开方面，该法规定所有的公务法人须在其电子网页上公布相关法规、章程或内部规范，领导人员信息包括其简历及薪酬，过去三年的活动计划以及活动报告，过去三年的预算账目，以及人员编制[⑥]。且各公务法人须向国家组织信息网

---

① 第六条。
② 第十条。
③ 第十一条。
④ 第十六条。
⑤ 第十七条。
⑥ 第四十四条。

提供有关信息包括其名称、设立法律、设立时间、曾有过的重组、领导人员组成等，以供其将有关信息置于公职及行政局的电子网页上。①

对现有公务法人的处理，该法规定，成立一委员会，对在通则法生效前已存在的公务法人应道研究其设立时的条件以考虑可能的重组、整合或裁撤，每个公务法人须向该委员会提交报告，最后由委员会向财政部以及其他阁员提交报告及处理现有公务法人的建议。②

（二）日本《独立行政法人通则法》

日本独立行政法人制度主要是于20世纪90年代行政改革的大背景中建立，主要目的是实现国家行政的精简化及效率化。独立行政法人制度背后的理念是将行政政策规划职能与具体实施职能分离，在因应事务之内容，追求最适当之组织、运营模式之同时，推动执行部门之一定事务的垂直减量，创设独立行政法人履行实施的职能，以谋求效率、提升质量以及透明度。[45]

《独立行政法人通则法》于1999年7月公布，于2001年1月6日与有关配套法规一并施行。有关配套法规包括"独立行政法人通则法施行之相关法律整备法"、"总务省设置法"、五十九个独立行政法人之个别法、"独立行政法人教育研修中心法"、"独立行政法人业务实施顺利化等相关法律整备法"、"独立行政法人制度之组织、营运及管理之共通事项政令"、独立行政法人通则法等施行之相关政令整备及其他过渡措施之政令、总务省组织令及政策评估独立行政法人评估委员会令。

设立独立行政法人的基本条件为："从国民生活及社会经济之安定等公共性之观点，有确实实施必要之事务/事业，且国家没有以主体地位直接实施之必要，但委诸民间者又恐有未实施之虞，或有必要由一主体独占实施者，政府得创设使其具备适于有效及效率实施之自律性、自发性及透明性之法人制度。"[46]必须由国家自己实施之事业主要是设计三类，对于私人权利义务有直接且强力限制之公权力者，例如警察，性质上因牵涉国家权威而必须以国家名义实施者，例如授予荣誉，与灾害等重大危机管理相关而必须直接由国家负起实施责任的事业，如国防。除此之外的事务如满足法定的标准，可创设独立行政法人。已独立的行政法人多为实验机构、研究机构、文教研习机构、医疗福利机构等。

《独立行政法人通则法》将独立行政法人分为普通及特定独立行政法人两类，两者之区别在于前者职员不具公务员身份，而后者职员具公务员身份，之所以两型化是

---

① 第四十九条。

② 第五十条，后被第5/2012号法令废止。

为避免行政阻力拖延改革而不得已为之的妥协。[47]

该法规定了主务大臣对独立行政法人的业务方法、中期、年度计划的实施的预先许可及监督的权力。第二十七条规定："独立行政法人在开始营运之际，应制作业务方法书，向主管大臣申请认可。变更时亦同。"第二十九条规定："主管大臣应设定以三年至五年期间之中期目标，并公告之。中期目标，应明定以下事项：1. 中期目标之期间；2. 业务营运效率化之相关事项；3. 对国民服务质量提升之相关事项；4. 财务改善之相关事项；5. 其他营运之相关事项。"第三十条规定："独立行政法人应依省令规定拟定为达成中期目标之计划，并经主管大臣之认可，变更时亦同。中期计划，应明记以下事项：1. 为达成营运效率化目标所必要之措施；2. 为达成提升国民服务质量目标所必要之措施；3. 预算、收支计划及资金计划；4. 短期借入款之限额；5. 重要资产转让或提供担保时之计划；6. 剩余金之使用目的；7. 其他主管省令所定业务营运之相关事项。"第三十一条规定，"独立行政法人，应于每事业年度开始前，依经认可之中期计划，订立其事业年度之业务营运计划，且向主管大臣报备，并公告之。变更时亦同。"第三十三条规定："独立行政法人，于中期目标期间终了后三个月内，应向主管大臣提出该中期目标之事业报告书，并公告之。"有关中期目标期间终了时之检讨，第三十五条规定："中期目标期间终了时，主管大臣应就该独立行政法人业务存续之必要性、应有之组织架构，及其他组织上及业务上全面性事项，并依其检讨结果，采取必要措施。"

独立行政法人通则法确立了双主体的绩效评鉴制度。首先在主管省设立独立行政法人评估委员会，委员会成员由主务大臣任命部会以外之有识者担任，以保障该委员会的客观、专业和中立性。该评估委员会对独立行政法人业务业绩及通则法及其他法律所定权限处理事项，实施评估，在业绩方面，对各事业年度之业务业绩以及中期目标之业务业绩实施评估，评估委员会于评估后，应将评估结果通知该独立行政法人。有必要时，也得对之为业务营运改善之劝告，且于通知或劝告后，应公告之。① 另外在总务省设立政策评估独立行政法人评估委员会，对各府省政策实施统一或综合评估，或实施为确保政策评估之客观性及严格性之评估，该委员会并无直接对法人进行评价之法定权限，而是对各部会之独立行政法人评估委员会之评估结果进行二度评估，并陈述意见，如此可避免评价机能之重叠，也不让其过度干涉各部会长之政策判断。政策评估独立行政法人评估委员会于法人中期目标终了时，有关该独立行政法人主要事务及事业之变更、废止，有权向主务大臣提出建议。[48]

内部组织制度方面，独立行政法人采取首长制，由主管部会首长任命独立行政法

---

① 第三十二条及第三十四条。

人首长与监事，独立行政法人首长则有权任命干部和职员。

财务及会计制度方面，在预算编列上，接受国家营运费及固定投资经费之财源，及弹性及效率之财务运行方式。① 独立行政法人采企业会计原则，每事业年度终了后三个月内，必须制作财务报表送经主管部会首长承认。财务监督除由其内部监事负责外，尚需由主管部会首长选任会计监察人对财务报表、事业报告书及决算报告书等进行审核。②

独立行政法人通则法确立了业务透明原则，规定"独立性之法人，应依本法规定将其业务内容等公告，使国民得知其组织及营运之状况"③，因此而须公开的事项包括理事之任命与卸任、业务方法书、中期计划和年度计划、评估委员会之评估结果、事业报告书、财务等报表、监察结果、理监事及职员俸给支给基准等。

（三）中国台湾地区《行政法人法》

中国台湾地区过去在行政体系中很少有公法人，除了地方自治团体以及农田水利会作为公法团体之外，是否有其他公法人，学界存在分歧。[49] 于21世纪初开始推动行政法人化，主要是为了改造政府组织，构建合理的政府职能及组织规模，及确保公共任务之妥善实施，"打破以往政府、民间体制上之二分法，让不适合或无需由行政机关推动之公共任务由行政法人来处理，俾使政府在政策执行方式之选择上，能更具弹性，并适当缩减政府组织规模，同时可以引进企业经营精神，使这些业务之推行更专业、更讲究效能，而不受现行行政机关有关人事、会计等制度之束缚"[50]。

中国台湾地区政府于2001年10月成立"政府改造委员会"，以"去任务化"、"行政法人化"、"地方化"和"委外化"为目标。2002年5月"行政院"成立"行政院组织改造推动委员会"，负责推动行政院组织改造各项工作至规划、协调和实施，"行政院"与"考试院"先后两次于2004年4月和2009年5月向"立法院"递交《行政法人法》草案，最终于2011年4月在"立法院"三读通过草案，该法于4月27日公布，并于同日施行。另外，于2011年12月21日施行《行政法人会计制度设置准则》，于2013年9月6日施行《政府机关（构）改制行政法人随同移转继续任用人员人事管理办法》。

《行政法人法》共六章四十二条。第一条规定其立法目的是"为规范行政法人之设立、组织、运作、监督及解散等共通事项，确保公共事务之遂行，并使其运作更具效率及弹性，以促进公共利益"。

---

① 第四十六条。
② 第三十七、三十八条。
③ 第三条。

该法将行政法人定义为"国家及地方自治团体以外，由中央目的事业主管机关，为执行特定公共事务，依法律设立之公法人"。特定公共事务指具有专业需求或须强化成本效益及经营效能的，且不适合由政府机关推动，亦不宜交由民间办理，所涉公权力行使程度较低的事务。①

除了行政法人法一般法外，行政法人受其组织法或统一适用于同一类型公务法人的通用性法律规范，后两类法律应该规定具体行政法人之监督机关。②

该法规定，行政法人应制定自己的制度，包括人事管理、会计制度、内部控制、稽核作业及其他规章，在提经董（理）事会通过后，报请监督机关备查。③

组织制度方面，行政法人应设董（理）事会、监事或监事会，董（理）事会负责审议"发展目标及计划、年度营运（业务）计划、年度预算及决算、规章、自有不动产处分或其设定负担以及其他重大事项"，监事或监事会负责审核年度营运（业务）决算、营运（业务），监督财务状况，稽核财务账册、文件及财产资料，以及审核或稽核其他重大事项。④

监督机关有以下监督权限：一、发展目标及计划之核定。二、规章、年度营运（业务）计划与预算、年度执行成果及决算报告书之核定或备查。三、财产及财务状况之检查。四、营运（业务）绩效之评鉴。五、董（理）事、监事之聘任及解聘。六、董（理）事、监事于执行业务违反法令时，得为必要之处分。七、行政法人有违反宪法、法律、法规命令时，予以撤销、变更、废止、限期改善、停止执行或其他处分。八、自有不动产处分或其设定负担之核可。九、其他依法律所为之监督。⑤

监督机关应邀集有关机关代表、学者专家及社会公正人士，办理行政法人之绩效评鉴。绩效评鉴之内容包括考核行政法人年度执行成果、评量行政法人营运（业务）绩效及目标达成率以及年度自筹款比率达成率、建议行政法人经费核拨。⑥

行政法人所任用的人员不具公务人员身份，由具体雇佣契约订定权利义务关系。⑦而改制前的具公务员任用资格的员工若继续留用就保留公务员身份，其任用、服务、惩戒等事项，均依原适用之公务人员相关法令办理。⑧

---

① 该法第二条。
② 第二条第三款及第三条。
③ 第四条第一款。
④ 第十条及第十一条。
⑤ 第十五条。
⑥ 第十六、十七条。
⑦ 第二十条。
⑧ 第二十一条。

会计及财务制度方面,行政法人之会计制度,依行政法人会计制度设置准则制定。① 政府机关核拨行政法人之经费,应依法定预算程序办理,并受审计监督。政府机关核拨之经费超过行政法人当年度预算收入来源50%者,应由监督机关将其年度预算书,送立法院审议。②

信息公开方面,该法规定行政法人之相关信息应依政府信息公开法相关规定公开之;其年度财务报表、年度营运(业务)信息及年度绩效评鉴报告,应主动公开。其年度绩效评鉴报告,应由监督机关提交分析报告,送立法院备查。必要时,"立法院"得要求监督机关首长率同行政法人之董(理)事长、首长或相关主管至立法院报告营运状况并备询。③

行政法人因情事变更或绩效不彰,致不能达成其设立目的时,由监督机关提请行政院同意后解散之。④

台湾地区于2004年1月通过并公布《国立中正文化中心设置条例》,设立了第一个行政法人。⑤截至2014年8月已设立的行政法人有"'国家'中山科学研究院""'国家'运动训练中心""'国家'表演艺术中心""'国家'灾害防救科技中心"[51]。"'国立'中正文化中心"已并入"'国家'表演艺术中心"。

需要指出的是,台湾学界认为行政法人制度源自新公共管理思潮,以"分权"及"绩效管理"为特征,而德国既有的公法人以及公营造物之建制,是为了保障自治权,而非旨在提升行政效率,强化成本效益与经营效能[52],因此以行政法人制度为新制度。笔者并不这样认为,葡萄牙的公法人制度以至公务法人继受德国制度,在21世纪初在同样的思潮下有所改革,乃枯木逢春,日本的独立行政法人与中国台湾地区的行政法人,虽然名称有所差异,但实质性质仍是一样的。

另外,关于中国台湾地区的行政法人制度,尚要提及的是行政法人并不包括公设财团法人,后者属于私法人,由政府透过预算编列出资捐助设立,有意见认为公社财团法人是最类似于行政法人的行政组织类型,故建议将其改制为行政法人,一并在"机关行政法人化"的过程中解决。[53]

---

① 第三十二条。
② 第三十五条。
③ 第三十八条。
④ 第四十条。
⑤ 中国台湾地区"立法院"于2014年1月通过《"国家"表演艺术中心设置条例》,成立"'国家'表演艺术中心",文化中心已于4月2日纳入"'国家'表演艺术中心",《"国立"中正文化中心设置条例》被废止。

五、借鉴

前述有关各国及地区公务法人通则法的介绍，对澳门特别行政区的公务法人制度建设可能有以下几点启发：

（一）行政任务极具多样性，各行政任务涉及的国家权力程度高低不同以及专业性不同，有不同的特性和需求，因此不能仅由单一的行政组织形态来执行各类行政任务，而应选择不同的行政组织形式。然而行政主体在设置行政组织时，不得恣意决定，应以所欲完成之行政任务与行政目的为取向，视其性质不同做出最适合达成行政目标之组织选择。[54]

（二）三个国家或地区在制定公务法人通则法时无一例外地都着眼于利用行政法人之独立法人格，以及其不受行政部门人事制度、预算、经费、采购等法令之拘束的特点，交予特定性质之行政任务，以追求更高效率地完成行政任务。对公务法人的建制及改革是为了建构具独立性、中立性、专业性、高效率、有成本效益分析观念的现代行政组织。

（三）当行政组织脱离行政科层体制，享有自治空间之后，也可能存在一些问题，例如浪费、信息不透明、董事任命和人员聘请私相授受等现象，因此为了杜绝这些风险，这些国家或地区在构建公务法人一般制度时，建立相应的配套监督机制和评鉴机制，强化公务法人的责任。

（四）具体的监督和方面，都强化了内部监督和外部监督两层监督机制，同时强调外部机构的事后监督，减少事前监督，加强事后监督，以保障公务法人的独立性。绩效评鉴制度方面，引进独立评鉴人或机关，并制定公平的评量指标，对公务法人之活动是否达成其组织目标予以评鉴。另外，无一例外都规定了公务法人信息公开和透明化机制，引进社会监督。[55]

（五）公务法人的人员制度会是公务法人制度建构中比较棘手的问题，因应其属于国家间接行政的性质，原则上应采非公务人员编制，除了改制其他行政机关或现有公务法人对现有工作人员保留其公务人员地位的情况之外。然而显而易见遇到了很大阻力，葡国法前后有修正，而日本则采取将独立行政法人两分法的机制，中国台湾地区虽然规定行政法人之人员不具公务人员身份，于契约中明定其权利义务关系，同时为现有编制内公务人员的转制订定了解决办法，但仍然因这些规定为推动行政法人化带来了不少的阻力。[56]从这些立法经验看出在改革公务法人制度时应小心处理人员制度，避免影响整个制度的实施。

事实上这些法律的一些具体的规定仍值得进一步研究和借鉴，而且关于公务法人制度值得思考的问题还有很多,例如作为公务法人的高等院校的特别制度;适当引进议会/立法会对于公务法人的监督等等。

六、结语

近年在社会上要求改革行政组织制度、提高行政效率的呼声越来越高,当审视一番澳门的公共行政组织结构后,发现有一独特的行政组织类型——公务法人,其设立理念在于实现行政的分权,以达到行政更灵活更有效率的目的,然而,多年实施下来的情况却与其初衷有了一定的偏离,因缺乏完善的制度性规定,往往存在监管过多已与直接行政机构无异,或监督不足的情形。

在澳门开展公共行政改革的大背景下,应该考虑开始对公务法人制度进行研究,参考国际上的改革趋势,制定订定公务法人基本原则和制度的法律,以及对现存的公务法人进行必要的评估、重组、改制或裁撤。

---

[1] 从行政学角度出发的研究,例如黄湛:《Quangos 与澳门政府自治机构:兼与香港比较》,第三届"21 世纪的公共行政管理:机遇与挑战"国际学术研讨会论文,2008 年;探讨澳门公法人与澳门教育机构的研究,如唐晓晴:《法人理论与澳门教育机构的组织模式》,《成大法学》第 24 期,2012 年 12 月。

[2] "间接国家行政是指国家不通过自己的行政机关自行执行行政任务,而是授权或者委任其他法律上具有权利能力的组织执行。"哈特穆特·毛雷尔:《行政法学总论》,高家伟译,第 546 页。德国法上,将公法人分为"公法社团""公法营造物""公法财团"三类,但亦引发为何在"公法营造物"之外承认"公法财团"的问题。参见李建良:《论公法人在行政组织建制上的地位与功能——以德国公法人概念与法制为借镜》,《月旦法学》第 84 期,2002 年 5 月,第 49 页。

[3] 关于间接行政与自治行政的概念与区分,参见 Vital Moreira, "Administração Autónoma e Associações Públicas", *Coimbra Editora*, 2003, p. 105ff。

[4] 关于法人的概念如何从私法演进到公法,参看唐晓晴:《法人理论与澳门教育机构的组织模式》,《成大法学》第 24 期,2012 年 12 月,第 80—84 页。

[5] 同注 5,第 84 页。

[6] Paulo Cardinal, A pessoa colectiva de Direito Publico ("公法人"),可下载于 http://www.odireito.com.mo/doutrina/9-doutrina/138-a-pessoa-colectiva-de-direito-publico.html。

[7] 唐晓晴教授曾指出,将 Insituto Público 译为"公务法人"有值得商榷之处,因不管从该概念的起源以及语义分析,都未突显"法人"的性质,因此建议译为"公共事业"或"公法事业"。唐晓晴:《法人理论与澳门教育机构的组织模式》,《成大法学》第 24 期,2012 年 12 月。事实上 Insituto Público 在中文译文中曾有过"公共机构""公务法人"两个译名,但多数公务法人的

组织法里采用"公务法人",笔者更倾向于公务法人,因这个名称指出了这个组织形式的本质特征,具法人资格,为执行特定行政/公共任务而设立,因此在全文中仍采用"公务法人"的名称。

[8] "o instituto publico e uma pessoa colectiva publica, de tipo institucional, criada para assegurar o desemphenho de determinadas funcoes administrativas de caracter nao empresarial, pertencentes ao Estado ou a outra pessoa colectiva publica."见注4,第363页。

[9] 见注4,第363—365页。

[10] Marcello Caetano, *Manual de Direito Administrativo*, Almedina – Coimbra, 1997, p. 188.

[11] 唐晓晴教授认为将其翻译为"公共机构"效果不好,建议将其译为"公共设施"。同注10,第101页。

[12] 关于公务法人的分类,参见注4,第366—373页。

[13] 例如港务局,第4/2005号行政法规《港务局的组织及运作》第一条:"港务局为具有行政自治权的公共部门,负责行使海事当局权力,促进及协调海事活动的发展。"又或澳门保安部队事务局,第9/2002号行政法规《澳门保安部队事务局的组织与运作》第一条,"澳门保安部队事务局,为澳门特别行政区公共行政当局的组织单位,具有行政自治权,且在运作上直属于保安司司长。""文化局",12月19日第63/94/M号法令。

[14] 见注4,第371页。

[15] 见注3,第126页及后续页数。

[16] 7月11日第33/94/M号法令第二条:澳门贸易投资促进局系一个具有公务法人性质之公法人,且具有法律人格、行政及财政自治权以及本身财产,并受自治实体制度规范。

[17] 第17/2013号行政法规《房屋局的组织及运作》第一条:"房屋局为一具有法律人格、行政及财政自治权,以及本身财产的公务法人。"

[18] 由第17/2001号法律通过的《民政总署章程》第一条:"民政总署为具有公务法人性质的公法人,受澳门特别行政区政府委托,根据本章程及其他适用的法律及规章的规定为居民服务。"

[19] 6月21日第24/99/M号法令第一条:"澳门社会工作司(葡文缩写为IASM)系具有法律人格、行政及财政自治权,以及拥有本身财产之公务法人,其宗旨系贯彻为本地区之社会政策而总体订定之活动方针。"

[20] 由2月4日第10/91/M号法令通过的《澳门民用航空局章程》第一条:"澳门民用航空局,简称为AACM,系受本章程及其他适用的法例管制,具有行政、财政及财产自主权的公共机构。"[该章程将葡文"instituto público"(公务法人)译为"公共机构"。]同样译为"公共机构"的尚有已废止的《澳门组织章程》(第六十三条)。

[21] 10月18日第59/93/M号法令第一条:"社会保障基金,葡文缩写为FSS,为一具有法律人格、行政暨财政自治权及本身财产之公务法人,并受本法规及其他适用法例规范。"

[22] 6月12日第4/95/M号法律《重组消费者委员会》第一条规定,"消费者委员会,是具有法律人格及行政和财政自治的公法人,且受本法规及其他适用法例管制。"然而,这里有一处误译,即将葡文的Instituto Público误译为"公法人",未采用惯常的"公务法人"。

[23] 第 9/2008 号行政法规《司法警察局福利会》第一条:"司法警察局福利会的性质为公务法人,具有法律人格、行政及财政自治权,拥有本身财产,其宗旨是向受益人提供补充性福利。"

[24] 第 18/2004 号行政法规《海关福利会》第一条:"海关福利会的性质为公务法人,具有法律人格及行政、财政自治权,拥有本身财产,其目的为向其受益人提供补充性福利。"

[25] 第 5/2005 号行政法规《港务局福利会》第一条:"港务局福利会的性质为公务法人,具有法律人格、行政及财政自治权,并拥有本身财产。"

[26] 8 月 3 日第 33/98/M 号法令治安警察厅福利会(葡文缩写为 OSPSP)之性质为公务法人,具有法律人格、行政及财政自治权,拥有本身财产,并旨在向其受益人提供补充性福利。

[27] 8 月 24 日第 37/98/M 号法令第一条:"消防队福利会(葡文缩写为 OSCB)之性质为公务法人,具有法律人格、行政及财政自治权,拥有本身财产,并旨在向其受益人提供补充性福利。"

[28] 3 月 11 日第 14/96/M 号法令第一条:"澳门货币暨汇兑监理署(葡文缩写为 AMCM)系具有行政、财政及财产自治权之公法人,且为具有法律人格之公共机关,并受本通则及其他适用法例管制。"

[29] 由 1 月 9 日第 2/89/M 号法令通过的《澳门邮电司组织规章》第一条:澳门邮电司(葡文缩写为 CTT),系一个获赋予法律人格以及具有行政及财政自主权之司级机构,其宗旨系在澳门地区提供邮政及电讯公共服务,而且透过其定名为"储金局"之厅,被视为《银行法》所规定之一个货币信用机构。

[30] 参见 Lino Ribeiro, *José Candido de Pinho*, *Código do Procedimento Administrativo de Macau-Anotado e Comentário*, p. 184. 作者称澳门基金会、退休基金会为具公务法人性质的公法人。文中列举的一些公共基金除了管理委员会之外并没有其他行政单位,在运作上需要其他政府部门提供行政及技术支援,是否应将其视为公务法人仍有一定的争议。

[31] 7 月 12 日第 34/93/M 号法令第二条规定,"一、本法规适用于一般劳工,包括公共行政当局、市政厅、公务法人及其他公法人之工作人员,亦适用于有关僱主。"

[32] 第 9/1999 号法律《司法组织纲要法》第三十条(行政法院):"二、在行政上的司法争讼方面,在不影响中级法院的管辖权的情况下,行政法院有管辖权审理:(一)对以下实体所作的行政行为或属行政事宜的行为提起上诉的案件:(1)局长以及行政当局中级别不高于局长的其他机关;(2)公务法人的机关;(3)被特许人;(4)公共团体的机关;(5)行政公益法人的机关;(6)市政机构或临时市政机构及其具法律人格与行政自治权的公共部门;"以及已废止的规范审计法院之组织、管辖、运作及程序的三月二日第 18/92/M 号法令也有相类似的提述:"澳门司法组织网要法——八月二十九日第 112/91 号法律——在本地区新司法体系内设立了审计法院,该法院不仅对行政当局各部门,亦对各公务法人、公共团体、地方自治团体、及行政公益法人等具有财政控制权力。"

[33] 第 8/2006 号法律《公务人员公积金制度》第一条(标的)规定:"二、为适用本法律的规定,公共部门指公共行政当局的机关及部门,包括行政长官办公室、政府主要官员的办公室

及行政辅助部门、自治基金、公务法人、立法会辅助部门、终审法院院长办公室及检察长办公室。"

[34] 第七条第一款第四项："（四）公共行政当局及其所有的部门及组织单位的架构和组织，包括咨询机关、具法律人格的公共部门、公务法人、公共实体、自治部门及基金组织、公共基金会、其他自治机构及同类性质机构的架构及组织，但不包括属于立法会、法院、检察院、审计署及廉政公署的机构或纳入其职能或组织范围内的机构，以及对基本权利和自由及其保障具有直接介入权限的机构，尤其是刑事调查机关"。

[35] 第一条第二项规定："为适用本法律的规定，公共部门指公共行政当局的机关及部门，包括行政长官办公室、政府主要官员的办公室及行政辅助部门、自治基金、公务法人、立法会辅助部门、终审法院院长办公室及检察长办公室。"

[36] 第一条第二款规定："为适用本法律的规定，公共部门指公共行政当局的机关及部门，包括行政长官办公室、政府主要官员的办公室及行政辅助部门、自治基金、公务法人、立法会辅助部门、终审法院院长办公室及检察长办公室。"

[37] 法案第一条第二款规定："为适用本法律的规定，公共部门指公共行政当局的机关及部门，包括行政长官办公室、主要官员的办公室及行政辅助部门、自治基金、公务法人、立法会辅助部门、终审法院院长办公室及检察长办公室。"

[38] 第三十六条（限制）规定："一、属于下列任一情况者不得被提名为候选人，但（二）至（八）项所指者在候选人提名开始日之前已辞职或退休者除外：七）公共行政工作人员，由行政长官委任在公务法人内、尤其在自治机关及自治基金组织内任职的全职人员，以及由行政长官委任在公共服务或使用属公产的财产的承批实体内及在澳门特别行政区有参资的公司内任职的全职人员"。

[39] 第11/2003号法律《财产及利益申报法律制度》第一条规定："公共职位据位人包括自治部门、自治基金及其他公务法人在内的公共行政部门的领导及主管人员，以及该等公共行政部门的领导、行政管理、管理及监察机关的主席及成员。"

[40] 第17/2013号行政法规《房屋局的组织及运作》第二条第二款第七、八项。

[41] 许昌：《澳门公共行政组织架构—二十年间的演变及未来的平稳过渡》，见娄胜华主编：《澳门人文社会科学研究文选（行政卷）》，社会科学文献出版社2009年版，第328—362页。另，关于澳门政治行政组织的历史与变革，也可参见吴志良：《20世纪澳门政治行政组织的变革》，见娄胜华主编：《澳门人文社会科学研究文选（行政卷）》，社会科学文献出版社2009年版，第613—639页。

[42] 周潭、陈瑞莲：《现代政府改革理念与澳门公共行政改革》，见娄胜华主编：《澳门人文社会科学研究文选（行政卷）》，社会科学文献出版社2009年版，第183页。

[43] 有学者认为澳门的自治机构有一定的调整和压缩空间，建议让大学院校脱离公务员体制，按学术自治原则管理，将一些基金会、福利会等划归有关局级部门统一领导，以精简编制，增加效率，参见刘伯龙：《澳门公共行政：有深层次改革的必要吗？》，见娄胜华主编：《澳门人文社会科学研究文选（行政卷）》，社会科学文献出版社2009年版，第38页。

[44] 转引自 José Henrique Rodrigues Polaco,"Os institutos públicos em Portugal"（葡萄牙的公务法人），网址：http://www. igf. min-financas. pt/inftecnica/75 _ anos _ IGF/josepolaco/josepolaco _ tema. htm。

[45] 转引自刘宗德：《日本公益法人、特殊法人及独立行政法人制度之分析》，《法治与现代行政法学——法治斌教授纪念论文集》，第 403 页。

[46] 《日本中央省厅等改革基本法》第三十六条。

[47] 蔡秀卿：《日本独立行政法人制度》，《月旦法学》第 84 期，2002 年 5 月，第 68 页。

[48] 关于日本独立行政法人的评鉴制度，可参见刘宗德、陈小兰：《官民共治之行政法人》，新学林出版 2008 年版，第 187—192 页。

[49] 参见詹镇荣：《变迁中之行政组织法——从"组织形式选择自由"到"组织最适诫命"》，《中研院法学期刊》第 6 期，第 10 页；翁岳生：《行政法》上册，"中国法制出版社"2002 年版，第 348 页。

[50] 台湾"行政院"《行政法人法草案总说明》。

[51] 其他待改制的机关有"国家教育研究院"、"国立台湾交响乐团"、"国家台湾文学馆"、"国家农业研究院"、警察广播电台、"国立科学工艺博物馆"、"国家龙潭研究院"劳工退休基金监理委员会。参见刘坤亿："台湾推动行政法人制度之经验分析"，可下载于 http://www. ntpu. edu. tw/pa/news/95news/attachment/951215/951215 – 02. pdf。

[52] 詹镇荣，见前注 49，第 18 页。

[53] 参见林三：《行政法人作为行政组织改造之选项》，见台湾行政法学会主编：《行政组织与人事法制之新发展》，2010 年 9 月，第 116 页。

[54] 有学者提出以"组织最适诫命"取代传统的"组织形式选择自由"理论，在考虑组织最适性时，除了行政合法性之外，考虑行政效率之提升以及人民基本权保障更臻完善等要素，参见詹镇荣，前注 72。

[55] 参见赖森本、许哲源：《行政法人监督机制之研究》，《月旦法学杂志》第 116 期，2005 年 1 月，第 77—94 页。

[56] 黄舒屏、黄依伟：《浅谈行政法人化》，《台湾"国立"国父纪念馆馆刊》第 21 期。

图书在版编目(CIP)数据

21世纪的公共管理：机遇与挑战：第六届国际学术研讨会文集/中山大学中国公共管理研究中心等主编. —北京：中央编译出版社，2017.6

ISBN 978-7-5117-3150-0

Ⅰ.①2… Ⅱ.①中… Ⅲ.①公共管理-国际学术会议-文集 Ⅳ.①D035-53

中国版本图书馆 CIP 数据核字(2016)第 254388 号

21 世纪的公共管理：机遇与挑战：第六届国际学术研讨会文集

出 版 人：	葛海彦
出版统筹：	贾宇琰
责任编辑：	王　琳
责任印制：	尹　珺
出版发行：	中央编译出版社
地　　址：	北京西城区车公庄大街乙 5 号鸿儒大厦 B 座（100044）
电　　话：	（010）52612345（总编室）　　（010）52612341（编辑室）
	（010）52612316（发行部）　　（010）52612346（馆配部）
传　　真：	（010）66515838
经　　销：	全国新华书店
印　　刷：	北京紫瑞利印刷有限公司
开　　本：	787 毫米×1092 毫米　1/16
字　　数：	449 千字
印　　张：	23
版　　次：	2017 年 6 月第 1 版
印　　次：	2017 年 6 月第 1 次印刷
定　　价：	102.00 元

网　　址：	www.cctphome.com　　邮　箱：cctp@cctphome.com
新浪微博：	@中央编译出版社　　　微　信：中央编译出版社（ID：cctphome）
淘宝店铺：	中央编译出版社直销店（http://shop108367160.taobao.com）　　（010）55626985

本社常年法律顾问：北京市吴栾赵阎律师事务所律师　闫军　梁勤
凡有印装质量问题，本社负责调换。电话：（010）55626985